APPLY YOUR KNOWLEDGE

```
    ►RETURN BOOLEAN IS
      dummy NUMBER;
BEGIN
      dummy := TO_NUMBER(Pstr);
      RETURN(TRUE);  -- conversion succeeded
EXCEPTION WHEN OTHERS THEN
      RETURN(FALSE); -- conversion failed
END is_number;
-- global public subroutines
    PROCEDURE clear_primes(Ptab IN OUT
INT_TAB) IS
      BEGIN
        Ptab := clear_tab;
      END clear_primes;
END blick;
```

A. The function is_number wasn't declared in the package header.

B. The function primes, found in the header, doesn't have an implementation.

C. The initialization section is missing.

D. The user-defined data type INT_TAB is out of scope.

9. What's wrong with this function?

```
CREATE OR REPLACE
FUNCTION strnum(Pstr   IN VARCHAR2,
               Pstatus OUT NUMBER,
               Pformat IN VARCHAR2 DEFAULT
NULL)
RETURN NUMBER IS
BEGIN
      Pstatus := 0;
      IF (Pformat IS NULL) THEN  -- use NLS
format
        RETURN(TO_NUMBER(Pstr));
      ELSE  -- use given format string
        RETURN(TO_NUMBER(Pstr, Pformat));
      END IF;  -- test format string
EXCEPTION
WHEN OTHERS THEN
      Pstatus :+ SQLCODE;
END strnum;
```

A. OUT parameters aren't allowed in a function parameter list.

B. IN parameters aren't allowed after OUT parameters.

C. A RETURN statement is needed in the exception handler.

D. The function TO_NUMBER is out of scope.

10. Which one of these statements is FALSE?

A. Global package variables are persistent between sessions.

B. Global public package variables are accessible to other packages.

C. If a function is used in a SQL statement, you must assert its purity with PRAGMA RESTRICT_REFERENCES following its declaration anywhere in the package specification.

D. If you grant EXECUTE on a package to another user, that user has access only to the package specification source code via the data dictionary view all_source.

Answers to Review Questions

1. **C.** Subprogram names can be overloaded only inside a package. With a standalone subprogram, the old routine simply gets replaced with the new one.

2. **B.** Packages offer persistence, encapsulation, and polymorphism.

3. **D.** A package can contain all PL/SQL program objects: constants, variables, user-defined types, and subprograms.

4. **D.** You must assert a pretty restrictive purity level in order to use a packaged function within SQL.

Answers to Review Questions: For each of the Review questions, you will find thorough explanations located at the end of the section. They are easily identifiable because they are in blue type.

Review Questions: These questions reflect the kinds of multiple-choice questions that appear on the Oracle exams. Use them to become familiar with the exam question formats and to help you determine what you know and what you need to review or study more.

OCP Training Guide: Oracle DBA

OCP Exam 1: Introduction to Oracle: SQL and PL/SQL

OCP Exam 2: Oracle7 Database Administration

OCP EXAM 3: ORACLE7 BACKUP AND RECOVERY WORKSHOP

OCP EXAM 4: ORACLE7 PERFORMANCE TUNING WORKSHOP

OCP

Oracle DBA

New Riders

Willard Baird

OCP Training Guide: Oracle DBA

International Standard Book Number: 1-56205-891-6

Library of Congress Catalog Card Number: 98-84813

Printed in the United States of America

First Printing: October, 1998

00 99 98   4   3   2   1

Trademarks

Warning and Disclaimer

EXECUTIVE EDITOR
Bryan Gambrel

ACQUISITIONS EDITOR
Angela C. Kozlowski

DEVELOPMENT EDITOR
Susan Shaw Dunn

MANAGING EDITOR
Sarah Kearns

PROJECT EDITOR
Mike La Bonne

COPY EDITORS
Keith Cline
Kristine Simmons

INDEXER
C.J. East

TECHNICAL EDITORS
Sundar Rajan
Sakhr Youness

SOFTWARE DEVELOPMENT SPECIALIST
Andrea Duvall

PROOFREADER
Maribeth Echard

PRODUCTION
Steve Balle-Gifford
Cheryl Lynch
Jeannette McKay
Louis M. Porter, Jr.

Contents at a Glance

PART V: Appendixes

Table of Contents

9 Database Recovery   357

PART IV: Tuning

About the Authors

Willard Baird has been working in data processing for 14 years, the past 10 years in the database arena. Willard has worked with the Oracle database since 1991 and has presented at the International Oracle Users Week (IOUW) and the NetSec security conference. He has created a one-day seminar on Oracle security that covers all aspects of defining and auditing an Oracle database environment. He teaches part time at the University of South Florida, where he has helped design and organize the Advance Database course. He has worked as an Oracle DBA for nine years in a banking environment, so he has strong experience in establishing controls, security policy, and performing security audits on an Oracle database.

Daniel J. Clamage has worked for 13 years as a software developer, in a wide range of industries on various platforms. He has worked with various relational databases, including Unify, R:Base, Informix, Ingres, and Oracle. Dan has spent the past three years as an Oracle developer, writing complex PL/SQL packages to automate software development, perform Y2K data conversions, perform data analysis, and build various software development tools. Dan contributed Chapters 2 and 3 for this book. Dan lives in Pittsburgh with his wife Robin and daughter Patty. Dan can be reached at **dclamage@telerama.com,** and maintains a Web site geared toward PL/SQL development at **http://www.telerama.com/~dclamage.**

Hasan Mir, a graduate of Brock University in Canada, is a senior Oracle consultant specializing in Oracle and its tools, Developer/2000 and Designer/2000. He has been working in Oracle RDBMS since 1993 and is a certified Oracle programmer and DBA. He is dedicated to training people in Oracle and is running a training institute, Andromeda Enterprises, for this purpose. Before starting this institute, he had been working as a training instructor in the Oracle Education Center. He has offered his services as a project leader to Marit Consultants and Gurusoft Consultants Inc., and worked for various Oracle application development projects. He is also working as a consultant for Gurusoft Consultants Inc., on a project to develop Oracle Virtual Training Center on the Web. Hasan contributed Chapters 1 and 10 for this book.

Kenny Smith graduated from the University of Alabama, Huntsville, with a bachelor's degree in electrical and computer engineering. He has developed Oracle applications since 1992 and has been involved in information technologies since 1989. During those years, he has been responsible for design, modeling, business analysis, project leadership, project development, implementation, construction, testing, and maintenance of Oracle database projects and systems. He has published numerous articles on Oracle database administration and tools and has conducted several training classes. Kenny is a senior consultant with Data General, in the company's Oracle Applications Practice. He contributed Chapter 6 for this book. He lives in Atlanta with his wife Tina and sons Tyler, Wesley, and Kevin.

Meghraj Thakkar works as a senior technical analyst at Oracle Corporation. He has been working with various Oracle products for the past six years. He has a master's degree in computer science and a bachelor's degree in electronics engineering. He has several industry vendor certifications, including Microsoft Certified Systems Engineer (MCSE), Novell Certified ECNE, and Lotus Certified Notes Consultant. He has taught several courses at the University of California, Irvine; developed and presented a two-day course, Supporting Oracle on Windows NT, to internal Oracle employees; and presented two papers at the ECO'98 in New York City in March 1998. He also coauthored several books for Macmillan Computer Publishing (*Special Edition Using Oracle8, Oracle8 Server Unleashed, Oracle8 for DBAs*, and *Using Oracle8*) and contributed Chapter 11 for this book.

Dedication

I thank **my family** for their loving support and understanding during this adventure called book writing. A special thanks to **my wife,** who believed I could do it, and **my son "Eagle Eyes"** and **daughter "Luv Dove,"** for all their sweet smiles.

Willard Baird

Acknowledgments

From *Willard Baird*: I thank Bill Sawyer for believing in a young professional who would stand on desks to make his point. I also thank Richard Carlson, who mentored me in the finer points of being a DBA in the wee hours of the morning.

From *Hasan Mir*: Special thanks to **Prof. Syed Javed Ahsraf** for his guidance that helped me in writing successful chapters for this book.

TELL US WHAT YOU THINK!

As the reader of this book, *you* are our most important critic and commentator. We value your opinion and want to know what we're doing right, what we could do better, what areas you'd like to see us publish in, and any other words of wisdom you're willing to pass our way.

As the Executive Editor for the Client/Server Database Team at Macmillan Computer Publishing, I welcome your comments. You can fax, email, or write me directly to let me know what you did or didn't like about this book—as well as what we can do to make our books stronger.

Please note that I cannot help you with technical problems related to the topic of this book, and that due to the high volume of mail I receive, I might not be able to reply to every message.

When you write, please be sure to include this book's title and author, as well as your name and phone or fax number. I will carefully review your comments and share them with the author and editors who worked on the book.

Fax: 317-817-7070

Email: cs_db@mcp.com

Mail: Executive Editor
            Client/Server Database Team
            Macmillan Computer Publishing
            201 West 103rd Street
            Indianapolis, IN 46290 USA

Introduction

OCP Training Guide: Oracle DBA is designed for database administrators whose goal is certification as an Oracle Certified Professional (OCP). The Database Administration track consists of four exams, and each exam has 60–70 questions and lasts 90 minutes. These exams measure your ability to use PL/SQL and administer, tune, and perform backup and recovery on Oracle 7.3 databases. This book is designed to help you meet these goals by preparing you for the OCP Database Administrator exam.

WHO SHOULD READ THIS BOOK

This book is your one-stop shop. Everything you need to know to pass the exam is in here. Depending on your personal study habits or learning style, however, you may benefit from taking a class in addition to reading the book or buying this book in addition to attending a class.

This book also can help advanced users and administrators who aren't studying for the exam but are looking for a single-volume reference on Oracle database administration.

HOW THIS BOOK HELPS YOU

This book provides a self-guided tour of all the areas covered by the OCP Database Administrators track exam and teaches you the specific skills you need to achieve your Oracle certification. You'll also find helpful hints, tips, real-world examples, exercises, and references to additional study materials. Specifically, this book is set up to help you in the following ways:

- **Organization.** This book is organized by major exam topics and individual exam objectives. Every objective you need to know for the OCP Database Administrator track exam is covered in this book; you can quickly locate each objective as they are addressed in the chapters. This information is also conveniently condensed on the tear-out card at the front of this book.

- **Study strategies.** Each chapter contains strategies for studying the topic covered. These strategies will help you study the chapter's more complex topics by summarizing the topic before you begin studying.

- **Extensive practice-test options.** Plenty of review questions appear at the end of each chapter to test your comprehension of the material covered within that chapter. An answer list follows the questions so you can check yourself. These review questions will help you determine what you understand thoroughly and what topics require further review.

You'll also get a chance to practice for the certification exams by using the Top Score test engine on the accompanying CD-ROM. The questions on the CD-ROM provide a more thorough and comprehensive picture of what the certification exams really are like.

For more information about the exam or the certification process, contact Oracle:

- Oracle Education: 1-650-506-7000

- World Wide Web: http://www.education.oracle.com/certification

UNDERSTANDING WHAT THE OCP DATABASE ADMINISTRATION TRACK COVERS

The Oracle Certified Professional Database Administrator track covers the main topic areas represented by the conceptual groupings of the test objectives. Each chapter represents a main topic area. The exam objectives are listed by topic area:

◆ The first exam will test your knowledge of SQL and PL/SQL language and usage. Because you must have a complete understanding of SQL to take this exam, Chapter 1, "Introduction to SQL," covers the components of the SQL language. Chapter 2, "PL/SQL Language Structure," contains the required information on PL/SQL, whereas Chapter 3, "PL/SQL in Use," covers how PL/SQL is implemented in programming entities. Finally, because the first exam also requires the understanding of the Oracle security model, Chapter 4, "Security," discusses using role-based security, auditing, and profiles (although auditing and profiles aren't tested until the second exam).

◆ The second exam covers Oracle7 database administration. You must be completely familiar with the Oracle7 architecture, including the different options for starting and stopping an instance, which is covered in Chapter 5, "Oracle Database Architecture." Managing database entities is covered in Chapter 6, "Managing Database Structures." You need to know how to implement SQL*Loader in order to load data, so Chapter 7, "Utilities," provides that information. The second exam also tests you on the security model by using the auditing and profile features, which are explained in Chapter 4.

◆ The third exam covers backing up and recovering an Oracle7 database. This includes the use of offline and online backups as well as the Export logical backup utility. Chapter 7, "Utilities," includes the Export and Import utilities as part of its discussion. Chapter 8, "Backing Up a Database," covers the architecture that Oracle provides for backing up the database in offline and online mode. Chapter 9, "Database Recovery," covers all levels of database recovery—database, tablespace, and datafile. It also includes key information on how Oracle manages the internal operation of recovering transactions.

◆ The fourth and final exam tests you on how to tune an Oracle database for peak performance. Chapter 10, "Database Tuning," covers optimal database configuration and application design. Chapter 11, "Tuning Memory Structures," explains how to tune the memory structures of an Oracle instance, how best to manage rollback segments and redo logs, and how to tune SQL statements.

HARDWARE AND SOFTWARE NEEDED

As a self-paced study guide, this book was designed with the expectation that you will use Oracle as you follow the exercises while you learn. Oracle designed the exams to operate in a wide range of actual situations, and the exercises in this book encompass that range.

Oracle runs on more than 70 platforms, but the exams aren't based on any specific operating system. You can use the Oracle DBMS or Personal Oracle in preparing for the exams.

It's somewhat easier to obtain access to the necessary computer hardware and software in a corporate business environment. It can be difficult, however, to allocate enough time within the busy workday to complete a self-study program. Most of your study time will occur after normal working hours, away from the everyday interruptions and pressures of your regular job.

TIPS FOR THE EXAM

Remember the following tips as you prepare for the certification exams:

◆ **Read all the material.** Oracle has been known to include material not expressly specified in the objectives. This course includes additional information not required by the objectives in an effort to give you the best possible preparation for the examination and for real-world experiences.

◆ **Complete the exercises in each chapter.** They will help you gain experience in understanding the Oracle7 DBMS. The OCP exams are experience based and require you to have used the Oracle DBMS. Exercises for each objective are placed at the end of each chapter.

◆ **Complete all the questions in the "Review Questions" sections.** Complete the questions at the end of each chapter; they help you remember key points. The questions are fairly simple, but be warned: Some questions require more than one answer.

◆ **Review the exam objectives.** Develop your own questions for each topic listed. If you can make and answer several questions for each topic, you shouldn't find it difficult to pass the exam.

NOTE

Although this book is designed to prepare you to take and pass the Oracle Certified Professional exam, there are no guarantees. Read this book, work through the questions and exercises, and when you feel confident, take a practice assessment exam with the Top Score test engine. This should tell you whether you're ready for the real thing.

When taking the actual certification exam, be sure to answer all the questions before your time limit expires. Don't spend too much time on any one question. If you are unsure about an answer, answer the question as best you can and mark it for later review, after you finish the rest of the questions.

Remember, the primary object isn't to pass the exam; it's to understand the material. After you understand the material, passing the exam should be simple. Knowledge is a pyramid; to build upward, you need a solid foundation. The Oracle Certified Professional programs are designed to ensure that you have that solid foundation.

Good luck!

NEW RIDERS PUBLISHING

The staff of New Riders Publishing is committed to bring you the best in computer reference material. Each New Riders book is the result of months of work by authors and staff who research and refine the information contained within its covers.

As part of this commitment to you, the NRP reader, New Riders invites your input. Please let us know whether you enjoy this book, whether you have trouble with the information or examples presented, or whether you have a suggestion for the next edition.

Note, however, that New Riders staff can't serve as a technical resource during your preparation for the OCP exams or for questions about software- or hardware-related problems. Please refer instead to the documentation that accompanies Oracle or to Oracle's help system.

If you have a question or comment about any New Riders book, there are several ways to contact New Riders Publishing. We will respond to as many readers as we can. Your name, address, or phone number will never become part of a mailing list or be used for any purpose other than to help us continue to bring you the best books possible. You can write to us at the following address:

New Riders Publishing
Attn: Executive Editor
Client/Server Database Team
201 W. 103rd Street
Indianapolis, IN 46290

If you prefer, you can fax New Riders Publishing at 317-817-7070.

You also can send email to New Riders at the following Internet address:

    cs-db@mcp.com

Thank you for selecting *OCP Training Guide: Oracle DBA*!

SQL AND PL/SQL

This chapter helps you prepare for the exam by covering the following objectives:

Understand the concept of tables and column constraints.

▶ This objective is necessary to understand how data is stored in relational databases. A beginner should understand the concept of tables, columns, and constraints before looking at the SQL commands.

Understand the characteristics of different Oracle data types.

▶ This objective is important so that you understand the behavior of different Oracle data types. After you understand their behavior and characteristics, you can use them in SQL commands.

Write SELECT statements to retrieve data from tables.

▶ This objective is necessary so that you understand how data is retrieved from the database with the SELECT statement. This chapter gives you the syntax of the SELECT statement and how the SELECT list and WHERE clause can be used to restrict output with certain criteria.

Use SQL functions in SELECT statements.

▶ This objective is necessary to understand the concept of functions and nested functions, and how built-in SQL functions can be used in SQL statements.

CHAPTER 1

Introduction to SQL

Use subqueries, join operations, and set operations in SELECT statements.

▶ This objective is necessary to understand the methods for retrieving related data from more than one table.

Insert, update, and delete data.

▶ This objective is important so that you understand how other manipulation tasks—such as data insertion, modification, and deletion—can be performed with SQL commands.

Understand the working of the optimizer and differentiate between cost-based and rule-based optimizing methods.

▶ This objective is important to understand how the Oracle optimizer works to determine the most efficient access path to execute SQL commands. You will learn different types of optimization methods available in Oracle and how they vary.

Run the ANALYZE command to gather statistics for tables, indexes, and clusters.

▶ This objective is necessary to understand how you can use the ANALYZE command to gather table statistics. Table statistics are used by the cost-based optimizer.

Run the EXPLAIN PLAN command to analyze the access path selected by Oracle.

▶ This objective is necessary to understand the working of the EXPLAIN PLAN command. This command shows you the access path that Oracle has chosen to execute the SQL.

STUDY STRATEGIES

▶ The best way to study this chapter is in front of a computer. You should have access to SQL*Plus, a database connection, and a text editor such as Notepad.

Many examples used in this chapter are based on particular sets of tables. Different sections of this chapter use different sets of tables to illustrate the use of SQL commands. You can create these tables yourself in your own user or in default user SCOTT before practicing the examples and playing with them. (The default password for the user SCOTT is TIGER.) Keep in mind that this chapter isn't using Oracle demonstration tables.

Feel free to experiment with the SQL statements. This is the best way you can learn more about the command and get a better understanding of its usage. Try to understand the concept first from the book before practicing and experimenting with it on SQL*Plus.

INTRODUCTION

Structured Query Language (SQL) is a set of commands used by programmers to access data within an Oracle database. Oracle tools such as Developer/2000 and application programs often enable programmers to access the data within Oracle database without writing SQL, but these applications in turn issue SQL commands to Oracle on behalf of the programmers when executing the user's request. To interact with an Oracle database, you must have a working knowledge of SQL.

Briefly, take a quick look at how SQL developed. In June 1970, Dr. E.F. Codd advanced his theory of relational database management in the paper, "A Relational Model of Data for Large Shared Data Banks," published in the *Association of Computer Machinery* journal. Codd's model is now accepted as the standard model for relational database management systems (RDBMS). IBM Corporation developed a language called Structured English Query Language (SEQUEL) to use Codd's model. Later this language came to be known as Structured Query Language (SQL). Oracle Corporation introduced the first commercially available implementation of SQL. SQL is now accepted as the standard language for relational database management system.

The purpose of SQL is to interface to a relational database such as Oracle. SQL statements are instructions to the database. The main characteristics of SQL are as follows:

- ◆ It processes sets of data as groups.

- ◆ It provides automatic navigation to the data.

- ◆ Its statements stand alone and can be very complex.

- ◆ It lacks flow-control statements like those provided by C and BASIC, although Oracle's extension to SQL, called PL/SQL, provides flow-control programming.

SQL enables you to work with data at the logical level and hides all details of the physical level from users. For example, users write in only the SQL command that they want to see, and only those rows that satisfy certain conditions. SQL retrieves the result in a single step and passes that result as a unit to users or to the application.

Users don't have to process each row one by one, nor do they have to mention how data is physically stored and how to retrieve them.

You can write commands in SQL for a variety of tasks:

◆ To query data

◆ To insert, update, and delete rows in a table

◆ To create, replace, alter, and drop objects

◆ To control access to the database and its objects

In Oracle, all SQL statements use an optimizer that determines the fastest means of accessing the given data. Oracle also provides techniques you can use to make the optimizer perform its job better.

TABLES AND COLUMNS

Understand the concept of tables and column constraints.

Before going into the SQL language, let's look at the concepts of tables, columns, Oracle data types, and SQL grammar. This creates the ground for understanding SQL statements.

In relational databases, data is stored in tables. A *table* is a set of columns. A table may represent an entity or an association between entities. Entity integrity and referential integrity are imposed by primary-key and foreign-key constraints on the table columns. In Figure 1.1, the tables Rooms and Workers represent entities, whereas the table Worker Room, in the logical view, represents an association.

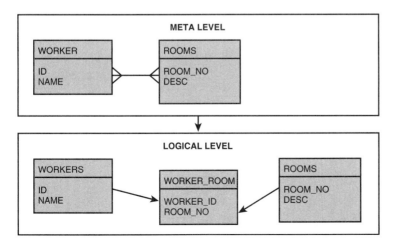

FIGURE 1.1
A table can represent an entity or an association.

In a relational concept, each row must be unique because it is representing a unique occurrence of the entity or association. Consider Figure 1.2. In the EMPLOYEES table, suppose that you have two rows exactly identical. You won't be able to identify the unique occurrence of either of the two workers and hence won't be able to do any calculations on the attributes of either worker. Primary keys are declared on one or more columns of the table to guarantee that all values in these columns will be unique and therefore all the rows of the table will be unique. Oracle doesn't let you insert duplicate values in a primary key column or columns.

In the EMPLOYEES table, the DEPTNO column contains IDs of the departments in which employees work. The DEPARTMENTS table has the detailed information of all the departments. Because the company has only four departments, the DEPTNO column in the EMPLOYEES table can contain only four values: 1, 2, 3, and 4. If this column contains the value 5, it would mean nothing because there's no such department in the company whose ID is 5. To maintain data integrity, foreign keys are declared on the columns so that they can store only those values now present in some other column. In this example, the DEPTNO column of the EMPLOYEES table is a foreign key referencing the DEPTNO column of the DEPARTMENTS table. When a foreign key is declared on a column, it becomes Oracle's responsibility to maintain the referential integrity, and you become headache-free.

In addition to the primary-key and foreign-key constraints, you also can declare other constraints on a column, such as not null, check constraint, and unique constraint. Table 1.1 summarizes the meaning of different constraint types.

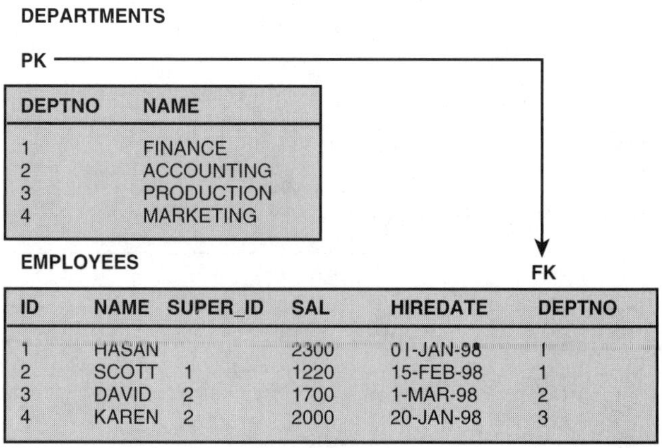

FIGURE 1.2
Primary key/foreign key relationship.

DEPARTMENTS

DEPTNO	NAME
1	FINANCE
2	ACCOUNTING
3	PRODUCTION
4	MARKETING

EMPLOYEES

ID	NAME	SUPER_ID	SAL	HIREDATE	DEPTNO
1	HASAN		2300	01-JAN-98	1
2	SCOTT	1	1220	15-FEB-98	1
3	DAVID	2	1700	1-MAR-98	2
4	KAREN	2	2000	20-JAN-98	3

TABLE 1.1

SUMMARY OF KEY CONSTRAINTS

Constraint	Description
Primary key (PK)	Only unique values can be inserted into a primary key. No nulls and no duplicates are allowed. A table can have only one primary key.
Foreign key (FK)	Only those values can be inserted into a foreign key column that exist in the primary key or unique key column this foreign key is referencing. Nulls and duplicates are allowed, however.
Unique key (UK)	Only unique values can be inserted into a unique column. Nulls are allowed in a unique key column. A table can have more than one unique key.
Not null (NN)	Nulls are not allowed in a not-null column.

In a relational database, the order of rows and columns is not important, as they used to be in flat-file systems. Rows and columns can be retrieved in any order irrespective of the order in which the data was stored. All the table names in a schema must be unique, and all the column names in a table must be unique. Table names and column names must start with an alphabetic character.

Data Types

Understand the characteristics of different Oracle data types.

Every column must be assigned a valid Oracle data type. The data types define the domain of values that each column can contain. Until Oracle7, SQL could use only predefined data types. In Oracle8, however, users can define their own data types.

A column can be assigned one of the following data types:

NUMBER	DATE
CHAR	RAW
VARCHAR2	LONG RAW
LONG	ROW ID

> **NOTE**
>
> **Precision and Scale**   When defining a column as INTEGER, you aren't allowed to define the limit for precision. Scale is automatically 0. Defining a column as INTEGER is the same as defining a column as NUMBER (*,0)—* means there's no limit on the precision, whereas 0 means scale is zero. When defining a column as DECIMAL, you can specify precision as well as scale.

The NUMBER Type

The NUMBER data type is used to store numeric data. It consists of two parts: precision and scale. *Precision* is the maximum number of digits to be stored. *Scale* indicates the position of the decimal number of digits. Precision can range from 1 to 38; scale can range from –84 to 127.

For compatibility with other database packages, Oracle offers two synonyms for NUMBER data types:

◆   DECIMAL

◆   INTEGER

Internally, Oracle converts the DECIMAL and INTEGER data types into NUMBER data types.

The VARCHAR2 Type

The VARCHAR2 data type is used to store variable-length character strings for up to 2,000 single-byte characters. Keep in mind that unlike the CHAR data type, VARCHAR2 is a variable-length data type, meaning that if you define a column as VARCHAR2(20) and store a value in this column that takes only 10 bytes, Oracle will occupy only 10 bytes to store this value, not 20 bytes. You are specifying the limit in terms of bytes, not characters. If a character is occupying a single byte in your system, the limit specified can be taken as a limit in terms of number of characters.

The synonym VARCHAR is available for the data type VARCHAR2. If a column is defined as VARCHAR, internally it will be converted into VARCHAR2. Oracle Corporation does not recommend the use of VARCHAR, because its meaning will be changed in upcoming versions.

The CHAR Type

The CHAR data type is used to store fixed-length character strings for up to 255 single-byte characters. If a column is defined as CHAR(20) and you store a value containing only 10 single-byte characters, Oracle will use 20 bytes in the memory to store this value and will append blank spaces to the value until it occupies 20 bytes. For efficient disk storage, the VARCHAR2 data type should be used rather than CHAR.

The LONG Type

The LONG data type is used to store variable-length character strings for up to 2GB. If a column is designed to store very large string values, you could define it as a LONG. Columns that store comments, text resumes, or notes are good candidates for the LONG data type.

One restriction on the usage of LONG data types is that you can't use them in SQL functions. The restriction also applies to SQL*Plus, where you can't use some of the functions (such as COPY) with this data type.

The DATE Type

The DATE data type is used to store date and time. Valid dates range from January 1, 4712 B.C. to A.D. December 31, 4712. Dates are discussed in detail later in this chapter.

The RAW Type

The RAW data type is used to store up to 255 bytes of binary data. Binary data can be used to store images, text documents, spreadsheets, sound files, and video clips.

The LONG RAW Type

The LONG RAW data type is used to store up to 2GB of variable-length binary data. Like the LONG data type, you can't use Oracle's built-in functions with the LONG RAW data type.

The ROWID Type

If you are storing row IDs in a column, you should define the data type of a column as ROWID. The rowid is the location of the row in the physical storage. Every row has a unique ID. The format of a rowid is *block-number.row-number.file-number*.

SQL GRAMMAR

Before going into the details of SQL statements, you need to keep in mind the following rules about the grammar of SQL:

◆ A SQL statement should be terminated by a semicolon(;). Until the semicolon is entered, the statement won't be executed.

◆ A SQL statement can be written in more than one line.

◆ SQL isn't case sensitive; keywords can be written in upper- or lowercase. If are referring to a string value stored in the database, however, case does matter—for example, the string value `'ORACLE'` isn't equal to `'oracle'` or `'Oracle.'`

SQL statements can be broadly categorized into three groups:

◆ Data Manipulation Language (DML)

◆ Data Definition Language (DDL)

◆ Data Control Language (DCL)

This chapter focuses on the DML statements in detail. For DCL and DDL statements, see Chapter 4, "Security," and Chapter 6, "Managing Database Structures," respectively. The following four basic statements fall under the category of DML statements:

◆ `SELECT`

◆ `INSERT`

◆ `UPDATE`

◆ `DELETE`

Figure 1.3 shows the grouping of different SQL commands into three main categories.

FIGURE 1.3
Grouping of SQL statements.

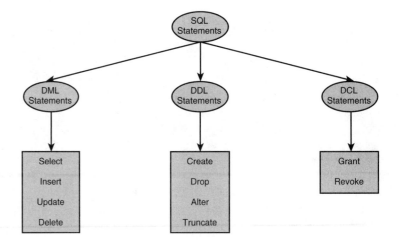

The SELECT Statement

Write SELECT statements to retrieve data from tables.

You use the SELECT statement to retrieve data from database tables. It is the most frequently used statement because data is retrieved more often than inserted, deleted, or updated.

A SELECT statement works on the concept of projection and restriction. *Projection* is the columns you want to see; *restriction* is the rows you want to retrieve. Figure 1.4 shows the concept of projection and restriction. By selecting the desired columns from the table and by restricting the rows with criteria, you can retrieve any desirable data from the table.

Consider the following table:

```
WORKERS
ID FNAME  LNAME    PHONE      CITY    ST   SAL  COMM BONUS
-- -----  -------  ---------- ------- ---- ---- ---- ---------

 1 HASAN  MIR      9056005410 ST PAUL KS   2250 1000 100
 2 LARRY  PHILLIPS 9057360123 ST PAUL KS    900 1000 200
 3 DAVID  PHILLIPS 4165329103 BUFFALO NY   1200  500
 4 AISHA  SHUJA    4169358051 BUFFALO NY   2300 1200 100
 5 KAREN  TAYLOR   9059356361 ST PAUL KS   1100  150
```

You can use the script in Listing 1.1 to create this table.

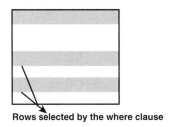

Restriction

Rows selected by the where clause

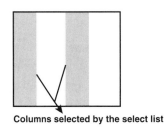

Projection

Columns selected by the select list

FIGURE 1.4
Concept of restriction and projection.

LISTING 1.1

CREATING THE WORKERS TABLE

```
DROP TABLE WORKERS;
CREATE TABLE WORKERS
     (ID NUMBER(3) PRIMARY KEY,
     FNAME VARCHAR2(15),
     LNAME VARCHAR2(15),
     PHONE VARCHAR2(10),
     CITY VARCHAR2(15),
     STATE VARCHAR2(2),
     SALARY NUMBER(6),
     COMM NUMBER(6),
     BONUS NUMBER(6));
INSERT INTO WORKERS VALUES
     (1,'HASAN','MIR','9056005410','ST PAUL','KS',
     ➡2250,1000,100);
INSERT INTO WORKERS VALUES
     (2,'LARRY','PHILLIPS','9057360123','ST PAUL','KS',
     ➡900,1000,200);
INSERT INTO WORKERS VALUES
     (3,'DAVID','PHILLIPS','4165329103','BUFFALO','NY',
     ➡1200,500,NULL);
```

continues

LISTING 1.1   *continued*

CREATING THE WORKERS TABLE

```
INSERT INTO WORKERS VALUES
     (4,'AISHA','SHUJA','4169358051','BUFFALO','NY',
     ➥2300,1200,100);
INSERT INTO WORKERS VALUES
     (5,'KAREN','TAYLOR','9059356361','ST PAUL','KS',
     ➥1100,150,NULL);
```

A simple SELECT statement tells Oracle which columns you want to project and from which table. The following query retrieves workers' first names:

```
SELECT FNAME FROM WORKERS;

FNAME
----------
HASAN
LARRY
DAVID
AISHA
KAREN
```

You can select more than one column in any order you want. Just write the column names in the SELECT list in any order you want. Commas must separate the column names:

```
SELECT FNAME, LNAME, PHONE FROM WORKERS;

FNAME       LNAME       PHONE
----------  ----------  ----------
HASAN       MIR         9056005410
LARRY       PHILLIPS    9057360123
DAVID       PHILLIPS    4165329103
AISHA       SHUJA       4169358051
KAREN       TAYLOR      9059356361
```

You can use * in the SELECT list as a shortcut for selecting all the columns in the default order:

```
SELECT * FROM WORKERS;

ID FNAME LNAME     PHONE       CITY     ST  SAL   COMM  BONUS
-- ----- --------  ----------  -------- --  ----- ----- -----
1  HASAN MIR       9056005410  ST PAUL  KS  2250  1000  100
2  LARRY PHILLIPS  9057360123  ST PAUL  KS   900  1000  200
3  DAVID PHILLIPS  4165329103  BUFFALO  NY  1200   500
4  AISHA SHUJA     4169358051  BUFFALO  NY  2300  1200  100
5  KAREN TAYLOR    9059356361  ST PAUL  KS  1100         150
```

The WHERE Clause

Along with projection, a SELECT statement can also define restriction of rows through criteria based on an optional WHERE clause. The following query brings the data of those workers whose salary is less than 2,000:

```
SELECT * FROM WORKERS WHERE SAL < 2000;

ID FNAME  LNAME     PHONE       CITY     ST   SAL   COMM  BONUS
-- ------ --------- ----------- -------  --  ----- ----- ------
 2 LARRY  PHILLIPS  9057360123  ST PAUL  KS   900  1000   200
 3 DAVID  PHILLIPS  4165329103  BUFFALO  NY  1200   500
 5 KAREN  TAYLOR    9059356361  ST PAUL  KS  1100   150
```

The WHERE clause can contain comparisons such as

=	Equal to
>	Greater than
<	Less than
>=	Greater than or equal to
<=	Less than or equal to
!=	Not equal to

The WHERE clause can also compare two columns:

```
SELECT * FROM WORKERS WHERE COMM >= SAL;

ID FNAME  LNAME     PHONE       CITY     ST   SAL   COMM  BONUS
-- ------ --------- ----------- -------  --  ----- ----- ------
 2 LARRY  PHILLIPS  9057360123  ST PAUL  KS   900  1000   200
```

You can specify very complex criteria in a WHERE clause by using the AND and OR keywords. Parentheses can be used if necessary:

```
SELECT * FROM WORKERS WHERE
    (SAL > 2000 OR (COMM > SAL AND BONUS > 100))
    AND STATE = 'KS';

ID FNAME  LNAME     PHONE       CITY     ST   SAL   COMM  BONUS
-- ------ --------- ----------- -------  --  ----- ----- ------
 1 HASAN  MIR       9056005410  ST PAUL  KS  2250  1000   100
 2 LARRY  PHILLIPS  9057360123  ST PAUL  KS   900  1000   200
```

The BETWEEN Operator

Suppose that you want to find out the names of all workers whose salary is between 1,000 and 2,000. You can write the following query:

```
SELECT FNAME FROM WORKERS WHERE SAL >= 1000 AND SAL <=
➥2000;

FNAME
- - - - - - - - - -
DAVID
KAREN
```

As a shortcut, you can use the BETWEEN operator to get the same result:

```
SELECT FNAME FROM WORKERS WHERE SAL BETWEEN 1000 AND 2000;

FNAME
- - - - - - - - - -
DAVID
KAREN
```

You can use the BETWEEN operator with other data types as well, such as CHAR, VARCHAR2, and DATE.

The IN Operator

If you were asked to retrieve the information of workers HASAN, ROBERT, and KAREN, you would write the following query:

```
SELECT * FROM WORKERS WHERE
FNAME = 'HASAN' OR FNAME = 'ROBERT' OR FNAME = 'KAREN';

ID FNAME  LNAME     PHONE       CITY     ST   SAL   COMM  BONUS
-- ------ -------   ----------  -------  --  ----- ----- ------
1  HASAN  MIR       9056005410  ST PAUL  KS   2250  1000  100
5  KAREN  TAYLOR    9059356361  ST PAUL  KS   1100        150
```

You can retrieve the same result by using the IN operator:

```
SELECT * FROM WORKERS WHERE FNAME IN
➥('HASAN', 'ROBERT', 'KAREN');

ID FNAME  LNAME     PHONE       CITY     ST   SAL   COMM  BONUS
-- ------ -------   ----------  -------  --  ----- ----- ------
1  HASAN  MIR       9056005410  ST PAUL  KS   2250  1000  100
5  KAREN  TAYLOR    9059356361  ST PAUL  KS   1100        150
```

If for any row the value of the FNAME column matches any of the values given in parentheses after the IN keyword, that row is displayed in the result. Similarly, if you want to see the information of all the workers except for HASAN, ROBERT, and KAREN, you can use a NOT IN operator:

```
SELECT * FROM WORKERS WHERE FNAME NOT IN
➥('HASAN', 'ROBERT', 'KAREN');
```

> **NOTE**
>
> **The ➥ Character** Macmillan Publishing uses a special character, ➥, which indicates that a code line has been continued to another line. Don't try to use a similar character in your actual code; instead, just move the code following that character to the preceding line.

```
ID FNAME  LNAME     PHONE        CITY      ST    SAL   COMM  BONUS
-- -----  --------  ----------  -------   --   -----  ----  ------
 2 LARRY  PHILLIPS  9057360123  ST PAUL   KS     900  1000  200
 3 DAVID  PHILLIPS  4165329103  BUFFALO   NY    1200   500
 4 AISHA  SHUJA     4169358051  BUFFALO   NY    2300  1200  100
```

The LIKE Operator

You have to rely on the LIKE operator when you aren't sure of the exact spelling of any word in the database. Suppose that many different data-entry operators enter data, and city names are entered in different ways throughout the WORKERS table:

```
ID FNAME  LNAME     PHONE        CITY      ST    SAL   COMM  BONUS
-- -----  --------  ----------  -------   -----  -----  ----  -----
 1 HASAN  MIR       9056005410  ST PAUL   KS    2250  1000  100
 2 LARRY  PHILLIPS  9057360123  ST.PAUL   KS     900  1000  200
 3 DAVID  PHILLIPS  4165329103  BUFFALO   NY    1200   500
 4 AISHA  SHUJA     4169358051  BUFFALO   NY    2300  1200  100
 5 KAREN  TAYLOR    9059356361  STPAUL    KS    1100   150
```

As you can see, St. Paul has been entered three different ways. When you are asked to retrieve all the names of those workers who live in St. Paul, you don't know whether the city name has been entered with a space between the first and second word of the city name, whether there's a period, or whether ST PAUL has been typed in as one word. The only thing you are certain about is that the city name starts with the letters ST and ends at PAUL. You issue the following query:

```
SELECT FNAME, CITY FROM WORKERS WHERE CITY LIKE 'ST%PAUL';
```

```
FNAME       CITY
----------  ----------
HASAN       ST PAUL
LARRY       ST.PAUL
KAREN       STPAUL
```

By using the LIKE operator, you could find the correct rows even though the city name was entered in an inconsistent manner.

The % character is a wildcard. By using % in 'ST%PAUL', you are telling Oracle to bring all the records where the city name starts with ST and ends with PAUL, and that anything could be between them, even nothing.

Another wildcard, _ (underscore), is available with the LIKE operator. Look at the result of the same query that uses _ rather than %:

NOTE

Changing the Table   Use the following commands to change the original WORKERS table for this section:

```
UPDATE WORKERS SET CITY =
➥'ST.PAUL' WHERE ID = 2;
UPDATE WORKERS SET CITY =
➥'STPAUL' WHERE ID = 5;
```

When you are done with this section, you can remove these temporary changes from the table with the following commands:

```
UPDATE WORKERS SET CITY =
➥'ST PAUL' WHERE ID = 2;
UPDATE WORKERS SET CITY =
➥'ST PAUL' WHERE ID = 5;
```

```
SELECT FNAME, CITY FROM WORKERS WHERE CITY LIKE 'ST_PAUL';

FNAME        CITY
----------   ----------
HASAN        ST PAUL
LARRY        ST.PAUL
```

By using an underscore in ST_PAUL, you are telling Oracle to bring all the records where city name starts with letters ST and ends at PAUL and only one letter is between them. You can use both wildcards at the same time with the LIKE operator, depending on the task you want to perform.

Similarly, you can use NOT LIKE to find all records that don't match your search criteria. The following query brings the names of those workers whose names don't start with the letter A:

```
SELECT FNAME FROM WORKERS WHERE FNAME NOT LIKE 'A%';

FNAME
----------
HASAN
LARRY
DAVID
KAREN
```

The DISTINCT Keyword

Suppose that you want find all the states in the WORKERS table. You would issue the following query:

```
SELECT STATE FROM WORKERS;

STATE
-----
KS
KS
NY
NY
KS
```

As you can see, you are also getting some duplicate values, even though you want to see only distinct values in the STATE column. For this purpose, you use the DISTINCT keyword after the SELECT keyword:

```
SELECT DISTINCT STATE FROM WORKERS;

STATE
-----
KS
NY
```

You can also use DISTINCT when projecting more than one column. Using DISTINCT on more than one column prevents the same combination of values to appear more than once.

```
SELECT DISTINCT CITY, STATE FROM WORKERS;

CITY        STATE
----------  -----
BUFFALO     NY
ST PAUL     KS
```

The SELECT List

The SELECT statement list can contain one or more of the following:

- ◆ Column names
- ◆ Literals
- ◆ Expressions
- ◆ String operators
- ◆ Functions
- ◆ Variables

Using Column Names

You have seen examples of the usage of column names in the SELECT list. There's no restriction on the number of times each column name is used. You can use one column name more than one time in the SELECT list:

```
SELECT ID, FNAME, ID FROM WORKERS;

ID FNAME              ID
-- ----------  ---------
 1 HASAN               1
 2 LARRY               2
 3 DAVID               3
 4 AISHA               4
 5 KAREN               5
```

Using Literals

You also can use literals in the SELECT list:

```
SELECT ID, ' IS A UNIQUE KEY FOR WORKER',
➥FNAME FROM WORKERS;

ID 'ISAUNIQUEKEYFORWORKER'     FNAME
-- -------------------------  -----
 1  IS A UNIQUE KEY FOR WORKER HASAN
 2  IS A UNIQUE KEY FOR WORKER LARRY
```

```
3  IS A UNIQUE KEY FOR WORKER DAVID
4  IS A UNIQUE KEY FOR WORKER AISHA
5  IS A UNIQUE KEY FOR WORKER KAREN
```

Using Expressions

Sometimes you need to see the result after performing some calculations on the column values. Expressions can be used in the SELECT list:

```
SELECT FNAME, SAL * 0.30 FROM WORKERS
WHERE SAL < 2000;

FNAME       SAL*0.30
---------- ---------
LARRY            270
DAVID            360
KAREN            330

SELECT ENAME, SAL + COMM FROM EMP WHERE COMM IS NOT NULL;

ENAME       SAL+COMM
---------- ---------
ALLEN           1900
WARD            1750
MARTIN          2650
TURNER          1500
```

Suppose that you want to calculate 5 * (3 + 2). Because it is an expression, you can use it in the SELECT statement. But the question is which table to select it from. If you select this expression from the WORKERS table, the result 25 will appear as many times as the number of rows in the WORKERS table. Therefore, to see the result only one time, the table that has only one row should be used. One such table, DUAL, exists in the database. It has only one column, DUMMY, and only one row. The DUAL table is used for the purpose of selecting something that doesn't have to be selected from any particular table—for example, the expression 5 * (3 + 2).

```
SELECT 5 * (3+2) FROM DUAL;

5*(3+2)
------
    25
```

Using String Operators

The || concatenation operator is one of the most important string operators. In a SELECT list, you can concatenate as many values as you want. To concatenate two strings, place || between them:

```
SELECT FNAME || ' HAS A HIGH SALARY AND LIVES IN ' ||
➥CITY FROM WORKERS
WHERE SAL > 2000;

FNAME¦¦'HASAHIGHSALARYANDLIVESIN'|| CITY
-------------------------------------------
HASAN HAS A HIGH SALARY AND LIVES IN ST PAUL
AISHA HAS A HIGH SALARY AND LIVES IN BUFFALO
```

Using Built-In Functions

Use SQL functions in SELECT statements.

Functions can be built-in or user-defined. Oracle's built-in functions are available to use in SQL statements. You also can write your own customized functions by using PL/SQL, although we won't cover that here.

No matter what language you use, the concept of functions is almost the same. A function will return a value of specific data type. One or more values can be passed to functions so that the return value is based on some calculations on the input values passed to the function. Figure 1.5 shows the concept of a function.

When functions are used in a SELECT statement, the returned value of the function is displayed in the result. Another powerful feature of functions is that the value returned by a function can be used as an input value to another function. By nesting the functions, you can perform powerful operations on the data. Figure 1.6 shows the concept of nested functions.

FIGURE 1.5
Concept of a function.

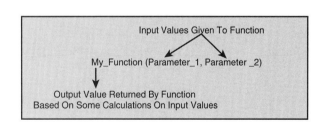

FIGURE 1.6
Concept of nested functions.

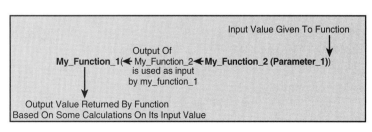

Built-in functions can be further divided into single-row functions and group functions. A single-row function returns a value for each row, whereas a group function returns one value for the whole column. The following sections show some examples of single-row functions; we will discuss group functions later when studying the GROUP BY clause.

The LENGTH Function

The LENGTH function takes a string value as input and returns its length as output.

```
SELECT LNAME, LENGTH (LNAME) FROM WORKERS;

LNAME        LENGTH(LNAME)
----------   -------------
MIR          3
PHILLIPS     8
PHILLIPS     8
SHUJA        5
TAYLOR       6
```

The UPPER and LOWER Functions

The UPPER function converts the input string value into uppercase; the LOWER function converts the input value into lowercase.

```
SELECT LOWER (FNAME), UPPER (FNAME) FROM WORKERS;

LOWER(FNAME) UPPER(FNAME)
------------ -----------
hasan        HASAN
larry        LARRY
david        DAVID
aisha        AISHA
karen        KAREN
```

The SUBSTR Function

You use the SUBSTR function to extract a string from another string. SUBSTR takes three parameters as input:

◆ The main string from which a substring must be extracted

◆ The starting position of extraction

◆ The number of characters to be extracted

The following query brings the first three characters of the workers' names:

```
SELECT SUBSTR (FNAME, 1, 3) FROM WORKERS;

SUB
- - -
HAS
LAR
DAV
AIS
KAR
```

You can write a query to bring the last three characters of the names by using nested functions:

```
SELECT SUBSTR (FNAME, LENGTH (FNAME) -2, 3) FROM WORKERS;

SUB
- - -
SAN
RRY
VID
SHA
REN
```

The following query brings the names of the employees in sentence case:

```
SELECT UPPER (SUBSTR (FNAME, 1,1)) ||
➥LOWER (SUBSTR (FNAME, 2, LENGTH (FNAME) ) ) )
➥FROM WORKERS;

UPPER(SUBS
- - - - - - - - - -
Hasan
Larry
David
Aisha
Karen
```

The GREATEST and LEAST Functions

The GREATEST function takes two values as input and returns the greater of the two. Similarly, the LEAST function takes two values as input and returns the smaller of the two. NUMBER data types are usually given as input, but these functions can also compare string values.

The following query brings the greatest of salary, commission, and bonus for each worker:

```
SELECT FNAME, GREATEST ( BONUS, GREATEST (SAL, COMM) )
➥FROM WORKERS;
```

> **Using Nested Functions** With GREATEST, you can compare only two values. This sample code uses one GREATEST function in another one to find the greatest among three values.

```
FNAME         GREATEST(BONUS,GREATEST(SAL,COMM))
----------    ------------------------------------
HASAN                                         2250
LARRY                                         1000
DAVID
AISHA                                         2300
KAREN
```

The following query brings the smaller of first name and last name in terms of their lengths:

```
SELECT LEAST (LENGTH (FNAME), LENGTH (LNAME ) )
➡FROM WORKERS;

LEAST(LENGTH(FNAME),LENGTH(LNAME))
----------------------------------
                                 3
                                 5
                                 5
                                 5
                                 5
```

The GREATEST and LEAST functions can also take CHAR and VARCHAR2 values as input arguments. The GREATEST function returns the one that precedes the other in alphabetic order. Similarly, the LEAST function returns the one that comes later in alphabetic order.

The ROUND Function

The ROUND function takes a number value as input and returns its rounded value as output.

```
SELECT ROUND (1.34) FROM DUAL;

ROUND(1.34)
-----------
          1
```

The DECODE Function

After reading all the preceding examples, you should have a clear idea of how functions are used in SQL statements. Before moving on, however, let's look at two very important functions—DECODE and NVL—that are used more than any other functions.

Consider the STATE column of the WORKERS table. It contains postal abbreviations of the states in which each worker lives. To see the full name of the state rather than the abbreviations, you can use the DECODE function:

```
SELECT FNAME, DECODE (STATE, 'NY', 'NEW YORK', 'KS',
➥'KANSAS', 'NOT KNOWN') FROM WORKERS;

FNAME       DECODE(ST
---------   ---------
HASAN       KANSAS
LARRY       KANSAS
DAVID       NEW YORK
AISHA       NEW YORK
KAREN       KANSAS
```

The value of the first parameter will be compared with NY. If the
value is NY, the function will return NEW YORK. If the value of the first
parameter isn't NY, it would be compared to KS. If the value is KS,
KANSAS will be returned. If the value of the first parameter isn't even
KS, the function would return the default value NOT KNOWN.

You can use the DECODE function with even more parameters,
depending on the number of items you want to decode. The simplest form of the DECODE function would contain three parameters:

```
SELECT FNAME, DECODE (STATE, 'NY', 'NEW YORK') FROM
➥WORKERS;

FNAME       DECODE(S
---------   --------
HASAN
LARRY
DAVID       NEW YORK
AISHA       NEW YORK
KAREN
```

In this case, if the value of the first parameter is NY, NEW YORK will be
returned as output; otherwise, a null value would be returned
because no default value is specified. (Null values are discussed in the
next section.)

You can use the DECODE function to perform complex tasks. To find
the greater of salary and commission for the workers, use the following simple statement:

```
SELECT FNAME, GREATEST (SAL, COMM) FROM WORKERS;

FNAME       GREATEST(SAL,COMM)
---------   ------------------
HASAN                     2250
LARRY                     1000
DAVID                     1200
AISHA                     2300
KAREN
```

If you are asked to find the greater of salary and commission as well as tell which one is greater, however, you could use DECODE to solve this problem:

```
SELECT FNAME, GREATEST (SAL, COMM) , DECODE ( GREATEST
➥(SAL, COMM), SAL, 'SALARY', 'COMMISSION') FROM WORKERS;

FNAME      GREATEST(SAL,COMM)   DECODE(GRE)
---------- ------------------   -----------
HASAN                    2250   SALARY
LARRY                    1000   COMMISSION
DAVID                    1200   SALARY
AISHA                    2300   SALARY
KAREN                           COMMISSION
```

The DECODE function compares the value given by GREATEST with the value of the SAL and COMM column. If this value equals the value of SAL, then SALARY is returned by the decode function; otherwise, COMMISSION is returned as the default value.

The Concept of the NULL Value and the NVL Function

Before studying the working of the NVL function, you have to understand the concept of the NULL value in RDBMSs such as Oracle.

In nonrelational databases, the absence of a value was indicated by a special character, such as * or 0. Relational databases introduced the concept of null. A null is used when the column value isn't yet available or is not applicable. A null value has special characteristics:

◆ NULL isn't equal to another NULL.

◆ The expression NULL = CONSTANT is always false. At the same time, the expression NULL != CONSTANT is also false.

◆ NULL isn't equal to 0 or a blank character.

◆ Multiplication, division, addition, or subtraction of any number by NULL results in a NULL.

You can easily see this behavior by looking at the results of the following query:

```
SELECT FNAME FROM WORKERS WHERE COMM != 500;

FNAME
----------
HASAN
LARRY
AISHA
```

The query was supposed to bring all the rows except the one where commission is 500. Those rows are also not shown in the result where the commission is null. The reason is very simple: The expression NULL != 500 resulted in false. Consider the following statements:

```
SELECT FNAME, GREATEST (SAL, COMM) FROM WORKERS;

FNAME        GREATEST(SAL,COMM)
----------   ------------------
HASAN                      2250
LARRY                      1000
DAVID                      1200
AISHA                      2300
KAREN


SELECT FNAME, LEAST (SAL, COMM) FROM WORKERS;

FNAME        LEAST(SAL,COMM)
----------   ---------------
HASAN                   1000
LARRY                    900
DAVID                    500
AISHA                   1200
KAREN
```

Similarly, the results of both statements contain null for those rows, where commission is null because the expressions SAL > NULL and SAL < NULL resulted in false.

You use the NVL function to convert the NULL value into the specified not-null value. This function takes two parameters as input:

◆ The value to be checked, regardless of whether it is null

◆ A not-null value that is to be returned if the first parameter value is NULL

The function returns the value of the second parameter if the value of the first parameter is null; otherwise, the value of the first parameter is returned.

```
SELECT NVL (COMM,0) FROM WORKERS;

NVL(COMM,0)
-----------
       1000
       1000
        500
       1200
          0
```

> **A NULL Workaround** Sometimes it is important to convert NULL values into 0 or some other constant before performing a calculation. For example, you would like to see the value of SAL to be returned by the GREATEST function when the value of COMM is NULL.

As you can see in the result, 0 is displayed, whereas the commission is null and commission's value is unchanged where it is not null. By using NVL in the following statement, you could get meaningful results:

```
SELECT FNAME, GREATEST (SAL,NVL (COMM,0)) FROM WORKERS;

FNAME          GREATEST(SAL,NVL(COMM,0))
----------     -------------------------
HASAN                               2250
LARRY                               1000
DAVID                               1200
AISHA                               2300
KAREN                               1100
```

If you want to use criteria in the WHERE clause that involves comparison with NULL, special keywords are used: IS and IS NOT. For example, the following queries bring all the names of the workers whose commission is null and not null, respectively:

```
SELECT FNAME FROM WORKERS WHERE COMM IS NULL;

FNAME
----------
KAREN

SELECT FNAME FROM WORKERS WHERE COMM IS NOT NULL;

FNAME
----------
HASAN
LARRY
DAVID
AISHA
```

Notice that the IS keyword is used rather than an = sign. Recall the characteristics of the NULL value: One NULL isn't equal to another. Therefore if we use WHERE COMM = NULL, logically it will always result in false. That's why IS and IS NOT are used rather than = and != when doing comparisons with NULLs.

The NVL function sometimes proves to be very helpful in preventing errors in the application that may be caused by the returned NULL.

Other Single-Row Functions

Other important single-row functions are as follows:

Function Syntax	Return Value
CEIL(n)	Smallest integer greater than or equal to n
EXP(n)	e raised to the nth power

Function Syntax	Return Value
FLOOR(n)	Largest integer equal to or less than n
MOD(m, n)	Remainder of m divided by n; returns the value of m if n is 0
POWER(m, n)	m raised to the nth power
ROUND(n[, m])	n rounded to m places right of the decimal point; if m is omitted, to 0 places
SQRT(n)	Square root of n
TRUNC(n[, m])	n truncated to m decimal places; if m is omitted, to 0 places
CONCAT(c1, c2)	c1 concatenated with c2.
INITCAP(char)	char, with the first letter of each word in uppercase, all other letters in lowercase

The following table points out the different ways the ROUND, TRUNCATE, FLOOR, and CEIL functions deal with decimal numbers:

	15.25	15.5	15.75	16.00	Comments
ROUND	15	16	16	16	Returns the rounded number
TRUNCATE	15	15	15	16	Returns the number after removing the decimals
FLOOR	15	15	15	16	Returns the highest integer less than the number
CEIL	16	16	16	16	Returns the highest integer greater than the number

We will look at few more functions in this chapter later when studying topics related to the DATE data type.

Using Variables

You can use user-defined variables in SQL*Plus. The variable name in the SELECT statement must be preceded by a & character. If the value of this variable is already defined, SQL*Plus will substitute the value; otherwise, it will prompt you to enter the value before executing the statement.

```
SELECT '&COLUMN_NAME' FROM WORKERS;

Enter value for column_name:
```

You can define the value for this variable as

```
DEFINE COLUMN_NAME = ID
```

Now, if you run the query again, you won't be prompted to enter the value for the user variable because it is already defined. Use the UNDEFINE command to remove its definition from the memory:

```
UNDEFINE COLUMN_NAME
```

Whenever a variable is defined with the DEFINE command, its data type is CHAR. In fact, user-defined variables can be used in any clause of the SELECT statement.

Column Aliases

By now, you must have noticed that the column names or the contents of the expression or functions become the default column heading in the displayed result. Sometimes you want the heading to be different from the column names, or you want to give meaningful headings to the complex expression used in the SELECT list. You can assign aliases to the columns that appear as result headings.

You can assign an alias to a column by writing a suitable alias after the column name in the SELECT list. If the alias consists of more than one word, it should be enclosed in double quotation marks:

```
SELECT FNAME "FIRST NAME", LNAME "LAST NAME",
➥SAL SALARY FROM WORKERS;

FIRST NAME    LAST NAME    SALARY
----------    ---------    ------
HASAN         MIR          2250
LARRY         PHILLIPS      900
DAVID         PHILLIPS     1200
AISHA         SHUJA        2300
KAREN         TAYLOR       1100

SELECT FNAME   NAME, SAL + NVL(COMM,0) + NVL (BONUS,0)
➥"TOTAL EARNINGS" FROM WORKERS;

NAME        TOTAL EARNINGS
----------  --------------
HASAN           3350
LARRY           2100
DAVID           1700
AISHA           3600
KAREN           1250
```

The ORDER BY Clause

No matter what the order of columns and rows in physical storage is, users can retrieve the data in any desired order. As you've seen when studying the SELECT statement, the columns will appear in the same order in the result as given in the SELECT list. Similarly, you can specify the desired row order according to which rows you want to appear in the result. The ORDER BY clause is used for this purpose.

ORDER BY must be the last clause of the SELECT statement. The name of the column that you want to use to order rows should follow the ORDER BY keyword.

```
SELECT * FROM WORKERS ORDER BY LNAME;

ID FNAME LNAME    PHONE       CITY    ST   SAL  COMM BONUS
-- ----- -------- ----------- ------- -- ----- ----- ------
 1 HASAN MIR      9056005410  ST PAUL KS  2250 1000  100
 2 LARRY PHILLIPS 9057360123  ST PAUL KS   900 1000  200
 3 DAVID PHILLIPS 4165329103  BUFFALO NY  1200  500
 4 AISHA SHUJA    4169358051  BUFFALO NY  2300 1200  100
 5 KAREN TAYLOR   9059356361  ST PAUL KS  1100       150
```

Sometimes you want to give more than one column name in an ORDER BY clause separated with commas. Suppose that you are using a last-name column to order the rows. If more than one worker has the same last name, you want to order the rows by using the first-name column. In this case, you want to include both column names in an ORDER BY clause.

```
SELECT * FROM WORKERS ORDER BY LNAME, FNAME;

ID FNAME LNAME    PHONE       CITY    ST   SAL  COMM BONUS
-- ----- -------- ----------- ------- -- ----- ----- ------
 1 HASAN MIR      9056005410  ST PAUL KS  2250 1000  100
 3 DAVID PHILLIPS 4165329103  BUFFALO NY  1200  500
 2 LARRY PHILLIPS 9057360123  ST PAUL KS   900 1000  200
 4 AISHA SHUJA    4169358051  BUFFALO NY  2300 1200  100
 5 KAREN TAYLOR   9059356361  ST PAUL KS  1100       150
```

You can also use ORDER BY for retrieving rows in descending order by using one or more columns. For this purpose, the DESC keyword is added after each column name. The following query brings the information of workers in descending order by using the last-name column, and if the last names are the same, by using the first-name column.

```
SELECT * FROM WORKERS ORDER BY LNAME DESC, FNAME DESC;

ID FNAME LNAME    PHONE       CITY    ST   SAL  COMM BONUS
-- ----- -------- ----------- ------- -- ----- ----- ------
 5 KAREN TAYLOR   9059356361  ST PAUL KS  1100       150
```

N
O
T
E

Ordering More Than One Column in Descending Order   Adding the DESC keyword after both column names is necessary if you want to use both in descending order. You can order one column as ascending and the other as descending, or vice versa.

```
4  AISHA  SHUJA     4169358051 BUFFALO NY    2300  1200 100
2  LARRY  PHILLIPS  9057360123 ST PAUL KS     900  1000 200
3  DAVID  PHILLIPS  4165329103 BUFFALO NY    1200  500
1  HASAN  MIR       9056005410 ST PAUL KS    2250  1000 100
```

Referring to Columns by Aliases

You can see the importance of column aliases in the ORDER BY clause. You can use column aliases in the ORDER BY clause when a column name is too big or the contents of an expression are too difficult to write again:

```
SELECT FNAME, SAL + NVL (COMM, 0) "EARNINGS" FROM WORKERS
ORDER BY EARNINGS;

FNAME        EARNINGS
---------    ---------
KAREN            1100
DAVID            1700
LARRY            1900
HASAN            3250
AISHA            3500
```

Note that it is not necessary to order the rows by using only those columns that you have used in the SELECT list. You can also use those columns in the ORDER BY clause that aren't projected in the query:

```
SELECT FNAME, LNAME FROM WORKERS
ORDER BY ID;

FNAME        LNAME
---------    ----------
HASAN        MIR
LARRY        PHILLIPS
DAVID        PHILLIPS
AISHA        SHUJA
KAREN        TAYLOR
```

Group Functions

As mentioned earlier, built-in functions can be divided into two categories: single-row functions and group functions. This section focuses on the usage of group functions. Group functions vary from single-row functions in that they return only one value for the whole column, after the rows are filtered out by the WHERE clause. Figure 1.7 illustrates the concept of group functions.

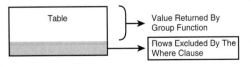

FIGURE 1.7
The concept of a group function.

Consider the table EMPLOYEES, which you can create with the script in Listing 1.2:

```
ID NAME   SUPER_ID SAL  HIREDATE   DEPTNO
-- -----  -------- ---- ---------- ------
 1 HASAN           2300 01-JAN-98       1
```

```
2 SCOTT        1 1220 15-FEB-98        1
3 DAVID        2 1700 01-MAR-98        2
4 KAREN        2 2000 20-JAN-98        3
```

LISTING 1.2

CREATING THE EMPLOYEES TABLE

```
DROP TABLE EMPLOYEES;
CREATE TABLE EMPLOYEES
     (ID NUMBER(3) PRIMARY KEY,
     NAME VARCHAR2(15),
     SUPER_ID NUMBER(3) REFERENCES EMPLOYEES (ID),
     SALARY NUMBER(6),
     HIREDATE DATE,
     DEPTNO NUMBER(3));
INSERT INTO EMPLOYEES VALUES (1,'HASAN',NULL,2300,
➡'01-JAN-98',1);
INSERT INTO EMPLOYEES VALUES (2,'SCOTT',1,1220,
➡'15-FEB-98',1);
INSERT INTO EMPLOYEES VALUES (3,'DAVID',2,1700,
➡'01-MAR-98',2);
INSERT INTO EMPLOYEES VALUES (4,'KAREN',2,2000,
➡'20-JAN-98',3);
```

The following query brings the sum of all the salaries in the EMPLOYEES table:

```
SELECT SUM (SAL) FROM EMPLOYEES;

SUM(SAL)
--------
    7220
```

The following query brings the sum of salaries for all the departments, except for department 3:

```
SELECT SUM (SAL) FROM EMPLOYEES WHERE DEPTNO != 3;

SUM(SAL)
--------
    5220
```

You can nest group functions within single-row functions, or single-row functions within group functions:

```
SELECT GREATEST (SUM(SAL), SUM(COMM)) FROM WORKERS;

SELECT SUM (GREATEST(SAL, COMM)) FROM WORKERS;
```

Some other important group functions are as follows:

Function Syntax	*Return Value*
AVG(*n*)	Average value
COUNT(*n*)	Number of rows
MAX(*n*)	Maximum value
MIN(*n*)	Minimum value
STDDEV(*n*)	Standard deviation
VARIANCE(*n*)	Variance

The GROUP BY Clause

You can split a table into groups and use a group function on each group. Figure 1.8 illustrates the concept.

Suppose that you want to find sum of salaries of each department rather than the whole company's sum of salaries. Therefore, you should use the GROUP BY clause to split the EMPLOYEES table into as many groups as there are distinct department numbers, and then apply the SUM group function to each group:

```
SELECT DEPTNO, SUM (SAL) FROM EMPLOYEES
GROUP BY DEPTNO;

   DEPTNO   SUM(SAL)
--------- ---------
        1      3520
        2      1700
        3      2000
```

This statement's GROUP BY clause tells Oracle that you want the sum of salaries for each department. If this statement is executed with the GROUP BY clause, however, an error will occur because the group function SUM (SAL) will bring only one result, whereas the DEPTNO column will bring as many rows as the number of rows in the EMPLOYEES table. Therefore, a group function can't be used in the SELECT list with other single row functions or columns without using the GROUP BY clause.

FIGURE 1.8

Using the GROUP BY clause to divide a table into groups.

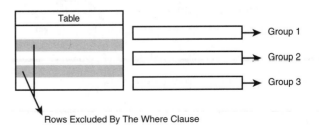

You also can use the WHERE clause when using GROUP BY. Suppose that you want the sum of salaries of all the departments and don't want to include salaries lower than 1,000 in the calculations:

```
SELECT DEPTNO, SUM (SAL) FROM EMPLOYEES
WHERE SAL >= 1000
GROUP BY DEPTNO;

DEPTNO   SUM(SAL)
-------- --------
       1     3520
       2     1700
       3     2000
```

In this case, the table will be split into groups after the rows not satisfying the WHERE clause criteria are filtered out.

The HAVING Clause

As you have seen, you can split a table into different groups and then apply group functions on individual groups. You can further restrict the group results returned by the group function by using the HAVING clause, as shown in Figure 1.9.

Suppose that you want to find the sum of salaries of all the departments and want to see the results for only those departments that have the sum of salaries equal to or more than 1,000:

```
SELECT DEPTNO, SUM (SAL) FROM EMPLOYEES
GROUP BY DEPTNO
HAVING SUM (SAL) >= 1000;

DEPTNO   SUM(SAL)
-------- --------
       1     3520
       2     1700
       3     2000
```

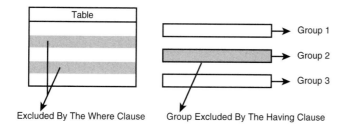

Excluded By The Where Clause   Group Excluded By The Having Clause

FIGURE 1.9

An illustration of a HAVING clause.

Notice that first you use a GROUP BY clause to split the table into as many groups as there are distinct department numbers. Then you apply the function SUM (SAL) on these groups. If the function resulted in a salary sum less than 1,000 on any group, that group is excluded from the final result.

Let's add few more requirements for the query. Now you want to find out the sum of salaries for all the departments, not including salaries lower than 1,200; see the results for only those departments that have the sum of salaries equal to or more than 2,000; and see the rows in the order of the department numbers:

```
SELECT DEPTNO, SUM (SAL) FROM EMPLOYEES
WHERE SAL >= 1200
GROUP BY DEPTNO
HAVING SUM (SAL) >= 2000
ORDER BY DEPTNO;

DEPTNO   SUM(SAL)
-------- ---------
       1      3520
       3      2000
```

As a rule of thumb, remember two things:

◆ You can't use a HAVING clause if the GROUP BY clause isn't used.

◆ If your criterion involves group functions, it must be placed in the HAVING clause, as in SUM (SAL) >= 2000. If your criterion involves a single-row function or column names, it must be placed in the WHERE clause, as in SAL >= 1200.

Selecting Data from More Than One Table

Use subqueries, join operations, and set operations in SELECT statements.

So far, you've extracted data from one table, first from the table WORKERS and then from the table EMPLOYEES. Another table, DEPARTMENTS, has all department information. The EMPLOYEES table has a DETPNO column that shows the department number of each employee and is also a foreign key referencing the DEPARTMENTS table's DEPTNO column. The DEPARTMENTS table is as follows:

```
DEPTNO   NAME
-------  -----------
      1  FINANCE
      2  ACCOUNTING
      3  PRODUCTION
      4  MARKETING
```

Use the script in Listing 1.3 to create this table.

LISTING 1.3

CREATING THE DEPARTMENTS TABLE

```
DROP TABLE DEPARTMENTS;
CREATE TABLE DEPARTMENTS
     (DEPTNO NUMBER(3) PRIMARY KEY,
     NAME VARCHAR2(15));
INSERT INTO DEPARTMENTS VALUES (1,'FINANCE');
INSERT INTO DEPARTMENTS VALUES (2,'ACCOUNTING');
INSERT INTO DEPARTMENTS VALUES (3,'PRODUCTION');
INSERT INTO DEPARTMENTS VALUES (4,'MARKETING');
ALTER TABLE EMPLOYEES ADD FOREIGN KEY (DEPTNO)
➥REFERENCES DEPARTMENTS (DEPTNO);
```

If you are asked to get the names of the employees and the department names in which they work, you have to extract data from two tables. You can extract data from more than one table by using one or a combination of the following methods:

◆ Join operation

◆ Subqueries

◆ Set operation

Join Operations

A *join operation* is a mechanism of relating two or more tables by giving the joining conditions. Join operations can be divided into three major types:

◆ Equi-joins

◆ Self-joins

◆ Outer joins

The following sections use the EMPLOYEES and DEPARTMENTS tables to discuss each type.

Equi-Joins

To join tables, you include their names in the FROM clause separated with commas. Figure 1.10 shows the concept of joins.

FIGURE 1.10

An equi-join of the DEPARTMENTS and EMPLOYEES tables. The joining condition is *WHERE* EMPLOYEES.DEPTNO = DEPARTMENTS.DEPTNO.

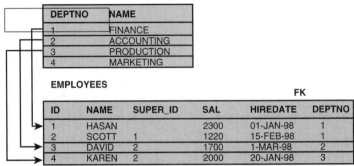

Consider the query that should bring the employees' names and the department names in which they work. Because the data should come from more than two tables, you must join the EMPLOYEES and DEPARTMENTS tables and specify the join condition:

```
SELECT EMPLOYEES.NAME, DEPARTMENTS.NAME
FROM EMPLOYEES, DEPARTMENTS
WHERE EMPLOYEES.DEPTNO = DEPARTMENTS.DEPTNO;
```

```
NAME        NAME
----------  ------------
HASAN       FINANCE
SCOTT       FINANCE
DAVID       ACCOUNTING
KAREN       PRODUCTION
```

Look at the SELECT list carefully. Because the NAME column is in both tables, you have to specify the column name as well as the table name so that Oracle can distinguish between the EMPLOYEES table's NAME column and the DEPARTMENTS table's NAME column. If you had used SELECT NAME, NAME, an error would have occurred because Oracle couldn't resolve the ambiguity of the columns. Similarly, the DEPTNO column also exists in both tables, so it is included in the WHERE clause with the table names. Another way of resolving the ambiguity is to assign an alias to the table name and use an alias to specify which column belongs to which table.

```
SELECT E.NAME, D.NAME
FROM EMPLOYEES E, DEPARTMENTS D
WHERE E.DEPTNO = D.DEPTNO;
```

```
NAME        NAME
----------  ------------
HASAN       FINANCE
SCOTT       FINANCE
DAVID       ACCOUNTING
KAREN       PRODUCTION
```

In this statement, alias E is assigned to the EMPLOYEES table and alias D is assigned to the DEPARTMENTS table. The alias is assigned by placing the alias after the table name. In the SELECT list and the WHERE clause, notice that aliases were used instead of table names to resolve the ambiguity.

You can further restrict rows by giving additional WHERE conditions. The following query brings only names and department names of those workers whose salary is more than 2,000:

```
SELECT E.NAME, D.NAME
FROM EMPLOYEES E, DEPARTMENTS D
WHERE E.DEPTNO = D.DEPTNO
AND E.SAL > 2000;


NAME        NAME
---------- ------------
HASAN       FINANCE
```

You have seen some examples of a type of join operation known as an equi-join, where the foreign key of one table is equated with the parent key of another table.

Let's look at the equi-join operation in other way. Try to execute the same query without the WHERE clause and select all the columns:

```
SELECT *
FROM EMPLOYEES E, DEPARTMENTS D;

ID NAME   SUPER  SAL    HIREDATE    DEPT  DEPT   NAME
          _ID                       NO    NO
-- -----  -----  -----  ---------   ----  ----   ----------
1  HASAN         2300   01-JAN-98   1     1      FINANCE
2  SCOTT  1      1220   15-FEB-98   1     1      FINANCE
3  DAVID  2      1700   01-MAR-98   2     1      FINANCE
4  KAREN  2      2000   20-JAN-98   3     1      FINANCE
1  HASAN         2300   01-JAN-98   1     2      ACCOUNTING
2  SCOTT  1      1220   15-FEB-98   1     2      ACCOUNTING
3  DAVID  2      1700   01-MAR-98   2     2      ACCOUNTING
4  KAREN  2      2000   20-JAN-98   3     2      ACCOUNTING
1  HASAN         2300   01-JAN-98   1     3      PRODUCTION
2  SCOTT  1      1220   15-FEB-98   1     3      PRODUCTION
3  DAVID  2      1700   01-MAR-98   2     3      PRODUCTION
4  KAREN  2      2000   20-JAN-98   3     3      PRODUCTION
1  HASAN         2300   01-JAN-98   1     4      MARKETING
2  SCOTT  1      1220   15-FEB-98   1     4      MARKETING
3  DAVID  2      1700   01-MAR-98   2     4      MARKETING
4  KAREN  2      2000   20-JAN-98   3     4      MARKETING
```

The result is called a *Cartesian product*. Whenever two or more tables are joined without the WHERE clause, the result will contain all the possible combinations of rows of the joining tables. Now consider this Cartesian product as a temporary table. If you apply the WHERE clause on this temporary table and select the desired columns, you will get the final result. It is good practice to think of it this way: The final result of a join operation is the projection and restriction of a Cartesian product based on the selection of columns given in the SELECT list and the restriction criteria specified in the WHERE clause.

Because these examples were joining two tables, you had only one joining condition. If you want to join three tables, you have to use two joining conditions. As a rule of thumb, remember that the number of joining conditions is equal to the number of joining tables minus 1.

Self-Joins

You have seen how two tables can be combined to result in a Cartesian product and how you can select desired columns and rows from the Cartesian product. This concept can also be applied to a single table. One table is combined with itself and results in a Cartesian product. The desired columns and rows can then be selected from the Cartesian product. This type of join operation is called a *self-join*. Figure 1.11 shows the concept of a self-join.

Self-joins can be very useful sometimes. To determine the Cartesian product, join the EMPLOYEES table with itself. To join a table with itself, its name is given twice in the FROM clause but different aliases are assigned to each name to resolve column ambiguity:

FIGURE 1.11

A self-join of the EMPLOYEES table. The joining condition is A.D = B.SUPER_ID.

EMPLOYEES A

ID	NAME	SUPER_ID	SAL	HIREDATE	DEPTNO
1	HASAN		2300	01-JAN-98	1
2	SCOTT	1	1220	15-FEB-98	1
3	DAVID	2	1700	1-MAR-98	2
4	KAREN	2	2000	20-JAN-98	3

EMPLOYEES B

ID	NAME	SUPER_ID	SAL	HIREDATE	DEPTNO
1	HASAN		2300	01-JAN-98	1
2	SCOTT	1	1220	15-FEB-98	1
3	DAVID	2	1700	1-MAR-98	2
4	KAREN	2	2000	20-JAN-98	3

```
SELECT * FROM EMPLOYEES A, EMPLOYEES B;
```

ID	NAME	SUPER _ID	SAL	HIREDATE	DEPT NO	ID	NAME	SUPER _ID	SAL	HIREDATE	DEPT NO
1	HASAN		2300	01-JAN-98	1	1	HASAN		2300	01-JAN-98	1
2	SCOTT	1	1220	15-FEB-98	1	1	HASAN		2300	01-JAN-98	1
3	DAVID	2	1700	01-MAR-98	2	1	HASAN		2300	01-JAN-98	1
4	KAREN	2	2000	20-JAN-98	3	1	HASAN		2300	01-JAN-98	1
1	HASAN		2300	01-JAN-98	1	2	SCOTT	1	1220	15-FEB-98	1
2	SCOTT	1	1220	15-FEB-98	1	2	SCOTT	1	1220	15-FEB-98	1
3	DAVID	2	1700	01-MAR-98	2	2	SCOTT	1	1220	15-FEB-98	1
4	KAREN	2	2000	20-JAN-98	3	2	SCOTT	1	1220	15-FEB-98	1
1	HASAN		2300	01-JAN-98	1	3	DAVID	2	1700	01-MAR-98	2
2	SCOTT	1	1220	15-FEB-98	1	3	DAVID	2	1700	01-MAR-98	2
3	DAVID	2	1700	01-MAR-98	2	3	DAVID	2	1700	01-MAR-98	2
4	KAREN	2	2000	20-JAN-98	3	3	DAVID	2	1700	01-MAR-98	2
1	HASAN		2300	01-JAN-98	1	4	KAREN	2	2000	20-JAN-98	3
2	SCOTT	1	1220	15-FEB-98	1	4	KAREN	2	2000	20-JAN-98	3
3	DAVID	2	1700	01-MAR-98	2	4	KAREN	2	2000	20-JAN-98	3
4	KAREN	2	2000	20-JAN-98	3	4	KAREN	2	2000	20-JAN-98	3

Look at the Cartesian product carefully. Look at the rows where A.SUPER_ID = B.ID. In all these rows, A.NAME is the name of the employee and B.NAME is the name of the supervisor:

```
SELECT A.NAME, B.NAME
FROM EMPLOYEES A, EMPLOYEES B
WHERE A.SUPER_ID = B.ID;


NAME    NAME
-----   -----
SCOTT   HASAN
DAVID   SCOTT
KAREN   SCOTT
```

Look at the Cartesian product again. Look at the rows where A.ID = B.SUPER_ID. In all these rows, A.NAME is the employee's name and B.NAME is the name of employee's subordinate:

```
SELECT A.NAME, B.NAME
FROM EMPLOYEES A, EMPLOYEES B
WHERE A.ID = B.SUPER_ID;


NAME    NAME
-----   -----
HASAN   SCOTT
SCOTT   DAVID
SCOTT   KAREN
```

Outer Joins

Look at the DEPARTMENTS table. The company has four departments, but there are no employees in department 4. To see all the department numbers, department names, and names of workers in each department, you would use the following query:

```
SELECT D.DEPTNO, D.NAME, E.NAME
FROM DEPARTMENTS D, EMPLOYEES E
WHERE D.DEPTNO = E.DEPTNO
ORDER BY D.DEPTNO;

DEPTNO    NAME          NAME
-------  ----------    ----------
      1  FINANCE       HASAN
      1  FINANCE       SCOTT
      2  ACCOUNTING    DAVID
      3  PRODUCTION    KAREN
```

Notice that the result shows all the department rows and their corresponding employees, except for department 4. This is because the EMPLOYEES table doesn't have 4 in its DEPTNO column. When the WHERE clause criteria was applied to the Cartesian product of tables DEPARTMENTS and EMPLOYEES, the row of department number 4 wasn't selected.

In the situation when one or more parent key column values haven't been used in the foreign key column at all and you still want the missing values to appear in the result, you can use outer joins. To use an outer join, place (+) in the join condition of the WHERE clause after the column name of the table with the missing values (usually the foreign key). In the example, department 4 is missing in the child table EMPLOYEES but exists in the parent table DEPARTMENTS.

```
SELECT D.DEPTNO, D.NAME, E.NAME
FROM DEPARTMENTS D, EMPLOYEES E
WHERE D.DEPTNO = E.DEPTNO(+)
ORDER BY D.DEPTNO;

DEPTNO    NAME          NAME
-------  ----------    ----------
      1  FINANCE       HASAN
      1  FINANCE       SCOTT
      2  ACCOUNTING    DAVID
      3  PRODUCTION    KAREN
      4  MARKETING
```

Notice that the value of E.NAME is NULL for department 4.

Outer joins are very useful in some queries. Suppose that you are asked to find the names of those departments that have no workers in them. You can use an outer-join operation on the tables EMPLOYEES and DEPARTMENTS by placing (+) after the foreign key of the EMPLOYEES table in the joining condition. This time, you want to see only those rows where E.NAME is null.

```
SELECT D.DEPTNO, D.NAME
FROM DEPARTMENTS D, EMPLOYEES E
```

```
WHERE D.DEPTNO = E.DEPTNO(+)
AND E.NAME IS NULL
ORDER BY D.DEPTNO;

DEPTNO NAME
------- ----------
      4 MARKETING
```

Both types of joins—equi-joins and self-joins—can come under the category of outer joins. The preceding example shows an equi-join operation used as an outer join. Let's see an example of how a self-join can be used as an outer join. The following query brings the names of those workers who aren't supervising anyone:

```
SELECT A.NAME
FROM EMPLOYEES A, EMPLOYEES B
WHERE A.ID = B.SUPER_ID(+)
AND B.SUPER_ID IS NULL;

NAME
----------
DAVID
KAREN
```

Subqueries

Subqueries are important in the sense that they can handle very complex tasks. Most tasks that can be performed by using join operations can also be performed by using subqueries.

The result returned by a subquery is used by the WHERE clause of the main query. If you are asked to find out the names of the departments in which the employee with the ID of 2 works, for example, the following query brings the desired result:

```
SELECT NAME
FROM DEPARTMENTS
WHERE DEPTNO =
(SELECT DEPTNO
FROM EMPLOYEES
WHERE ID = 2);

NAME
----------
FINANCE
```

Look at the statement carefully. First, Oracle will solve the subquery that will give the number of that department in which the employee with the ID of 2 works—that is, department 1. Then main query will find the name of the department whose department number is 1.

The following query brings those department names in which there's at least one employee:

```
SELECT NAME
FROM DEPARTMENTS
WHERE DEPTNO IN
    (SELECT DEPTNO
    FROM EMPLOYEES);


NAME
- - - - - - - - - -
FINANCE
ACCOUNTING
PRODUCTION
```

Notice that the WHERE clause of the main query is using the IN operator, whereas the WHERE clause of the preceding query was using the = operator. That's because the subquery of the second statement can bring more than one result, whereas the subquery of the first statement was guaranteed to bring at most one result. Similarly, you can use the NOT IN operator in subqueries. The following query brings the name of those departments that have no employees:

```
SELECT NAME
FROM DEPARTMENTS
WHERE DEPTNO NOT IN
    (SELECT DEPTNO
    FROM EMPLOYEES);

NAME
- - - - - - - - - -
MARKETING
```

Sometimes it is very useful to use group functions in a subquery. The following query brings the name of the worker with the highest salary:

```
SELECT NAME
FROM EMPLOYEES
WHERE SAL IN
    (SELECT MAX(SAL)
    FROM EMPLOYEES);

NAME
- - - - - - - - - -
HASAN
```

Again you are using the IN operator, not the = sign, because logically more than one worker can have the highest salary.

The EXISTS Operator

The EXISTS operator is useful when you aren't concerned with what value is returned by a subquery but are concerned only with whether the subquery returns any row. If the subquery has returned at least one row, the EXISTS operator returns true to the main query's WHERE clause and the row is included in the result. On the other hand, if the subquery doesn't return any row, the EXISTS operator returns false to the main query and the row isn't included in the result.

Suppose that you are asked to retrieve all the department names in which there's at least one employee. You have solved this problem by using join operation and subqueries with the IN operator. Now you will see how to solve this problem by using the EXISTS operator:

```
SELECT NAME
FROM DEPARTMENTS D
WHERE EXISTS
    (SELECT E.DEPTNO
    FROM EMPLOYEES E
    WHERE E.DEPTNO = D.DEPTNO);


NAME
----------
FINANCE
ACCOUNTING
PRODUCTION
```

Notice that the subquery is using the value of D.DEPTNO provided by the main query. To understand the working of this query, understand the process in this way:

◆ The main SELECT statement is checking each row of the DEPARTMENTS table one by one.

◆ If the row being assessed by the main query satisfies the WHERE clause criteria, or if the EXISTS operator returns true, the row is selected for display; otherwise, the row is rejected. After this row is selected or rejected, the next row is assessed. This process continues until all the rows are assessed.

◆ When the main query is checking any row, the decision to select or accept the row is based on the value returned by the EXISTS operator. The value returned by EXISTS is based on the number of rows returned by the subquery. If the subquery returns at least one row, EXISTS returns true; otherwise, it returns false.

◆ Each time the main query is assessing a new row, the subquery is executed and D.DEPTNO has the number of that department that belongs to the row being assessed by the main query. If the subquery finds any department number equal to the value of D.DEPTNO in the EMPLOYEES table, it will return at least one row, and the EXISTS operator will return true to the WHERE clause of the main query. Therefore, the row now being assessed by the main query will be selected for the display. On the other hand, if the subquery doesn't find any department number equal to the value of D.DEPTNO in the EMPLOYEES table, it won't return any rows. EXISTS will return false to the WHERE clause of the main query, and the row now being assessed by the main query won't be selected for display.

Similarly, you can find names of those departments in which there are no employees by using the NOT EXISTS operator. NOT EXISTS returns true if no rows are returned by the subquery and returns false when at least one row is returned by the subquery:

```
SELECT NAME
FROM DEPARTMENTS D
WHERE NOT EXISTS
    (SELECT E.DEPTNO
    FROM EMPLOYEES E
    WHERE E.DEPTNO = D.DEPTNO);


NAME
----------
MARKETING
```

Set Operations

Set operations can be performed on the results of two or more SELECT statements. The following set operations can be performed in SQL:

◆ UNION

◆ INTERSECTION

◆ SUBTRACTION

Figure 1.12 shows the concept of major set operations.

Following examples explain the usage of set operations. Consider the following three tables:

```
CUSTOMERS
ID CNAME      PHONE
-- -------- ----------
 1 STELCO     7135264364
 2 DORASCO    7139234562
 3 CMIC       4167360123
```

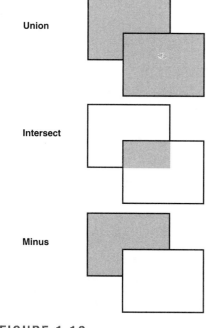

Union

Intersect

Minus

FIGURE 1.12
Concept of set operations.

```
SUPPLIERS
ID SNAME        PHONE
-- ---------- ----------
 1 STELCO       7135264364
 2 ABC INC.     9051453243
 3 AUTO PARTS   4165325325

CREDITORS
ID CRNAME   PHONE
-- ------- ----------
 1 STELCO  7135264364
 2 DOFASCO 7139234562
```

You can use the scripts in Listings 1.4, 1.5, and 1.6 to create the three tables.

LISTING 1.4

CREATING THE CUSTOMERS TABLE

```
DROP TABLE CUSTOMERS;
CREATE TABLE CUSTOMERS
     (ID NUMBER(3),
      CNAME VARCHAR2(15),
      PHONE VARCHAR2(10));
INSERT INTO CUSTOMERS VALUES (1,'STELCO','7135264364');
INSERT INTO CUSTOMERS VALUES (2,'DOFASCO','7139234562');
INSERT INTO CUSTOMERS VALUES (3,'CMIC','4167360123');
```

LISTING 1.5

CREATING THE SUPPLIERS TABLE

```
DROP TABLE SUPPLIERS;
CREATE TABLE SUPPLIERS
     (ID NUMBER(3),
      SNAME VARCHAR2(15),
      PHONE VARCHAR2(10));
INSERT INTO SUPPLIERS VALUES (1,'STELCO','7135264364');
INSERT INTO SUPPLIERS VALUES (2,'ABC INC.','9051453243');
INSERT INTO SUPPLIERS VALUES (3,'AUTO
PARTS','4165325325');
```

LISTING 1.6

CREATING THE CREDITORS TABLE

```
DROP TABLE CREDITORS;
CREATE TABLE CREDITORS
     (ID NUMBER(3),
      CRNAME VARCHAR2(15),
      PHONE VARCHAR2(10));
INSERT INTO CREDITORS VALUES (1,'STELCO','7135264364');
INSERT INTO CREDITORS VALUES (2,'DOFASCO','7139234562');
```

UNION

As you can see, some companies are customers as well as suppliers. Also, some companies are customers *or* suppliers. Now you will see how set operations can combine results from two or more SELECT statements.

The following query brings up names of all customers and suppliers:

```
SELECT CNAME FROM CUSTOMERS
UNION
SELECT SNAME FROM SUPPLIERS;

CNAME
-----------
ABC INC.
AUTO PARTS
CMIC
DOFASCO
STELCO
```

In the set operations, the number of columns in the SELECT list of all the queries must be the same and of the same data type. They don't have to have the same name—for example, one column is CNAME, but the other column is SNAME. The column names of the first statement also becomes the default column headings in the result. You use column aliases to give your own headings.

You can use the ORDER BY clause in two different ways: by specifying the column names or aliases of the first statement in the clause, or by specifying the position of columns you want to use in the ORDER BY clause. The following queries bring the same result:

```
SELECT CNAME, PHONE FROM CUSTOMERS
UNION
SELECT SNAME, PHONE FROM SUPPLIERS
ORDER BY PHONE;
```

```
CNAME         PHONE
-----------   ----------
AUTO PARTS    4165325325
CMIC          4167360123
STELCO        7135264364
DOFASCO       7139234562
ABC INC.      9051453243


SELECT CNAME FROM CUSTOMERS
UNION
SELECT SNAME FROM SUPPLIERS
ORDER BY 2;

CNAME         PHONE
-----------   ----------
AUTO PARTS    4165325325
CMIC          4167360123
STELCO        7135264364
DOFASCO       7139234562
ABC INC.      9051453243
```

UNION ALL

Notice that the names of the companies that are customers as well as suppliers appear only once in the final result of the preceding UNION query. This is because the UNION operator shows only distinct values. UNION ALL won't filter out the duplicate values:

```
SELECT CNAME FROM CUSTOMERS
UNION ALL
SELECT SNAME FROM SUPPLIERS;

CNAME
-----------
ABC INC.
AUTO PARTS
CMIC
DOFASCO
STELCO
STELCO
```

INTERSECT

The INTERSECT operator shows only the common value of the two results. The following query brings the name of those companies that are customers as well as suppliers:

```
SELECT CNAME FROM CUSTOMERS
INTERSECT
SELECT SNAME FROM SUPPLIERS;
```

```
CNAME
- - - - - - - - - - -
STELCO
```

MINUS

The MINUS operator subtracts one result from another. The following query brings all the names of companies that are customers, but not suppliers:

```
SELECT CNAME FROM CUSTOMERS
MINUS
SELECT SNAME FROM SUPPLIERS;

CNAME
- - - - - - - - - - -
CMIC
DOFASCO
```

Using More Than Two Queries with Set Operations

Just like the WHERE clause, you can make the set operations very complex by using parentheses. The following query brings all the names of customers and suppliers, but not creditors:

```
(SELECT CNAME FROM CUSTOMERS
UNION
SELECT SNAME FROM SUPPLIERS)
MINUS
SELECT CRNAME FROM CREDITORS;

CNAME
- - - - - - - - - - -
ABC INC.
AUTO PARTS
CMIC
```

> **NOTE**
>
> **The Syntax of a Complete SELECT Statement: A Summary** What follows is the complete syntax for a SELECT statement. Some clauses are required. The items enclosed in [ ] are optional.
>
> ```
> SELECT [DISTINCT] select list
> FROM TABLE_NAME[, TableName2],...
> [WHERE conditions]
> [GROUP BY clause]
> [HAVING clause]
> [ORDER BY clause]
> ```

THE INSERT STATEMENT

Insert, update, and delete data.

The INSERT statement is used to add new rows to a table:

```
INSERT INTO CUSTOMERS (ID, CNAME, PHONE) VALUES
➡(10, 'CMIC','9055600541');
```

You can specify the column names in any order you want. The sequence of column values must be the same as their corresponding column names. The following INSERT statement adds the same row with sequence of column given in a different way, for example:

```
INSERT INTO CUSTOMERS (ID, PHONE, CNAME) VALUES
➡(10, '9055600541','CMIC');
```

Suppose that you have a new customer, Dofasco, who doesn't have a telephone. You can insert NULL in the PHONE column for Dofasco in two ways:

```
INSERT INTO CUSTOMERS (ID, CNAME, PHONE) VALUES
➡(11, 'DOFASCO', NULL);
```

```
INSERT INTO CUSTOMERS (ID, CNAME) VALUES (11, 'DOFASCO');
```

In the latter case, the default value for the PHONE column would be inserted automatically if specified at table creation time. If any column is declared NOT NULL, you can't enter NULL in that column.

You can omit the column names from the INSERT statement if you are inserting values in all the columns in their default sequence:

```
INSERT INTO CUSTOMERS VALUES (12, 'GURUSOFT',
➡'9059848693');
```

Inserting Rows with the SELECT Statement

You can use a SELECT statement within the INSERT statement to read data from a table and insert into another table. Suppose that your suppliers with IDs 1, 2, and 4 have become your customers, also. The following statement inserts their rows from SUPPLIERS table into the CUSTOMERS table:

```
INSERT INTO CUSTOMERS
SELECT * FROM SUPPLIERS WHERE ID IN (1,2,4);
```

In this statement, you know that the SUPPLIERS table has the same number of columns and same sequence as the CUSTOMERS table. Therefore, you don't specify the column names in the preceding INSERT statement. If you aren't sure about the sequence of columns in the SUPPLIERS and CUSTOMERS tables, you can write the following statement to be on the safe side:

```
INSERT INTO CUSTOMERS (ID, CNAME, PHONE)
SELECT (ID, SNAME, PHONE) FROM SUPPLIERS
➡WHERE ID IN (1,2,4);
```

You can also insert selected columns from one table into another:

```
INSERT INTO CUSTOMERS (ID, CNAME)
SELECT (ID, SNAME) FROM SUPPLIERS WHERE ID IN (1,2,4);
```

This statement will insert only suppliers' IDs and names into CUSTOMERS table where the ID is 1, 2, or 4. In the PHONE column, NULL will be inserted or the default value will be inserted if specified at table creation time.

THE UPDATE STATEMENT

The UPDATE statement is used to modify already existing data. Suppose that the phone number of customer Dofasco, whose ID is 1, has changed from 9055600541 to 4165329103. The following statement updates the table with new information:

```
UPDATE CUSTOMERS SET PHONE = '4165329103'
WHERE ID = 1;
```

Notice that a unique ID identifies each customer. You could have used CNAME = 'DOFASCO' in the WHERE clause, but that would have changed the phone number of all customers whose name is Dofasco. That's why you should use primary key columns to identify each record uniquely.

One UPDATE statement can make more than one change at the same time. Suppose that customer Dofasco has changed its phone number as well as complained about the spelling mistake of its name in the database. The name is supposed to be Dofasco Inc., not Dofasco. The following statement makes both corrections at the same time:

```
UPDATE CUSTOMERS SET NAME = 'DOFASCO INC.',
➡PHONE = '4165329103'
WHERE ID = 1;
```

You can specify an expression in UPDATE statements as you can in SELECT statements. Suppose that the company's manager has announced a 10% salary increase for all workers in department 10. You can update this information in the WORKERS table as follows:

```
UPDATE WORKERS SET SAL = SAL * 1.1
WHERE DEPTNO = 1;
```

If you remove the WHERE clause from the UPDATE statement, the changes will then be made to each and every row of the table.

THE DELETE STATEMENT

The DELETE statement is used to delete already existing rows from the table. The syntax for the DELETE statement is a bit different from other DML statements in that you don't include column names. You don't need to because in delete operations, whole rows are deleted from the table, not selected column values. Assume that customer Gurusoft has broken the contract with you and found another supplier. Because Gurusoft is no more your customer, you can delete its row from the CUSTOMERS table:

```
DELETE FROM CUSTOMERS WHERE ID = 3;
```

If you don't include the WHERE clause in the DELETE statement, all the rows from the table would be deleted.

WORKING WITH DATES

This section covers the methods of selecting and inserting DATE data types. The DATE data type causes confusion for many users because they are told that Oracle stores the time and date in the appropriate columns; when they use a SELECT statement on the column, however, they see only the date and no time. Remember that the DATE data type stores the following information in it:

- ◆ Century
- ◆ Year
- ◆ Month
- ◆ Day
- ◆ Hour
- ◆ Minute
- ◆ Second

Also remember that Oracle's default format to display a date value as a result of a SELECT statement or to accept a date value from an INSERT statement is DD-MON-YY:

```
Select HIREDATE column from the EMPLOYEES table:

SELECT HIREDATE FROM EMPLOYEES;

HIREDATE
---------
01-JAN-98
15-FEB-98
01-MAR-98
20-JAN-98
```

Notice that Oracle has displayed the value for this column in its default format. Similarly, you can add a new row in the EMPLOYEES table by giving the HIREDATE value in Oracle's default format:

```
INSERT INTO EMPLOYEES VALUES
➥(5,'SCOTT', 2, 1200,'01-JAN-98',4);
```

If you want to see the values in the HIREDATE column in the format of your choice, you have to convert these values into the desired format by using the TO_CHAR function. The first parameter of the TO_CHAR function takes the value of the DATE data type as input. The second parameter specifies the format in which the first parameter value has to be converted. The function converts the date value into the desired format and returns the result as character data type. Suppose that you want to see the hire dates of the employees in the format DD/MM/YY:

```
SELECT NAME, TO_CHAR(HIREDATE, 'DD/MM/YY') FROM EMPLOYEES;

NAME         TO_CHAR(HIREDATE,'DD/MM/YY')
----------   ----------------------------
HASAN        01/01/98
SCOTT        15/02/98
DAVID        01/03/98
KAREN        20/01/98
```

Following are the other format elements you can use in the TO_CHAR and TO_DATE functions:

```
FORMAT
ELEMENT        MEANING

D              Day of week (1-7)
DAY            Name of day
DD             Day of month (1-31)
HH24           Hour of day (0-23)
MI             Minute (0-59)
MM             Month (01-12)
MONTH          Name of month
MON            Abbreviated name of month
SS             Second (0-59)
Y YYY          Year (e.g. 1999)
```

Similarly, you can see the time values stored in the HIREDATE column by converting it into a desirable format:

```
SELECT NAME, TO_CHAR (HIREDATE, 'HH:MI SS') FROM EMPLOYEES;

NAME        TO_CHAR(HIREDATE,'HH:MISS')
----------  ---------------------------
HASAN       12:00 00
SCOTT       12:00 00
DAVID       12:00 00
KAREN       12:00 00
```

You can also see date and time values at the same time:

```
SELECT NAME, TO_CHAR (HIREDATE, 'DD/MM/YY HH-MM-SS')
➥FROM EMPLOYEES;

NAME        TO_CHAR(HIREDATE,'DD/MM/YYHH-MM-SS')
----------  ------------------------------------
HASAN       01/01/98 12-01-00
SCOTT       15/02/98 12-02-00
DAVID       01/03/98 12-03-00
KAREN       20/01/98 12-01-00
```

Similarly, you can enter date or time values in the DATE data type column in any format you want, but you have to use the TO_DATE function to tell Oracle what format you are using. If you are using the default format, you don't have to use TO_DATE and can enter the date directly in single quotation marks. The first parameter of the TO_DATE function takes a character data type as input. The second parameter specifies the format in which the date and time are given in the first parameter value. The TO_DATE function uses the second parameter to understand the values given in the first parameter and converts it into the DATE data type, which is returned as output by the function. The following INSERT statement inserts the date and time in the HIREDATE column:

```
INSERT INTO EMPLOYEES VALUES (6, 'DAVID', 1, 1500, TO_DATE
➥('12/01/97 12:23:13 AM', 'DD/MM/YY HH:MI:SS AM'), 1);
```

Sometimes the DATE data type columns are used to store date and time; sometimes they are used to store date *or* time, depending on the nature of the application. If only a date value is inserted into DATE data type column without any time values specified, Oracle inserts 12:00 am as a default time value:

```
INSERT INTO EMPLOYEES VALUES (7, 'WILIAM', 1800, 4,
➥TO_DATE ('14-02-98','DD-MM-YY'), 4);
```

```
SELECT TO_CHAR (HIREDATE, 'DD/MM/YY HH:MI SS AM')
➥FROM EMPLOYEES WHERE ID =7;

TO_CHAR(HIREDATE,'DD/MM/YYHH:MISSAM')
-----------------------------------------
14/02/98 12:00 00 AM
```

Similarly, if you insert only time value in the DATE data type and insert nothing for date values, Oracle will insert the first day of the current month as a default date value:

```
INSERT INTO EMPLOYEES VALUES (8, 'JAVED', 6,2000, TO_DATE
➥('01 23 11 PM','HH-MI-SS AM'),4);

SELECT TO_CHAR (HIREDATE, 'DD/MM/YY HH:MI SS AM')
➥FROM EMPLOYEES WHERE ID =8;

TO_CHAR(HIREDATE,'DD/MM/YYHH:MISSAM')
-----------------------------------------
01/06/98 01:23 11 PM
```

THE ORACLE OPTIMIZER

Understand the working of the optimizer and differentiate between cost-based and rule-based optimizing methods.

The first part of this chapter discussed the methods of data manipulation through SQL. In addition to knowing how to write SQL, you need to know how the Oracle optimizer optimizes a SQL statement's performance and what access path Oracle chooses to execute your query.

Before executing a SQL statement, Oracle chooses an execution plan. The Oracle optimizer determines this execution plan by using a rule-based approach or a cost-based approach. The initialization parameter or ALTER SESSION command specifies which method to use. SQL hints can overwrite the method specified in the initialization parameter or by the ALTER SESSION command. The method you choose depends on the application you are using.

Cost-based approach is more efficient than rule-based approach, but the latter is provided for backward compatibility. Applications written in older versions of Oracle are well-tuned for rule-based optimization; therefore, rule-based optimization may result in better performance. With the passage of time as statistics are gathered for the database objects, the optimization method should be migrated from rule-based to cost-based approach. Unlike rule-based optimization, cost-based optimization uses statistics about the database objects that are stored in the data dictionary by the ANALYZE command.

Let's get a quick overview of how the optimizer works. First, the optimizer evaluates the SQL statement and makes modifications, if necessary, to improve the query's performance. Some examples of the modifications follow:

```
SELECT * FROM WORKERS
WHERE DEPTNO IN
(SELECT DEPTNO FROM DEPARTMENTS);
```

If the DEPTNO column of the DEPARTMENTS table is a primary key or has a UNIQUE constraint, the optimizer can transform the complex query into this join statement that is guaranteed to return the same data:

```
SELECT WORKERS.*
FROM WORKERS, DEPARTMENTS
WHERE WORKERS.DEPTNO = DEPARTMENT.DEPTNO;

SELECT * FROM WORKERS WHERE ID IN (1,2);
```

The IN operator is converted into one or more OR operators:

```
SELECT * FROM WORKERS WHERE ID = 1 OR ID = 2;

SELECT * FROM WORKERS WHERE ID BETWEEN 1 AND 4;
```

The BETWEEN operator is converted into two AND operators:

```
SELECT * FROM WORKERS WHERE ID >= 1 AND ID <= 4;
```

If the statement is using a view, the optimizer sometimes merges the statement's query with the query in the view before optimization. Now the optimizer makes a choice of which method to use. You can specify one of four options:

CHOOSE   This option causes Oracle to make the decision by itself between rule-based and cost-based optimization for best throughput. If statistics are available for a particular object, cost-based optimization for best throughput will be used; otherwise, rule-based optimization will be used.

RULE   This option causes Oracle to use rule-based optimization regardless of whether statistics for the objects are available. If no method is specified, Oracle uses rule-based optimization by default.

ALL_ROWS   This option causes Oracle to always use cost-based optimization for best throughput performance.

> **NOTE**
>
> **Save Yourself Some Worry** It is best to use CHOOSE because you don't have to worry about whether statistics are available for the object. If it is available, Oracle automatically executes the query by using cost-based optimization for best throughput performance. If it is not available, rule-based optimization is used.

Even if statistics aren't available for the object, Oracle uses other information, such as the number of blocks in a table, to estimate the statistics.

FIRST_ROWS   This option causes Oracle to always use cost-based optimization for best response time. If statistics of the objects aren't available, Oracle estimates the statistics from other information, such as the number of blocks in a table.

You can specify one of these optimization options in one of three ways:

◆ Set the initialization parameter OPTIMIZATION_MODE:

```
OPTIMIZATION_MODE = CHOOSE
```

◆ Use the ALTER SESSION command and set the OPTIMIZER_GOAL parameter:

```
ALTER SESSION SET OPTIMIZER_GOAL = CHOOSE;
```

◆ Specify the optimization method in a hint:

```
SELECT /*+ CHOOSE */ *
FROM WORKERS WHERE SAL < 1000;
```

Specifying an optimization method in a hint will override the specifications of the initialization parameter and ALTER SESSION command. If an optimization method isn't specified in a hint, by an ALTER SESSION command, or by an initialization parameter, rule-based optimization is used by default.

If rule-based optimization is used, the optimizer will determine all the possible access paths, rank them from least costly to most costly, and choose the least costly access path. This cost is determined by the fixed set of rules. For example, reading a single row by ROWID is least costly, for example, and a full table scan is most costly. Other access paths fall between them in terms of cost. Users can force Oracle to use an access path of their choice by using hints. Rule-based optimization calculates the cost totally on the basis of SQL statement and hence doesn't need table statistics.

If cost-based optimization is used, the statistics of the object used in the SQL is read from the data dictionary. You have to use the ANALYZE command on the particular object to store its statistics in the data dictionary. Cost-based optimization uses this information to determine the most efficient access path. The default goal of cost-based optimization is to maximize throughput performance, although you can force cost-based optimization instead to minimize performance time.

The ANALYZE Command

Run the ANALYZE command to gather statistics for tables, indexes, and clusters.

As mentioned earlier, the ANALYZE command is used to store statistics of a particular object in data dictionary performance tables. These statistics are then used by cost-based optimization to determine the most efficient access path. You can access the data in data dictionary performance tables through different views such as ALL_TABLES, ALL_CLUSTERS, and ALL_INDEXES. You can also use ANALYZE for other purposes, such as checking data integrity and gathering chained-row statistics.

To gather statistics, you can use the ANALYZE command in two different modes. The first mode scans the whole table, index, or cluster. Although this method is the most accurate, it consumes a great deal of system resources and temporary space to hold all the table rows. The following examples show the ANALYZE command used with the full scan option:

```
ANALYZE TABLE MY_TABLE COMPUTE STATISTICS;

ANALYZE INDEX MY_INDEX COMPUTE STATISTICS;

ANALYZE CLUSTER MY_CLUSTER COMPUTE STATISTICS;
```

The second mode of the ANALYZE command estimates statistics by scanning a sample of the table, index, or cluster. The following examples show the command used with estimation mode:

```
ANALYZE TABLE MY_TABLE ESTIMATE STATISTICS;

ANALYZE INDEX MY_INDEX ESTIMATE STATISTICS;

ANALYZE CLUSTER MY_CLUSTER ESTIMATE STATISTICS;
```

You can specify the size of the sample to be used in terms of rows or percentage:

```
ANALYZE TABLE MY_TABLE ESTIMATE STATISTICS
SAMPLE 2000 ROWS;

ANALYZE TABLE MY_TABLE ESTIMATE STATISTICS
SAMPLE 30 PERCENT;
```

Although estimating statistics doesn't give you accurate results, it consumes fewer system resources. You can increase the effectiveness of the statistics by increasing the sample size.

You can also use the ANALYZE command to check the structural integrity of tables, indexes, and clusters. Hardware or software problems can cause structural integrity problems. By analyzing the structure, you can take effective measures before the system crashes. If there's a problem in the structure of any object, it should be dropped and re-created again. The following examples show the ANALYZE command being used to check structural integrity:

```
ANALYZE TABLE MY_TABLE VALIDATE STRUCTURE;

ANALYZE INDEX MY_INDEX VALIDATE STRUCTURE;

ANALYZE CLUSTER MY_CLUSTER VALIDATE STRUCTURE;
```

You can also use ANALYZE to determine the existence and extent of any chained rows in a table or cluster. Chained rows cause serious performance problems because a single row has to be read from two different blocks on the hard disk. Before running ANALYZE to analyze the chained rows, you have to create a table that has a proper structure required by ANALYZE to store the data in it. You can create a table called CHAINED_ROWS by running the UTLCHAIN.SQL script that comes with Oracle. The following example shows the usage of ANALYZE command for this purpose:

```
ANALYZE TABLE MY_TABLE LIST CHAINED ROWS INTO CHAINED_ROWS;

ANALYZE CLUSTER MY_CLUSTER LIST CHAINED ROWS INTO
➥CHAINED_ROWS;
```

The EXPLAIN PLAN Command

Run the EXPLAIN PLAN command to analyze the access path selected by Oracle.

Now that you understand how the Oracle optimizer works, you need to know how you can see what data access path Oracle is using to execute your query. This information may help you rewrite queries to improve performance.

The EXPLAIN PLAN command shows the execution plan that the Oracle optimizer has chosen for SELECT, INSERT, UPDATE, and DELETE statements. After looking at the execution plan, you can check whether the statement is fully optimized. You might decide to rewrite SQL statement in a different way to improve the performance or to add some hints in the query to force Oracle to choose a particular access path that you think will improve the performance.

When you run EXPLAIN PLAN, the result is stored in a table that must have a particular structure. You can create a table called PLAN_TABLE by running the script UTLXPLAN.SQL that comes with Oracle. This script will run the following CREATE TABLE statement:

```
CREATE TABLE PLAN_TABLE (
STATEMENT_ID          VARCHAR2(30),
TIMESTAMP             DATE,
REMARKS               VARCHAR2(80),
OPERATION             VARCHAR2(30),
OPTIONS               VARCHAR2(30),
OBJECT_NODE           VARCHAR2(128),
OBJECT_OWNER          VARCHAR2(30),
OBJECT_NAME           VARCHAR2(30),
OBJECT_INSTANCE       NUMERIC,
OBJECT_TYPE           VARCHAR2(30),
OPTIMIZER             VARCHAR2(255),
SEARCH_COLUMNS        NUMERIC,
ID                    NUMERIC,
PARENT_ID             NUMERIC,
POSITION              NUMERIC,
COST                  NUMERIC,
CARDINALITY           NUMERIC,
BYTES                 NUMERIC,
OTHER_TAG             VARCHAR2(255),
OTHER                 LONG);
```

After this table is created, you are ready to run EXPLAIN PLAN. The syntax for EXPLAIN PLAN is as follows:

```
EXPLAIN PLAN
SET STATEMENT_ID = 'STATEMENT ID'
INTO OUTPUT_TABLE_NAME
FOR
    SQL STATEMENT;
```

The statement ID is the label you give to each task, so that the particular output can be identified within the PLAN_TABLE. The following is another EXPLAIN PLAN example:

```
EXPLAIN PLAN
SET STATEMENT_ID = 'TESTING 1'
INTO PLAN_TABLE
FOR
    SELECT * FROM EMPLOYEES WHERE SAL < 2000;
```

After EXPLAIN PLAN executes, you can select the output from PLAN_TABLE for a particular statement ID. You can select the desired data in table or nested format. The following queries show the examples of each.

Table format:

```
SELECT OPERATION, OPTIONS, OBJECT_NAME, ID, PARENT_ID,
➥POSITION
FROM PLAN_TABLE
WHERE STATEMENT_ID = 'TESTING 1';

OPERATION          OPTIONS OBJECT_NAME ID PARENT_ID POSITION
---------------    ------- ----------- -- --------- --------
SELECT STATEMENT                        0
TABLE ACCESS       FULL    EMPLOYEES    1  0           1
```

Nested format:

```
SELECT LPAD(' ',2*(LEVEL-1))||OPERATION||' '||OPTIONS||'
➥'||OBJECT_NAME||' '||
DECODE(ID, 0, 'COST = '||POSITION) "EXECUTION PLAN"
FROM PLAN_TABLE
START WITH ID = 0 AND STATEMENT_ID = 'TESTING 1'
CONNECT BY PRIOR ID = PARENT_ID AND STATEMENT_ID
➥='TESTING 1';

EXECUTION PLAN
---------------------------
SELECT STATEMENT    COST =
TABLE ACCESS FULL EMPLOYEES
```

By looking at the output, you can see exactly how your SQL statement has been executed and whether full advantage of indexes, clusters, or hash clusters has been taken. You might decide to rewrite the SQL statement differently again if you think that the execution plan can be maximized that way, or you might decide to place hints in the SQL statement if you think that forcing optimizer to use a particular access path will further improve performance.

CHAPTER SUMMARY

KEY TERMS

Before you take the exam, be sure you are familiar with the following terms and how they apply to SQL statements:

- constraints
- variable and fixed-length datatypes
- Data Manipulation Language (DML)

This chapter has covered two main topics: usage of the SQL Data Manipulation Language and the Oracle optimizer. The Data Manipulation Language consists of four main SQL statements: SELECT, INSERT, UPDATE, and DELETE.

SELECT statements are used to retrieve data from one or more database tables. To retrieve data from more than one table, three main methods are available: join operations, subqueries, and set operations. A query can use one or a combination of these methods, depending on the nature of the task. Join operations link two or more tables via a joining condition. The main concept behind join

CHAPTER SUMMARY

operations is the concept of the Cartesian product, in which the main query uses output of the subquery to process the final results. Set operations consist of UNION, INTERSECTION, and subtraction operations on two or more results of SELECT statements. INSERT statements are used to add new rows to database tables. SELECT statements can be used within INSERT statements to read data from one table and to insert that data into another table. UPDATE statements are used to modify already existing data in database tables. An UPDATE statement can make changes on more than one column at a time. Rows are deleted from database tables by using the DELETE statement.

Before executing SELECT, INSERT, UPDATE, or DELETE statements, the Oracle optimizer make necessary modifications in the query for best performance. If a view is involved, the optimizer might merge the view query with the statement query. After the changes are made, the Oracle optimizer decides which optimization method to use: rule-based or cost-based. The decision is made based on specifications given in the initialization parameter, by the ALTER SESSION command, or by a query hint. After the optimizer decides which method to use, it lists all the possible access paths for the execution of query. The least-costly access path is selected. The criteria of selection differ in each of the three methods. Rule-based optimization uses a fixed set of rules to decide which access path is less costly than others. Cost-based optimization uses object statistics to make the same decision. The ANALYZE command stores the object's statistics in data dictionary tables and hence has to be run before cost-based optimization can be used efficiently. You can use the EXPLAIN PLAN command to see what access path Oracle has chosen to execute your query. Based on this information, you can decide to rewrite the query for better performance or decide to use hints in SQL statements to force Oracle to use the access path of your choice.

KEY TERMS

- Data Definition Language (DDL)
- Data Control Language (DCL)
- select list
- WHERE clause
- group function
- single-row function
- nested function
- NULL value
- user-defined variable
- column alias
- join operation
- set operation
- subquery
- default date format
- cost-based optimizer
- rule-based optimizer
- data dictionary
- access path

APPLY YOUR KNOWLEDGE

This section enables you to assess how well you understood the material in the chapter. Review questions test your knowledge of the tasks and concepts specified in the objectives. The exercises provide you with opportunities to engage in the sorts of tasks that comprise the skill sets the objectives reflect.

Exercise

1.1 Using the Oracle Optimizer

For this exercise, choose cost-based optimization for best throughput and look at the access path Oracle chose to execute the following query:

```
SELECT * FROM EMPLOYEES
WHERE ID NOT IN
      (SELECT SUPER_ID FROM EMPLOYEES);
```

This exercise assumes that the WORKERS table is already created in your user. Refer to the section "The SELECT Statement" for the script that creates this table.

Estimated Time: 15 minutes

1. Because you have to use cost-based optimization, make sure that table statistics have been stored in the data dictionary:

   ```
   ANALYZE TABLE WORKERS COMPUTE STATISTICS;
   ```

2. When you execute the query, use a hint in the SQL statement to tell Oracle to use the cost-based optimizer:

   ```
   SELECT /*+ CALL_ROWS*/ * FROM EMPLOYEES
   WHERE ID NOT IN
         (SELECT SUPER_ID FROM EMPLOYEES);
   ```

3. Create the PLAN_TABLE either by running the UTLXPLAN.SQL script that comes with Oracle or by entering the following statement at the SQL prompt:

```
CREATE TABLE  PLAN_TABLE (
STATEMENT_ID       VARCHAR2(30),
TIMESTAMP          DATE,
REMARKS            VARCHAR2(80),
OPERATION          VARCHAR2(30),
OPTIONS            VARCHAR2(30),
OBJECT_NODE        VARCHAR2(128),
OBJECT_OWNER       VARCHAR2(30),
OBJECT_NAME        VARCHAR2(30),
OBJECT_INSTANCE    NUMERIC,
OBJECT_TYPE        VARCHAR2(30),
OPTIMIZER          VARCHAR2(255),
SEARCH_COLUMNS     NUMERIC,
ID                 NUMERIC,
PARENT_ID          NUMERIC,
POSITION           NUMERIC,
COST               NUMERIC,
CARDINALITY        NUMERIC,
BYTES              NUMERIC,
OTHER_TAG          VARCHAR2(255),
OTHER              LONG);
```

4. Run the EXPLAIN PLAN command by giving a suitable STATEMENT_ID to your SQL statement:

   ```
   EXPLAIN PLAN
   SET STATEMENT_ID = 'EXERCISE1'
   INTO PLAN_TABLE
   FOR
   SELECT /*+ CALL_ROWS*/ * FROM EMPLOYEES
   WHERE ID NOT IN
         (SELECT SUPER_ID FROM EMPLOYEES);
   ```

5. To see the access path, query the PLAN_TABLE:

   ```
   SELECT OPERATION, OPTIONS, OBJECT_NAME, ID,
   ➡PARENT_ID, POSITION
   FROM PLAN_TABLE
   WHERE STATEMENT_ID = 'EXERCISE1';
   ```

You should get something like this:

OPERATION	OPTIONS	OBJECT_NAME	ID	PARENT_ID	POSITION
SELECT STATEMENT			0		
FILTER			1	0	1
TABLE ACCESS	FULL	EMPLOYEES	2	1	1
TABLE ACCESS	FULL	EMPLOYEES	3	1	2

APPLY YOUR KNOWLEDGE

Review Questions

1. Which of the following functions isn't a single-row function?

   A. GREATEST

   B. LEAST

   C. AVG

   D. ROUND

2. What's the function of the DISTINCT keyword?

   A. To eliminate duplicate rows in a table

   B. To eliminate duplicate columns in a table

   C. To eliminate duplicate rows in the result

   D. To eliminate duplicate columns in the result

3. Which two functions can be used on the CHAR or VARCHAR2 data type?

   A. ROUND

   B. CEIL

   C. GREATEST

   D. LEAST

4. What data type is created with the DEFINE command?

   A. CHAR

   B. VARCHAR2

   C. NUMBER

   D. DATE

5. If one column of the EMPLOYEES table stores employee IDs and another column stores supervisor IDs, by using which methods can you find out employee names and their supervisor names?

   A. UNION

   B. Subquery

   C. Join

   D. INTERSECT

6. How many join conditions are required in a join query?

   A. Number of tables

   B. Number of columns in both tables

   C. Number of tables plus one

   D. Number of tables minus one

7. What type of condition can't be specified in a WHERE clause?

   A. SUM(SAL) > 1000

   B. SAL * 2 > 1000

   C. ROUND (SAL) > 1000

   D. SAL > COMM

8. Which clause is used to exclude values returned by a group function?

   A. WHERE

   B. HAVING

   C. ORDER BY

   D. GROUP BY

9. The following command is issued to Oracle:
   SELECT NVL(&MY_VARIABLE, 0) FROM DUAL;

   What will be the output if MY_VARIABLE is defined as DEFINE MY_VARIABLE = NULL

APPLY YOUR KNOWLEDGE

A. NULL

B. MY_VARIABLE

C. 0

D. Nothing

10. The following query is issued to Oracle:

```
SELECT NAME FROM EMPLOYEES WHERE NAME
➥LIKE '%A_';
```

What names are likely to be displayed?

A. Names that have A as the next-to-last letter

B. Names that end at letter A

C. Names that include letter A

D. Names that have at least one letter A

11. For which task is the function TO_CHAR likely to be used?

A. To convert the character string into date value

B. To convert date value into character string

C. To convert character string into number

D. To insert data value in the database

12. Which of the following values can't go into a foreign key column?

A. NULL

B. A value that already exists in foreign-key column

C. DATE data type

D. None of the above

13. Which of the following statements is false?

A. A table can't have more than one unique constraint.

B. A table can't have more than one primary key constraint.

C. More than one foreign key can refer to one primary key column.

D. Foreign-key and primary-key columns can both be in one table.

14. Which of the following table names is invalid?

A. .EMP

B. EMP_

C. EM#P

D. THISISEMPTABLE

15. The concatenation operator won't work on which of the following data types?

A. LONG

B. LONG RAW

C. NUMBER

D. DATE

16. What are the two main advantages of using column aliases?

A. Reasonable headings can be given.

B. Distinct values are eliminated in columns.

C. The result is displayed in uppercase.

D. The ORDER BY clause can use aliases.

17. Which of the following methods can't be used to extract data from more than one table?

A. Outer joins

B. Subqueries

C. Set operations

D. Self-joins

APPLY YOUR KNOWLEDGE

18. Which of the following methods can't be used to specify an optimization method?

    A. Specify in initialization parameters

    B. Specify in hints

    C. Specify in data dictionary table

    D. Use ALTER SESSION command

19. What's the major difference between cost-based and rule-based optimization?

    A. Cost-based optimization uses tables statistics.

    B. Cost-based optimization is the default method.

    C. Rule-based optimization is more efficient.

    D. Cost-based optimization is twice as fast as rule-based optimization.

20. The major purpose of the EXPLAIN PLAN command is to

    A. Check the structural integrity of the objects

    B. Explain the errors in SQL

    C. Explain the data access path Oracle has chosen

    D. Tell Oracle which data access path you want to use

21. Which of the following can't be performed by the ANALYZE command?

    A. Check the structural integrity of tables

    B. Show the existence of chained rows

    C. Show access path for SQL

    D. Store table's statistics in data dictionary

Answers to Review Questions

1. **C.** AVG is a group function. Unlike single-row functions, group functions return only one result, no matter how many rows there are in the table. The section "Group Functions" discusses group functions in detail.

2. **C.** The DISTINCT keyword in a SELECT statement eliminates duplicate rows in the returned result. The section "The DISTINCT Keyword" discusses the concept in detail.

3. **C, D.** The GREATEST and LEAST functions can work on NUMBER as well as CHAR and VARCHAR2 data types. For example, GREATEST('USA','CANADA') will return CANADA, because the letter C comes before the letter U. The section "The GREATEST and LEAST Functions" provides more information on these functions.

4. **A.** When you define a variable using the DEFINE command, it always creates a variable with the CHAR data type. Refer to the section "Using Variables" for more information.

5. **B** and **C.** You can use subqueries and join operations to select data from more than one column that have some relationship between them. The columns can be in one table or in different tables. For more information, refer to the sections "Self-Joins" and "Subqueries."

6. **D.** In an equi-join query, the number of join conditions should be equal to one less the number of tables being joined. In this way, the relationship between all the tables can be specified. Refer to the section "Join Operations" for more details.

APPLY YOUR KNOWLEDGE

7. **A.** Conditions involving GROUP functions can't be specified in the WHERE clause. You have to use the HAVING clause for this purpose. Refer to the sections "The WHERE Clause" and "The HAVING Clause" for details.

8. **B.** The HAVING clause is used to restrict the groups created by the GROUP BY clause from the final result. The section "The HAVING Clause" provides more details.

9. **C.** If the value of the variable given in the first argument of the NVL function is NULL, NVL returns whatever is the value given in the second argument; otherwise, the original value in the first argument is returned. In this case, the value of MY_VARIABLE is defined as NULL, so NVL will return the value given in the second argument—that is, 0. Refer to the section "The Concept of the NULL Value and the NVL Function" for details.

10. **A.** Two wildcards can be used with the LIKE operator: % and _. The % wildcard matches everything, whereas the _ wildcard matches only one character. In this case, all names will be displayed that have A as a second-to-last letter. For more information, refer to the section "The LIKE Operator."

11. **B.** The TO_CHAR function is used to convert date and number data types into character data types. It is mainly used to convert dates into characters. The section "Working with Dates" provides more information.

12. **D.** The only restriction a foreign column has is that all the values coming into this column should already exist in the corresponding primary key column. Refer to the section "Tables and Columns" for more details.

13. **A.** A table can have more than one unique key, but only one primary key. Refer to the section "Tables and Columns" for details.

14. **A.** A table name should start with an alphabetic character. This is discussed further in the section "Tables and Columns."

15. **A** and **B.** One disadvantage of using the LONG and LONG RAW data types is that functions and concatenation operators can't work on them. Refer to the section "Data Types" for details.

16. **A** and **D.** The two main advantages of using column aliases are that they become column headings in the result and that the ORDER BY clause can use column aliases rather than the column names. The section "Column Aliases" discusses this concept in detail.

17. **D.** Self-joins are used to join a table with itself if it has two columns with a relationship between them. Refer to the section "Self-Joins" for more information.

18. **C.** You can specify the optimization method in an initialization parameter, in hints, or in an ALTER SESSION statement. Refer to the section "The Oracle Optimizer" for details.

APPLY YOUR KNOWLEDGE

19. **A.** Unlike rule-based optimization, cost-based optimization uses table statistics to find the most efficient access path for the query. The section "The Oracle Optimizer" provides more details.

20. **C.** The EXPLAIN PLAN command shows what access path Oracle has chosen to execute the query. Refer to the section "The EXPLAIN PLAN Command" for details.

21. **C.** The major functions performed by the ANALYZE command are

    - Storing a table's statistics in the data dictionary

    - Checking structural integrity

    - Showing the existence of chained rows

    The EXPLAIN PLAN command shows the access path for SQL. Refer to the sections "The ANALYZE Command" and "The EXPLAIN PLAN Command" for details.

This chapter helps you prepare for the exam by covering the following objectives:

Understand and use the program components that comprise syntactically correct PL/SQL anonymous blocks.

▶ This objective is necessary for understanding the basic construction of PL/SQL programs.

Write exception handlers for anonymous blocks.

▶ This objective is necessary for understanding how to process exceptions in a PL/SQL program.

Use cursors and looping constructs within PL/SQL programs.

▶ This objective is necessary for understanding how a PL/SQL program interacts with the database.

Define complex data structures and use data typing effectively.

▶ This objective is necessary because efficient data structures result in efficient programs.

Make use of various built-in functions and the Oracle-supplied DBMS_OUTPUT package.

▶ This objective is necessary for understanding the use of specific features of the language.

CHAPTER 2

PL/SQL Language Structure

OUTLINE

▶ The best way to study this material is in front of a computer. You should have access to SQL*Plus, a database connection, and a simple text editor such as Notepad. Follow along in the book by running the listings provided. Make sure you understand what each program is doing before trying the next one.

Some of the listings are dependent on objects owned by user SCOTT, which is created when the demo database is installed. If this account does not exist on your database, you can re-create it by using the script found in <ORACLE_HOME>\RDBMS<version>\ADMIN\ SCOTT.SQL, where <ORACLE_HOME> is the directory where Oracle was installed and <version> is the version of your database. On my system, for example, this file is found at D:\ORANT\RDBMS80\ADMIN\ SCOTT.SQL.

Most important, play around with the programs as your curiosity dictates. Take the time to try out different things. Feel free to edit the scripts provided. Write your own that perform some simple, useful operation. The best way to get a handle on a new language is to observe the differences between valid and invalid syntax and explore various approaches to a problem.

At the time of this writing, Oracle8 is not covered by the exam. However, some material covered here is pertinent to Oracle8. New keywords, new data types, and nested tables and varrays (short for variable-size arrays), for example, are elements introduced in Oracle8. This material is included here because of its impact on the PL/SQL language. If you declare a variable name that happens to be the same as a reserved word in Oracle8, for instance, your program will stop working properly when you move to Oracle8. All Oracle8 material is well identified as such, and it will not negatively impact your preparation for the exam. If the exam is modified to include Oracle8 material, you won't find your reference material suddenly out of date.

INTRODUCTION

Oracle Server supports a built-in language known as *PL/SQL (Procedural Logic/SQL)*. PL/SQL provides a procedural wrapper for SQL statements. A procedural language is one in which programmers specify step-by-step statements to be carried out or evaluated. In contrast, SQL (Structured Query Language) describes what data to get, not how to get it. SQL isn't a procedural language, but rather a declarative one.

PL/SQL was initially developed for automating SQL transactions but has since been transformed into a substantial development platform for complex applications. It is a robust language that supports a wide range of data types, extensions through user-defined data types, strong data-typing enforcement, subroutines, conditional and iterative logic, and sophisticated error handling. Using PL/SQL has many benefits, including the following:

- ◆ You can automate and repeat complex data manipulation.
- ◆ You can compile and store programs in the database that can be run by multiple users.
- ◆ You can reduce network traffic by performing complex logic directly on the database server.
- ◆ You can break down complex or unmanageable SQL statements into simpler steps.
- ◆ Code can be shared, thus reducing development time.
- ◆ You can embed PL/SQL blocks in host languages to simplify and standardize client software development.

RESERVED WORDS

The PL/SQL language uses a set of reserved words that have special syntactical meaning (see Table 2.1). These words can't be used as variable or program names. SQL reserved words are restricted in the same manner.

TABLE 2.1

PL/SQL AND SQL RESERVED WORDS

ABORT	CLUSTER*	DIGITS
ACCEPT	CLUSTERS	DISPOSE
ACCESS*	COLAUTH	DISTINCT*
ADD*	COLUMN*!	DO
ALL*	COLUMNS	DROP*
ALTER*	COMMENT*!	ELSE*
AND*	COMMIT	ELSIF
ANY*	COMPRESS*	END
ARRAY	CONNECT*	ENTRY
ARRAYLEN	CONSTANT	EXCEPTION
AS*	COUNT*+	EXCEPTION_INIT
ASC*	CRASH	EXCLUSIVE*#
ASSERT	CREATE*	EXISTS*
ASSIGN	CURRENT*	EXIT
AT	CURRVAL	FALSE
AUDIT*!	CURSOR	FETCH
AUTHORIZATION	DATA_BASE	FILE*!
AVG	DATABASE	FLOAT*
BASE_TABLE	DATE*	FOR*
BEGIN	DBA	FORM
BETWEEN*	DEBUGOFF	FROM*
BINARY_INTEGER	DEBUGON	FUNCTION
BODY	DECIMAL*	GENERIC
BOOLEAN	DECLARE	GOTO
BY*	DEFAULT*	GRANT*
CASE	DEFINITION	GROUP*
CHAR*	DELAY	HAVING*
CHAR_BASE	DELETE*	IDENTIFIED*
CHECK*	DELTA&	IF
CLOSE	DESC*	IMMEDIATE*!

continues

TABLE 2.1	*continued*

PL/SQL AND SQL RESERVED WORDS

IN[*]	NOCOMPRESS[*]	REAL
INCREMENT[*!]	NOT[*]	RECORD
INDEX[*]	NOWAIT[*!]	REF
INDEXES	NULL[*]	RELEASE
INDICATOR	NUMBER[*]	REMR
INITIAL[*!]	NUMBER_BASE	RENAME[*]
INSERT[*]	OF[*]	RESOURCE[*]
INTEGER[*]	OFFLINE[*!]	RETURN
INTERFACE[!]	ON[*]	REVERSE
INTERSECT[*]	ONLINE[*!]	REVOKE[*]
INTO[*]	OPEN	ROLLBACK
IS[*]	OPTION[*]	ROW[*!]
LEVEL[*]	OR[*]	ROWID[*]
LIKE[*]	ORDER[*]	ROWLABEL[*]
LIMITED	OTHERS	ROWNUM[*]
LOCK[*!]	OUT	ROWS[*]
LONG[*]	PACKAGE	ROWTYPE
LOOP	PARTITION	RUN
MAX	PCTFREE[*]	SAVEPOINT
MAXEXTENTS[*!]	PLS_INTEGER[!]	SCHEMA
MIN	POSITIVE	SELECT[*]
MINUS[*]	POSITIVEN[!]	SEPARATE
MLSLABEL	PRAGMA	SESSION[*!]
MOD	PRIOR[*]	SET[*]
MODE[*]	PRIVATE	SHARE[*!]
MODIFY[*!]	PRIVILEGES[*!]	SIZE[*]
NATURAL	PROCEDURE	SMALLINT[*]
NATURALN[!]	PUBLIC[*]	SPACE
NEW	RAISE	SQL
NEXTVAL	RANGE	SQLCODE
NOAUDIT[*#]	RAW[*]	SQLERRM

START*	THEN*	VARCHAR*
STATEMENT	TO*	VARCHAR2*
STDDEV	TRIGGER*	VARIANCE
SUBTYPE	TRUE	VIEW*
SUCCESSFUL*!	TYPE	VIEWS
SUM	UID*!	WHEN
SYNONYM*!	UNION*	WHENEVER*!
SYSDATE*!	UNIQUE*	WHERE*
TABAUTH	UPDATE*	WHILE
TABLE*	USE	WITH*
TABLES	USER*!	WORK
TASK	VALIDATE*!	WRITE!
TERMINATE	VALUES*	XOR

*   SQL reserved word
\+   Dropped as a reserved word after Oracle Server 7.1
!   Introduced as a reserved word in Oracle Server 7.3
\#   Introduced as a reserved word in Oracle Server 8.0.3
&   Dropped as a reserved word in Oracle Server 8.0.3

MODULAR TOP-DOWN DESIGN SYNTAX

Top-down design refers to the practice of defining procedural actions first at a general, high level and then recursively refining the actions by creating more detailed routines at lower and lower levels until the actions are fully specified. Such a design approach has been used successfully on small-, medium-, and large-scale applications since the 1970s. PL/SQL supports this design method through the concept of *blocks*.

PL/SQL programs are organized in blocks. Like other block-oriented programming languages, PL/SQL blocks follow strict *scoping rules*, which refer to the visibility of programming objects (such as variables, constants, and cursors) within and between blocks. A programmatic object is in scope if it is defined at or above (in nesting depth) the current block.

NOTE

Running the Sample Code You can run all the examples throughout this chapter in SQL*Plus. To receive output from the `put_line` statements, first run the following command in SQL*Plus:

> SET SERVEROUTPUT ON

Output will then be enabled for the duration of the session.

Some of the examples will also work from Oracle Enterprise Manager's SQL Worksheet. However, SQL Worksheet doesn't support certain features found in SQL*Plus, such as `ACCEPT`. Also, it won't prompt you for input for host variables, which is indicated with a preceding ampersand (&). For this reason, it is best to just use SQL*Plus when running the examples.

Blocks

To understand and use the program components that comprise syntactically correct PL/SQL anonymous blocks.

An *anonymous block* is the general name for a body of PL/SQL code submitted to the database server for immediate compilation and execution. An anonymous block is different from stored subprograms and packages, which are compiled once and can then be executed repetitively in a separate step. In contrast, an anonymous block is compiled and executed every time it is submitted to the server. This chapter deals exclusively with anonymous blocks; stored subprograms and packages are the subject of Chapter 3, "PL/SQL in Use."

A PL/SQL block begins with BEGIN and ends with END. You can think of a BEGIN...END sequence as a single statement. You can have an unlimited number of statements within the block as long as each one ends with a semicolon (;). The following is a simple Hello program:

```
BEGIN
  DBMS_OUTPUT.put_line('Hello, DBA!');
END;
/
```

This statement says to display the string Hello, DBA! on its own line. The slash tells SQL*Plus to submit the block for compilation and execution.

A block can optionally have a DECLARE section. All variables, constants, cursors, and so on are defined only within the declaration section. The following code is an example of the DECLARE statement:

```
DECLARE
  hello CONSTANT VARCHAR2(20) := 'Hello, DBA!';
BEGIN
  DBMS_OUTPUT.put_line(hello);
END;
/
```

This statement says to define a constant of type VARCHAR2, initialize it to the string Hello, DBA!, and then display the contents of the constant on its own line.

Exception Handling

To write exception handlers for anonymous blocks.

A block can optionally have an *exception block,* which is the section of code that program execution immediately jumps to when a PL/SQL or SQL error condition arises. Table 2.2 lists Oracle's predefined exceptions. Any named exception, such as the ones listed in this table, can be tested for in the exception block.

TABLE 2.2

PREDEFINED ORACLE EXCEPTIONS

Exception Name	SQLCODE Value
CURSOR_ALREADY_OPEN	ORA-06511
DUP_VAL_ON_INDEX	ORA-00001
INVALID_CURSOR	ORA-01001
INVALID_NUMBER	ORA-01722
LOGIN_DENIED	ORA-01017
NO_DATA_FOUND	ORA-01403 or +100
NOT_LOGGED_ON	ORA-01012
PROGRAM_ERROR	ORA-06501
STORAGE_ERROR	ORA-06500
TIMEOUT_ON_RESOURCE	ORA-00051
TOO_MANY_ROWS	ORA-01422
TRANSACTION_BACKED_OUT	ORA-00061
VALUE_ERROR	ORA-06502
ZERO_DIVIDE	ORA-01476

The exception block consists of one or more exception handlers. You can define a specific exception handler for one or more exceptions, as well as a default handler for any other exceptions. The exception handler contains statements to further process or manage an exception. Think of a set of exception handlers as a CASE or SWITCH statement, where only one case is performed based on the value of the SQL exception code. The program in Listing 2.1 illustrates an exception block with three exception handlers.

LISTING 2.1

EXCEPTION HANDLING (EXCEPT.SQL)

```
DECLARE
  x NUMBER;
BEGIN
  x := 10000;   -- this will generate VALUE_ERROR exception
EXCEPTION
  WHEN ZERO_DIVIDE THEN   -- divide by zero error
    DBMS_OUTPUT.put_line('ZERO_DIVIDE');
  WHEN VALUE_ERROR THEN   -- overflow
    DBMS_OUTPUT.put_line('VALUE_ERROR');
  WHEN OTHERS THEN   -- anything else
    DBMS_OUTPUT.put_line('OTHER ERROR');
END;
/
```

Only the statement within the WHEN VALUE_ERROR THEN block is executed because the exception handlers are processed exclusively. You can write one exception handler for multiple exceptions by putting them in an OR condition:

```
WHEN ZERO_DIVIDE OR VALUE_ERROR THEN
```

However, an exception can appear in only one exception handler.

The exception handler WHEN OTHERS is used as a default to pick up any other exception that may arise. (The WHEN OTHERS clause must always be the last exception handler in a series.) There are more than 25,000 exceptions; defining them all would be undesirable, so this catchall is used instead.

Nesting Blocks and Scope

Blocks can be nested to any depth (see Listing 2.2). A block can be given a label so that objects within it can be explicitly referenced. This is important when objects are ambiguously defined.

LISTING 2.2

NESTING BLOCKS (NESTING.SQL)

```
<<TOP BLOCK>>
DECLARE
  x NUMBER := 50;
  z NUMBER := 10;
BEGIN
```

```
    DBMS_OUTPUT.put_line('x (TOP_BLOCK): ' || x);
    DBMS_OUTPUT.put_line('z (TOP_BLOCK): ' || z);
    <<BLOCK_ONE>>
    DECLARE
      x NUMBER := 3;
    BEGIN
      DBMS_OUTPUT.put_line('x (BLOCK_ONE): ' || x);
      x := TOP_BLOCK.x;
      DBMS_OUTPUT.put_line('x (BLOCK_ONE): ' || x);
    END;  -- BLOCK ONE
    <<BLOCK_TWO>>
    DECLARE
      x NUMBER := 100;
    BEGIN
     DBMS_OUTPUT.put_line('x (BLOCK_TWO): ' || x);
     <<BLOCK_THREE>>
     DECLARE
      w NUMBER;
      x NUMBER;
      y NUMBER;
     BEGIN
      x := BLOCK_TWO.x;  -- qualifier resolves ambiguous reference
      y := TOP_BLOCK.x;  -- at any depth
      w := z;  -- unambiguous reference doesn't need qualifier
      DBMS_OUTPUT.put_line('x (BLOCK_THREE): ' || x);
      DBMS_OUTPUT.put_line('y (BLOCK_THREE): ' || y);
      DBMS_OUTPUT.put_line('w (BLOCK_THREE): ' || w);
     END;  -- BLOCK THREE
     x := z;  -- this is BLOCK_TWO.x
     DBMS_OUTPUT.put_line('x (BLOCK_TWO): ' || x);
    END;  -- BLOCK TWO
   END;
   /
```

The program in Listing 2.2 illustrates the following points about valid and invalid references between blocks:

◆ Variables in inner blocks are completely independent of variables of the same name declared in outer blocks (they define separate storage).

◆ Variables in inner blocks can reference variables declared in any enclosing block.

◆ Variables can't reference variables declared in other blocks at the same level (that aren't nested, but are sequential).

◆ A reference to a variable in an outer block can be qualified with the name of the outer block.

◆ Variables declared in outer blocks can't reference variables defined in inner blocks.

◆ Forward variable references aren't allowed.

When a block goes out of scope, any variables declared within it cease to exist. Also, the memory allocated for them is released. When the block is reentered, the variables are again allocated memory and initialized. This explains why blocks defined at the same nesting level can't "see" into each other, and blocks at a higher level can't "see" into blocks nested within them.

IDENTIFIERS AND VARIABLE DECLARATIONS

To be able to define complex data structures and use data typing effectively.

Identifier is the general name for programmatic objects (items that are operated on): variables, constants, cursors, exceptions, and so on.

When you declare variables, you must specify a legal name, a data type, and (optionally) an initial value or constraint. Legal names must begin with a letter (upper- or lowercase) and contain any combination of subsequent letters, numbers, underscores, dollar signs ($), or pound signs (#)—up to 30 characters. They can't contain embedded blanks (spaces), special characters, or unprintable characters. Table 2.3 illustrates valid and invalid variable declarations.

TABLE 2.3

SPECIFYING LEGAL AND ILLEGAL IDENTIFIERS

Legal Variable Names	*Illegal Variable Names*
MyVariable	MyVariable
Variable$Name	Variable Name
var123	123var
var_123_$	var-123
v#dept#	dept_no!

PL/SQL is *not* case sensitive. It converts all identifiers to uppercase; therefore, you can't distinguish variable names by case alone. Listing 2.3, for example, gives a compilation error because the same variable name is being declared.

LISTING 2.3

DUPLICATE DECLARATIONS (DUPDECL.SQL)

```
DECLARE
  danclamage VARCHAR2(30);
  DANCLAMAGE VARCHAR2(20);
BEGIN
  DanClamage := 'Dan Clamage';
EXCEPTION
WHEN OTHERS THEN
  NULL;
END;
/

ERROR at line 1:
ORA-06550: line 5, column 3:
PLS-00371: at most one declaration for 'DANCLAMAGE'
➥is permitted in the declaration section
ORA-06550: line 5, column 3:
PL/SQL: Statement ignored
```

A meaningful error message is provided by the PL/SQL engine. Such errors have the prefix PLS. Oracle Server, in turn, returns the general error code ORA-06550, which states that some PL/SQL problem on line 5 has occurred and the program can't continue. Because this is a compilation error and not a runtime error, the exception block can't trap it.

For readability, I standardize all my PL/SQL code to follow a handful of casing rules.

Literal Strings

Literal strings are always denoted by single quotation marks and represent CHAR constants. Only literal strings aren't converted to uppercase. The two following strings aren't equivalent, for example (they represent different values):

```
DECLARE
  name1 VARCHAR2(30) := 'dan clamage';
  name2 VARCHAR2(30) := 'DAN CLAMAGE';
BEGIN
  IF (name1 = name2) THEN -- test fails
```

Literal strings are also used to denote date and number formats (such as 'DD-MON-YYYY' and '999.00') and default date values (such as '18-MAY-98'). They can contain any printable character. Other literals include fixed decimal numbers, NULL, FALSE, and TRUE.

Special Characters

PL/SQL uses certain special printable characters for specific purposes. Table 2.4 briefly describes these special characters.

TABLE 2.4

SPECIAL CHARACTERS ORGANIZED BY TYPE

Character	Description
	Arithmetic Operators
+	Addition and unary positive
-	Subtraction and unary negation
*	Multiplication
/	Division
**	Exponentiation
	Relational Operators (Used in Boolean Expressions)
=	Equivalence
<	Less than
>	Greater than
<>	Not equal
!=	Not equal (alternate)
~=	Not equal (alternate)
^=	Not equal (alternate)
<=	Less than or equal
>=	Greater than or equal
	Expressions and Lists
:=	Assignment
(	Start list or subexpression
)	End list or subexpression
,	Separate list items (as in parameter lists)
..	Range operator (used in FOR...IN loops)
||	String concatenation
=>	Association (used in parameter lists)
;	Statement end

> **NOTE**
>
> **Using Expressions and Lists**   The expressions and lists are used in statements, data type declarations, parameter list declarations, and variable and table references.

	Expressions and Lists
%	Cursor attribute or object type
.	Member specifier for qualified references
@	Remote database indicator
'	Start/end of character string
"	Start/end of quoted identifier
:	Host variable indicator
&	Bind variable indicator
	Comments and Labels
—	Single-line comment
/*	Start multiline comment
*/	End multiline comment
<<	Start label
>>	End Label

Initialization and Variable Constraints

After a PL/SQL block is compiled, all declared variables are initialized before the first executable statement is processed. Any variables not explicitly initialized to some value are initialized to NULL. In this manner, programmers can expect all variables to contain some value, even if value is NULL (and not garbage).

Variables are initialized only once. They can be assigned a literal value or any legal expression. A variable can be assigned a value from a previously declared variable, for example:

```
PI CONSTANT NUMBER(8,7) := 3.1415927;
radius NUMBER(2,0) := 10;
area NUMBER(6,3) := PI * radius**2; -- 314.159
circumf NUMBER(5,3) := PI * 2 * radius; --  62.832
```

Two valid variable constraints are CONSTANT and NOT NULL. CONSTANT indicates that the variable is strictly read-only; it must never appear on the left side of an assignment. NOT NULL indicates that the variable must never contain a NULL value.

```
E CONSTANT NUMBER(13,12) := 2.718281828459;  -- requires initializer
SSN CHAR(11) NOT NULL := '123-45-6789';  -- requires initializer
MB CONSTANT NUMBER NOT NULL := 10241000;  -- redundant
NULL_DATE CONSTANT DATE := NULL;
```

Initialization is required for the CONSTANT variable, even if it is set to NULL. Also, carefully notice the placement of the CONSTANT and NOT NULL constraints before and after the data type, respectively.

| NOTE | **NOT NULL Processing Overhead** The NOT NULL constraint incurs additional runtime overhead because it must be tested for. For this reason, you should avoid using it. |

Supported Data Types

PL/SQL supports all the database types for Oracle7.x and 8. The level of data type support between PL/SQL versions heavily depends on the database version. For example, large object binaries (LOBs) were introduced in Oracle8 and are supported by PL/SQL8, but not previous versions of PL/SQL. A LOB is used to store binary data such as images, sounds, and video.

A *subtype* is a data type derived from a parent type. A subtype has the same internal representation as the parent, but typically has some additional constraint.

The supported lengths under PL/SQL for the data types CHAR (and its subtype NCHAR), VARCHAR2, LONG, and RAW (and its subtype LONG RAW) vary from the database (see Table 2.5).

TABLE 2.5

DIFFERENCES BETWEEN PL/SQL AND DATABASE TYPES

Data type	Subtype	PL/SQL Value Limits	Database Value 7.x	Limits 8.0
CHAR (s)		32,767 bytes	255 bytes	255 bytes
	NCHAR	32,767 bytes	Not available	2,000 bytes
VARCHAR2 (s)	32,767 bytes	2,000 bytes	4,000 bytes	
LONG		32,760 bytes	2,147,483, 647 bytes	2,147,483, 647 bytes
RAW (s)		32,767 bytes	255 bytes	255 bytes
	LONG RAW	32,760 bytes	2,147,483, 647 bytes	2,147,483, 647 bytes

PL/SQL also defines data types not compatible with the database (see Table 2.6).

TABLE 2.6

PL/SQL Data Types Not Supported by the Database

Data type	Subtypes	Value Range
BINARY_INTEGER		12 ±2,147,483,647
	NATURAL	0–2,147,483,647
	POSITIVE	1–2,147,483,647
	NATURALN	Same as NATURAL but NOT NULL
	POSITIVEN	Same as POSITIVE but NOT NULL
	SIGNTYPE	(−1, 0, +1)
PLS_INTEGER (available in 7.3)		12 ±2,147,483,647 used for fast machine arithmetic
BOOLEAN		TRUE, FALSE, NULL
REF CURSOR		Cursor variable (handle)

Finally, Table 2.7 illustrates the rest of the data types that are precisely compatible with the database.

TABLE 2.7

Data Types Common to PL/SQL and the Database

Data type	Subtype	Value Limits
NUMBER(p,s)	NUMERIC	Magnitude range is $1.0\mathrm{E}129$–$9.99\mathrm{E}+125$.
	DEC	
	DECIMAL	Precision is 1–38.
	INT[*]	Scale is −84 to 127.
	INTEGER[*]	
	FLOAT[*]	
	REAL	
	DOUBLE PRECISION	
	SMALLINT[*]	
DATE		January 1, 4712 B.C. to December 31, 4712 A.D.
LOB (Large object binary) available in Oracle8		0–4GB
	BFILE (read-only)	External file
	BLOB (read/write)	Internal/external
	CLOB (read/write)	Internal/external single byte
	NCLOB (read/write)	Internal/external fixed-width, multibyte data

*No scale

Given the valid data types, here are some more valid variable declarations:

```
tax_amount NUMBER(11, 2);
tax_rate REAL(5,3);
status NUMERIC;
system_date DATE;
big_str VARCHAR2(32767);
qty INTEGER(7);
idx BINARY_INTEGER;
word_doc LONG;
```

Collections

PL/SQL enables programmers to define complex data structures to suit their needs. One such construct is the *collection*—an ordered group of data elements, all having the same data type. PL/SQL supports two kinds of collections: nested tables (formerly known just as *PL/SQL Tables* in Oracle7.*x* and now referred to as *index-by tables*) and varrays (short for variable-size arrays). Here's the syntax for declaring nested and index-by tables:

```
TYPE nested_type IS TABLE OF datatype [NOT NULL]
    [INDEX BY BINARY_INTEGER];  -- defines type
variable_name nested_type;      -- defines storage
```

In this syntax, nested_type is a valid identifier representing the name of the new type, and datatype is any valid PL/SQL or user-defined data type, except for the following:

BOOLEAN	Object types containing TABLE or VARRAY data types
NCHAR	REF CURSOR
NCLOB	TABLE
NVARCHAR2	VARRAY

The nested table can optionally have a NOT NULL constraint or indicate that it is an index-by table with INDEX BY BINARY_INTEGER.

Here's the syntax for varrays:

```
TYPE varray_type IS {VARRAY | VARYING ARRAY} (size)
    OF datatype [NOT NULL];  -- defines type
variable_name varray_type;   -- defines storage
```

In this syntax, size is the maximum size allowable.

After you declare a suitable type, you declare a variable to be of that type.

Collections behave something like arrays, with some semantic differences, as shown in Table 2.8.

TABLE 2.8

COLLECTION COMPARISON

Nested Table (Oracle8)	*Index-By Table (Oracle7.x)*	*Varray (Oracle8)*
Behaves like a linked list whose elements can be referenced with an index (offset).	Behaves like a linked list whose elements can be referenced with an index (offset).	Behaves like a bounded array whose consecutive elements are referenced with an index (offset).
Uses collection methods to traverse linked lists.	Uses collection methods to traverse linked list (7.3); or tests an element for no_data_found (before 7.3).	Uses collection methods to traverse linked lists.
When uninitialized, the nested table itself is NULL.	When uninitialized, elements don't exist but the table exists.	When uninitialized, the varray itself is NULL.
When set to NULL or another uninitialized nested table, the nested table itself is NULL.	When set to another index-by table that's uninitialized, all elements are freed (but table itself can't be NULL).	When set to NULL or another uninitialized varray, the varray itself is NULL.
Initialized with a constructor of the nested table name (explicit constructor).	Initialized by assigning values to elements (implicit constructor).	Initialized by using a constructor of the varray name (explicit constructor).
Can have 1 to 2,147,483,647 elements.	Can have ±2,147,483,647 elements.	Can have 1 to 2,147,483,647 elements.
Number of elements aren't declared.	Number of elements aren't declared.	Number of elements must be declared.
Attempting to reference an unassigned element raises ORA-06533: Subscript beyond count.	Attempting to reference an unassigned element raises ORA-01403: no data found.	Attempting to reference an unassigned element raises ORA-06533: Subscript beyond count.

continues

TABLE 2.8   *continued*

COLLECTION COMPARISON

Nested Table (Oracle8)	Index-By Table (Oracle7.x)	Varray (Oracle8)
Attempting to use an offset value out of range raises ORA-06532: Subscript outside of limit.	All BINARY_INTEGER values are valid offsets.	Attempting to use an offset value out of range raises ORA-06532: Subscript outside of limit.
Can be referenced within SQL (except in DISTINCT, GROUP BY, or ORDER BY lists)	Can't be referenced within SQL.	Can be referenced within SQL (except in DISTINCT, GROUP BY, or ORDER BY lists).
Can store objects, records, records, and scalars.	Can't store objects but can store records (7.3) or simple scalars (before 7.3).	Can store objects, and scalars.
Uses the collection method EXTEND to add elements.	Just assigns values to an element to extend.	Uses the collection method EXTEND to add elements.
Uses the collection method TRIM to remove elements from end.	Can't use TRIM.	Uses the collection method TRIM to remove elements from end.

Listing 2.4 illustrates initializing nested tables as well as some behavior pitfalls.

LISTING 2.4

INITIALIZING NESTED TABLES (NEST1.SQL)

```
DECLARE
  status NUMERIC;
  TYPE   BYTE_TABLE IS TABLE OF VARCHAR2(1);
  alpha  BYTE_TABLE;
  i        BINARY_INTEGER;
BEGIN
  BEGIN  -- Test 1: uninitialized nested table is NULL
   DBMS_OUTPUT.put_line(
     'Test 1: uninitialized nested table is NULL');
   alpha(1) := 'A';  -- try to write to uninitialized table
  EXCEPTION
  WHEN OTHERS THEN
    status := SQLCODE;
    DBMS_OUTPUT.put_line('Test 1: ' || SQLERRM(status));
  END;
```

```
   BEGIN   -- Test 2: subscripts must start at 1
     DBMS_OUTPUT.put_line(
       'Test 2: subscripts must start at 1');
     alpha := BYTE_TABLE('A');  -- use constructor
     DBMS_OUTPUT.put_line(alpha(0));  -- bad subscript
   EXCEPTION
   WHEN OTHERS THEN
     status := SQLCODE;
     DBMS_OUTPUT.put_line('Test 2: ' || SQLERRM(status));
     DBMS_OUTPUT.put_line(alpha(1));  -- was stored OK
   END;

   BEGIN   -- Test 3: subscript past end of nested table
     DBMS_OUTPUT.put_line(
       'Test 3: subscript past end of nested table');
     -- alpha(1) on left hand side
     -- is illegal when using constructor
     alpha := BYTE_TABLE('A');  -- use constructor
     alpha := BYTE_TABLE('B');  -- but how to set any off-
set?
     i := 1;  -- nested tables always start at 1
     -- how many elements did I just set?
     WHILE alpha(i) IS NOT NULL AND i < 10 LOOP
       DBMS_OUTPUT.put_line(alpha(i)); -- print index
       i := i + 1;  -- next offset
     END LOOP;
     DBMS_OUTPUT.put_line('Found ' || i);
   EXCEPTION
   WHEN OTHERS THEN
     status := SQLCODE;
     DBMS_OUTPUT.put_line('Test 3: ' || SQLERRM(status));
     DBMS_OUTPUT.put_line('Found ' || i);
   END;

   -- Test 4: legal assignment once initialized
   DBMS_OUTPUT.put_line(
     'Test 4: legal assignment once initialized');
   alpha := BYTE_TABLE('A');  -- use constructor
   DBMS_OUTPUT.put_line(alpha(1));
   alpha(1) := 'B';  -- legal assignment (once initialized)
   DBMS_OUTPUT.put_line(alpha(1));
 END;
 /
```

The server then responds with this:

```
Test 1: uninitialized nested table is NULL
Test 1: ORA-06531: Reference to uninitialized collection
Test 2: subscripts must start at 1
Test 2: ORA-06532: Subscript outside of limit
A
Test 3: subscript past end of nested table
B
Test 3: ORA-06533: Subscript beyond count
Found 2
```

```
Test 4: legal assignment once initialized
A
B

PL/SQL procedure successfully completed.
```

Nested and index-by tables are said to be *sparse*, meaning that stored values don't need to be consecutive and there's no wasted storage between those elements having stored values. A nested table could be loaded up with data stored in consecutive elements, for example, and then have some of those elements deleted. These deleted elements cease to exist and don't take up storage. In contrast, a varray's elements themselves can't be deleted; they're merely assigned a new value or set to NULL. For this reason, varrays are said to be *dense*. Arrays in most other programming languages are dense; you must allocate storage for the entire array before using it. If some elements are never written to, the elements take up storage nonetheless.

You can use the collection methods to traverse sparse nested tables and work with them in general. Collection methods are a set of procedures and functions used for manipulating collections. They have the following syntax:

```
collection.method(optional_parameters)
```

Table 2.9 illustrates the collection methods, and Listing 2.5 illustrates the use of some of these methods.

TABLE 2.9

COLLECTION METHODS

Method	Description	Returns	Syntax
EXISTS	Tests for the existence of an element (7.3) or collection (8.0 only)	TRUE/FALSE (returns FALSE if offset is out of bounds)	collection.EXISTS [(offset)]
COUNT	Number of elements in a collection (same as LAST for varrays)	BINARY_INTEGER	collection.COUNT
FIRST	Offset of first element	BINARY_INTEGER	collection.FIRST
LAST	Offset of last element	BINARY_INTEGER	collection.LAST
PRIOR	Offset of preceding element from given offset	BINARY_INTEGER	collection.PRIOR (offset)
NEXT	Offset of next element from given offset	BINARY_INTEGER	collection.NEXT (offset)

Method	*Description*	*Returns*	*Syntax*
DELETE	Removes a specified element, range, or all (nested tables only)	None	collection.DELETE [(m[,n])]
LIMIT (Oracle8 only)	Maximum number of elements that a varray can contain (from its declaration)	BINARY_INTEGER or NULL for nested tables	collection.LIMIT
EXTEND (Oracle8 only)	Increases the size of a collection by one NULL element, *n* NULL elements or *n* copies of element m.	None	collection.EXTEND [(n[,m])]
TRIM	Remove one or more elements from the end	None	collection.TRIM[]

LISTING 2.5

MORE NESTED TABLE METHODS (NEST2.SQL)

```
DECLARE
  status NUMERIC;
  TYPE   BYTE_TABLE IS TABLE OF VARCHAR2(1);
  alpha  BYTE_TABLE;
  i        BINARY_INTEGER;
BEGIN
  -- Test 5: initializing and traversing multiple elements
  DBMS_OUTPUT.put_line(
    'Test 5: initializing and traversing multiple
➥elements');
  alpha := BYTE_TABLE('A', 'B', 'C');  -- use constructor
  i := alpha.FIRST;  -- table attribute
  WHILE (i <= alpha.LAST) LOOP
    DBMS_OUTPUT.put_line(alpha(i));
    i := alpha.NEXT(i);  -- find next element from here
  END LOOP;

  -- Test 6: extending and trimming nested table
  DBMS_OUTPUT.put_line(
    'Test 6: extending and trimming nested table');
  alpha := BYTE_TABLE('A', 'B', 'C');  -- use constructor
  alpha.EXTEND(5,2); -- use element 2 to make 5 more
➥elements
  i := alpha.FIRST;  -- table attribute
  WHILE (i <= alpha.LAST) LOOP
    DBMS_OUTPUT.put_line(alpha(i));
    i := alpha.NEXT(i);  -- find next element from here
  END LOOP;
  DBMS_OUTPUT.put_line('-- TRIM --');
```

continues

LISTING 2.5	*continued*

MORE NESTED TABLE METHODS (NEST2.SQL)

```
    alpha.TRIM;   -- remove last 2 entries
    i := alpha.FIRST;   -- table attribute
    WHILE (i <= alpha.LAST) LOOP
      DBMS_OUTPUT.put_line(alpha(i));
      i := alpha.NEXT(i);   -- find next element from here
    END LOOP;
  END;
  /
```

The server then responds with this:

```
Test 5: initializing and traversing multiple elements
A
B
C
Test 6: extending and trimming nested table
A
B
C
B
B
B
B
B
-- TRIM --
A
B
C
B
B
B

PL/SQL procedure successfully completed.
```

A general approach to using nested tables and varrays that are expected to contain a relatively small number of elements might be in the following order:

1. Initialize the nested table or varray, either in its declaration or by calling its constructor. Assigning a NULL value suits this purpose.

2. Extend the nested table or varray to the number of elements desired using the value of the first element assigned in the previous step.

3. Assign values to individual elements, delete or trim elements, extend new elements, and so on.

This is also suitable for a potentially large collection that starts out small. By initializing elements in chunks, you can simplify your allocation scheme. In this manner, collections can be worked with safely, without your having to write complex code that keeps extending or trimming elements. In contrast, index-by tables are a bit easier to work with, especially because you don't have to extend them to be able to store more values. They do not, however, make as efficient use of memory as nested tables and varrays.

When an element is deleted, it ceases to exist; therefore, references to it raise the NO_DATA_FOUND exception. However, the element can be set again to a new value explicitly. The table procedure TRIM, however, completely removes elements from the end of a nested table; therefore, merely assigning a new value will fail.

Records

PL/SQL supports user-defined record types. A *record type* is a user-defined composite data type that's composed of one or more members. These members are declared as a list inside the record type definition, similar to regular variables. Record declarations have the following syntax:

```
TYPE record_type IS RECORD (
  member member_type
  [, member member_type ...]);   -- defines datatype
variable_name record_type;       -- defines storage
```

You can list as many members as you need.

Using records is a two-step process: You declare the record type, and then declare a variable as having that type. Here's an example:

```
TYPE ADDR_TYPE IS RECORD (   -- defines a pattern

    name     VARCHAR2(30),
    address  VARCHAR2(40),
    city     VARCHAR2(30),
    state    VARCHAR2(2),
    zip      VARCHAR2(10));
  cust_rec ADDR_TYPE;   -- defines storage
```

Members are referenced by using dot notation:

```
cust_rec.name := 'Dan Clamage';
cust_rec.city := 'Pittsburgh';
```

You can name the record variables anything you like; I usually add the suffix _rec to aid readability.

Records can be nested to any depth. To do this, you first declare the supporting record types and then include them in the definition of the main record type. Forward references aren't allowed. Here's an example:

```
-- example continued
TYPE ACCOUNT_TYPE IS RECORD (   -- describes account
  branch_code NUMBER(5),
  route_code VARCHAR2(9),
  account_no VARCHAR2(12),
  branch_addr ADDR_TYPE);
TYPE CUST_ACCOUNT_TYPE IS RECORD (   -- customer account
  cust_no NUMBER(8),
  account_info ACCOUNT_TYPE,
  cust_addr ADDR_TYPE);
new_cust_rec CUST_ACCOUNT;
BEGIN
  new_cust_rec.cust_no := 100;
  new_cust_rec.account_info.branch_code := 113;
```

You can assign one record variable to another only if the variables are declared as the same type:

```
old_cust_rec CUST_ACCOUNT;
new_cust_rec CUST_ACCOUNT;
BEGIN
...
old-cust_rec := new_cust_rec;
```

You can't assign a dissimilar record variable to another record variable, even if their members match precisely. To perform a copy between two such variables, you must copy one member at a time. Also, you can't initialize a record variable or set it to NULL except by assigning a value to each member in turn.

You can set a default value to a member in the type declaration. The value can be any expression that evaluates to the proper data type. When a variable is then declared of that record type, the member is initialized to the default value. Here's an example:

```
TYPE ORDER_TYPE IS RECORD (
  quantity NUMBER(6)  := 1,
  price NUMBER(9,2)  := 0.0,
  ext_price NUMBER(10,2)  := 0.0,
  item_no NUMBER(6),
  cust_no NUMBER(6));
new_order ORDER_TYPE;
```

The members quantity, price, and ext_price of the record variable new_order are initialized to non-NULL values. You could also use the keyword DEFAULT in place of the assignment operator; they are equivalent for initialization.

You can fetch directly from a cursor into a record variable, provided the members match the cursor's columns precisely in number and type. You can't insert an entire record with an INSERT statement. Instead, you must list each member in the VALUES clause.

You can use collections in records or declare collections of records (except in version 7.2 and earlier). A record of nested tables would be treated as parallel arrays. A nested table of record enables you to collect a variety of disparate, but related data in each element; you can't have a nested table of record of nested tables, however: PL/SQL doesn't support multidimensional arrays.

Based Variables

PL/SQL allows a variable's data type to be based on an existing variable, database table, or database column. This is accomplished by using %TYPE for scalar variables and %ROWTYPE for record variables:

Explicit Data Type	*Based Data Type*
n_deptno NUMBER(2); DEPT.deptno%TYPE;	n_deptno
v_dname VARCHAR2(14)	v_dname DEPT.dname%TYPE;
v_loc VARCHAR2(13)	v_loc DEPT.loc%TYPE;

TYPE DEPT_TYPE IS RECORD (
  deptno NUMBER(2),
  dname VARCHAR2(14),
  loc   VARCHAR2(13));
dept_rec DEPT_TYPE;
	dept_rec DEPT%ROWTYPE;

When you base a variable on some column or variable's type, you get (for free) the data type, the length of the type, and the constraints, but you don't get a default value. When you base a variable on a table or cursor row type, you get members for all the columns in the table or the cursor's SELECT clause.

The benefit of using this technique is highly maintainable code. Suppose that a variable's data type is defined the same as that of a database column, because it is intended to be used to store a value from this column. In the event the column definition changes, this variable's declaration must also be modified. If a similar variable is used in hundreds of modules, you will have the rather daunting task of modifying the variable everywhere. On the other hand, if the variables are properly based, little or no code changes are required.

Also note that to declare a record variable without basing it on the table ROWTYPE, a two-step method is employed. First, a RECORD type, with members matching precisely the table columns and their types, is defined. Then, a variable is declared of that RECORD type. This method can be very expensive to maintain when table changes affect all types and variables implicitly defined as supporting that table. In contrast, using the table or cursor ROWTYPE obviates these problems.

Comments

PL/SQL supports two kinds of comments: single line and multiline. The PL/SQL compiler ignores everything after a single-line comment or between multiline comments. Comments can't be nested. I use multiline comments at the beginning of each PL/SQL program module to convey some basic information:

```
/*
  Program Name:
  Author:
  Date Written:
  Description:
  Modification History::
*/
```

Inside the declaration section, I group similar variables together under common single-line comment headings:

```
-- global constant variables
PI CONSTANT NUMBER(8,7) := 3.1415927;
-- global user-defined types
-- global cursors
-- global record variables
-- global variables
radius REAL(11,2);
```

Good programmers sprinkle comments liberally throughout their programs to aid understanding and make dense logic more readable:

```
-- linear approximation of an FFT
-- Accounting rules require notification of Manager
-- required business logic for Inventory Control
```

The more time you have while developing software, the better your comments tend to be. In many large shops, the person who originally writes a program is rarely the person who has to maintain it six months or a year down the road. What's more, you may find yourself scratching your head about why you wrote a program a certain way after even just a short time away from the code. This is why good commenting habits are very important.

When I build a new module, I usually enter some single-line comments highlighting the overall program structure in the places where I expect to add code later. Frequently, I will write the pseudocode for a specification and then use it to organize my program. I tend to add comments to my code as I go along or add them shortly thereafter. In this manner, I keep the task of commenting code at a manageable level. Imagine trying to go back over a thousand-line program adding comments! In my experience, I have found it is better to comment code incrementally.

EXECUTABLE STATEMENTS

All executable statements are found within the block body. Here, you can perform the following tasks:

◆ Evaluate expressions and assign their values to variables

◆ Perform conditional and unconditional logic (program branching) based on Boolean expressions

◆ Iterate statements (loops)

◆ Call subprograms (that is, subroutines: procedures and functions)

A *subprogram* is just another generic name for subroutine. Subprograms are covered in Chapter 11, "Tuning Memory Structures."

Each and every executable statement must end with a semicolon. A statement can be written to span multiple lines, or more than one statement can be written per line. A good programming habit is to write just one statement per line and to place LOOP...END LOOP, IF...ELSE...END IF, and BEGIN...END markers on their own lines so that they stand out for better readability.

Executable statements are evaluated at runtime, whereas declarative statements (except for their assignments) are evaluated at compile time.

Assignment

You can assign values to variables by using the assignment operator (:=). The expression on the right side is evaluated, and the resulting value is stored in the variable to the left of the operator. Only one variable can appear on the left side of an assignment. The expression on the right side must evaluate to a single scalar value of the data type of the variable on the left side.

Assignments can't be nested or compounded inside other statements. C programmers are used to being able to write something like this, for example:

```
while ((ch=getchar()) != EOF) {
   i = j = 0;
```

However, these sorts of idioms aren't allowed in PL/SQL.

Implicit Data Type Conversion

For certain mixes of data types in expressions, the PL/SQL compiler can implicitly convert them to a common data type. In the following code, for example, the compiler converts the number variable to a string, using the default number NLS format, before performing the concatenation:

```
DECLARE
   str1 VARCHAR2(10) := 'amount: ';
   str2 VARCHAR2(20);
   num NUMBER(4, 2) := 20.05;
BEGIN
   str2 := str1 || num;
```

The result of the expression is now of the proper data type to store in the variable on the left side of the assignment operator. As another example, here the compiler performs the string concatenation and then converts the result into a number for storage in the number variable:

```
DECLARE
   str1 VARCHAR2(10) := '10';
   str2 VARCHAR2(10) := '33';
   num NUMBER;
BEGIN
   num := str1 || str2;
   dbms_output.put_line(num);
end;
/
```

```
1033

PL/SQL procedure successfully completed.
```

Table 2.10 enumerates the data types that can be converted implicitly to one another.

TABLE 2.10

IMPLICIT DATA TYPE CONVERSIONS

TO FROM	BINARY INTEGER	CHAR	DATE	LONG	NUMBER	RAW	ROWID	VARCHAR2
BINARY INTEGER	×		×	×			×	
CHAR	×		×	×	×	×	×	×
DATE	×	×				×		
LONG		×				×		×
NUMBER	×	×		×				×
RAW		×		×				×
ROWID	×						×	
VARCHAR2	×	×	×	×	×	×	×	

In general, everything converts to a VARCHAR2 as the lowest common denominator. If the compiler can't determine a common data type to which to reduce an expression, it will issue an error message. Here's an example:

```
DECLARE
   str1 VARCHAR2(10) := 'amount: ';
   num NUMBER(4, 2) := 20.05;
   dte DATE;
BEGIN
   dte := str1 || num;
end;
/

ERROR at line 1:
ORA-01858: a non-numeric character was found where a
           numeric was expected
ORA-06512: at line 6
```

In these situations, you may need to perform an explicit data type conversion.

Explicit Data Type Conversion

To make use of various built-in functions.

When the PL/SQL compiler can't reduce an expression to a particular data type, you can help the compiler by performing an explicit data type conversion. To do so, you use a conversion function. Table 2.11 enumerates the various explicit data type conversion functions at your disposal.

TABLE 2.11

EXPLICIT DATA TYPE CONVERSION FUNCTIONS

TO FROM	VARCHAR2	CHAR	NUMBER	DATE	RAW	ROWID
VARCHAR2			TO_NUMBER (vc[, fmt[, lang]])	TO_DATE (vc[, fmt[, lang]])	HEXTORAW (vc)	CHARTOROWID (vc)
CHAR			TO_NUMBER (c[, fmt[, lang]])	TO_DATE (c[, fmt[, lang]])	HEXTORAW (c)	CHARTOROWID (c)
NUMBER	TO_CHAR (n[, fmt[, lang]])	TO_CHAR (n[, fmt[, lang]])		TO_DATE (n[, fmt[, lang]])		
DATE	TO_CHAR (dt[, fmt[, lang]])	TO_CHAR (dt[, fmt lang]])				
RAW	RAWTOHEX (raw)	RAWTOHEX (raw)				
ROWID	ROWIDTOCHAR (rowid)	ROWIDTOCHAR (rowid)				

You are probably already familiar with several conversion functions—such as TO_CHAR(), TO_NUMBER(), and TO_DATE()—just from using SQL.

MORE ON EXCEPTION HANDLING

To write exception handlers for anonymous blocks.

Here are some other considerations for handling exceptions in addition to just writing exception handlers for specific blocks:

◆ Exception propagation

◆ Avoiding infinite loops

◆ Capturing SQLCODE

◆ Performing cleanup (for example, closing the cursor and resetting variables)

◆ Raising your own exception

◆ Defining other exceptions

The following sections delve into these somewhat more complex aspects of program design.

Exception Propagation

If a nested block doesn't have an exception-handler section and experiences an exception, the exception is passed up the call stack to the outer block. If this block, in turn, has no exception handler, the exception is passed further up the call stack until a suitable exception handler is found or the exception propagates all the way up the call stack to the calling context, which might be SQL*Plus or some other executable program. This behavior is called *exception propagation*. The exception "bubbles up" through the call stack until it is handled or else just returned to the calling program.

You can stop exception propagation by providing a suitable exception handler for the block experiencing the exception. By *suitable*, I mean an explicit exception handler of the name of the exception that occurred or the OTHERS handler.

You can take advantage of this behavior by trapping the exception, performing some logic, and then again raising the exception to the calling context. You would do this when you want the calling block to terminate its processing by going to its exception handler. This technique is illustrated by the following skeleton code:

```
BEGIN
   ...   -- normal processing
   BEGIN
      ...   - nested block processing
   EXCEPTION
   WHEN NO_DATA_FOUND THEN
      -- process the exception here
      RAISE;   -- re-raise exception to break outer block
   END;
EXCEPTION
WHEN OTHERS THEN   -- traps the re-raised exception
   -- some error processing
END;
```

In general, however, you shouldn't use exception propagation as a means of passing error values between blocks, because it can be very difficult to follow the logic. Instead, you should create a subprogram and return the error status in the parameter list. Subprograms are dealt with in Chapter 11.

Avoiding Infinite Loops

It is perfectly legitimate to perform SQL or complex logic inside an exception handler. However, you must be very aware of the potential for such code to generate an exception as well. If this occurs, your program might be thrown into an infinite loop.

To resolve this situation, you can just nest a block with its own exception handler inside the exception handler. Here's an example:

```
EXCEPTION   -- for main block
WHEN NO_DATA_FOUND THEN   -- no main phone#
   BEGIN   -- nested block
      SELECT phone_no   -- look for alternate phone#
      INTO v_phone_no
      FROM alt_phone_numbers
      WHERE indiv_no = v_indiv_no;
   EXCEPTION   -- for nested block
   WHEN OTHERS THEN
      V_phone_no := NULL;   -- no phone# available
   END;   -- nested block
WHEN OTHERS THEN   -- main's default handler
   ...   - some other handling
END;   -- main block
```

In this case, if the nested block with the exception handler had been omitted and the query inside the NO_DATA_FOUND exception handler also raised NO_DATA_FOUND, the program would loop forever.

Capturing SQLCODE

If you need to do something with the exception value, you should capture this value immediately, because the SQL error code changes on every SQL statement execution. You can capture the SQL error code with the built-in function SQLCODE, which returns the number of the exception. Here's an example:

```
DECLARE
  status NUMERIC;
  v_empno emp.empno%TYPE := 9999;
  v_ename emp.ename%TYPE;
BEGIN
  SELECT ename
  INTO v_ename
  FROM emp
  WHERE empno = v_empno;
EXCEPTION
WHEN OTHERS THEN
  Status := SQLCODE;
  DBMS_OUTPUT.put_line(v_empno || ': ' ||
                        SQLERRM(status));
END;
/

9999: ORA-01403: no data found

PL/SQL procedure successfully completed.
```

For production programs, you will usually dump these error messages into some sort of error table for postmortem analysis. Note the use of the built-in function SQLERRM, which returns a string containing the error number and a brief explanation.

Performing Cleanup

Other additional processing you may need to perform in an exception handler involves closing any potentially open cursors and clearing up variables so that they don't contain any previous or misleading values:

```
OPEN dept_cursor;
LOOP
  FETCH dept_cursor INTO dept_rec;
  ... - process dept data
END LOOP;  -- dept_cursor
CLOSE dept_cursor;  -- normal termination
...
EXCEPTION
WHEN OTHERS THEN
```

```
    IF (dep_cursor%ISOPEN) THEN
       CLOSE dept_cursor;   -- potentially open cursor
    END IF;
    dept_rec := NULL;   -- clear any previous values
END;   -- main dept block
```

You need to close any potentially open cursors because the next time you enter the block, if you try to open an already open cursor, you get the following exception:

```
ORA-06511: PL/SQL: cursor already open.
```

Even if you are convinced that logically an exception is very unlikely and that you don't need to provide an exception handler or close a potentially open cursor, you are setting yourself up for a tough time debugging some unexpected problem that might be difficult to re-create. Instead, you should get in the habit of making your code bulletproof. Then if a problem should arise, you will know immediately what it *isn't*. Also, you will have the structure in place to quickly localize the bug.

If a code block is normally expected to provide a value, you will also want to reset or provide a default value for it in the exception handler. Suppose that you are getting an individual's name from a table. If no row is found, you can use a default name string of 'N/A' (or some other suitable value) to indicate that a value wasn't available. When an implicit cursor fails with NO_DATA_FOUND, any current values stored in the variables in the INTO clause are unchanged. Here's an example to help illustrate this point:

```
DECLARE
   ename emp.ename%type;
   status NUMERIC;
BEGIN
   ename := 'GARBAGE';   -- initialize
   BEGIN
     SELECT ENAME INTO ENAME
     FROM EMP
     WHERE empno = 9999;
   EXCEPTION
   WHEN OTHERS THEN
     status := SQLCODE;
     DBMS_OUTPUT.put_line(SQLERRM(STATUS));
   END;   -- nested block
   DBMS_OUTPUT.put_line(ename);
END;
/

ORA-01403: no data found
GARBAGE

PL/SQL procedure successfully completed.
```

If such an exception occurs, you probably don't want the previous value left in the variable.

Raising Your Own Exceptions

You can define your own exceptions, raise them based on some business rules, and trap them in the exception block:

```
DECLARE
  BAD_SALARY EXCEPTION;  -- user-defined exception
BEGIN  -- perform data validation
  IF (some_salary NOT BETWEEN lo_sal AND hi_sal) THEN
    RAISE BAD_SALARY;  -- salary out of range
  ...
EXCEPTION
  WHEN BAD_SALARY THEN  -- process bad salary here
```

By defining business rules in this manner, you can collect all error-handling logic in one place. This keeps the main body of logic clean and readable. This is more maintainable than sprinkling error logic throughout the code and writing logic around these errors.

Another method of raising application-specific errors is to use the Oracle-supplied procedure RAISE_APPLICATION_ERROR. This procedure has the following syntax:

```
RAISE_APPLICATION_ERROR(error_number,
                        message_string
                        [, TRUE ¦ FALSE]);
```

Here, error_number is a negative integer between −20000 and 20999, and message_string can be up to 2,048 bytes long. The optional third parameter determines whether the error is placed on the stack of previous errors (TRUE) or the error replaces all previous errors (FALSE, the default). RAISE_APPLICATION_ERROR is found in the DBMS_STANDARD package, an extension of the STANDARD package, so you don't have to qualify the reference to it.

This method has the advantage of providing a text message with a user-reserved error number. The disadvantage to using it is that you have to track all unique error values yourself and apply them consistently throughout an application. The other shortcoming is that you have only 1,000 unique error values at your disposal.

Here's an example of RAISE_APPLICATION_ERROR in action:

```
DECLARE
  ename emp.ename%type;
  status NUMERIC;
```

```
          v_empno emp.empno%TYPE := 9999;
BEGIN
  ename := 'GARBAGE';  -- initialize
  BEGIN
    SELECT ENAME INTO ENAME
    FROM EMP
    WHERE empno = v_empno;
  EXCEPTION
  WHEN OTHERS THEN
    status := SQLCODE;
    DBMS_OUTPUT.put_line('nested: ' || SQLERRM(STATUS));
    raise_application_error(-20001,
        'EMPNO ' || v_empno || ' NOT FOUND',
        FALSE);  -- clear error stack
  END;  -- nested block
  DBMS_OUTPUT.put_line(ename);
EXCEPTION
WHEN OTHERS THEN
  status := SQLCODE;
  DBMS_OUTPUT.put_line('outer: ' || SQLERRM(STATUS));
END;
/

nested: ORA-01403: no data found
outer: ORA-20001: EMPNO 9999 NOT FOUND

PL/SQL procedure successfully completed.
```

If the third parameter is TRUE (meaning *don't clear the error stack*), you get this:

```
nested: ORA-01403: no data found
outer: ORA-20001: EMPNO 9999 NOT FOUND
ORA-01403: no data found
```

Naming Exceptions

Oracle predefines some exceptions for you (see Table 2.2 earlier in this chapter). If you want to name other Oracle exceptions so that you can test them explicitly in an exception handler, you must follow these steps:

1. Define your own exception.

2. Associate this user-defined exception with an Oracle exception value, using the pragma EXCEPTION_INIT.

Then, whenever this exception occurs, you can trap it by the name you gave it.

A *pragma* is a compiler directive that specifies how to handle language-specific conditions. This information is applied at compile time, not runtime. Here's the syntax for this pragma:

```
PRAGMA exception_init(exception_name, oracle_error_value);
```

Here's an example:

```
DECLARE
   -- ORA-01438: value larger than specified precision
   -- allows for this column
   COL_VAL_TOO_BIG EXCEPTION;   -- user-defined exception
   pragma exception_init(COL_VAL_TOO_BIG, -1438);
   bad_empno NUMBER(5) := 10000;   -- this will fail insert
   status NUMERIC;
BEGIN
   INSERT INTO emp (empno) VALUES (bad_empno);
EXCEPTION
WHEN COL_VAL_TOO_BIG THEN   -- trap error
 DBMS_OUTPUT.put_line('empno: ' || bad_empno || ' too big');
WHEN OTHERS THEN
   status := SQLCODE;
   DBMS_OUTPUT.put_line('some other error: ' ||
                        SQLERRM(status));
END;
/

empno: 10000 too big

PL/SQL procedure successfully completed.
```

In practice, you will probably use this feature sparingly. The list of predefined exceptions should take care of most of the situations you are likely to handle.

SQL WITHIN PL/SQL

To use cursors and looping constructs within PL/SQL programs.

The SQL language is integrated very well into PL/SQL. You can write SQL inline (where the SQL statements are mixed in with the PL/SQL code) with implicit cursors, for example, and you can perform complex row-level operations by using explicit cursors.

Implicit Cursors

An *implicit cursor* is a SQL statement embedded inline in PL/SQL code. An implicit cursor has the following form:

```
SELECT column_list
INTO variable_list
FROM table_list
WHERE where_clause ...;
```

The variable list must precisely match the SELECT clause's column list in both number and data type.

Here's a short example:

```
DECLARE
  user_name VARCHAR2(30);
  local_date DATE;
BEGIN
  SELECT USER, SYSDATE
  INTO user_name, local_date
  FROM DUAL;
  DBMS_OUTPUT.put_line('Hello, ' || user_name ||
                      ' on ' || local_date);
END;
/
```

The server then returns this:

```
Hello, SCOTT on 23-MAY-98

PL/SQL procedure successfully completed.
```

An implicit cursor must always return a single row. If more than one row is fetched, Oracle returns the exception TOO_MANY_ROWS.

An implicit cursor is generally the fastest way to obtain a single row from the database, because the implicit OPEN...FETCH...CLOSE operation is optimized.

You can use the SQL attributes FOUND, NOTFOUND, and ROWCOUNT to get information about the last SQL statement processed. Here's an example:

```
BEGIN
  UPDATE dept
  SET dname= 'Accounting '
  WHERE deptno = 10;
  IF (SQL%ROWCOUNT > 1) THEN  -- too many rows affected
    DBMS_OUTPUT.PUT_LINE('ROLLBACK');
  ELSIF (SQL%FOUND) THEN  -- exactly one row affected
    DBMS_OUTPUT.PUT_LINE('COMMIT');
  ELSE  -- no rows affected
    DBMS_OUTPUT.PUT_LINE('NO DATA FOUND');
  END IF;
END;
/
```

Here are two very good uses for implicit cursors:

◆ Performing single-row lookups on a unique index or primary key

◆ Getting the next value from a sequence object

Because implicit cursors must return only a single row, they are ideal for unique index scans, which are expected to return a single row for a given criterion. Here's an example:

```
SELECT *
INTO dept_rec
FROM dept
WHERE deptno = 20;   -- uses unique index PK_DEPT

SELECT seq_obj1.NEXTVAL
INTO next_seq
FROM DUAL;   -- uses temp table having 1 row

SELECT seq_obj1.CURRVAL
INTO curr_seq
FROM DUAL;   -- must have gotten NEXTVAL first
```

A good habit to get into is putting an implicit cursor inside its own block so that you can perform exception handling inline. This way, even if an error occurs on the update, processing can continue normally. Here's an example:

```
LOOP
   FETCH orderitem_cursor INTO orderitem_rec;
   EXIT WHEN orderitem_cursor%NOTFOUND;
   BEGIN   -- nested block for update statement
     UPDATE orderheader
     SET total_order_amount = orderitem_rec.order_amount
     WHERE orderno = orderitem_rec.orderno;
   EXCEPTION
   WHEN OTHERS THEN
     ... -- error processing here ***
   END;   -- nested update block
   ...   - continue processing order items
END LOOP;
```

Explicit Cursors

Explicit cursors are used to process queries (SELECT statements only) that return more than one row. An explicit cursor enables you to process one row at a time.

Here's the syntax for an explicit cursor declaration:

```
CURSOR cursor_name [(parameter_list)]
[RETURN row_type] IS
   select_statement;
```

When you are using cursors, a normal sequence of operation is as follows:

1. Declare the cursor and optionally a return type, as well as variables or a record variable to return each row into.

2. Open the cursor and provide optional parameters.

3. Within a loop, fetch the cursor into the variables or record variable. Test the cursor to detect when all the rows have been fetched and then break out of the loop.

4. Close the cursor.

Listing 2.6 illustrates these steps.

LISTING 2.6

A SIMPLE EXPLICIT CURSOR (GETDEPT.SQL)

```
DECLARE
  CURSOR get_dept IS SELECT * FROM dept;
  dept_rec get_dept%ROWTYPE;   -- based on cursor return
type
BEGIN
  OPEN get_dept;
  LOOP  -- process dept
    FETCH get_dept INTO dept_rec;  -- get a row
    EXIT WHEN get_dept%NOTFOUND;   -- finished yet?
    -- display some column values
    DBMS_OUTPUT.put_line('deptno= ' || dept_rec.deptno ||
                         ' dname= ' || dept_rec.dname);
  END LOOP;  -- done processing dept
  CLOSE get_dept;  -- finished with cursor
END;
/
```

The code in Listing 2.6 returns this:

```
deptno= 10 dname= Accounting
deptno= 20 dname= RESEARCH
deptno= 30 dname= SALES
deptno= 40 dname= OPERATIONS

PL/SQL procedure successfully completed.
```

By basing a record variable on the cursor row type, you get (for free) all the columns as members of the record variable. This makes the FETCH statement very easy to maintain. If you should add or remove columns in the cursor's SELECT clause, you won't have to maintain a separate list of matching variables.

Cursors have four attributes: NOTFOUND, FOUND, ROWCOUNT, and ISOPEN. Here's the syntax for using them:

```
cursor_name%attribute
```

They return Boolean or integer values, which you can test to determine the present state of the cursor. The following list is a summary of cursor attributes, their possible values, and the meaning of these values:

Attribute	Value	Meaning
NOTFOUND	TRUE	No more rows are available to fetch.
	FALSE	More rows are available to fetch.
FOUND	TRUE	A row has been fetched.
	FALSE	A row wasn't fetched.
ROWCOUNT	An integer	The number of rows fetched so far.
ISOPEN	TRUE	The cursor is now open.
	FALSE	The cursor isn't open.

Cursors can optionally take parameters. Here's an example:

```
    CURSOR emp_by_dept(Cdeptno emp.deptno%TYPE) IS
      SELECT empno, ename
      FROM emp
      WHERE deptno = Cdeptno;
BEGIN
  OPEN emp_by_deptno(20);
```

The scope of the cursor parameter is strictly local to the cursor. By basing the parameter's type on the database column, you are guaranteed of getting the correct matching data type, even if it changes down the road. You can name the parameter anything you like, except it can't be the same as a column name. It would be a programming error to use the column name exactly because the query would match the column value against itself, and thus return every row.

CONDITIONAL STATEMENTS

To understand and use the program components that comprise syntactically correct PL/SQL anonymous blocks.

NOTE

END IF Syntax Notice the space between the END and IF. This isn't a typo! END IF denotes the end of the conditional statement. The next statement to be processed after the conditional statement (regardless of whether the antecedent was executed) immediately follows END IF.

A conditional statement (test-and-branch) is one where a Boolean expression is evaluated, and one set of statements is executed if true while another set is executed if false. Three basic forms for conditional statements are discussed in the following sections.

The first and simplest form executes one or more statements if an expression is true or skips them if false:

```
IF (condition_is_true) THEN  -- perform the antecedent
   statements;
END IF;
```

The parentheses around the condition are optional. I always use them for readability, especially for complex expressions.

The antecedent can be one or more statements. No BEGIN...END block is needed, as is the case with some other languages. Here are some simple examples:

```
DECLARE
   having_fun BOOLEAN := TRUE;
   x NUMBER := 3;
   y NUMBER := 2;
   str VARCHAR2(10) := 'STRING';
BEGIN
   IF (having_fun) THEN  -- Boolean is an atomic expression
     x := x - y;  -- antecedent can be one statement
   END IF;
   IF (x = y) THEN  -- can test numbers
     NULL;  -- this statement does nothing (placeholder)
   END IF;
   IF (str = 'STRING') THEN  -- can test strings, constants
     x := y;  -- antecedent can have many statements
     str := 'EMPTY';
   END IF;
```

The second form executes one or more statements if an expression is true or another set if false. Only one or the other set of statements is executed; they're mutually exclusive. No matter which one is performed, execution subsequently jumps to the next instruction after END IF. Here's an example:

```
IF (condition_is_true) THEN  -- perform the antecedent
   statements;
ELSE  -- condition was false; perform the consequent
   statements;
END IF;  -- test some condition
```

I comment the test (ELSE) and END IF for readability. This is especially useful for long conditional blocks.

In the next example, the nested blocks provide a local scope for local variables. PL/SQL doesn't actually allocate storage for these variables unless the block is actually entered:

```
<<OUTER>>
DECLARE
  x NUMBER(3) := 5;
BEGIN
  IF (x < 10) THEN   -- test an inequality
    DBMS_OUTPUT.put_line('ANTECEDENT');
    DECLARE
      x NUMBER(3) := 5; -- this is a different x!
    BEGIN
      OUTER.x := x;
    END;
  ELSE    -- x is >= 10
    DECLARE
      y NUMBER(3) := 1;  -- may not be allocated at runtime
    BEGIN
      x := y;  -- this is OUTER.x
    END;
    DBMS_OUTPUT.put_line('CONSEQUENT');
  END IF;
  DBMS_OUTPUT.put_line('x = ' || x);
END;
/

ANTECEDENT
x = 5

PL/SQL procedure successfully completed.
```

The expression tested is computed left to right, using *short-circuit evaluation*, a compiler design technique for reducing expression evaluation time. In a series of OR expressions, as soon as one of them evaluates to TRUE, the entire expression must be TRUE, and evaluation stops. In a series of AND expressions, as soon as one of them evaluates to FALSE, the entire expression must be FALSE, and evaluation stops. Here's an example:

```
-- short-circuits to FALSE on third expression
IF (10 > 9) AND (9 > 8) AND (5 > 7) AND (7 > 6) THEN
-- short-circuits to TRUE on second expression
IF (10 < 9) OR (7 < 8) or (8 < 7) OR (7 < 6) THEN
```

Table 2.12 illustrates Boolean logic with the values TRUE, FALSE, and NULL.

TABLE 2.12

TRUTH TABLES FOR AND, OR, XOR, AND NOT

p	q	p AND q	p OR q	p XOR q	NOT p
TRUE	TRUE	TRUE	TRUE	FALSE	FALSE
TRUE	FALSE	FALSE	TRUE	TRUE	FALSE
TRUE	NULL	NULL	TRUE	NULL	FALSE
FALSE	TRUE	FALSE	TRUE	TRUE	TRUE
FALSE	FALSE	FALSE	FALSE	FALSE	TRUE
FALSE	NULL	FALSE	NULL	NULL	TRUE
NULL	TRUE	NULL	TRUE	NULL	NULL
NULL	FALSE	FALSE	NULL	NULL	NULL
NULL	NULL	NULL	NULL	NULL	NULL

Testing for NULL Values

Because NULL represents an indeterminate value, you can't test it for equality or inequality. You might make the mistake of writing this, for example:

```
IF (lname = NULL) THEN
IF (lname != NULL) THEN
```

Instead, you should use the special syntax IS NULL and IS NOT NULL to find out whether a variable or expression has the NULL value.

```
IF (lname IS NULL) THEN
IF (lname IS NOT NULL) THEN
```

Because of this special syntax, listing NULL in an IN expression (such as can be used in SQL) doesn't buy you anything:

```
IF bird IN (NULL, 'robin', 'peacock', 'cardinal') THEN
```

Such an expression is expanded to a group of OR expressions. If the variable to test is NULL, this test won't detect it. If the variable contains a value that matches one in the list, the test will succeed. The only way to properly test for NULL in a list is to expand the list yourself:

```
IF (bird IS NULL) OR
    (bird = 'robin') OR
    (bird = 'peacock') OR
    (bird = 'cardinal') THEN
```

The short-circuit evaluation you saw earlier is especially handy with NULL values. Here's a typical idiom I use:

```
IF ((x IS NULL) OR (x = y) OR ...) THEN
```

When x is NULL, the expression short-circuits to TRUE and stops evaluating there.

Nested Logic

IF statements can be nested to any depth. Very complex logic can therefore be evaluated. Here's an example:

```
IF (a > b OR c < d) THEN
  IF (a > b) THEN
    -- some statements
  ELSE  -- c < d
    -- some other statements
  END IF;
ELSE  -- not ((a > b) OR (c < d))
  -- some more statements
  IF (a = d AND b != c) THEN  -- do this
    -- further statements
  END IF;
  -- last thing to do
END IF;
```

As you can see, such logic might be rather opaque to new programmers who must maintain this code. Good comments are essential for keeping complex logic straight.

Sequential Logic

Rather than nest logic to test mutually exclusive expressions, you can use the special sequential logic syntax:

```
IF (expression) THEN  -- perform the antecedent
  statements;
ELSIF (expression) THEN  -- perform the antecedent
  statements;
[ELSIF (expression) THEN  -- perform the antecedent
  statements; ...]
[ELSE  -- perform the consequent
  statements;]
END IF;
```

Notice the unusual spelling ELSIF (not ELSE IF). The entire compound statement is terminated by a single END IF. Here's an example:

```
IF (test_score < 60) THEN
  DBMS_OUTPUT.put_line('FLUNKED');
```

```
    ELSIF (test_score < 70) THEN
      DBMS_OUTPUT.put_line('PASSED');
    ELSIF (test_score < 80) THEN
      DBMS_OUTPUT.put_line('AVERAGE');
    ELSIF (test_score < 90) THEN
      DBMS_OUTPUT.put_line('ABOVE AVERAGE');
    ELSIF (test_score <= 100) THEN
      DBMS_OUTPUT.put_line('EXCELLENT');
    ELSE
      DBMS_OUTPUT.put_line('INVALID SCORE');
    END IF;
```

When used to test overlapping inequalities, the order of the tests is significant.

UNCONDITIONAL STATEMENTS

In a very few cases, you may choose to use an unconditional branch to skip a large, complex body of logic. You perform an unconditional branch by using

```
GOTO label
```

where label indicates the place to jump to. Here's an example:

```
    IF (status != 0) THEN
      GOTO SKIPIT;
    END IF;
    -- lots of complex logic you don't want to mess with
    <<SKIPIT>>
    NULL;
END;
```

If the label precedes any END statement, a NULL statement is required before it in the manner shown. (It is a syntax error to place a label immediately before an END statement.)

The label must be within the scope of the GOTO statement; otherwise, you will get a compilation error. It is illegal, for example, to jump from the antecedent to the consequent of a conditional statement, to an outer block into an inner block, or from one block to another block at the same level.

One situation in which you might be compelled to use GOTO is to simulate a CONTINUE statement in a complex While loop, such as you can do with FORTRAN and C. PL/SQL doesn't have such a mechanism:

```
LOOP
  ...
  IF (SQL%NOTFOUND) THEN   -- last SQL failed
    GOTO NEXT_LOOP;
  END IF;
  ...
  <<NEXT_LOOP>>
  NULL;   -- the obligatory No-Op
END LOOP;
```

Although using GOTO simplifies coding in this specific instance, its use should be generally avoided (in the interest of maintainability).

ITERATIVE STATEMENTS

To use cursors and looping constructs within PL/SQL programs.

PL/SQL supports four flavors of iterative statements:

◆ FOR loops

◆ Cursor FOR loops

◆ Unconditional loops

◆ WHILE loops

In general, loops allow programmers to repeat a set of executable statements a finite number of times until some condition is met.

FOR Loops

A FOR loop is an iterative statement that enables you to loop over a range of integer values. You use the FOR loop when you need to iterate a precise number of times. The general syntax is

```
FOR loop_control_variable IN [REVERSE]
    range_low .. range_high LOOP
  executable statements
END LOOP;
```

where the loop control variable is an implicitly defined, read-only, integer variable.

Everything between the keywords FOR and LOOP (the loop control variable and the range condition) is called an *iteration scheme*.

Here are a couple of simple examples:

```
DECLARE
  x NUMBER;
BEGIN
  FOR k IN 1..10 LOOP   -- do 10 loops
    x := k;   -- capture loop control variable value
    DBMS_OUTPUT.put_line(x);
  END LOOP;
END;
DECLARE
  lo NUMBER := 10;
  hi NUMBER := 20;
  cnt NUMBER := 0;
BEGIN
  FOR i in REVERSE lo..hi LOOP   -- backward from hi to lo
    cnt := cnt + i;   -- 0+20+19+18+17...
    DBMS_OUTPUT.put_line(cnt);
  END LOOP;
END;
```

From these examples, you can discern some FOR loop characteristics:

◆ The loop control variable (k and i in the examples) is declared implicitly, strictly local in scope to the loop.

◆ The loop control variable is always an integer.

◆ The loop control variable can be referenced only inside the loop; it doesn't exist outside the loop.

◆ The loop control variable is read-only; it can appear only in expressions or on the right side of an assignment (never on the left side).

◆ You can name the loop control variable anything you want.

◆ The range must be specified from the low value to the high value, even when you are using the REVERSE keyword.

◆ The range can be numeric constants, variable expressions, or a combination of the two.

◆ The loop control variable increments (or decrements when using REVERSE) by 1 only; there's no STEP facility (although it can easily be simulated).

The FOR loop evaluates the low- and high-range expressions, initializes the loop control variable to the first value in the range, iterates through the range values, and then exits. If the program runs the FOR loop again (for instance, if the FOR loop were enclosed within a larger loop), this process is repeated.

If need be, you can prematurely exit the loop with an EXIT state-ment, although this is generally considered an abuse of the FOR loop.

The loop control variable is always an integer incremented (or decremented) by 1. Here's an example:

```
DECLARE
   lo NUMBER(2,1) := 1.1;
   hi NUMBER(2,1) := 2.9;
BEGIN
   FOR i In lo .. hi LOOP
      DBMS_OUTPUT.put_line(TO_CHAR(i, '0.0'));
   END LOOP;
END;
```

This just returns:

```
1.0
2.0
3.0
```

If you needed to simulate stepping by 0.1 (or some other offset), you could divide the loop control variable by 10 and make sure that the iteration scheme provides the correct number of loops, or you could use another variable to compute the step value.

Listing 2.7 uses FOR loops to find all the prime numbers between 2 and a user-supplied number. The algorithm used, known as the *Sieve of Eratosthenes*, was discovered by the Greek geographer Eratosthenes, chief librarian of the Library at Alexandria, Egypt, c.276–195 B.C.

LISTING 2.7

THE SIEVE OF ERATOSTHENES

```
-- Program Name: Sieve of Eratosthenes
-- Written By  : Daniel J. Clamage
-- Date        : May 16, 1998
-- Description : This program computes prime numbers
➥between
--               2 and a user-supplied number, using the
--               algorithm discovered by Eratosthenes.
SET ECHO OFF
SET SERVEROUTPUT ON SIZE 1000000
ACCEPT NUM PROMPT 'Enter a number between 2 and 99999 [2]:
'
DECLARE
   -- user-defined datatypes
TYPE SIEVE_TAB IS TABLE OF BOOLEAN INDEX BY BINARY_INTEGER;

   -- constants
   LAST_NUM  CONSTANT BINARY_INTEGER :=
              LEAST(GREATEST(NVL('&&NUM','2'),2),99999);
```

continues

continued

```
    PRIME        CONSTANT BOOLEAN          := TRUE;

  -- variables
  sieve       SIEVE_TAB;        -- array used to compute
primes
  last_mult BINARY_INTEGER; -- check primes <= SQRT(NUM)
BEGIN
  -- initialization
  last_mult := CEIL(SQRT(LAST_NUM));  -- check primes
  FOR i IN 2 .. LAST_NUM LOOP  -- reset array
    sieve(i) := PRIME;  -- indicates potential prime number
  END LOOP;  -- initialization

  -- compute prime numbers
  FOR i IN 2 .. last_mult LOOP  -- check multiples of
these
   IF (sieve(i) = PRIME) THEN  -- process multiples
   FOR j IN 2 .. FLOOR(LAST_NUM / i) LOOP -- multiples of
i
     sieve(i * j) := NOT PRIME;  -- mark as NOT PRIME
   END LOOP;
  END IF;  -- already marked as NOT PRIME
 END LOOP;

  -- display prime numbers found
  FOR i IN 2 .. last_num LOOP
    IF (sieve(i) = PRIME) THEN
      DBMS_OUTPUT.put_line(i);
    END IF;
  END LOOP;  -- display primes
END;
/
-- DONE
```

A typical session in SQL*Plus might go like this:

```
SQL> @c:\docs\word\mcp\sieve
Enter a number between 2 and 99999 [2]: 20
old   8:    LAST_NUM  CONSTANT SIEVE_TYPE :=
➥LEAST(GREATEST(NVL('&&NUM','2'),2),99999);
new   8:    LAST_NUM  CONSTANT SIEVE_TYPE :=
➥LEAST(GREATEST(NVL('20','2'),2),99999);
2
3
5
7
11
13
17
19

PL/SQL procedure successfully completed.
```

The complex-looking business with the constant declaration for LAST_NUM is just some bounds validation on the user's input. If a user attempts to enter a number less than 2 or greater than 99,999, these lower and upper bounds will be used instead. If the user enters nothing, it is treated as a NULL, and the input defaults to 2. The literal strings are implicitly converted to BINARY_INTEGER.

> **Loop Control Variables**   The variables controlling the loop are BINARY_INTEGER, the correct type to use for PL/SQL table indexing. The loop control variables also implicitly receive this data type.

Cursor FOR Loops

A *cursor* FOR *loop* is an easy method for executing a multirow query in PL/SQL. Here's the general syntax:

```
FOR loop_control_variable IN cursor_or_query LOOP
   executable statements
END LOOP;
```

There are two basic flavors of cursor FOR loops. The simplest version embeds the query directly into the iteration scheme:

```
FOR x IN (SELECT * FROM SCOTT.dept) LOOP
   executable statements
END LOOP;
```

The cursor FOR loop implicitly opens the cursor, fetches its result set into the loop control variable, and then implicitly closes the cursor when the set is exhausted.

In this example, the implicit loop control variable, x, is a record variable based on the cursor's ROWTYPE—that is, every column in the SELECT clause. Like any record variable, its members are referenced with dot notation. The parentheses around the query are required.

As with regular FOR loops, the loop control variable can be named anything you like. Its scope is strictly limited to the FOR loop; it doesn't exist outside the loop.

A slightly more complex version of a cursor FOR loop requires you to declare the cursor beforehand and then reference it in the iteration scheme:

```
DECLARE
   CURSOR my_cursor IS SELECT * FROM SCOTT.dept;
BEGIN
   FOR rec IN my_cursor LOOP
     executable statements
   END LOOP;
```

You must omit parentheses from around the cursor in the iteration scheme.

Here are some benefits to using this method:

◆ The cursor FOR loop is easier to read, especially if the cursor statement is particularly lengthy.

◆ The cursor can be used in more than one place, if needed.

◆ Cursors can be defined together in one place, making them easier to find and maintain.

If you need to see the values contained in the loop control variable outside the loop, you must assign it to another variable whose scope is defined outside the cursor FOR loop:

```
DECLARE
    CURSOR my_cursor IS SELECT * FROM SCOTT.dept;
    my_rec my_cursor%ROWTYPE;
BEGIN
    FOR rec IN my_cursor LOOP
      some executable statements
      my_rec := rec;  -- capture row
    END LOOP;
```

Although they're very fast and easy to code, cursor FOR loops have their limitations. If you need full control of the OPEN...FETCH...CLOSE process, you can issue these statements explicitly, usually along with an unconditional loop.

Unconditional Loops

Unconditional loops are the simplest form of loops to use. They're most typically used with explicit cursors. They have the following general syntax:

```
LOOP
    some code
END LOOP;
```

Notice that the method of exiting the loop is unspecified, as is the number of iterations to perform. You decide whether to check the exit condition near the top or bottom (or in the middle) of the loop, according to your requirements. Here are the general methods for exiting a loop:

◆ EXIT WHEN some Boolean expression is TRUE;

◆ IF (some condition is TRUE) THEN
    EXIT;
    END IF;

You will find yourself using the first method very heavily, especially with explicit cursors, by testing the cursor's NOTFOUND attribute. Here's an example:

```
DECLARE
   CURSOR my_cursor IS SELECT * FROM SCOTT.dept;
   my_rec my_cursor%ROWTYPE;
BEGIN
   OPEN my_cursor;
   LOOP
     FETCH my_cursor INTO my_rec;
     EXIT WHEN my_cursor%NOTFOUND;
     other statements go here
   END LOOP;
   CLOSE my_cursor;
END;
```

The OPEN...FETCH...CLOSE sequence shown here is functionally equivalent to the cursor FOR loop.

You may need the second exit method when the exit logic is very complex. For example, if you are trying to detect a control break on a certain column, you are more likely to use a sequential IF statement to determine whether to exit, skip processing the row, or process the row.

These loops don't have their own scope like blocks do. This means you can't declare local variables inside the loop unless you specifically code a block inside the loop. If needed, you could use something like the following code, which is useful for trapping exceptions inside a loop so that processing can continue:

```
LOOP
   FETCH my_cursor INTO my_rec;
   EXIT WHEN my_cursor%NOTFOUND;
   DECLARE
     i NUMBER;
   BEGIN
     now the variable i is local to this block
   EXCEPTION
   WHEN OTHERS THEN
     <error-handling code here>
   END;
END LOOP;
```

> **NOTE**
>
> **Avoiding Infinite Loops**   I placed the FETCH and EXIT WHEN statements outside the nested block. Had I placed them inside the block and an error occurred during the FETCH (for example, a VALUE_ERROR), I might get trapped in an infinite loop. The exception handler would continue to trap exceptions and offer no opportunity to exit the loop. Always make sure you have a way to break out of these loops.

WHILE Loops

Another iterative statement having the exit condition evaluated right at the top of the loop is the WHILE loop. It has the following general form:

```
WHILE <some Boolean condition is TRUE> LOOP
   executable code goes here
END LOOP;
```

The condition is evaluated once before each loop iteration. The loop will continue to iterate until the condition fails to be met. This means that inside the loop, something had better change at some point that causes the condition to become false.

Listing 2.8 provides a simple example.

LISTING 2.8

SIMPLE WHILE LOOP

```
DECLARE
    x NUMBER := 0;
BEGIN
  WHILE (x <= 100) LOOP
    IF (MOD(x, 5) = 0) THEN   -- display multiples of 5
      DBMS_OUTPUT.put_line(x);
    END IF;
    x := x + 1;   -- increment loop counter
  END LOOP;
END;
/
```

When you run this from SQL*Plus, you get this:

```
0
5
10
15
20
25
30
35
40
45
50
55
60
65
70
75
80
85
90
95
100

PL/SQL procedure successfully completed.
```

If the condition for the WHILE loop fails on the first iteration, none of the loop code is executed. If you need a loop that tests the exit condition at the bottom of the loop, use an unconditional loop and place the EXIT WHEN statement at the bottom of this loop.

GETTING OUTPUT

To make use of various built-in functions and the Oracle-supplied DBMS_OUTPUT package.

PL/SQL wasn't designed with input/output in mind; it was intended to operate on tables and database objects only. Consequently, there's no facility for program output. Oracle has, however, built such a facility to be used from SQL*Plus. You use the procedures found in the Oracle-supplied database package DBMS_OUTPUT to perform program output.

Most other programming languages have a feature to write a single line of output to the console: for example, write and writeln in Pascal, printf in C, and format in FORTRAN. With PL/SQL, you use DBMS_OUTPUT.put and DBMS_OUTPUT.put_line to write out string text. Both can buffer up to 255 byte strings. If the string exceeds 255 bytes, you will get the following exception:

```
ORA-20000: ORU-10028: line length overflow, limit of
                      255 bytes per line
```

The procedure put buffers a non-newline–terminated string. You can call put multiple times to concatenate text into one long string. At some point, you must then call put_line or new_line to terminate the string with a newline character.

put_line buffers a newline-terminated string. Multiple calls to put_line buffers multiple newline-terminated strings, which will be displayed by SQL*Plus as separate text lines.

The DBMS_OUTPUT package uses an internal PL/SQL table (nested table) to implement this feature. The strings are buffered up in this table until the program completes. Then, SQL*Plus can get these strings and display them. SQL*Plus must wait until the program finishes because the internal table exists in a private memory area in the SGA. SQL*Plus can only indirectly access its session's memory objects in the SGA through the server. Until the server finishes its work, this PL/SQL table isn't available.

After the program completes, SQL*Plus calls `get_lines` to get all the buffered terminated strings. It reads all these strings into its own memory until no more strings are available. Then, SQL*Plus dumps them to the screen.

To activate this feature, you must first enter the following command in SQL*Plus:

```
SET SERVEROUTPUT ON
```

This SQL*Plus command (not a SQL command) takes optional parameters:

```
SIZE n    -- buffer size, where n is 2000 - 1000000
FORMAT WRAPPED    -- leave leading spaces untrimmed
```

The buffer size is the entire size, in bytes, of all output strings. The full command, along with any parameters, must be entered on a single line.

If you don't take this first step, you will get no output from SQL*Plus, even if the program writes output.

The `DBMS_OUTPUT` package also has two commands—`enable` and `disable`—to manage whether the facility is on or off, respectively. A program can use `enable` to activate output and set the buffer size (the total number of bytes stored in the internal table). Conversely, `disable` turns buffering off, even when `SERVEROUTPUT` is on. It also clears any previous entries. If the buffer size is exceeded, the exception

```
ORA-20000: ORU-10027: buffer overflow,
                        limit of buf_size bytes
```

is raised, where `buf_size` is the value supplied with `enable` or `2,000` (the default).

CHAPTER SUMMARY

KEY TERMS

Before you take the exam, make sure you are familiar with the following terms. You should be able to understand how they apply to or how to implement them in PL/SQL programs:

This chapter introduced you to the PL/SQL language. In addition to familiarizing yourself with the syntax and various language features, you should be comfortable with the following concepts:

- ◆ PL/SQL programs are designed in logical blocks. Blocks can be nested to any depth. Blocks are made up of a declaration section (where variables, cursors, and types are declared), the executable section (between `BEGIN...END`, where executable code is placed), and an exception section (where exception handlers are written).

CHAPTER SUMMARY *continued*

◆ PL/SQL blocks follow strict scoping rules. Program objects, such as variables and cursors, can be referenced only within the block where they are declared.

◆ PL/SQL enables you to declare your own data types, such as records and scalar types that are based on a parent data type, with optional constraints.

◆ Instead of declaring a variable to be of some data type explicitly, you can base it on the data type of an existing object, such as a database column or table, a cursor row type, or another variable. Basing variables makes your code more maintainable—if a database object changes, for example, the based variable's type changes without code modification.

◆ In expressions, when variables of different data types are used, PL/SQL can often convert their data types implicitly to match so that the expression can be properly evaluated. In some cases, however, you will have to use the explicit conversion functions to avoid compiler or runtime errors.

◆ Runtime errors (exceptions) can be trapped and processed during program execution. Exception handlers can be tailored to trap only certain exceptions so that program behavior can be modified as needed. You can declare your own exceptions as well as raise exceptions yourself when business rules are violated. Use the function SQLCODE to trap the exception's numeric value.

◆ Database table queries are processed with cursors. Use implicit cursors when exactly one row is expected to be returned by a query. Use explicit cursors when zero or more rows are expected, or you need to perform special logic for each row. Use cursor attributes to determine the state of a cursor. DML (Data Manipulation Language) is done with implicit UPDATE, INSERT, and DELETE statements.

◆ PL/SQL supports conditional logic (if a condition is true, then do something) with IF and ELSIF statements.

◆ PL/SQL supports these language constructs to perform looping: WHILE (condition_is_true) LOOP, FOR iteration_scheme LOOP, and the unconditional LOOP. Looping is especially important for processing multirow queries.

KEY TERMS *continued*

- Block structure
- Scope (also *scoping rules*)
- PL/SQL table (also called *index-by* or *nested tables*)
- User-defined types and subtypes
- Based variables
- Implicit and explicit data type conversion
- Exception block and exception handlers
- Implicit and explicit cursors
- Conditional logic
- Iteration

APPLY YOUR KNOWLEDGE

This section enables you to assess how well you understand the material in this chapter. Review questions test your knowledge of the tasks and concepts specified in the objectives. The exercises provide you with opportunities to engage in the sorts of tasks that comprise the skill sets the objectives reflect.

Exercises

1.1   Listing the Tables Visible to You

Write a PL/SQL program to list the tables visible to you that were created by a specific schema (hint: Use the all_tables view). The program should prompt the user for the schema name and convert it to uppercase. Only print the schema name once, followed by a columnar list of tables in alphabetic order. If no tables for the given schema exist, display a suitable message, such as No tables for schema_name are visible to you. (This exercise addresses objectives 1, 3, 4, and 5.)

Time Estimate: 15 minutes

1.2   Query a Table

Write a PL/SQL program to query the SCOTT.EMP table for just those employees whose job is MANAGER and who have a monthly salary greater than $2,500 (use an explicit cursor). Then, give each of these managerial employees a 5% raise. Be sure to enclose the UPDATE statement in its own block so that you can trap any errors that might occur. If the UPDATE block traps an error, display the error text and the current employee number. Count the number of employees updated, and then perform a COMMIT every fifth update. Also include an exception handler for the main block so that you can display error text, the current manager's employee number, and close the explicit cursor (if it is

open). During processing, display the manager's name once, the employee name, and the old and new salary. At the end of the program, display the number of employees updated. (This exercise addresses all the objectives.)

Time Estimate: 30 minutes

Review Questions

1. Suppose you have a loop that's processing a cursor. Inside the loop is an UPDATE statement for a related table. You discover that for certain rows, the UPDATE statement fails and the loop is exited prematurely, leaving the cursor open. How would you fix this bug? Here's a sample loop:

```
OPEN prod_cursor;
LOOP
   FETCH prod_cursor INTO prod_rec;
   EXIT WHEN prod_cursor%NOTFOUND;
   UPDATE customers
   SET last_item_purchased = prod_rec.item_no
   WHERE cust_no = prod_rec.cust_no;
END LOOP;
CLOSE dept_cursor;
```

A. Enclose LOOP...END LOOP in a block with its own exception handler.

B. Check the SQLCODE value immediately after the UPDATE statement and call ROLLBACK if it is a nonzero value.

C. Enclose the UPDATE statement in a block with its own exception handler.

D. Enclose all statements inside the loop within a block and close the cursor in the exception handler.

2. What value of the variable z will be displayed upon executing the following code?

APPLY YOUR KNOWLEDGE

```
DECLARE
  x NUMBER := 1;
  y NUMBER := 2;
  z NUMBER := 3;
BEGIN
  IF (z = 0) THEN
    z:= z + y;
  ELSE
    DECLARE
      x NUMBER;
    BEGIN
      z := x + z;
    END;
  END IF;
  DBMS_OUTPUT.put_line('z = ' ||
➥TO_CHAR(NVL(z, -1)));
END;
```

A. 1

B. 4

C. –1

D. NULL

3. What message will the following program display?

```
DECLARE
  v_hello CONSTANT VARCHAR2(10) := 'hello!
➥';
  c_hello CONSTANT CHAR(10) := 'hello! ';
BEGIN
  IF (v_hello = c_hello) THEN
    DBMS_OUTPUT.put_line('EQUAL');
  ELSIF (v_hello != c_hello) THEN
    DBMS_OUTPUT.put_line('NOT EQUAL');
  ELSE
    DBMS_OUTPUT.put_line('DON''T KNOW');
  END IF;
END;
```

A. EQUAL

B. NOT EQUAL

C. DON'T KNOW

D. Nothing; the program has a syntax error.

4. In the declaration, what value are variables automatically initialized to?

A. NULL

B. They aren't initialized; they contain garbage until you assign a value to them.

C. It depends on their data type: zero for NUMBER, empty string for VARCHAR2 and CHAR, and '01-JAN-00' for DATE.

D. Indeterminate

5. Suppose a column in a table is named the same as an Oracle reserved word. How can you specify it in a PL/SQL program so as to avoid a syntax error?

A. Just specify the name; no syntax error will occur because Oracle reserved words are okay as column names.

B. There's no method for specifying it in PL/SQL; the column will have to be renamed.

C. It is impossible to name columns the same as Oracle reserved words, so this problem couldn't occur.

D. Place double quotation marks around the column name, making sure that it is all in uppercase.

6. Which of the following IF statement's antecedents will be executed, given the following declaration for x?

```
x VARCHAR2(1) := 'A';
```

A. IF (x <> NULL) THEN

B. IF (x NOT IN (NULL, 'B', 'C')) THEN

C. IF (x IS NOT NULL) THEN

D. IF (x ~= NULL)) THEN

APPLY YOUR KNOWLEDGE

7. Which of the following declarations contains a syntax error?

   A. `dept_rec SCOTT.dept%TYPE;`

   B. `dept_name VARCHAR2(20) DEFAULT 'NOT` ↪`AVAILABLE';`

   C. `emp_name SCOTT.emp.name%TYPE;`

   D. `PI CONSTANT REAL(9, 8) NOT NULL :=` ↪`3.14159265;`

8. Which of these declarations *won't* generate an exception?

   A. `w NUMBER(3) NOT NULL := 'ABC';`

   B. `x NUMBER(4,2) := 1.2345;`

   C. `y NUMBER(4,2) := 123.45;`

   D. `z VARCHAR2(4) := 'FALSE';`

9. Which of these statements *doesn't* contain a syntax error?

   A. `IF (x := (dept_cursor%NOTFOUND)) THEN`

   B. `x := y := z + 1;`

   C. `IF (dept_rec.deptno = ANY (10, 20, 30,` ↪`40)) THEN`

   D. `FOR rec IN (SELECT deptno FROM dept) LOOP`

10. Suppose the exception `NO_DATA_FOUND` occurs. What will the following exception handler display?

```
EXCEPTION
   status := SQLCODE;
WHEN NO_DATA_FOUND THEN
   DBMS_OUTPUT.put_line('NO_DATA_FOUND');
WHEN VALUE_ERROR THEN
   DBMS_OUTPUT.put_line('VALUE_ERROR');
WHEN OTHERS THEN
   DBMS_OUTPUT.put_line('OTHER');
END;
```

A. All three messages

B. The first and third message

C. Just the first message

D. The third message

Answers to Review Questions

1. **C.** By enclosing just the UPDATE statement in its own block, you can handle any exception the UPDATE might suffer inline. Regardless of how the UPDATE statement is processed, control passes to the statement immediately following the block the UPDATE statement is located in.

2. **C.** The assignment z := x + z computes a value of NULL for z because the value of the local variable x (not the x declared in the outer block) is used. By default, the compiler assigns NULL to declared variables when no explicit assignment is given (such as was done for the outer x). By definition, any expression containing a NULL results in NULL. The output statement uses the NVL function to convert a NULL value into the –1 value.

3. **B.** Although it looks like both variables, v_hello and c_hello, are given the same value ('hello! '), the variable c_hello actually contains 'hello!   ', which has four trailing blanks, not one. Variables of type CHAR are always given enough trailing blanks to fill in the total length of the variable, whereas VARCHAR2 variables only contain exactly as many characters as you assign them. Literal strings are always of type CHAR.

4. **A.** Unless you explicitly assign a value in the variable declaration, variables are always initialized to NULL by the compiler.

APPLY YOUR KNOWLEDGE

5. **D**. The only way to specify a column name that's also a PL/SQL reserved word is to surround the name in double quotation marks. The name has to be uppercase because that's how all names are stored in the data dictionary. For example, TO_DATE is a typical column name given by inexperienced Oracle designers. Although perfectly legal in SQL, it is a reserved PL/SQL word.

6. **C**. The antecedent is the section of code that's executed when an IF condition is TRUE. The consequent is the ELSE section (the condition evaluated to FALSE or NULL). Because the variable was assigned a value ('A'), it is TRUE that it is NOT NULL.

7. **A**. The correct declaration is

   ```
   dept_rec SCOTT.dept%ROWTYPE;
   ```

   because dept is a table.

8. **B**. The value for x just gets rounded to 1.23. The precision of a number declaration states the number of significant digits, which must include all digits to the left of a decimal. Digits to the right of a decimal can be rounded.

9. **D**. The first two answers have nested assignments, and nested assignments are not supported. The third uses = ANY, which is a SQL expression; the proper keyword should have been IN.

10. **C**. Exception handlers are mutually exclusive. When one is performed, control skips past the rest to the end of the block. For this reason, the order of exception handlers is unimportant (except for WHEN OTHERS THEN, which is the catchall handler, and therefore must come last).

This chapter helps you prepare for the exam by covering the following objectives:

Write syntactically correct subprograms, stored procedures, functions, and packages.

▶ This objective is necessary so that you understand how to build modular program components that will compile properly.

State the benefits of using stored procedures, functions, and packages.

▶ You must understand how using stored program objects improves application performance and developer productivity.

State the benefits of using packages versus standalone subprograms.

▶ Understand when to use packages and standalone stored subprograms.

Locate and correct syntax errors within stored subprograms and packages.

▶ This objective covers how to troubleshoot, debug, and fix program errors.

Obtain information about stored subprograms and packages by using various data dictionary views.

▶ This objective is necessary to understand how to check the status, size, and components of stored program units.

Use stored and packaged functions in SQL statements.

▶ Being able to create your own PL/SQL functions for use in SQL is a powerful feature that is in high demand.

CHAPTER 3

PL/SQL in Use

STUDY STRATEGIES

▶ The best way to study this material is in front of a computer. You should have access to SQL*Plus, a database connection, and a simple text editor such as Notepad. Follow along with the text by running the listings provided and typing the queries shown.

Some listings depend on objects owned by user SCOTT that's created when the demo database is installed. If this account doesn't exist on your database, you can re-create it by using the script found in *ORACLE_HOME*\RDBMSversion\ADMIN\SCOTT.SQL, where *ORACLE_HOME* is the directory where Oracle was installed and version is the version of your database. For example, on my system, this file is found at D:\ORANT\RDBMS80\ADMIN\SCOTT.SQL.

Most importantly, play around with the programs as your curiosity dictates. Take the time to try different things. The best way to get a handle on a new language is to observe the difference between valid and invalid syntax and explore various approaches to a problem.

INTRODUCTION

This chapter introduces subprograms, stored subprograms, and packages. These features of PL/SQL extend the concept of modularity and "top-down" design by allowing you to break a program into functional units. By taking advantage of stored subprograms and packages, your compiled PL/SQL programs are readily deployed through the database server.

Stored subprograms and packages are used to

◆ Encode and enforce business rules

◆ Control access to database objects

◆ Simplify client applications by moving complex logic to the server, where it can be reused

◆ Provide a simple interface to complex database operations

In Chapter 2, "PL/SQL Language Structure," I discussed *anonymous PL/SQL blocks*, programs typically run manually from SQL*Plus to perform an immediate operation. If a user needs to run the operation again, the block must be submitted again. If a related operation must use some of the logic found in the anonymous block, you must cut and paste that piece of logic into the new block. Such programming methods are primitive at best. Stored subprograms and packages provide an alternative to hacking out new code based on existing code by making executable subroutines available to developers. Rather than reinvent the wheel, developers can incorporate work that has gone before. Such program units are immediately deployable to users through the database.

SUBPROGRAMS, PROCEDURES, AND FUNCTIONS

Write syntactically correct subprograms, stored procedures, functions, and packages.

A *subprogram* is a program unit, callable by name. Another word for a subprogram is a *subroutine*. The two kinds of subprograms are procedures and functions. Oracle uses subprogram as a generic term to mean both functions and procedures.

Subprograms are defined in the declaration section of a program block, after all the other declarations. Placing variables or other declarations after subprogram declarations causes a syntax error.

Procedure declarations have the form

```
PROCEDURE procedure_name (optional_parameter_list) IS
   declarative statements
BEGIN
   executable statements;
END [procedure_name];
```

In this syntax, the optional parameter list has the form

```
parameter_name [mode] datatype
[, parameter_name [mode] datatype ...]
```

Mode

The mode (also known as flow) can have one of three values:

Mode	Direction	Description
IN	Input	Read-only
OUT	Output	Write-only
IN OUT	Input/output	Read and write

The mode indicates how the parameter can be used inside the subprogram. If the mode isn't supplied, it defaults to IN.

You can use an IN parameter only in an expression or on the right side of an assignment. You use an OUT parameter only on the left side of an assignment. You can use an IN OUT parameter anywhere. Note this example:

```
PROCEDURE div (numerator    IN NUMBER,   -- read-only
               denominator IN NUMBER,
               result      OUT NUMBER,    -- write-only
               status IN OUT NUMBER) IS  -- both read-write
BEGIN
  status := 0;
  result := numerator / denominator;
EXCEPTION
WHEN OTHERS THEN
  status := SQLCODE;  -- trap error
  DBMS_OUTPUT.put_line('div: ' || SQLERRM(status));
END div;
```

Should the denominator be zero, the exception handler traps it and displays the message div: ORA-01476: divisor is equal to zero.

The parameter variable named status receives the exception value from the built-in function SQLCODE and then is read (passed into the built-in function SQLERRM) to display the message text. As a rule of thumb, restrict the mode to the actual usage of each parameter.

Using Procedures

You use a procedure anywhere you want to encapsulate a set of actions and optionally return one or more values in the parameter list. By encapsulating the actions, you can call the procedure as often as needed, perhaps with different parameter values each time. You call the procedure as a single statement, providing actual values (in the form of literals and variables) in place of the parameters. Listing 3.1 shows an example.

LISTING 3.1

GETDEPT.SQL; GET DEPARTMENT DATA

```
DECLARE
  -- local variables
  dept_rec dept%ROWTYPE;    -- variable to return row into
  status NUMBER;            -- success or failure of lookup

  -- perform a single row lookup on DEPT
  PROCEDURE get_dept(Pdeptno IN dept.deptno%TYPE,
                     Prec    OUT dept%ROWTYPE,
                     Pstatus IN OUT NUMBER) IS
  BEGIN
    Pstatus := 0;  -- OK
    SELECT *
    INTO Prec
    FROM SCOTT.dept
    WHERE dept.deptno = Pdeptno;
  EXCEPTION
  WHEN OTHERS THEN
    Pstatus := SQLCODE; -- trap error
    Prec := NULL;       -- clear record
    DBMS_OUTPUT.put_line('get_dept: ' || SQLERRM(Pstatus));
  END get_dept;

BEGIN  -- anonymous block
  get_dept(10, dept_rec, status);
  IF (status = 0) THEN  -- found row
    DBMS_OUTPUT.put_line(dept_rec.dname || ': ' ||
                         dept_rec.loc);
  END IF;
```

continues

LISTING 3.1 | *continued*

GETDEPT.SQL; GET DEPARTMENT DATA

```
  get_dept(30, dept_rec, status);
  IF (status = 0) THEN  -- found row
    DBMS_OUTPUT.put_line(dept_rec.dname || ': ' ||
                         dept_rec.loc);
  END IF;

  get_dept(50, dept_rec, status);
  IF (status = 0) THEN  -- found row
    DBMS_OUTPUT.put_line(dept_rec.dname || ': ' ||
                         dept_rec.loc);
  END IF;

END;  -- anonymous block
/
```

When Listing 3.1 is run from SQL*Plus, you get

```
SQL> @c:\docs\word\mcp\ch3\getdept
Accounting : NEW YORK
SALES: CHICAGO
get_dept: ORA-01403: no data found

PL/SQL procedure successfully completed.
```

In this example, a literal value for deptno is passed into the procedure, and a record is returned via the parameter list upon success. If the query fails for whatever reason, the record variable is cleared so that a previous value won't be mistaken for a successful operation. The status parameter variable (whose mode is IN OUT so that it can also be used by SQLERRM) tells the calling context whether the lookup was successful. The exception handler displays an error message.

In general, I prefer to perform the error handling at the point of occurrence, inside the routine that generated the error. This way, the main body of code needs to perform logic only around the error, rather than perform the error handling itself. For a production system, I dump the error to an error table, including the user name, program name, procedure name, and usually the input parameters as well.

Using Functions

A *function* has a syntax very similar to a procedure, except that the function name returns a value of a specified data type:

```
FUNCTION function_name (optional_parameter_list)
RETURN datatype IS
  declarative statements
BEGIN
  executable statements;
  RETURN(datatype);
END [procedure_name];
```

When writing a function, consider that it must always return a value
of the specified data type. If the function has an exception handler,
you must make sure that a RETURN statement is also found in the
exception handler. Listing 3.2 shows an example. Notice the local
variables declared before the BEGIN keyword. The scope of a local
variable is limited strictly to the body of the subprogram. When program execution enters the subprogram, local variables are created
and initialized. When execution exits the subprogram, the variables
are destroyed and their memory freed.

LISTING 3.2

**GETDEPTF.SQL; GET DEPARTMENT DATA WITH A
FUNCTION**

```
DECLARE
  -- local variables
  dept_rec dept%ROWTYPE;

  -- perform a single row lookup on DEPT
  FUNCTION get_dept(Pdeptno IN dept.deptno%TYPE)
  RETURN dept%ROWTYPE IS
    rec dept%ROWTYPE;
    status NUMBER;
  BEGIN
    SELECT *
    INTO rec
    FROM SCOTT.dept
    WHERE deptno = Pdeptno;

    RETURN(rec);

  EXCEPTION
  WHEN OTHERS THEN
    status := SQLCODE;  -- trap error
    rec := NULL;  -- clear record
    DBMS_OUTPUT.put_line('get_dept: ' ¦¦ SQLERRM(status));
    RETURN(rec);  -- now cleared
  END get_dept;

BEGIN  -- anonymous block
  dept_rec := get_dept(10);
  IF (dept_rec.deptno IS NOT NULL) THEN
```

continues

LISTING 3.2	*continued*

GETDEPTF.SQL; GET DEPARTMENT DATA WITH A FUNCTION

```
      DBMS_OUTPUT.put_line(dept_rec.dname || ': ' ||
                             dept_rec.loc);
  END IF;

  dept_rec := get_dept(30);
  IF (dept_rec.deptno IS NOT NULL) THEN
    DBMS_OUTPUT.put_line(dept_rec.dname || ': ' ||
                           dept_rec.loc);
  END IF;

  dept_rec := get_dept(50);
  IF (dept_rec.deptno IS NOT NULL) THEN
    DBMS_OUTPUT.put_line(dept_rec.dname || ': ' ||
                           dept_rec.loc);
  END IF;

END;  -- anonymous block
/
```

The results are exactly as before:

```
SQL> @c:\docs\word\mcp\ch3\getdeptf
Accounting : NEW YORK
SALES: CHICAGO
get_dept: ORA-01403: no data found

PL/SQL procedure successfully completed.
```

Compare this solution to the procedure example. I'm not returning a status variable; instead, the primary key column in the record variable is used to test whether the lookup succeeded. In general, it's considered poor programming practice to have a function return more than one value, such as additional values on the parameter list, along with the value returned by the function name itself.

There are two RETURN statements: one in the function body and one in the function's exception handler. If I neglect to include the RETURN statement in the exception handler, at runtime I get the error

```
ORA-06503: PL/SQL: Function returned without value
```

but only for the input value for which no row exists. For the two valid values, no error is detected. It's only when the exception handler is invoked that the missing RETURN statement is detected.

Using Procedures Rather Than Functions

Use a procedure instead of a function when you expect more than one value to be returned.

Use a function instead of a procedure when you need to use the function in an expression, such as in an IF or WHILE statement. The built-in functions were designed with this capability in mind, such as

```
IF (SUBSTR(str, pos, len) = old_str) THEN ...
numstr := TO_CHAR(num, '0000') || CHR(10);
```

You can also write functions to be used in SQL statements, as long as the functions don't have side effects such as writing to the database.

Suppose that you want to test two record variables for equivalence. You can write a function to test them, member-by-member:

```
FUNCTION same_dept(dept1 IN dept%ROWTYPE,
                   dept2 IN dept%ROWTYPE)
RETURN BOOLEAN IS
BEGIN
  RETURN (dept1.deptno = dept2.deptno AND
          dept1.dname  = dept2.dname AND
          dept1.loc    = dept2.loc);
END same_dept;
```

Notice that the expression within the RETURN statement reduces to a single Boolean value. Then, you can use the function in a condition:

```
IF (NOT same_dept(old_dept, new_dept))  -- control break
THEN ...
```

This makes the condition very readable and has the added benefit of being available for other tests (perhaps with different values) as well.

Parameters and Local Variables

Subprograms can take as parameters any scalar value (VARCHAR2, NUMBER, DATE, variables based on database columns, and so on) or composite values (RECORD, record variables based on a database table, or a nested table). There's no limit on the number of parameters a subprogram can have (if any).

The scope of the parameters is strictly local to the subprogram. You can reference the parameter variables only inside the subprogram.

When you call the subprogram, you provide actual values or variables in place of the parameter names. As far as calling the subprogram is concerned, you can think of the parameters as placeholders, telling you their order and data types. As far as declaring the subprogram is concerned, the parameters are used strictly inside the subprogram. The parameter values are passed back and forth between the subprogram and the calling context via the stack.

Many other programming languages, such as C and Pascal, use the stack model for passing parameter values between the subroutine and the calling context. Just before the subroutine call, the parameters are pushed onto the stack. Inside the subroutine, the parameters are popped off the stack (in reverse order) and used as needed. If any parameters are used to return values, their values are pushed back onto the stack at the end of the subroutine. These return values are popped back off the stack after the subroutine returns to the calling context.

Some older languages, such as COBOL, don't use a stack to pass parameters. Instead, programmers define a global data area to store, by convention, inputs to and outputs from a particular paragraph. Then, the paragraph is designed to know to use this global data block for input and output variables. The problem with this scheme is that there's no guarantee that some other code block won't also read or write this global data. Hence, debugging such code can be extremely difficult. Programmers must verify that the data isn't accidentally overwritten by another code section. In contrast, languages that use the stack when making subroutine calls are isolating the subroutine internals from possible interference from other modules.

Although you can use global variables inside subprograms, you should strive to minimize such use. The more dependencies your subprograms have with external programming objects, the more difficult it becomes to maintain and reuse code. When generalizing subprograms, you should take the attitude that everything needed by the subroutine will be passed in the parameter list.

To avoid confusion, standardize your parameter names so that it's obvious what their scope is. For example, I prefix all parameters with the letter P for *parameter* and make the rest of the name lowercase so the prefix stands out. Also, any variables declared inside the subprogram are typically prefixed with L or local_ to indicate their temporary status.

Like blocks in general, when a subprogram is exited, any local variables cease to exist; their memory is relinquished. When the subprogram is re-entered, the local variables are again allocated and initialized.

Default Values

You can define parameters with default values; should the parameter value be omitted, the default value is provided in its place. A familiar example of this is the built-in function TO_CHAR. The second parameter, a format string, is optional. If you leave it off, the value is converted to a string using the significant digits. If you provide the format string, the number is converted according to the format

TO_CHAR(99.99) returns the string '99.99'.

TO_CHAR(99.9900) returns the string '99.99'.

TO_CHAR(99.99, '000.000') returns the string '099.990'.

TO_CHAR(99.99, '0.00') cannot be converted to a string.

You can declare some or all parameters to have default values in like fashion. You use the keyword DEFAULT or the assignment operator (they both work equally well) after the data type, along with the default value expression. The expression must be able to be determined at runtime, as in the following example:

```
FUNCTION run_date(Pval_date IN DATE DEFAULT SYSDATE)
RETURN DATE IS
BEGIN  -- compute last day of previous month
  RETURN (LAST_DAY(ADD_MONTHS(Pval_date, -1)));
END run_date;
```

Then, you can call this function with or without a parameter:

```
valuation_date := run_date(some_date);
valuation_date := run_date;  -- uses default (SYSDATE)
```

When a subprogram takes no parameters, leave the parentheses off.

Positional Notation

By default, parameters are given in positional notation. That is, you don't need to give the name of the parameter when providing a value; its position relative to the other parameters is sufficient. If the parameter list shows a VARCHAR2 as the first parameter, a DATE for the second, and a NUMBER for the third parameter, when you call the subprogram, you must provide a VARCHAR2 value, a DATE value and a NUMBER value, exactly in that order.

If you want to change the order of the parameters or skip a parameter entirely, you use named notation.

Named Notation

Sometimes, a subprogram is defined with several default parameters, and you'd like to supply values for only some parameters. You can omit the last parameters in the parameter list without a problem. What if you need to skip some and supply values for following parameters? You can't just leave the parameter out, as in the following:

```
proc(P1, P2, , P4);  -- SYNTAX ERROR!
```

Supplying NULL isn't really what you want either because NULL might be a legitimate value.

Instead, you use named notation to supply parameters in any order or skip parameters that have default values. You indicate named notation by providing the parameter name as defined, followed by the association operator =>, followed by the value:

```
-- build up to a 6-digit number in any base
-- using power series
FUNCTION pwr(Pbase IN INTEGER,
            P0     IN INTEGER DEFAULT 0,
            P1     IN INTEGER DEFAULT 0,
            P2     IN INTEGER DEFAULT 0,
            P3     IN INTEGER DEFAULT 0,
            P4     IN INTEGER DEFAULT 0,
            P5     IN INTEGER DEFAULT 0)
RETURN INTEGER IS
  local_num INTEGER;
BEGIN
  IF (Pbase <= P0 OR Pbase <= P1 OR Pbase <= P2 OR
      Pbase <= P3 OR Pbase <= P4 OR Pbase <= P5) THEN
    RAISE VALUE_ERROR;  -- illegal power series
  END IF;
  local_num := P5 * Pbase**5 +
               P4 * Pbase**4 +
               P3 * Pbase**3 +
               P2 * Pbase**2 +
               P1 * Pbase +
               P0;
  RETURN(local_num);
END pwr;
...
num := pwr(2, P2=>1, P0=>1);  -- returns 5 (101 base 2)
```

You can start a parameter list by using positional notation and then switch to named notation, as with the preceding example. This is known as *mixed notation*. However, once you go to named notation, you can't revert to positional notation; such a switch generates a syntax error.

You can't use named notation when calling a function from a SQL statement.

Calling a Subprogram

You can call any function or procedure that's within the scope of the current block. You can nest subprogram declarations as well. You can also call subroutines recursively. Listing 3.3 shows an example of a function that calls itself to compute factorials elegantly.

LISTING 3.3

FACTORL.SQL; USE OF RECURSION

```
DECLARE
  FUNCTION factorial (Pnum IN NATURAL) RETURN NATURAL IS
  BEGIN
    IF (Pnum > 1) THEN
      RETURN (factorial(Pnum - 1) * Pnum);
    ELSE
      RETURN (1);   -- handles 0!
    END IF;
  END factorial;

BEGIN
  DBMS_OUTPUT.put_line('0! = ' || factorial(0));
  DBMS_OUTPUT.put_line('1! = ' || factorial(1));
  DBMS_OUTPUT.put_line('2! = ' || factorial(2));
  DBMS_OUTPUT.put_line('3! = ' || factorial(3));
  DBMS_OUTPUT.put_line('4! = ' || factorial(4));
  DBMS_OUTPUT.put_line('5! = ' || factorial(5));
  DBMS_OUTPUT.put_line('6! = ' || factorial(6));END;
/
```

The server responds with

```
0! = 1
1! = 1
2! = 2
3! = 6
4! = 24
```

```
5! = 120
6! = 720
```

```
PL/SQL procedure successfully completed.
```

Here, the function is calling itself. Known as *recursion*, this technique offers an elegant solution for many iterative problems. The most important consideration with recursion is that you must provide some means of ending a recursive call to avoid an infinite loop. In this example, the function calls itself until the input value is decremented to 1. Then, each recursive call is exited, starting with the most deeply nested call, returning a value to the previous call.

Notice the use of the NATURAL data type to make a negative input illegal (but try using NUMBER and see how high a factorial you can compute).

Another consideration with recursion is nesting depth. Recursion by nature makes heavy use of the program stack. This can become a memory-intensive operation when hundreds or thousands of recursive calls are made. In this situation, using a loop will provide faster throughput.

You nest subprogram declarations when you want to limit the scope of a subprogram to a particular block. In theory, it's good programming practice to limit the scope of a programming object to only where it's needed. In practice, you can overdo this and make your programs harder to understand. You should limit this practice to reasonably short subprograms. A series of nested subprograms might have the form

```
PROCEDURE w IS
  -- w declarations
  PROCEDURE x IS
    -- x declarations
    PROCEDURE y IS
      -- y declarations
      PROCEDURE z IS
        -- z declarations
      BEGIN  -- z
        -- z statements
        NULL;
      END z;
    BEGIN  -- y
      -- y statements
      z; -- this is in scope
    END y;
  BEGIN  -- x
    -- x statements
    y; -- this is in scope
```

```
    END x;
  BEGIN  -- w
    -- w statements
    x;  -- this is in scope
  END w;
```

As you can see, although technically feasible, this can lead to obfus-
cated code. Although procedure w may be in y's scope, for y to call w
would cause an infinite recursion, sucking up all available memory
and bringing the server to its knees (as I just found out!).

Built-In Functions and Operators

PL/SQL uses most of the built-in functions and operators available
in SQL. Notable exceptions are DECODE, ANY, DUMP, and VSIZE and the
aggregate functions AVG, SUM, COUNT, MIN, MAX, UNIQUE, DISTINCT,
STDDEV, and VARIANCE, which can appear only in SQL statements.
Table 3.1 lists the functions and operators that you can use in
PL/SQL statements.

TABLE 3.1

BUILT-IN FUNCTIONS

ABS	ACOS	ADD_MONTHS
ASCII	ASIN	ATAN
ATAN2	BETWEEN	CEIL
CHARTOROWID	CHR	CONCAT
CONVERT	COS	COSH
DUMP	EXP	FLOOR
GREATEST	GREATEST_LB	HEXTORAW
IN	INITCAP	INSTR
INSTRB	LAST_DAY	LEAST
LEAST_UB	LENGTH	LENGTHB
LIKE	LN	LOG
LOWER	LPAD	LTRIM
MOD	MONTHS_BETWEEN	NEW_TIME
NEXT_DAY	NLS_CHARSET_ID	NLS_CHARSET_NAME
NLS_INITCAP	NLS_LOWER	NLS_UPPER

continues

TABLE 3.1	*continued*	
BUILT-IN FUNCTIONS		
NLSSORT	NOT	NVL
POWER	RAWTOHEX	REPLACE
ROUND	ROWIDTOCHAR	RPAD
RTRIM	SIGN	SIN
SINH	SOUNDEX	SQLCODE
SQLERRM	SQRT	SUBSTR
SUBSTRB	SYSDATE	TAN
TANH	TO_CHAR	TO_DATE
TO_LABEL	TO_MULTI_BYTE	TO_NUMBER
TO_SINGLE_BYTE	TRANSLATE	TRUNC
UID	UPPER	USER
USERENV	VSIZE	XOR

STORED SUBPROGRAMS

Write syntactically correct subprograms, stored procedures, functions, and packages.

State the benefits of using stored procedures, functions, and packages.

Defining functions and procedures inside a PL/SQL block is useful but still quite limiting. To call subprograms, you must include them inside every PL/SQL anonymous block that needs to use them. You can imagine how inefficient this becomes—multiple scripts repeating the same code for a generally useful subprogram. This is certainly wasteful, time-consuming, and error-prone. What would be better is to put a subprogram someplace once, where it could be called repeatedly by all PL/SQL programs. If the algorithm inside the subprogram needs to be modified, you then need change it in only one place, and all the programs that call the subprogram would immediately benefit without your rewriting them. This is precisely what stored subprograms are for.

A *stored subprogram* is a named PL/SQL block whose executable code is in the database. Stored subprograms are owned by whoever creates them, although the owner can always grant EXECUTE privilege to another user or role.

Users must have the CREATE PROCEDURE system privilege to create stored functions and procedures in their own schemas. To create stored subprograms in any schema, users must have the CREATE ANY PROCEDURE privilege.

The Edit-Compile-Test Cycle

Typically, programmers follow a program development cycle similar to other languages: edit a source file, compile the source file, run the compiled program, and test it. Programmers must fix any compilation errors before the program can be executed. When all syntax errors are fixed, the program can be run. Unexpected or undesirable runtime errors that are discovered during testing must be fixed before you use the program in production. This cycle of edit-compile-test is generally known as the *waterfall methodology* or *paradigm* of software development, and it has been around as compilers have been around (more than 40 years).

The CREATE FUNCTION or PROCEDURE Syntax

The syntax for submitting a subprogram for compilation is

```
CREATE [OR REPLACE]
FUNCTION function_name(optional_parameter_list)
RETURN datatype IS
  declarative statements
BEGIN
  executable statements
END [function_name];

CREATE [OR REPLACE] PROCEDURE
procedure_name(optional_parameter_list) IS
  declarative statements
BEGIN
  executable statements
END [procedure_name];
```

As you can see, the syntax for creating functions and procedures is very similar. I use indentation and white space as an aid to readability.

Submitting a Subprogram Repeatedly for Compilation Although the OR REPLACE clause is optional, you should always include it in your declaration so you can submit a compilation unit repeatedly. Without it, you would have to first drop the program unit, even if it fails to compile successfully.

Although it's optional, you should always provide the subprogram name at the end for purposes of clarity.

The optional parameter list follows the same syntax as for regular subprograms: a comma-separated list of [variable name mode datatype]. By using the parameter list, you can make stored subprograms more generic, as well as provide a limited scope for the variables used inside the stored subprogram.

Let's convert the get_dept procedure I wrote earlier (Listing 3.1) into a stored procedure. Listing 3.4 shows how.

LISTING 3.4

GETDEPTP.SQL; A SIMPLE STORED PROCEDURE

```
-- perform a single-row lookup on DEPT
CREATE OR REPLACE PROCEDURE get_dept(
    Pdeptno IN dept.deptno%TYPE,
    Prec    OUT dept%ROWTYPE,
    Pstatus IN OUT NUMBER) IS
  BEGIN
    Pstatus := 0;  -- OK
    SELECT *
    INTO Prec
    FROM SCOTT.dept
    WHERE dept.deptno = Pdeptno;
  EXCEPTION
  WHEN OTHERS THEN
    Pstatus := SQLCODE;  -- trap error
    Prec := NULL;         -- clear record
    DBMS_OUTPUT.put_line('get_dept: ' ¦¦ SQLERRM(Pstatus));
  END get_dept;
/
SHOW ERRORS
GRANT EXECUTE ON get_dept TO PUBLIC;
```

This stored procedure is functionally equivalent to the subroutine as it was declared inside the anonymous block. When we submit this script via SQL*Plus, we get

```
SQL> @C:\DOCS\WORD\MCP\CH3\GETDEPTP

Procedure created.

No errors.

Grant succeeded.
```

The program isn't run but rather compiled, and it is ready for execution.

Notice that in addition to compiling the stored subprogram, I've added a couple of other things to the script. This is for the convenience of the developer as well as the DBA (who may be different people). The SQL*Plus command SHOW ERRORS checks whether the compilation was successful and provides a list of errors if otherwise. The GRANT statement allows other users to execute the stored procedure.

Getting Information About Stored Subprograms

Obtain information about stored subprograms and packages by using various data dictionary views.

If I want to see the calling convention for this stored procedure, I can describe it from SQL*Plus:

```
SQL> desc get_dept;
PROCEDURE get_dept
 Argument Name          Type              In/Out Default?
 -----------------------------------------------------------
 PDEPTNO                NUMBER(2)         IN
 PREC                   RECORD            OUT
   DEPTNO               NUMBER(2)         OUT
   DNAME                VARCHAR2(14)      OUT
   LOC                  VARCHAR2(13)      OUT
 PSTATUS                NUMBER            IN/OUT
```

This tells me how to call the stored procedure. If I want more information about the stored procedure, I can run the following query:

```
SELECT
  OBJECT_TYPE, CREATED, LAST_DDL_TIME, TIMESTAMP, STATUS
FROM USER_OBJECTS
WHERE OBJECT_NAME='GET_DEPT';
```

The server responds with

```
OBJECT_TYPE   CREATED     LAST_DDL_ TIMESTAMP           STATUS
-----------------------------------------------------------------
PROCEDURE     06-JUN-98 06-JUN-98 1998-06-06:11:33:36 VALID
```

If the stored procedure had failed to compile properly, its status would have been INVALID. Other events that will invalidate an otherwise successfully compiled subprogram are when tables and other stored subprograms—on which the subprogram may depend—are modified, dropped, or re-created. When a subprogram is invalidated

> **NOTE**
>
> **A DESCRIBE Bug** The SQL*Plus DESCRIBE command (which can be shortened to DESC) has a bug in Oracle 8.03. It may not function properly or at all. For example, you can't describe data dictionary views unless you're connected as SYS.

in this manner, you can recompile it without having to resubmit the source file (which could in turn invalidate other dependent modules) by executing

```
ALTER FUNCTION [schema.]function_name COMPILE;

ALTER PROCEDURE [schema.]procedure_name COMPILE;
```

The stored subprogram must be in your own schema, or you must have the ALTER ANY PROCEDURE system privilege.

When you recompile a stored subprogram in this manner, here's what happens:

1. Oracle recompiles any invalid dependent modules.

2. Oracle invalidates the subprogram being recompiled, which further invalidates any subprograms that call it.

3. The stored subprogram is recompiled. If successful, the stored subprogram is valid; otherwise, Oracle will return an error, and the stored subprogram will remain invalid.

Another way of recompiling invalid stored subprograms is with the alter_compile procedure found in the DBMS_DDL package. You can use it as shown in Listing 3.5.

> **NOTE**
>
> **Beware of Circular References** You can quickly visualize the trouble you can get into if you have a series of subprograms that all reference one another in circular fashion. If procedure A references B, which references C, which references A, you'll never be able to compile them successfully.

LISTING 3.5

PCOMPILE.SQL; STORED PROCEDURE TO COMPILE STORED PROCEDURES

```
-- stored procedure to recompile any stored object:
-- FUNCTION, PROCEDURE, PACKAGE or PACKAGE BODY
-- NOTE alter_compile DOES NOT RETURN ERROR
-- IF RECOMPILE FAILS!
CREATE OR REPLACE PROCEDURE pcompile(
     Pobj_type IN all_objects.object_type%TYPE,
     Pobj_name IN all_objects.object_name%TYPE,
     Powner    IN all_objects.owner%TYPE DEFAULT USER) IS

VALID CONSTANT all_objects.status%TYPE := 'VALID';
v_status all_objects.status%TYPE;
status NUMERIC; -- for error code
obj_type CONSTANT all_objects.object_type%TYPE :=
                   UPPER(Pobj_type);
obj_name CONSTANT all_objects.object_name%TYPE :=
                   UPPER(Pobj_name);
```

```
    obj_ownr CONSTANT all_objects.owner%TYPE :=
                        NVL(UPPER(Powner), USER);
    FUNCTION get_obj_status(
        Powner IN all_objects.owner%TYPE,
        Pname  IN all_objects.object_name%TYPE,
        Ptype  IN all_objects.object_type%TYPE)
    RETURN all_objects.status%TYPE IS
      obj_status all_objects.status%TYPE;
    BEGIN
      SELECT status
      INTO obj_status
      FROM all_objects
      WHERE
        owner=Powner AND
        object_name=Pname AND
        object_type=Ptype;
      RETURN(obj_status);
    END get_obj_status;

BEGIN
  IF (get_obj_status(obj_ownr, obj_name, obj_type) =
      VALID) THEN
    DBMS_OUTPUT.put_line('No need to recompile ' ||
                        obj_type || ' ' ||
                        obj_ownr || '.' ||
                        obj_name || '.');
  ELSE -- must be invalid so recompile
    DBMS_OUTPUT.put_line('Recompiling ' ||
                        obj_type || ' ' ||
                        obj_ownr || '.' ||
                        obj_name || '...');
    DBMS_DDL.alter_compile(obj_type, obj_ownr, obj_name);
    DBMS_OUTPUT.put_line(obj_type || ' ' ||
                        obj_ownr || '.' ||
                        obj_name || ' status is now ' ||
                        get_obj_status(obj_ownr, obj_name,
                                        obj_type));
  END IF;   -- need to recompile?
EXCEPTION
WHEN NO_DATA_FOUND THEN   -- no such animal
  DBMS_OUTPUT.put_line(obj_type || ' ' ||
                        obj_ownr || '.' ||
                        obj_name || ' does not exist!');
WHEN OTHERS THEN
  status := SQLCODE;
  DBMS_OUTPUT.put_line('PCOMPILE: ' || SQLERRM(status));
END pcompile;
/
SHOW ERRORS
```

You can then run this anonymous PL/SQL block to test the stored procedure, as shown in Listing 3.6.

LISTING 3.6

COMP.SQL; TESTING A STORED PROCEDURE

```
SET ECHO OFF
SET SERVEROUTPUT ON
SET TIMING ON
ACCEPT owner       PROMPT "Enter OWNER of stored object: "
ACCEPT object_name PROMPT "Enter NAME  of stored object: "
ACCEPT object_type PROMPT "Enter TYPE  of stored object: "
BEGIN
  pcompile('&&object_type', '&&object_name', '&&owner');
END;
/
```

Then, run the script a few times to exercise it. The idea is to try each logic path in order to verify the stored subprogram's correct execution under various expected conditions. After all, the point to using stored subprograms is to make automation available to those who need it. Timing is run to show that stored subprograms work very fast, typically much faster than anonymous blocks. These tests were run under Oracle 8.0.3 on a Pentium 133MHz with 128MB RAM—not exactly a screamer, but it suffices.

The following session illustrates how to use Listing 3.6 to run the pcompile stored procedure from SQL*Plus. You're prompted to provide the owner, name, and type of the stored object to recompile. The line marked new shows how your entries replace the placeholders (prefixed with the double ampersands) in the anonymous block. I'll run a variety of cases so that you can see that the stored procedure handles each situation correctly and that it is robust.

I start by compiling an object that's already valid:

```
SQL> @c:\docs\word\mcp\ch3\comp
Enter OWNER of stored object: scott
Enter NAME  of stored object: get_dept
Enter TYPE  of stored object: procedure
old   2:    pcompile('&&object_type', '&&object_name',
            ➥'&&owner');
new   2:    pcompile('procedure', 'get_dept', 'scott');
No need to recompile PROCEDURE SCOTT.GET_DEPT.
PL/SQL procedure successfully completed.
real: 121
```

Next, I compile an object that doesn't even exist to make sure the stored procedure handles this case properly:

```
SQL> @c:\docs\word\mcp\ch3\comp
Enter OWNER of stored object:
Enter NAME  of stored object: get_dept
Enter TYPE  of stored object: function
old   2:    pcompile('&&object_type', '&&object_name',
            ➡'&&owner');
new   2:    pcompile('function', 'get_dept', '');
FUNCTION SCOTT.GET_DEPT does not exist!
PL/SQL procedure successfully completed.
real: 151
```

The next test shows that I can successfully recompile an invalid object. First, I verify that the stored procedure is valid; then, I invalidate the procedure by recompiling a module on which it's dependent. Finally, I recompile it and verify the success of the operation:

```
-- prove that recompiling an invalid subprogram works
CREATE OR REPLACE PROCEDURE JUNK IS
  DEPT_REC DEPT%ROWTYPE;
  STATUS NUMBER;
BEGIN
  GET_DEPT(10, DEPT_REC, STATUS);
END;
/
Procedure created.
real: 551

SQL> SELECT status FROM user_objects WHERE
     ➡object_name='JUNK';
STATUS
------
VALID
real: 140
-- this will invalidate the dependent JUNK
SQL> ALTER PROCEDURE get_dept COMPILE;
Procedure altered.
real: 511
SQL> SELECT status FROM user_objects WHERE
     ➡object_name='JUNK';
STATUS
------
INVALID
real: 110
SQL> @c:\docs\word\mcp\ch3\comp
Enter OWNER of stored object:
Enter NAME  of stored object: junk
Enter TYPE  of stored object: procedure
old   2:    pcompile('&&object_type', ➡'&&object_name',
            ➡'&&owner');
new   2:    pcompile('procedure', 'junk', '');
Recompiling PROCEDURE SCOTT.JUNK...
PROCEDURE SCOTT.JUNK status is now VALID
```

```
PL/SQL procedure successfully completed.
real: 400
```

Now, I recompile a stored procedure that has a syntax error in it. Its status should remain invalid.

```
-- prove that recompiling an erroneous module
-- will remain invalid
SQL> CREATE OR REPLACE PROCEDURE JUNK IS
  2  BEGIN
  3    x := 0;  -- deliberate error so it won't compile OK
  4* END;
SQL> /
Warning: Procedure created with compilation errors.
real: 240
SQL> @c:\docs\word\mcp\ch3\comp
Enter OWNER of stored object: scott
Enter NAME  of stored object: junk
Enter TYPE  of stored object: procedure
old   2:    pcompile('&&object_type', '&&object_name',
           ➡'&&owner');
new   2:    pcompile('procedure', 'junk', 'scott');
Recompiling PROCEDURE SCOTT.JUNK...
PROCEDURE SCOTT.JUNK status is now INVALID
PL/SQL procedure successfully completed.
real: 291
```

Finally, I illustrate the error generated by alter_compile when you recompile an object you don't own and don't have ALTER ANY PROCEDURE privilege for:

```
-- show an error generated by alter_compile
SQL> CONN BOOKS/BOOKS@DEV
Connected.
SQL> CREATE OR REPLACE PROCEDURE JUNK IS
  2  BEGIN
  3    x := 0;  -- deliberate error so it won't compile OK
  4* END;
/
Warning: Procedure created with compilation errors.
real: 511
-- make stored subprogram visible
SQL> GRANT EXECUTE ON JUNK TO SCOTT;
Grant succeeded.
real: 200
SQL> CONN SCOTT/TIGER@DEV
Connected.
SQL> SELECT STATUS FROM ALL_OBJECTS
  2  WHERE OWNER='BOOKS' AND OBJECT_NAME='JUNK';
STATUS
-------
INVALID
real: 241
```

```
-- try to recompile an object you're not allowed to
SQL> @c:\docs\word\mcp\ch3\comp
Enter OWNER of stored object: BOOKS
Enter NAME  of stored object: JUNK
Enter TYPE  of stored object: PROCEDURE
old    2:    pcompile('&&object_type', '&&object_name',
             ➥'&&owner');
new    2:    pcompile('PROCEDURE', 'JUNK', 'BOOKS');
Recompiling PROCEDURE BOOKS.JUNK...
PCOMPILE: ORA-20000: Unable to compile PROCEDURE
             ➥"BOOKS"."JUNK", insufficient privileges
             ➥or does not exist
PL/SQL procedure successfully completed.
real: 260
```

Debugging Compilation Errors from SQL*Plus with SHOW ERRORS

Locate and correct syntax errors within stored subprograms and packages.

SQL*Plus has a simple facility for showing the line/column and error message for when your procedure or function fails to compile. Immediately after submitting a compilation unit, run SHOW ERRORS (as some of the preceding listings have done). For example, when I compile the faulty JUNK procedure, I get the following with SHOW ERRORS:

```
SQL> show errors
Errors for PROCEDURE JUNK:

LINE/COL ERROR
--------------------------------------------------------------
3/3      PLS-00321: expression 'X' is inappropriate as the
         left hand side of an assignment statement

3/3      PL/SQL: Statement ignored
```

This tells you what line suffered the error but doesn't show you the code line itself.

Where Source and Errors Are Stored

Obtain information about stored subprograms and packages by using various data dictionary views.

The source code for your compiled subprograms is exposed via the data dictionary view user_source. This view has these columns:

```
NAME     VARCHAR2(30)
TYPE     VARCHAR2(12)
LINE     NUMBER
TEXT     VARCHAR2(4000)
```

You could run this query:

```
SELECT text
FROM user_source
WHERE name= 'JUNK' AND line=3
ORDER BY line;
```

and you get

```
TEXT
------------------------------------------------------------
    x := 0;   — deliberate error so it won't compile OK
```

In a big program, you might have difficulty locating the faulty line, for lack of context. Furthermore, the PL/SQL compiler strips out double-spacing in the stored source code. Your source file on disk will quickly become unsynchronized with the database stored code if you use a lot of double-spacing for readability.

The error information is stored in user_errors. This view has these columns:

```
NAME      VARCHAR2(30)
TYPE      VARCHAR2(12)
SEQUENCE  NUMBER
LINE      NUMBER
POSITION  NUMBER
TEXT      VARCHAR2(4000)
```

You can run this query to list all the error information:

```
column text format a25
SELECT line, position, text
FROM user_errors
WHERE name = 'JUNK'
ORDER BY sequence;

LINE  POSITION TEXT
---------------------------------------------
3       3         PLS-00321: expression 'X'
                  is inappropriate as the
                  left hand side of an assi
                  gnment statement

3       3         PL/SQL: Statement ignored
```

POSITION is the column position (counting characters from left to right) where the error was detected within the line. Note that I sort by SEQUENCE, not by LINE; the sequence is a more accurate representation of the order in which the error was detected.

Calling Stored Subprograms

You can call stored subprograms from two places:

◆ PL/SQL anonymous blocks and other stored subprograms

◆ SQL or DML statements

There are some considerations for both. They also have some common elements.

Use the schema qualifier to call stored subprograms owned by another user. The stored subprogram will be visible to you only if that user or a role grants you the EXECUTE privilege. For example, another user can call SCOTT.get_dept if SCOTT granted EXECUTE privileges to this user or to PUBLIC. You can omit the schema qualifier if you own the stored subprogram. You can tell whether you have EXECUTE privilege on a stored subprogram if it appears in the view all_objects. In this case, you can see the subprogram declaration in all_source but won't have access to its code.

Use stored and packaged functions in SQL statements.

One major restriction of calling PL/SQL subprograms from SQL is that they must be functions. You can't call stored procedures from SQL because the SQL statement expects a return value to use in the expression. You can pass in values on the parameter list, as long as they are in-scope literals or variables. For example, if the SQL is embedded in PL/SQL, you can use any variables defined within the scope of the SQL statement. The parameter values can also be columns from a table listed in the FROM clause. In this case, the value of the column for each row would be passed into the function. For example, a stored function, strnum (in Listing 3.7), is used to trap the exception that results when converting a string to a number, when the string doesn't represent a valid number. The function returns a NULL when such a string can't be converted.

LISTING 3.7

STRNUM.SQL; STRING-TO-NUMBER CONVERSION

```
CREATE OR REPLACE
FUNCTION strnum(Pstr IN VARCHAR2,
               Pformat IN VARCHAR2 DEFAULT NULL)
RETURN NUMBER IS
BEGIN
  IF (Pformat IS NULL) THEN   -- use NLS format
    RETURN(TO_NUMBER(Pstr));
  ELSE  -- use given format string
    RETURN(TO_NUMBER(Pstr, Pformat));
  END IF;  -- test format string
EXCEPTION
WHEN OTHERS THEN
  RETURN(NULL);  -- indeterminate value
END strnum;
/
Function created.
```

Now test this function from a SQL statement. First, create a table with a string associated with a numeric value and populate it with a couple of rows:

```
CREATE TABLE test_strnum (str VARCHAR2(2), num NUMBER(2));
Table created.
INSERT INTO test_strnum (str) VALUES ('10');
1 row created.
INSERT INTO test_strnum (str) VALUES ('AA');
1 row created.
COMMIT;
```

The next two UPDATE statements show the different results you get when you use the supplied function TO_NUMBER, which fails abruptly when it attempts to convert a non-numeric string, and STRNUM, which handles the error gracefully. Because STRNUM returns NULL on an error, you can substitute a default value by using the function NVL, and the UPDATE can complete successfully.

```
UPDATE test_strnum
SET num = NVL(TO_NUMBER(str),0);
ERROR at line 2:
ORA-01722: invalid number
UPDATE test_strnum
SET num = NVL(strnum(str),0);
2 rows updated.
SELECT * FROM test_strnum;
ST        NUM
------------
10         10
AA          0
```

Another restriction is that the stored function can't have any side effects, such as writing to the database, in order to preserve read consistency with the database. For example, if a function used in an UPDATE statement deleted the current row, how would this affect the UPDATE? For this reason, writing to the database in stored functions called by SQL and DML statements is forbidden.

Stored procedures must be called as a single statement. You can't use them in expressions or assignments; therefore, you can't use them inside SQL or DML statements. You can call them from other PL/SQL programs, from a 3GL language such as C or COBOL, or even from SQL*Plus.

You can use stored subprograms to implement applications that perform complex analysis and data manipulation. You might have a stored subprogram gather data from various tables, perform complex logic on it, and then write the results to a heavily denormalized table. This table can then be read from a querying or reporting tool. This typical technique makes heavy use of PL/SQL. If you write the program as a stored procedure rather than an anonymous block, users are guaranteed that it's compiled and available for execution.

PACKAGES

State the benefits of using packages versus standalone subprograms.

A *package* is a container for a collection of related subprograms and data. Packages provide certain benefits that standalone subprograms can't:

◆ **Encapsulation.** Programmers decide which subroutines and data to expose to execution and manipulation, making some public and others private, as needed.

◆ **Polymorphism.** A subprogram name can be overloaded, having multiple copies that vary only by the parameter list.

◆ **Persistence.** Variables declared as global (whether private or public) exist and hold their values for the duration of the session. In contrast, variables declared inside subprograms exist only when the subprogram is executed; their memory is freed when the subprogram is exited.

Packages actually have two parts: the package header (or specification) and the package body. The header is where public variable, cursor, and program declarations are located, whereas the body is where private cursor declarations are located and program implementation is performed.

When any element within the package is referenced, the entire package is loaded into memory, making all subprograms inside the package readily available for execution. Like stored subprograms, code is re-entrant; one image in memory is sharable among users.

Package Header

The *package header* (also known as the *package specification*) contains all subprogram declarations, user-defined types, global variables, and cursor declarations visible to users. Items placed in the package header are global and public—global in that their scope is at the broadest level and therefore they are persistent for the duration of the session and public in that they are accessible to users and other subprograms. The actual implementation of these subprograms and cursor are deferred to the package body.

Write syntactically correct subprograms, stored procedures, functions, and packages.

The package header has the following syntax:

```
CREATE [OR REPLACE] PACKAGE package_name IS
    declarations
END [package_name];
/
```

In SQL*Plus, you submit the compilation by using the forward slash.

Subprograms declared inside the package header follow the syntax

```
PROCEDURE procedure_name(optional_parameter_list);
FUNCTION  function_name(optional_parameter_list)
          RETURN datatype;
```

When subprograms are located inside packages, the CREATE procedure is implied. These declarations specify only the name of the subprogram, its parameter list (if any), and the return type for a function.

Cursor declarations have the following forms:

```
CURSOR cursor_name(optional_parameter_list)
RETURN datatype_list_or_record_type;

CURSOR cursor_name(optional_parameter_list) IS
  select_statement;

CURSOR cursor_name(optional_parameter_list)
RETURN datatype_list_or_record_type IS
  select_statement;
```

In the first method, the cursor body is deferred to the package body; therefore, the return type must be given. In the second method, the cursor body is also given. In the third, the return type and body are specified.

All three methods are valid. The first method is generally preferred because it provides for *encapsulation*, also known as *information hiding*. The third type is used typically when a record type was previously defined to match the cursor's select clause.

Variables and user-defined types can also be declared inside the package header. You must list all variables before any subprograms are declared. Placing variables after the first subprogram is a syntax error. You can place cursor and type declarations anywhere, but forward declarations aren't permitted. For example, to base a variable on a record type, the type must be declared before any variables that use it.

You can take advantage of persistence by placing data values inside public global variables. For example, if a large volume of data is needed between several packages, you could locate the necessary variables inside the package header. These variables are then available to other subprograms.

In general, it's considered good programming practice to minimize the use of global data. Using a lot of global data tends to make programs more difficult to debug and maintain because of the potential for data to be read or written by so many outside agents. A better practice is to make the data private (by placing it inside the package body) and then provide read and write routines for them. In this way, access to persistent data is controlled.

For example, you might define a package header to support several operations on a single database table. Listing 3.8 shows a package header that declares typical operations for the Dept table: Select, Insert, Update, and Delete.

LISTING 3.8

DEPT_PKG.SQH; PACKAGE HEADER FOR THE TABLE DEPT

```
CREATE OR REPLACE PACKAGE dept_pkg AS
/*
 Module: dept_pkg.sqh (Dept Table Operations Specification)
 Author: Daniel J. Clamage
 Description:
 This package defines all the table operations desired for
 table SCOTT.DEPT.
 History:
 10-JUN-1998 - djc - Original draft.
*/
  -- global public variables
  dept_rec dept%ROWTYPE;  -- handy global record variable

  -- global public subroutines
  -- single row lookup by primary key
  PROCEDURE get_dept(Pdeptno IN     dept.deptno%TYPE,
                     Prec       OUT dept%ROWTYPE,
                     Pstatus IN OUT NUMBER);

  -- non unique lookup by location
  PROCEDURE get_dept(Ploc     IN     dept.loc%TYPE,
                     Prec       OUT dept%ROWTYPE,
                     Pstatus IN OUT NUMBER);

  -- return every row one at a time
  -- state is for test purposes to prove correct operation
  -- on an error, state shows what operation
  -- was being attempted
  PROCEDURE get_dept(Prec       OUT dept%ROWTYPE,
                     Pstate     OUT NUMBER,
                     Pstatus IN OUT NUMBER);

  -- update specified row
  PROCEDURE upd_dept(Prowid   IN     ROWID,
                     Prec     IN     dept%ROWTYPE,
                     Pstatus IN OUT NUMBER);

  -- delete specified row
  PROCEDURE del_dept(Prowid   IN     ROWID,
                     Pstatus IN OUT NUMBER);

  -- insert specified row
  PROCEDURE ins_dept(Prec     IN     dept%ROWTYPE,
                     Pstatus IN OUT NUMBER);

END dept_pkg;
/
```

The slash at the end tells SQL*Plus to submit the package for compilation. The indentation and double spacing are just for readability.

I placed the multiline comment block within the package declaration so that it will be stored with the source text in the database. Comments placed outside the package are stripped. You can see the stored source text with

```
SELECT text FROM user_source
WHERE name='DEPT_PKG'
AND type='PACKAGE'
ORDER BY line;
```

Notice the use of subprogram overloading with get_dept. At runtime, the correct version will be executed, depending on the number of parameters and their data types.

If there are any dependent stored objects, such as stored procedures that call any procedures contained within the package, a recompilation of the package header will also require a recompilation of these dependent objects. For this reason, it's highly desirable to minimize package header recompilation.

The actual implementation for the subprograms defined in this package is deferred to the package body.

Package Body

The package body contains the implementation of all subprograms declared in the package header. The package body has the following syntax:

```
CREATE [OR REPLACE] PACKAGE BODY package_name IS
  implementation
[BEGIN]
  optional initialization code
END [package_name];
/
```

You can use the optional initialization section to execute one-time-only code when the package is first instantiated. Such code is performed only once for the session. You might use it to enable output, initialize some global variables, or load some initial data.

If a subprogram is declared in the package header, the package body must contain an implementation for it. Such a subprogram must match exactly by name and parameter list between the specification in the package header and body.

> **NOTE**
>
> **Designing Useful Packages**   A good plan for package design is to determine all the operations needed for a clearly defined domain—for example, the set of table operations, the set of business rules for one department, or the set of interfaces for a single application. After these operations (and any related public global variables and user-defined data types) are defined, the package header will require little maintenance.

You can declare global variables, user-defined data types, and cursors inside the package body, outside of any subprograms. Such programmatic objects, although global within the package body, are private to the package body—that is, they can't be referenced outside the scope of the package body. Private global variables must follow the same placement restrictions as package headers. Private global variables are also persistent; they will retain their values for the duration of the session.

You can also declare private subprograms that are callable to other subprograms within the package body yet aren't exposed via the procedure header. Any private subprograms must precede the subprograms that reference them; forward references aren't allowed.

One workaround for the forward reference restriction is to place the subprogram declaration in the package header for the subprogram that must be referenced. Because it's considered public global, a reference to it by a subprogram in the package body is no longer a forward reference.

A typical problem experienced by programmers occurs when the package header and body are placed in the same text file. If subprograms in two different package bodies (for two different packages) make references to objects in the other package, a circular reference results. This will always leave one or the other package invalid because recompiling an object on which other packages depend always invalidates the dependent packages.

The workaround for this problem is to place the header and body in separate files. All the package headers are compiled first and the bodies compiled afterward. Because the packaged subprograms reference objects declared in the headers, the references are valid (assuming the header compiled successfully).

Completing the example for the package header given earlier, an implementation might look like the one in Listing 3.9.

LISTING 3.9

DEPT_PKG.SQB; PACKAGE BODY FOR THE TABLE DEPT.

```
CREATE OR REPLACE PACKAGE BODY dept_pkg AS
/*
```

```
     Module: dept_pkg.sql (Dept Table Operations)
     Author: Daniel J. Clamage
     Description:
     This package defines all the table operations desired for
     table SCOTT.DEPT.
     History:
     10-JUN-1998 - djc - Original draft.
*/
   -- global private declarations
   -- used by get_dept (with location parameter)
   CURSOR dept_by_loc(Cloc dept.loc%TYPE) IS
     SELECT *
     FROM dept
     WHERE loc = Cloc;

   -- used by get_dept (all rows)
   CURSOR dept_all IS
     SELECT *
     FROM dept
     ORDER BY deptno;

   -- global public subroutines
   -- single row lookup by primary key
   PROCEDURE get_dept(Pdeptno IN      dept.deptno%TYPE,
                      Prec      OUT dept%ROWTYPE,
                      Pstatus IN OUT NUMBER) IS
   BEGIN
     Pstatus := 0;
     SELECT *
     INTO Prec
     FROM dept
     WHERE deptno = Pdeptno;
   EXCEPTION
   WHEN OTHERS THEN
     Pstatus := SQLCODE;
   END get_dept;

   -- non unique lookup by location
   PROCEDURE get_dept(Ploc    IN      dept.loc%TYPE,
                      Prec      OUT dept%ROWTYPE,
                      Pstatus IN OUT NUMBER) IS
   BEGIN
     Pstatus := 0;
     OPEN dept_by_loc(Ploc);
     FETCH dept_by_loc INTO Prec;    -- get one row
     CLOSE dept_by_loc;
   EXCEPTION
   WHEN OTHERS THEN
     Pstatus := SQLCODE;
   END get_dept;

   -- return every row one at a time
   -- state is for test purposes to prove correct operation
```

continues

LISTING 3.9 *continued*

DEPT_PKG.SQB; PACKAGE BODY FOR THE TABLE DEPT.

```
-- on an error, state shows what operation
-- was being attempted
PROCEDURE get_dept(Prec      OUT dept%ROWTYPE,
                   Pstate    OUT NUMBER,
                   Pstatus IN OUT NUMBER) IS
BEGIN
  Pstatus := 0;
  IF (NOT dept_all%ISOPEN) THEN   -- State 1: CLOSED
    Pstate := 1;
    OPEN dept_all;
  END IF;
  Pstate := 2;
  FETCH dept_all INTO Prec;       -- State 2: FETCHING
  IF (dept_all%NOTFOUND) THEN     -- State 3: RESTART
    Pstate := 3;
    CLOSE dept_all;
    OPEN dept_all;  -- reopen
    FETCH dept_all INTO Prec;
    IF (dept_all%NOTFOUND) THEN   -- State 4: EMPTY TABLE
      Pstate := 4;
      RAISE NO_DATA_FOUND;
    END IF;
  END IF;
EXCEPTION
WHEN OTHERS THEN
  Pstatus := SQLCODE;
END get_dept;

-- update specified row
PROCEDURE upd_dept(Prowid IN      ROWID,
                   Prec   IN      dept%ROWTYPE,
                   Pstatus IN OUT NUMBER) IS
BEGIN
  Pstatus := 0;
  UPDATE dept
  SET
    dname = Prec.dname,
    loc   = Prec.loc
  WHERE ROWID = Prowid;
EXCEPTION
WHEN OTHERS THEN
  Pstatus := SQLCODE;
END upd_dept;

-- delete specified row
PROCEDURE del_dept(Prowid  IN      ROWID,
                   Pstatus IN OUT NUMBER) IS
BEGIN
  Pstatus := 0;
  DELETE FROM dept
  WHERE ROWID = Prowid;
```

```
   EXCEPTION
   WHEN OTHERS THEN
     Pstatus := SQLCODE;
   END del_dept;

   -- insert specified row
   PROCEDURE ins_dept(Prec     IN      dept%ROWTYPE,
                      Pstatus IN OUT NUMBER) IS
   BEGIN
     Pstatus := 0;
     INSERT INTO dept (
       deptno,
       dname,
       loc)
     VALUES (
       Prec.deptno,
       Prec.dname,
       Prec.loc);
   EXCEPTION
   WHEN OTHERS THEN
     Pstatus := SQLCODE;
   END ins_dept;

END dept_pkg;
/
```

This implementation illustrates the use of an implicit cursor for exact match on the primary key, a local explicit cursor for exact match on a non-unique column, and a private global cursor for consecutive calls getting all the rows, one at a time. To allow multiple calls to obtain all the rows, the cursor is declared private global so that it's persistent. If the cursor had been declared locally, it would lose state every time the procedure exited. Only global package objects, whether private (in the body) or public (in the header), are persistent.

Listing 3.10 gives a partial test plan.

LISTING 3.10

TESTDEPT.SQL. PROGRAM TO TEST DEPT_PKG

```
DECLARE
  status NUMBER;
  state  NUMBER;  -- subprogram state
```

continues

LISTING 3.10 *continued*

TESTDEPT.SQL. PROGRAM TO TEST DEPT_PKG

```
BEGIN
  -- TEST get_dept (unique lookup)
  dept_pkg.get_dept(30, dept_pkg.dept_rec, status);
  DBMS_OUTPUT.put_line('30=' || dept_pkg.dept_rec.dname);
  dept_pkg.get_dept(40, dept_pkg.dept_rec, status);
  DBMS_OUTPUT.put_line('40=' || dept_pkg.dept_rec.dname);

  -- TEST dept_dept (by location)
  dept_pkg.get_dept('NEW YORK', dept_pkg.dept_rec, status);
  DBMS_OUTPUT.put_line('NEW YORK=' ||
                    dept_pkg.dept_rec.dname);
  dept_pkg.get_dept('CHICAGO', dept_pkg.dept_rec, status);
  DBMS_OUTPUT.put_line('CHICAGO=' ||
                    dept_pkg.dept_rec.dname);

  -- TEST dept_dept (all rows)
  FOR rec IN 1..10 LOOP
    dept_pkg.get_dept(dept_pkg.dept_rec, state, status);
    DBMS_OUTPUT.put_line('DEPT=' ||
                    dept_pkg.dept_rec.deptno ||
                    ', STATE=' || TO_CHAR(state));
  END LOOP;

END;
/
```

The server responds with

```
30=SALES
40=OPERATIONS
NEW YORK=Accounting
CHICAGO=SALES
DEPT=10, STATE=2
DEPT=20, STATE=2
DEPT=30, STATE=2
DEPT=40, STATE=2
DEPT=10, STATE=3
DEPT=20, STATE=2
DEPT=30, STATE=2
DEPT=40, STATE=2
DEPT=10, STATE=3
DEPT=20, STATE=2

PL/SQL procedure successfully completed.
```

Additional items that should be added are tests for insert, update, and delete and boundary and error conditions (such as a failed lookup).

Calling from SQL

Use stored and packaged functions in SQL statements.

To call a packaged function from SQL, you must assert the *purity* level of the function. Purity is an assurance to the compiler that the function has no side effects, such as reading from or writing to the database. Purity is important in assuring the read consistency of the database. With standalone stored functions, the compiler can check the body of the function. Because the body of a package is hidden, however, you must tell the compiler that the function has no side effects.

You assert purity by adding the pragma RESTRICT_REFERENCES in the package specification (not the body) following the packaged function's declaration. A *pragma* is a compiler directive that tells the compiler how to handle language-specific conditions and similar information.

The syntax for asserting the purity of a packaged function is

```
PRAGMA RESTRICT_REFERENCES (
    function_name, WNDS[, RNDS][, WNPS][, RNPS]);
```

In this syntax,

◆ WNDS means Writes No Database State (no inserts, updates, deletes, commits, or rollbacks).

◆ RNDS means Reads No Database State (no selects).

◆ WNPS means Writes No Package State (doesn't modify the values of any packaged variables).

◆ RNPS means Reads No Package State (doesn't use any packaged variables in expressions).

The order of the assertion parameters is insignificant, but you must always specify at least WNDS. The rule of thumb is to assert the highest purity level possible for the packaged function. If you assert a purity level that is inconsistent with the actual execution of the function—such as RNPS when the function uses some packaged variable in an expression—the compiler will generate an error.

A standalone or packaged function called from SQL has these restrictions:

◆ The function must not write to the database (insert, update, delete, commit, or rollback) directly or indirectly by calling another routine. Any routine called by the function must also assert an appropriate purity level.

◆ Only functions referenced in a SELECT, VALUES, or SET clause can write to packaged variables.

◆ If a function reads or writes the values of packaged variables, it can't be executed in parallel or remotely.

◆ The function must not call another routine or reference a view, which violates any of these purity rules.

◆ The function must return a valid SQL data type. Some valid data types in PL/SQL aren't valid in SQL—such as BOOLEAN.

One workaround for WNDS is to send data via an Oracle pipe to another session, which then performs a DML statement on behalf of the sending function. Reading from and writing to an Oracle pipe is transactionless; the operation is independent of any transaction and isn't affected by commits or rollbacks.

Getting Information on a Stored Object

Obtain information about stored subprograms and packages by using various data dictionary views.

You can check on the status and date of the last compilation for a particular stored object by querying the data dictionary view USER_OBJECTS:

```
SELECT object_type, status, timestamp
FROM user_objects
WHERE object_name = 'DEPT_PKG';
```

For this example, the server returns

```
OBJECT_TYPE      STATUS   TIMESTAMP
-------------------------------------------------
PACKAGE          VALID    1998-06-25:22:31:43
PACKAGE BODY     VALID    1998-06-25:22:52:04
```

You can check on the source, parsed object code, and error sizes for a particular stored program unit by querying the USER_OBJECT_SIZE view:

```
SELECT
   TYPE,
   SOURCE_SIZE,
```

```
    PARSED_SIZE,
    CODE_SIZE,
    ERROR_SIZE
FROM USER_OBJECT_SIZE
WHERE
    NAME = 'DEPT_PKG';
```

Returns (in bytes):

TYPE	SOURCE_SIZE	PARSED_SIZE	CODE_SIZE	ERROR_SIZE
PACKAGE	1456	1452	609	0
PACKAGE BODY	3109	0	2458	0

You can see all compilation errors for a particular stored object by using the data dictionary view USER_ERRORS:

```
SELECT text
FROM user_errors
WHERE name = 'DEPT_PKG' AND
type = 'PACKAGE BODY'
ORDER BY line;
```

You can see the source code for a particular stored object by using the data dictionary view USER_SOURCE:

```
SELECT text
FROM user_source
WHERE name = 'DEPT_PKG' AND
type = 'PACKAGE BODY'
ORDER BY line;
```

If you grant another user EXECUTE privilege on a package you own, all she will see in ALL_SOURCE and ALL_OBJECTS is the package header. Because she doesn't own it, the implementation of the stored object isn't available to her. If you grant other users EXECUTE privilege on a stored procedure or function you own, the code body is visible to them. For example, from user DEMO,

```
SELECT
    owner, object_name, object_type
FROM all_objects
WHERE
    owner != USER AND
    object_type IN ('PROCEDURE','FUNCTION',
                    'PACKAGE','PACKAGE BODY');
```

returns the following

OWNER	OBJECT_NAME	OBJECT_TYPE
SYS	DBMS_APPLICATION_INFO	PACKAGE
SYS	DBMS_AQ	PACKAGE
SYS	DBMS_AQADM	PACKAGE
SYS	DBMS_DDL	PACKAGE

continues

continued

SYS	DBMS_DEBUG	PACKAGE
SYS	DBMS_DESCRIBE	PACKAGE
SYS	DBMS_EXPORT_EXTENSION	PACKAGE
SYS	DBMS_JOB	PACKAGE
SYS	DBMS_LOB	PACKAGE
SYS	DBMS_OUTPUT	PACKAGE
SYS	DBMS_REFRESH	PACKAGE
SYS	DBMS_ROWID	PACKAGE
SYS	DBMS_SESSION	PACKAGE
SYS	DBMS_SNAPSHOT	PACKAGE
SYS	DBMS_SNAPSHOT_UTL	PACKAGE
SYS	DBMS_SPACE	PACKAGE
SYS	DBMS_SQL	PACKAGE
SYS	DBMS_STANDARD	PACKAGE
SYS	DBMS_TRANSACTION	PACKAGE
SYS	DBMS_UTILITY	PACKAGE
SYS	DIUTIL	PACKAGE
SYS	GET_INDEX	PROCEDURE
SYS	PBRPH	PACKAGE
SYS	PBSDE	PACKAGE
SYS	PLITBLM	PACKAGE
SYS	PSTUB	PROCEDURE
SYS	PSTUBT	PROCEDURE
SYS	REV_ENG	PACKAGE
SYS	SHOWERR	PROCEDURE
SYS	SUBPTXT	PROCEDURE
SYS	ULOOKUP	PACKAGE
SYS	UTL_FILE	PACKAGE
SYS	UTL_HTTP	PACKAGE
CTXSYS	DR_REWRITE	PACKAGE
SCOTT	GET_DEPT	PROCEDURE
SCOTT	STRNUM	FUNCTION
DRSYS	DR_REWRITE	PACKAGE

In SQL*Plus, you can get a quick list of a stored subprogram's parameters with DESCRIBE (DESC):

```
desc scott.strnum
FUNCTION scott.strnum RETURNS NUMBER
 Argument Name          Type          In/Out Default?
 ---------------------------------------------------
 PSTR                   VARCHAR2      IN     DEFAULT
 PFORMAT                VARCHAR2      IN     DEFAULT
```

The default means the parameter has a default value (although what it is isn't shown).

If you want to see the parameters for all subprograms inside a package, you can still use DESCRIBE:

```
desc scott.dept_pkg
PROCEDURE DEL_DEPT
 Argument Name            Type              In/Out Default?
------------------------------------------------------------
 PROWID                   ROWID             IN/OUT
 PSTATUS                  NUMBER            IN/OUT
PROCEDURE GET_DEPT
 Argument Name            Type              In/Out Default?
------------------------------------------------------------
 PDEPTNO                  NUMBER(2)         IN/OUT
 PREC                     RECORD            N/OUT
   DEPTNO                 NUMBER(2)         IN/OUT
   DNAME                  VARCHAR2(14)      IN/OUT
   LOC                    VARCHAR2(13)      IN/OUT
 PSTATUS                  NUMBER            IN/OUT
PROCEDURE GET_DEPT
 Argument Name            Type              In/Out Default?
------------------------------------------------------------
 PLOC                     VARCHAR2(13)      IN/OUT
 PREC                     RECORD            IN/OUT
   DEPTNO                 NUMBER(2)         IN/OUT
   DNAME                  VARCHAR2(14)      IN/OUT
   LOC                    VARCHAR2(13)      IN/OUT
 PSTATUS                  NUMBER            IN/OUT
PROCEDURE GET_DEPT
 Argument Name            Type              In/Out Default?
------------------------------------------------------------
 PREC                     RECORD            IN/OUT
   DEPTNO                 NUMBER(2)         IN/OUT
   DNAME                  VARCHAR2(14)      IN/OUT
   LOC                    VARCHAR2(13)      IN/OUT
 PSTATE                   NUMBER            IN/OUT
 PSTATUS                  NUMBER            IN/OUT
PROCEDURE INS_DEPT
 Argument Name            Type              In/Out Default?
------------------------------------------------------------
 PREC                     RECORD            IN/OUT
   DEPTNO                 NUMBER(2)         IN/OUT
   DNAME                  VARCHAR2(14)      IN/OUT
   LOC                    VARCHAR2(13)      IN/OUT
 PSTATUS                  NUMBER            IN/OUT
PROCEDURE UPD_DEPT
 Argument Name            Type              In/Out Default?
------------------------------------------------------------
 PROWID                   ROWID             IN/OUT
 PREC                     RECORD            IN/OUT
   DEPTNO                 NUMBER(2)         IN/OUT
   DNAME                  VARCHAR2(14)      IN/OUT
   LOC                    VARCHAR2(13)      IN/OUT
 PSTATUS                  NUMBER            IN/OUT
```

NOTE

DESCRIBE and Oracle 7   For Oracle 7.x, you must list each subprogram separately with DESCRIBE, as with

```
DESCRIBE SCOTT.DEPT_PKG.
GET_DEPT.
```

CHAPTER SUMMARY

KEY TERMS

Before you take the exam, make sure that you're familiar with the following terms. You should be able to understand how they apply to, or how to implement them in, PL/SQL programs.

• Calling context

• Function

• Mode (or flow)

• Named notation

• Package

• Package body

• Package header (or specification)

• Parameter list

• Persistence

• Positional notation

• Procedure

• Pragma

• Purity

• Recursion

• Stored subprogram

• Subprogram

In this chapter, you reviewed how to design, build, and debug subprograms, stored subprograms, and packages.

◆ Repetitive logic can be abstracted into procedures and functions, code that can be invoked multiple times. This makes programs leaner and more efficient.

◆ Logic that many clients need to reuse can be compiled into stored procedures and functions. This organization is more efficient in its use of memory. Stored subprogram code is re-entrant, meaning multiple clients can invoke it, but only one code image resides in memory.

◆ Packages have the additional benefit of offering persistence, encapsulation, and polymorphism.

◆ The data dictionary views USER_OBJECTS and USER_OBJECT_SIZE help you observe and manage your code base.

◆ SQL*Plus offers the SHOW ERRORS feature to help locate and debug syntax errors. The data dictionary views USER_SOURCE and USER_ERRORS help you look into and debug your stored programs.

APPLY YOUR KNOWLEDGE

This section allows you to assess how well you understand the material in the chapter. Review questions test your knowledge of the tasks and concepts specified in the objectives. The exercises provide you with opportunities to engage in the sorts of tasks that compose the skill sets the objectives reflect.

Exercises

3.1 Creating a Stored Procedure

Write a stored procedure that performs a single-row lookup on the SCOTT.EMP table, given the unique key (or a table of your choice). Be sure to include an exception handler, and return the success or error value through the parameter list. Use a record variable for the return data type. (This exercise addresses the objectives "Write syntactically correct subprograms, stored procedures, functions, and packages" and "Locate and correct syntax errors within stored subprograms and packages.")

Time Estimate: 15 minutes

3.2 Creating a Stored Function

Write a stored function that safely converts a string to a DATE value to be used in a SQL statement. On an error, return a NULL. Provide an optional parameter for the format string. (This exercise addresses the objectives "Locate and correct syntax errors within stored subprograms and packages" and "Use stored and packaged functions in SQL statements.")

Time Estimate: 15 minutes

3.3 Creating a Package

Write a package to handle various queries on a table of your choice, one with multiple indexes. Give the

routines the same name but different parameter lists. Write one routine per index. Unique indexes (or primary/unique constraints) should be implemented as single-row lookups by using an implicit cursor. Non-unique indexes should use explicit cursors. Be sure to make the cursors persistent so that you can track their state. The only items exposed in the header should be the procedures. Finally, obtain a listing of the package and the exposed routines with DESCRIBE in SQL*Plus or the data dictionary views. (This exercise addresses the objectives "Write syntactically correct subprograms, stored procedures, functions, and packages," "State the benefits of using packages versus standalone subprograms," "Locate and correct syntax errors within stored subprograms and packages," and "Obtain information about stored subprograms and packages by using various data dictionary views.").

Time Estimate: 1 hour

Review Questions

1. Which one of the following is not a characteristic of standalone stored subprograms?

    A. The code is re-entrant, available to other users.

    B. Information hiding (encapsulation).

    C. Subprogram name overloading (one interface with multiple uses).

    D. Functions can be used in SQL.

2. What benefits do you get with packages that you don't get with standalone stored subprograms?

    A. The executable code in memory is sharable among users.

APPLY YOUR KNOWLEDGE

B. Variables defined globally are persistent for the duration of the session.

C. You can expose normally inaccessible data dictionary objects.

D. You can read and write from another user's global data.

3. What kinds of objects can you place in a package?

A. Cursors

B. Persistent data

C. Subprograms

D. All of the above

4. What must be true in order to use a packaged function in SQL?

A. No read/write operations on the database are allowed.

B. No read/write operations on packaged global data are allowed.

D. The function must return a Boolean value.

D. You must assert Write No Database State, Read No Database State, Write No Package State, and Read No Package State.

5. What pragma is used to assert the purity level of a packaged subprogram?

A. PRAGMA exception_init

B. PRAGMA assert

C. PRAGMA restrict_references

D. PRAGMA serially_reusable

6. What's wrong with the following standalone function?

```
CREATE OR REPLACE FUNCTION get_user_info IS
    user_rec user_users%ROWTYPE;
BEGIN
  SELECT *
  INTO user_rec
  FROM user_users;
  RETURN(user_rec);
END get_user_info;
```

A. user_users isn't a valid data dictionary view.

B. The EXCEPTION section is missing.

C. The implicit cursor returns more than one row.

D. The RETURN clause is missing in the declaration.

7. What's wrong with the following package header?

```
CREATE OR REPLACE PACKAGE blick IS
-- global public user-defined data types
  TYPE INT_TAB IS TABLE OF INTEGER INDEX
      ➥BY BINARY_INTEGER;
  -- global public subroutines
  FUNCTION primes RETURN INT_TAB;
  PROCEDURE clear_primes(Ptab IN OUT
INT_TAB);
  -- global public variables
  an_int INTEGER;
END;
```

A. Variable declarations aren't allowed after subprogram declarations.

B. The package name must be included after the END statement.

C. Functions must always take parameters.

D. The initialization section is missing.

8. Given the package header in Question 7, what's missing from the following package body?

```
CREATE OR REPLACE PACKAGE BODY blick IS
  -- global private user-defined data types
  clear_tab INT_TAB;  -- leave empty!
  -- global private subroutines
  FUNCTION is_number(Pstr IN VARCHAR2)
```

APPLY YOUR KNOWLEDGE

```
➤RETURN BOOLEAN IS
  dummy NUMBER;
BEGIN
  dummy := TO_NUMBER(Pstr);
  RETURN(TRUE);  -- conversion succeeded
EXCEPTION WHEN OTHERS THEN
  RETURN(FALSE); -- conversion failed
END is_number;
-- global public subroutines
PROCEDURE clear_primes(Ptab IN OUT
INT_TAB) IS
  BEGIN
    Ptab := clear_tab;
  END clear_primes;
END blick;
```

A. The function is_number wasn't declared in the package header.

B. The function primes, found in the header, doesn't have an implementation.

C. The initialization section is missing.

D. The user-defined data type INT_TAB is out of scope.

9. What's wrong with this function?

```
CREATE OR REPLACE
FUNCTION strnum(Pstr    IN VARCHAR2,
               Pstatus OUT NUMBER,
               Pformat IN VARCHAR2 DEFAULT
NULL)
RETURN NUMBER IS
BEGIN
  Pstatus := 0;
  IF (Pformat IS NULL) THEN  -- use NLS
format
    RETURN(TO_NUMBER(Pstr));
  ELSE  -- use given format string
    RETURN(TO_NUMBER(Pstr, Pformat));
  END IF;  -- test format string
EXCEPTION
WHEN OTHERS THEN
  Pstatus :+ SQLCODE;
END strnum;
```

A. OUT parameters aren't allowed in a function parameter list.

B. IN parameters aren't allowed after OUT parameters.

C. A RETURN statement is needed in the exception handler.

D. The function TO_NUMBER is out of scope.

10. Which one of these statements is FALSE?

A. Global package variables are persistent between sessions.

B. Global public package variables are accessible to other packages.

C. If a function is used in a SQL statement, you must assert its purity with PRAGMA RESTRICT_REFERENCES following its declaration anywhere in the package specification.

D. If you grant EXECUTE on a package to another user, that user has access only to the package specification source code via the data dictionary view all_source.

Answers to Review Questions

1. **C.** Subprogram names can be overloaded only inside a package. With a standalone subprogram, the old routine simply gets replaced with the new one.

2. **B.** Packages offer persistence, encapsulation, and polymorphism.

3. **D.** A package can contain all PL/SQL program objects: constants, variables, user-defined types, and subprograms.

4. **D.** You must assert a pretty restrictive purity level in order to use a packaged function within SQL.

Standalone stored subprograms don't need to assert purity because the code body is available for inspection by the SQL engine.

5. **C.** You must issue PRAGMA restrict_references following the declaration of a packaged function that you intend to use in SQL. The pragma is used only in the package header and doesn't need to immediately follow the function.

6. **D.** The RETURN keyword followed by a valid data type must be part of the declaration of a function. Also, you must code a RETURN statement at every exit point.

7. **A.** All subprogram declarations are coded after variables, constants, and user-defined types. A syntax error may result otherwise.

8. **B.** All subprograms declared in the header must have a corresponding implementation in the body. The converse isn't true; you may have private helping routines in the body that aren't exposed in the header.

9. **C.** A RETURN statement must be coded at every exit point, such as for every exception handler defined, as well as in the function body. A good programming style is to have exactly one exit point in the body.

10. **A.** When a session is terminated, all memory allocated for it in the SGA is released, and any program objects in memory are purged.

This chapter helps you prepare for the exam by covering the following objectives:

Learn end-user management, including creating, altering, and dropping users.

▶ The Data Control Language (DCL) that's part of the SQL language is used to administer end users and their privileges.

Learn how to implement a role-based security plan.

▶ The implementation of a security plan is complex but becomes manageable when roles are defined and used.

Learn how to manage system and object privileges.

▶ The two categories of privileges are system and object. System privileges give users access to the system and the authority to administer the system. Object privileges allow users to manage objects.

Learn dynamic implementation of roles by using the SET ROLE command.

▶ You can ensure that users have access only to the database objects by using the application software.

Create and maintain profiles to manage resource limits.

▶ Profiles, when defined, control the amount of system resources at the user level.

Implement Oracle's auditing facility for objects and sessions.

▶ Auditing allows you to know who did what and when on the database, but it won't show you what data they changed.

CHAPTER 4

Security

STUDY STRATEGIES

▶ Oracle's security architecture centers around the least-privilege model. It's important to understand the two categories of privileges to avoid giving users too much authority in the database.

Roles are the centerpiece of Oracle's security model, so you need to understand how to administer roles with the SET ROLE command.

Oracle's audit facility is often misunderstood. For the exam, you must understand the different categories of the audit model. You also have to prepare an Oracle database for auditing. Finally, you need to understand what the audit facility does not do.

Profiles are straightforward; they're created and assigned to users to control system resources. What gets confusing is which parameters you use for security.

INTRODUCTION

Oracle security is extremely granular and complex to implement and manage. This chapter explores all the aspects of creating and managing a secure Oracle database. Creating users is the basis of the Oracle security architecture. A user is created without any privilege on the database; this is called the least-privilege security architecture. Privileges fall into two categories: system and object. A system privilege allows a user to perform some type of action on the system. Object privileges control who can access an object and who can modify the structure of an object. You can control database resources with Oracle's profiles, which can be associated to users. Once a profile is associated with a user, the resource limits are enforced on the user. The database objects are assets to the business that is running the Oracle database. You can protect these assets with Oracle's built-in auditing.

USERS

Learn end-user management, including creating, altering, and dropping users.

A *user* is a name that Oracle uses to determine whether a database session has the privilege to perform a database activity. Security domain settings that you must address when creating a user include default tablespaces, temporary tablespaces, tablespace quotas, and system resource limits:

◆ The *user default tablespace* specification is used by any object requiring storage that's created without appropriate storage parameters.

◆ The *user temporary tablespace* is used for any data activity that requires sorting. This includes building indexes and the SQL ORDER BY and aggregate functions.

◆ A *tablespace quota* specifies the maximum amount of storage a user can use in a tablespace. A quota set to zero prevents the user from creating any objects in that tablespace. Once an object is created, you can remove the quota from the user, because a user who has been granted privileges to update the data doesn't need a quota for the tablespace.

◆ When a user is created, you must decide how he will be authenticated. Oracle can authenticate the user by using the password provided when the user was created; if you use the keyword externally in the password clause, the operating system will do the authentication. Listing 4.1 shows the syntax of assigning operating-system authentication.

◆ When you create a profile, you assign it resource limits. You then assign the profile to a user, who inherits the profile's resource limits.

LISTING 4.1

DDL FOR THE CREATE USER STATEMENT OPERATING-SYSTEM AUTHENTICATION

```
CREATE USER username
IDENTIFIED BY user_password¦external
DEFAULT TABLESPACE tablespace_name
TEMPORARY TABLESPACE tablespace_name
PROFILE profile_name;

CREATE USER barnes
IDENTIFIED BY external
DEFAULT TABLESPACE books_ts
TEMPORARY TABLESPACE temp_ts
PROFILE manager_pf;
```

The init.ora parameter REMOTE_OS_AUTHENT must be set to True (default is false) to allow Oracle to use the user name from a non-secure connection. This keeps a potential computer vandal from masquerading as a valid user.

The CREATE USER Data Definition Language (DDL) can have multiple quotas defined (see Listing 4.2).

LISTING 4.2

DDL FOR THE CREATE USER STATEMENT

```
CREATE USER noble
IDENTIFIED BY barnes
DEFAULT TABLESPACE books_ts
TEMPORARY TABLESPACE temp_ts
QUOTA 10M ON new_releases_ts
QUOTA 5M  ON old_books_ts
PROFILE manager_pf;
```

You can modify all the security domain settings by using the ALTER USER command (see Listing 4.3).

LISTING 4.3

DDL FOR THE ALTER USER STATEMENT

```
ALTER USER username SECURITY DOMAIN SETTING new value;
ALTER USER barnes IDENTIFIED BY new_password;
```

To remove a user from a database, issue the DROP USER command (see Listing 4.4).

LISTING 4.4

DDL FOR THE DROP USER STATEMENT

```
DROP USER username;
```

If a user owns objects in a database, you must use the keyword CASCADE with the DROP USER command (see Listing 4.5).

> **NOTE** When you remove a user from the database, there's no second chance when the drop is complete; the user is immediately removed from the database.

LISTING 4.5

DDL FOR THE DROP USER STATEMENT WITH THE CASCADE OPTION

```
DROP USER username CASCADE;
```

Real-World Problems

Users are implemented without any of the security domain settings modified from their default settings. The default settings use the system tablespace because it's the only tablespace that Oracle can be sure exists. Implementing users with the default settings will cause excessive fragmentation of the system tablespace and can possibly cause an unplanned outage of the database. A good practice is to always modify the default settings when creating a user. Using quotas is a good way to limit users with an excessive appetite for storage.

A better policy is to allow only administrators to create objects in a production database. Using operating-system authentication on an operating system that's less secure than an Oracle database will reduce overall security. Oracle's security is based on least privilege, so when users are created, they don't have rights to the Oracle database or database objects. This tempts some uninformed administrators to give users more privileges than they need.

The DROP USER command won't drop a user if the CASCADE option isn't specified. The user may still own objects.

If the CASCADE option is specified and the user still isn't removed from the database, the user might be logged on to the database. Another reason might be that when the command was issued, the database didn't have enough rollback segment space to complete the drop operation.

ROLES

Learn how to implement a role-based security plan.

A *role* is a database entity that can be granted privileges; you then grant the role to users or other roles. The granted privileges are called the *privilege domain*. The role name must be unique within the database. A role can use a password for authentication. You initiate password authentication by using the IDENTIFIED BY clause when the role is created (see Listing 4.6).

LISTING 4.6

DDL FOR THE CREATE ROLE STATEMENT

```
CREATE ROLE manager_rl
IDENTIFIED BY password;
```

When you do not specify the optional IDENTIFIED BY clause, the role isn't authenticated. Whoever creates the role must have the admin option to grant the role. The admin option provides the following special privileges:

◆ Revoke the role from another user or role

◆ Alter the role to change the authorization needed to access it

For added security, you can activate a role dynamically by using the SET ROLE command. The user must first be granted the role. When a role is granted, it automatically becomes part of the user's default role set, meaning that the role's privileges are active whenever the user signs on to the database. If a role isn't part of the user default role set but has been granted to the user, Oracle allows you to use the SET ROLE command to activate the privileges for that role, if properly authenticated. This allows the application to control when a user has access to the data and prevent unwanted access via other nonsecured programs. Oracle's built-in roles are described in Table 4.1.

TABLE 4.1

ORACLE'S BUILT-IN ROLES

Role Name	Description
CONNECT	Allows you to create a session
RESOURCE	Allows users to create objects
DBA	Provides complete authority in the database
EXP_FULL_DATABASE	Allows you to fully export the database
IMP_FULL_DATABASE	Allows you to fully import the database

Real-World Problem

Suppose that the parameter MAX_ENABLED_ROLES limits the number of roles users can have in their default role sets. You can modify this parameter in init.ora.

If this happens, modify the parameter in the init.ora file and restart the instance. An application that uses the SET ROLE command experiences unexplained privilege violations. Check the timeout parameters on Oracle profiles, open database connectivity (ODBC) on the client machine, and SQL*Net.

PRIVILEGES

Learn how to manage system and object privileges.

A *privilege* can be object or system level and, when specifying object-specific columns, can be secured. A schema object includes clusters, database links, indexes, tables, views, sequences, synonyms, stored procedures, and database triggers. You can create a user with the Security Manager utility and any Oracle tool that supports SQL, such as Server Manager, SQL*DBA, SQL Worksheet, and SQL*Plus. An object privilege allows you to modify the structure or data of the object.

Privileges are administered with the GRANT and REVOKE DCL commands. GRANT gives the privilege to a user or role (see Listing 4.7); REVOKE removes the privilege (see Listing 4.8). The REVOKE command's CASCADE CONSTRAINTS option drops any referential integrity constraint that's defined by using the references privilege. Also, users who revoke the privilege can revoke only the privilege that they originally granted. The revoke will have a cascading effect on the user to whom it was originally granted.

LISTING 4.7

DCL FOR GRANT STATEMENT

```
GRANT object_priv/all (column) optional
    ON schema.object_name TO user/role/PUBLIC
    WITH GRANT OPTION;
```

LISTING 4.8

DCL FOR REVOKE STATEMENT

```
REVOKE object_priv
    ON schema.object_name FROM user/role/PUBLIC
    CASCADE CONSTRAINTS;
```

Object privileges can be in the form of database manipulation language (DML) and DDL. The keyword all gives all object privileges to the grantee. When you specify PUBLIC in the statement, all users receive the granted privilege. If you grant the privilege with WITH

GRANT OPTION, the grantee can grant the privilege to another user or role; a role can't be granted a privilege with WITH GRANT OPTION. When an object is created, it's owned by the schema that created it.

More than 60 distinct system privileges let users perform administrative activities on the database (see Table 4.2). Many different categories of users can have different privileges. Any user who will perform database activity on an object must have object privileges (see Table 4.3).

TABLE 4.2

SYSTEM PRIVILEGES

System Privilege	Description
Analyze	
ANALYZE ANY	Analyze any table, cluster, or index in the database.
Audit	
AUDIT ANY	Audit any schema object in the database.
AUDIT SYSTEM	Enable and disable statement and privilege audit options.
Cluster	
CREATE CLUSTER	Create a cluster in own schema.
CREATE ANY CLUSTER	Create a cluster in any schema. Behaves similarly to CREATE ANY TABLE.
ALTER ANY CLUSTER	Alter any cluster in the database.
DROP ANY CLUSTER	Drop any cluster in the database.
ALTER DATABASE	Alter the database; add files to the operating system via Oracle, regardless of operating system privileges.
CREATE DATABASE LINK	Create private database links in own schema.
Index	
CREATE ANY INDEX	Create an index in any schema on any table.
ALTER ANY INDEX	Alter any index in the database.
DROP ANY INDEX	Drop any index in the database.
Library	
CREATE LIBRARY	Create callout libraries in own schema.
CREATE ANY LIBRARY	Create callout libraries in any schema
DROP LIBRARY	Drop callout libraries in own schema.
DROP ANY LIBRARY	Drop callout libraries in any schema.

continues

TABLE 4.2	*continued*

SYSTEM PRIVILEGES

System Privilege	Description
Privilege	
GRANT ANY PRIVILEGE	Grant any system privilege (not object privileges).
Procedure	
CREATE PROCEDURE	Create stored procedures, functions, and packages in own schema.
CREATE ANY PROCEDURE	Create stored procedures, functions, and packages in any schema (requires that user also have ALTER ANY TABLE, BACKUP ANY TABLE, DROP ANY TABLE, SELECT ANY TABLE, INSERT ANY TABLE, UPDATE ANY TABLE, DELETE ANY TABLE, or GRANT ANY TABLE privilege).
ALTER ANY PROCEDURE	Compile any stored procedure, function, or package in any schema.
DROP ANY PROCEDURE	Drop any stored procedure, function, or package in any schema.
EXECUTE ANY PROCEDURE	Execute any procedure or function (standalone or packaged), or reference any public package variable in any schema.
Profile	
CREATE PROFILE	Create profiles.
ALTER PROFILE	Alter any profile in the database.
DROP PROFILE	Drop any profile in the database.
Resource	
ALTER RESOURCE COST	Set costs for resources used in all user sessions.
Public	
CREATE PUBLIC DATABASE LINK	Create public database links.
DROP PUBLIC DATABASE LINK	Drop public database links.
CREATE PUBLIC SYNONYM	Create public synonyms.
DROP PUBLIC SYNONYM	Drop public synonyms.
Role	
CREATE ROLE	Create roles.
ALTER ANY ROLE	Alter any role in the database.

System Privilege	Description
Role	
DROP ANY ROLE	Drop any role in the database.
GRANT ANY ROLE	Grant any role in the database.
Rollback Segment	
CREATE ROLLBACK SEGMENT	Create rollback segments.
ALTER ROLLBACK SEGMENT	Alter rollback segments.
DROP ROLLBACK SEGMENT	Drop rollback segments.
Session	
CREATE SESSION	Connect to the database.
ALTER SESSION	Issue ALTER SESSION statements.
RESTRICTED SESSION	Connect when the database has been started by using STARTUP RESTRICT. (OSOPER and OSDBA roles contain this privilege.)
Sequence	
CREATE SEQUENCE	Create a sequence in own schema.
CREATE ANY SEQUENCE	Create any sequence in any schema.
ALTER ANY SEQUENCE	Alter any sequence in any schema.
DROP ANY SEQUENCE	Drop any sequence in any schema.
SELECT ANY SEQUENCE	Reference any sequence in any schema.
Snapshot	
CREATE SNAPSHOT	Create snapshots in own schema. (User must also have the CREATE TABLE privilege.)
CREATE ANY SNAPSHOT	Create snapshots in any schema. (User must also have the CREATE ANY TABLE privilege.)
ALTER SNAPSHOT	Alter any snapshot in any schema.
DROP ANY SNAPSHOT	Drop any snapshot in any schema.
Synonym	
CREATE SYNONYM	Create a synonym in own schema.
CREATE ANY SYNONYM	Create any synonym in any schema.
DROP ANY SYNONYM	Drop any synonym in any schema.
System	
ALTER SYSTEM	Issue ALTER SYSTEM statements.

continues

| TABLE 4.2 | *continued* |

SYSTEM PRIVILEGES

System Privilege	Description
Table	
CREATE TABLE	Create tables in own schema; also allows grantee to create indexes (including those for integrity constraints) on table in own schema. (Grantee must have a quota for the tablespace or the UNLIMITED TABLESPACE privilege.)
CREATE ANY TABLE	Create tables in any schema. (If grantee has CREATE ANY TABLE privilege and creates a table in another user's schema, the owner must have space quota on that tablespace. The table owner need not have the CREATE [ANY] TABLE privilege.)
ALTER ANY TABLE	Alter any table in any schema and compile any view in any schema.
BACKUP ANY TABLE	Perform an incremental export by using the Export utility on tables in any schema.
DROP ANY TABLE	Drop or truncate any table in any schema.
LOCK ANY TABLE	Lock any table or view in any schema.
COMMENT ANY TABLE	Comment on any table, view, or column in any schema.
SELECT ANY TABLE	Query any table, view, or snapshot in any schema.
INSERT ANY TABLE	Insert rows into any table or view in any schema.
UPDATE ANY TABLE	Update rows in any table or view in any schema.
DELETE ANY TABLE	Delete rows from any table or view in any schema.
Tablespace	
CREATE TABLESPACE	Create tablespaces; add files to the operating system via Oracle, regardless of the user's operating system privileges.
ALTER TABLESPACE	Alter tablespaces; add files to the operating system via Oracle, regardless of the user's operating system privileges.
MANAGE TABLESPACE	Take any tablespace offline, bring any tablespace online, and begin and end backups of any tablespace.
DROP TABLESPACE	Drop tablespaces.

System Privilege	Description
Tablespace	
UNLIMITED TABLESPACE	Use an unlimited amount of any tablespace. This privilege overrides any specific quotas assigned. If revoked, the grantee's schema objects remain, but further tablespace allocation is denied unless allowed by specific tablespace quotas. This system privilege can be granted only to users and not to roles. In general, specific tablespace quotas are assigned rather than granted this system privilege.
Transaction	
FORCE TRANSACTION	Force the commit or rollback of own in-doubt distributed transaction in the local database.
FORCE ANY TRANSACTION	Force the commit or rollback of any in-doubt distributed transaction in the local database.
Trigger	
CREATE TRIGGER	Create a trigger in own schema.
CREATE ANY TRIGGER	Create any trigger in any schema associated with any table in any schema.
ALTER ANY TRIGGER	Enable, disable, or compile any trigger in any schema.
DROP ANY TRIGGER	Drop any trigger in any schema.
User	
CREATE ANY USER	Create users; assign quotas on any tablespace, set default and temporary tablespaces, and assign a profile as part of a CREATE USER statement.
BECOME ANY USER	Become another user (required by any user performing a full database import).
ALTER USER	Alter other users: Change any user's password or authentication method, assign tablespace quotas, set default and temporary tablespaces, assign profiles and default roles. (Not required to alter own password.)
DROP USER	Drop another user.
View	
CREATE VIEW	Create a view in own schema.
CREATE ANY VIEW	Create a view in any schema. To create a view in another user's schema, you must have CREATE ANY VIEW privileges, and the owner must have the required privileges on the objects referenced in the view.
DROP ANY VIEW	Drop any view in any schema.

TABLE 4.3

OBJECT PRIVILEGES

Object Privilege	Commands
ALTER	ALTER object (table or sequence).
DELETE	DELETE FROM object (table or view).
EXECUTE	EXECUTE object (procedure or function). Refers to public package variables.
INDEX	CREATE INDEX ON object (tables only).
INSERT	INSERT INTO object (table or view).
REFERENCES	CREATE statement defining a FOREIGN KEY integrity or ALTER TABLE constraint on object (tables only).
SELECT	SELECT...FROM object (table, view, or snapshot).
SQL	Statements using a sequence.
UPDATE	UPDATE object (table or view).

Assume that the following examples refer to a production environment. End users can establish a session and have DML-level object privileges. Developers can select an object. DBAs have all authority on the database except the ability to create, alter, and drop users. Security administrators have only the ability to create, alter, and drop users.

Reports on Roles and Privileges

For a report on user information, use the dba_users view.

For a report on roles granted to roles, use the role_role_privs view. For a report on roles granted to users, use the dba_role_privs view.

For a report on system privileges granted to roles, use the role_sys_privs view. For a report on table privileges granted to roles, use a SQL statement to join the view dba_tab_privs to dba_roles. For reports on system privileges granted to users, join the dba_sys_privs and all_users tables on *username*. For a report on table privileges granted to roles, use dba_tab_privs and dba_roles table, joining *grantee* to *role*. For a report on table privileges granted to users, use the dba_tab_privs and dba_users tables, joining *grantee* to *username*.

The following SELECT statement will list all users in the database, showing key information about the user:

```
SELECT username, default_tablespace,

  temporary_tablespace, created

FROM dba_users

ORDER BY created,username;

REPORT
Security user report_
USER        DEFAULT_        TEMPORARY_
NAME        TABLESPACE      TABLESPACE      CREATED
--------    ----------------  --------------------  ---------

SYS         SYSTEM          PSTEMP          02-DEC-97
SYSTEM      SYSTEM          PSTEMP          02-DEC-97
PS          SYSTEM          SYSTEM          02-DEC-97
OTxx001     USERS           PSTEMP          02-DEC-97
```

The following SQL statement will show roles that have been granted to other roles:

```
select * from role_role_privs

order by role

/
Security report roles granted to roles        page          1
ROLE                    GRANTED_ROLE                ADM
----------------------  --------------------------------  ---

DBA                     EXP_FULL_DATABASE           NO
DBA                     IMP_FULL_DATABASE           NO
DBA                     MONITORER                   YES
SEC_RL                  CONNECT                     NO
```

The following SQL statement will show system privileges that have been granted to roles:

```
SELECT
  role,
  privilege,
  admin_option
FROM role_sys_privs
order by role,privilege;

REPORT
SECURITY REPORT SYSTEM PRIVILEGE GRANTED TO ROLE page      1
ROLE                PRIVILEGE           ADM
--------------------------------  ----------------------  ---

APPL_PSHR_QRY       CREATE SESSION      NO
APPL_PSHR_UPDATE    CREATE SESSION      NO
DBA                 ALTER ANY CLUSTER   YES
```

```
select grantee,privilege,admin_option
from dba_sys_privs,all_users
where grantee=username
order by grantee,privilege;
ttitle off
btitle off
spool off

SECURITY SYSTEM PRIVILEGE GRANTED TO USER REPORT PAGE          1
GRANTEE       PRIVILEGE               ADM
----------    --------------------    ---
ADM_DBA       UNLIMITED TABLESPACE    NO
AUD_USER      AUDIT ANY               NO
AUD_USER      AUDIT SYSTEM            NO
AUD_USER      CREATE SESSION          NO
DBVISION      ANALYZE ANY             YES
DBVISION      BECOME USER             YES
DBVISION      CREATE ANY SYNONYM      YES
DBVISION      CREATE ANY VIEW         YES
DBVISION      CREATE PUBLIC SYNONY    YES
```

The following SQL statement will show object-level privileges that have been granted to roles:

```
SELECT grantor,grantee, owner,
table_name,privilege,grantable
FROM dba_tab_privs,dba_roles
where grantee=role
ORDER BY grantor,grantee, owner, table_name
/
SECURITY TABLE PRIVILEGE GRANTED TO ROLE REPORT PAGE      30

GRANTOR   GRANTEE     OWNER    TABLE_NAME          PRIVILEGE   adm
--------  ----------  ------   ----------------    ----------  ---
UXCLP1    APPL_PS_R   PHCL     PX_HOLIDAY_DATE     SELECT      NO
UXCLP1    APPL_PS_R   PHCL     PX_HOLIDAY_TBL      SELECT      NO
UXCLP1    APPL_PS_R   PHCL     PX_HR_ACCTG_LINE    SELECT      NO
UXCLP1    APPL_PS_R   PHCL     PX_IMP_GTL_DPL      SELECT      NO
UXCLP1    APPL_PS_R   PHCL     PX_INCDNT_ACTN_T    SELECT      NO
```

The following SQL will show object privileges that have been granted directly to users, not using roles:

```
SELECT grantor,grantee,owner,
table_name,privilege,grantable
FROM dba_tab_privs,all_users
where grantee=username
ORDER BY grantor,grantee, owner, table_name
/
SECURITY TABLE PRIVILEGE GRANTED TO USER REPORT PAGE          1
GRANTOR     GRANTEE     OWNER    TABLE_NAME       PRIVILEGE   adm
--------    ----------  -------- ---------------  ----------  ---
XHCLP1      ADM_DBA     XHCLP1   PSTREENODE       ALTER       NO
XHCLP1      ADM_DBA     XHCLP1   PSTREENODE       DELETE      NO
```

```
XHCLP1    ADM_DBA   XHCLP1   PSTREENODE   INDEX    NO
XHCLP1    ADM_DBA   XHCLP1   PSTREENODE   INSERT   NO
```

SYSTEM RESOURCE LIMITS

Create and maintain profiles to manage resources limits.

System resource limits are implemented with a database entity called a *profile*. A profile name must be unique within the database, and the database must have the init.ora option `resource_limit` set to true, or you can use the `ALTER SYSTEM` command to enable resource limits. The profile can limit the amount of CPU time, number of I/O operations, memory space (private SQL area/MTS only), number of concurrent sessions of a user, and idle time for a user session. Listing 4.9 shows the `CREATE/ALTER PROFILE` statement.

LISTING 4.9

DDL FOR PROFILE STATEMENT

```
CREATE/ALTER PROFILE           profile_name LIMIT
SESSIONS_PER_USER              integer/UNLIMITED/DEFAULT
CPU_PER_SESSION                integer/UNLIMITED/DEFAULT
CPU_PER_CALL                   integer/UNLIMITED/DEFAULT
CONNECT_TIME                   integer/UNLIMITED/DEFAULT
IDLE_TIME                      integer/UNLIMITED/DEFAULT
LOGICAL_READS_PER_SESSION      integer/UNLIMITED/DEFAULT
LOGICAL_READS_PER_CALL         integer/UNLIMITED/DEFAULT
COMPOSITE_LIMIT                integer/UNLIMITED/DEFAULT
PRIVATE_SGA                    integer in kilobytes   or
                               ➥megabytes /UNLIMITED/DEFAULT
```

A profile controls resources at two levels: session level (see Table 4.4) and call level (see Table 4.5).

TABLE 4.4

SESSION-LEVEL RESOURCES

Resource	Description
CPU_PER_SESSION	Total CPU time in hundredths of seconds.
SESSIONS_PER_USER	Amount of concurrent sessions allowed for each username.
CONNECT_TIME	Time measured in minutes for total amount of time user was connected.
IDLE_TIME	Time measured in minutes for total amount of time user's server process was idle with no application activity.
LOGICAL_READS PER_SESSION	Number of data blocks read from memory and disk.
PRIVATE_SGA	Measured in bytes for private space in the System Global Area (SGA) for Multithreaded Server (MTS) only.

TABLE 4.5

CALL-LEVEL RESOURCES

Resource	Description
CPU_PER_CALL	CPU time measured in hundredths of seconds per call.
LOGICAL_READS_PER_CALL	Number of data blocks read from memory and disk.

When a user exceeds a profile session limit, the current statement is rolled back and only a commit, rollback, or disconnect is allowed. The session must be re-established to continue work. When a call limit is exceeded, the offending statement is rolled back, but the session remains active.

You remove profiles from a database with the DROP PROFILE command. You need the SYSTEM privilege to drop a profile. If a profile has been assigned to users, you must use the CASCADE option:

```
DROP PROFILE profile_name cascade
```

Real-World Problems

Setting the profile limit too low hinders users from doing their tasks. Gather statistics on CONNECT_TIME, LOGICAL_READS_PER_SESSION, and LOGICAL_READS_PER_CALL by using the AUDIT SESSION option (discussed later in this chapter). These statistics will provide real-world information on your database and help you set the profile limits accurately.

DATABASE ADMINISTRATOR (DBA) AUTHENTICATION

Oracle gives DBAs additional authentication with the special password file.

Oracle recommends that DBAs be placed in a special group so it can check the group ID of the user who's trying to perform a DBA task. You can set up an optional password file for DBAs using the ORAPWD password utility. The password file will restrict administration privilege to only the users who know the password and have been granted a special role, either SYSDBA or SYSOPER. Table 4.6 lists privileges by role.

TABLE 4.6

SPECIAL DBA ROLES

DBA Roles	Privilege
SYSOPER	STARTUP, SHUTDOWN, ALTER DATABASE OPEN/MOUNT, ALTER DATABASE BACKUP, ARCHIVE LOG, RECOVER, and RESTRICTED SESSION.
SYSDBA	Contains all system privileges with ADMIN OPTION and the SYSOPER system privilege; permits CREATE DATABASE and time-based recovery.

Using the ORAPWD Utility

You execute the ORAPWD utility at the command prompt of an operating system to create a password for additional authentication of database administrators.

1. Create the password file by using the following ORAPWD syntax:

   ORAPWD FILE=*filename* PASSWORD=*password* ENTRIES=*max_users*

   filename is the actual filename for the password file, *password* is the password that must be used to log on to the database as a DBA, and *max_users* is the maximum number of users that can have the DBA privilege.

2. Set the REMOTE_LOGIN_PASSWORDFILE initialization parameter to a valid value (see Table 4.7).

3. Add users to the password file by using the GRANT command (see Listing 4.10). The database must have exclusive rights to the password file.

TABLE 4.7

VALID VALUES FOR REMOTE_LOGIN_PASSWORDFILE

Valid Value	*Description*
NONE	Behaves as though there isn't a password file.
SHARED	A password file can be used by multiple databases. The only users recognized by a SHARED password file are SYS and INTERNAL.
EXCLUSIVE	Restricts the password file to one database. Allows users to be granted the roles SYSDBA and SYSOPER.

LISTING 4.10

DCL TO ADD DBA USERS TO SPECIAL DBA ROLES

```
GRANT SYSDBA TO BARNES;
GRANT SYSOPER TO NOBEL;
```

Users are removed from the DBA roles with the REVOKE command, as shown in Listing 4.11.

DCL TO REMOVE DBA USERS FROM SPECIAL DBA ROLES

```
REVOKE SYSDBA FROM BARNES;
REVOKE SYSOPER FROM NOBLE;
```

The role SYSDBA permits users to perform the same operations as OSDBA. Also, the role SYSOPER permits users to perform the same operations as OSOPER.

DBA users can use a command similar to the following:

```
CONNECT BARNES/password@prddb.hq.com AS SYSDBA
```

Operating system authentication is still used for the users that have been specified with it.

Listing Password File Members

The view V$PWFILE_USERS will show all the users granted SYSDBA and SYSOPER roles.

AUDITING DATABASE ACTIVITY

Implement Oracle's auditing facility for objects and sessions.

Oracle can audit database activity at four different levels:

◆ Level one, logins auditing:

```
audit session whenever not successful;
audit session whenever successful;
```

◆ Level two, statement auditing:

```
AUDIT statement_option [BY user]
BY SESSION/ACCESS    WHENEVER [NOT] SUCCESSFUL;
```

◆ Level three, privilege auditing:

```
AUDIT system_privilege [BY user]
BY SESSION/ACCESS    WHENEVER [NOT] SUCCESSFUL;
```

◆ Level four, object auditing:

```
AUDIT object_option
          ON schema.object
BY SESSION/ACCESS   WHENEVER [NOT] SUCCESSFUL;
```

You can specify that auditing activity record only when the activity is successful or unsuccessful. If you specify the successful option, an audit record is generated only when that operation is successful. When you specify unsuccessful, the inverse is true.

You can further focus audit activity to collect at the session or access level. The session-level option records only one audit record for the user session of an audited activity, no matter how many times the activity occurs. This is a good way to keep the audit information manageable. The BY ACCESS audit option creates an audit record every time the audited activity happens. By default, statement options, system privileges, and DDL are audited at the access level.

You must do several things to the database to prepare it to audit database activity. Set the init.ora file parameter audit_trail to OS (for operating system) or DB (for database). This is where all auditing information is kept. If the audit information is kept on the database, it is kept in the SYS.AUD$ table. You must run a special script, CATAUDIT.SQL, as SYS to create the audit table and associated views.

The AUDIT SQL command is how you enable auditing at any audit level. You can stop auditing at a particular level by using the NOAUDIT SQL command. You should modify the tablespace storage parameter of the SYS.AUD$ table from the system tablespace to a tablespace created for auditing purposes. You can issue all the audit commands from SQL Worksheet, SQL*Plus, or any Oracle tool that will accept SQL commands.

Auditing Logins

You must have the AUDIT ANY privilege to issue audit commands. Use the AUDIT SESSION command to audit logins. The successful and not successful options of the audit command can record all attempts made to establish a connection with the database. Examples in a previous section show the syntax for monitoring unsuccessful attempts and successful attempts.

Reports of the recorded audit data are stored in the SYS.AUD$ table if the data is being stored on the database. Listing 4.12 shows a report on login attempts.

LISTING 4.12

AUDIT REPORT ON LOGIN ATTEMPTS

```
SELECT
os_username, /* O/S user name*/
user name,   /* Oracle user name */
to_char(timestamp,'DD-MON-YY HH24:MI'), /* Login time */
to_char(logoff_time, 'DD-MON-YY HH24:MI') /* Logoff time C2 */
FROM dba.audit_session
ORDER BY os_username;

OUTPUT TO QUERY
OS_USERNAME    USERNAME    TIMESTAMP       LOGOFF
BARNES         BARNES      04-MAR-98 09:00 04-MAR-98 13:05
```

Auditing Database Actions

You can audit database actions at the statement and system privilege level without regard to a specific database object, but you can specify a user ID. Auditing at the statement level allows you to audit more than one SQL statement at a time. By issuing the audit statement on ROLE, you can audit the CREATE ROLE, ALTER ROLE, SET ROLE, and DROP ROLE SQL statements.

To audit system privileges, you must specify the privilege. The system privilege ALTER DATABASE isn't included in the statement-level audit option, but you can still audit it because it's a system privilege. Some statement audit options use the same name as the system privileges. You can specify the AUDIT statement for a user, session, or access. You can further refine the audit to include only successful or unsuccessful statements. Table 4.8 lists statements that you can audit.

TABLE 4.8

STATEMENT AUDIT OPTIONS

Statement	Option
ALTER SYSTEM	ALTER SYSTEM.
CLUSTER	CREATE CLUSTER, ALTER CLUSTER, TRUNCATE CLUSTER, DROP CLUSTER.

continues

TABLE 4.8 | *continued*

STATEMENT AUDIT OPTIONS

Statement	Option
DATABASE LINK	CREATE DATABASE LINK, DROP DATABASE LINK.
INDEX	CREATE INDEX, ALTER INDEX, DROP INDEX.
NOT EXISTS	All SQL statements that return an Oracle error because the specified structure or object doesn't exist.
PROCEDURE	CREATE [OR REPLACE] FUNCTION, CREATE [OR REPLACE] PACKAGE, CREATE [OR REPLACE] PACKAGE BODY, CREATE [OR REPLACE] PROCEDURE, DROP PACKAGE, DROP PROCEDURE.
PUBLIC DATABASE	CREATE PUBLIC DATABASE LINK, DROP PUBLIC LINK DATABASE LINK.
PUBLIC SYNONYM	CREATE PUBLIC SYNONYM, DROP PUBLIC SYNONYM.
ROLE	CREATE ROLE, ALTER ROLE, SET ROLE, DROP ROLE.
ROLLBACK SEGMENT	CREATE ROLLBACK SEGMENT, ALTER DROPBACK SEGMENT, DROP ROLLBACK SEGMENT.
SEQUENCE	CREATE SEQUENCE, DROP SEQUENCE.
SESSION	CONNECTS and DISCONNECTS.
SYNONYM	CREATE SYNONYM, DROP SYNONYM.
SYSTEM AUDIT	AUDIT, NO AUDIT.
SYSTEM GRANT	GRANT *system_privileges*/*role* TO user/role, REVOKE *system_privileges*/*role* FROM *user*/*role*.
TABLE	CREATE TABLE, ALTER TABLE, DROP TABLE.
TABLESPACE	CREATE TABLESPACE, ALTER TABLESPACE, DROP TABLESPACE.
TRIGGER	CREATE TRIGGER, ALTER TRIGGER, ENABLE or DISABLE, ALTER TABLE with ENABLE, DISABLE, and DROP clauses.
USER	CREATE USER, ALTER USER, DROP USER.
VIEW	CREATE [OR REPLACE] VIEW, DROP VIEW.0.

Auditing Database Objects

You can audit a specific schema object. Objects that you can audit are tables, views, sequences, packages, standalone stored procedures, and standalone stored functions.

You can specify an object option, such as insert or update, or use the keyword ALL to specify all object options. Valid object options appear in Table 4.9, and examples appear in Listing 4.13.

TABLE 4.9

VALID OBJECT OPTIONS

Option	Table	View	Sequence	Snapshot	Stored Procedure
ALTER	×	×			
AUDIT	×	×	×	×	×
COMMENT	×	×			
DELETE	×	×			
EXECUTE					×
GRANT	×	×	×		×
INDEX	×				
INSERT	×	×			
LOCK	×	×			
RENAME	×	×			×
SELECT	×	×	×		
UPDATE	×	×			

LISTING 4.13

EXAMPLES OF THE OBJECT AUDIT COMMAND

```
AUDIT insert,update
ON scott.emp_table
WHENEVER NOT SUCCESSFUL;

AUDIT ALL
  ON scott.emp_table
  WHENEVER NOT SUCCESSFUL;
```

Administrating Auditing

Audit records should have reports compiled on a daily basis and then removed. You should record all activity against the SYS.AUD$ table if the repository chosen for audit records is DB. The following statement will audit all activity on this special table:

```
AUDIT INSERT, UPDATE, DELETE, SELECT
ON sys.aud$
BY ACCESS;
```

Auditing doesn't come without an overhead cost, so be selective on what you chose to audit. The BY SESSION clause in the audit statement is more efficient than BY ACCESS because BY SESSION has to write only a single record for all SQL statements of the same type used in the same session. The BY ACCESS clause, on the other hand, causes Oracle to write one record for each audited statement. If you audit data definition language (DDL) statements, Oracle automatically uses BY ACCESS no matter which clause is specified. To maintain a secure environment, you should implement a policy about which actions to audit.

Turning Auditing Off

The NOAUDIT command is how you turn off auditing for all auditing options. Listing 4.14 shows the syntax statement, and Listing 4.15 shows the syntax for disabling object auditing.

LISTING 4.14

NOAUDIT COMMAND STATEMENT SYNTAX

```
NOAUDIT statement/system_priv [by user]
  WHENEVER [NOT] SUCCESSFUL;
```

LISTING 4.15

NOAUDIT COMMAND OBJECT SYNTAX

```
NOAUDIT object_option ON schema.object
  WHENEVER [NOT] SUCCESSFUL;
```

Reporting on Auditing Activity

To report on privilege auditing, use the SYS.DBA_PRIV_AUDIT_OPTS
view. To report on statement auditing, use the
SYS.DBA_STMT_AUDIT_OPTS view. To report on object auditing, use the
USER_OBJ_AUDIT_OPTS view.

Real-World Problems

If auditing doesn't work, make sure that you've set the init.ora parameters to turn on auditing and that you've stopped and started the
database.

If the database is frozen and won't allow anyone to log on except the
SYS user account, the audit repository is full and the audit function
can't write any data to it. It's time to run audit reports and clear out
the repository.

If you connect as internal, the user SYS can't be audited by design.

If you omit the whenever clause, both successful and unsuccessful
attempts are audited. Unsuccessful attempts don't include invalid
syntax errors, which are still recorded if the error is due to a lack of
authorization.

You cannot audit remote database activity with the local database.
You should use database triggers to audit data changes on a table.

Auditing objects generate audit records for all users. You need the
system AUDIT ANY privilege to audit objects outside your schema.

CHAPTER SUMMARY

KEY TERMS

Before you take the exam, make sure that you're comfortable with the definitions and concepts for each of the following key terms:

- Role
- Privilege
- Audit
- NOAUDIT
- System resources
- Profile
- User
- DCL
- Grant
- Revoke

Oracle's security architecture consists of object-owning users who must have privileges to access the system or to access other user objects. Roles are how you implement the privileges using a role-based security plan. You can even grant roles to roles.

You implement limits on computing resources by using a database entity called a profile. Once a profile is created, it can be granted to one or many users. Each user will inherit the resource restrictions of that profile. You can add authentication to the database administrator privilege user account by using the ORAPWD utility.

Oracle's built-in auditing will monitor objects, logins, or database actions. This system provides a complete approach to Oracle's security model.

APPLY YOUR KNOWLEDGE

This section allows you to assess how well you understand the material in the chapter. Review questions test your knowledge of the tasks and concepts specified in the objectives. The exercises provide you with opportunities to engage in the sorts of tasks that compose the skill sets the objectives reflect.

Exercise

4.1   Implement Auditing

The following steps will show you how to implement the audit facility. This exercise fulfills the objective of implementing Oracle's auditing facility for objects and sessions.

Time Estimate: 15 minutes

1. Shut down the instance with the `normal` or `immediate` option.

2. Set the init.ora file parameter `audit_trail` to `OS` (for operating system) or `DB` (for database).

3. Restart the instance.

4. Connect as `SYS` and run the CATAUDIT.SQL script to create the audit table and associated views. You can find CATAUDIT in most operating systems in the directory ORACLE_HOME/ rdbms/admin.

Review Questions

1. When creating a user in Oracle, which of the following decisions should be made?

    A. Assigning a temporary tablespace

    B. Assigning a default tablespace

    C. Assigning a password

    D. All of the above

2. What does it mean when a user password is defined as external?

    A. The password is external.

    B. The password must be changed on the next login.

    C. The operating system is doing the authentication for the user.

    D. External isn't a valid syntax.

3. What command do you use to reset a user password?

    A. `ALTER USER`

    B. `UPDATE USER`

    C. `MODIFY USER`

    D. `CHANGE USER`

4. What option or command is used to remove a user that owns objects from a database?

    A. `REMOVE USER`

    B. `DROP USER`

    C. `DROP USER` with the `CASCADE` option

    D. `CHANGE USER`

5. Which one of the following roles gives complete authority in an Oracle database?

    A. Resource

    B. `DBA`

    C. `SYSTEM`

    D. `SYS`

6. Roles can be authenticated by a password with which clause in the ROLE statement?

    A. ALTER ROLE *role_name* PASSWORD

    B. ALTER ROLE *role_name* IDENTIFIED BY

    C. UPDATE ROLE *role_name* IDENTIFIED BY

    D. CHANGE ROLE *role_name* PASSWORD

7. Privileges are added to a user with which command?

    A. ALTER

    B. REVOKE

    C. UPDATE

    D. GRANT

8. Privileges are removed from a user with which command?

    A. ALTER

    B. REVOKE

    C. UPDATE

    D. GRANT

9. What happens when a user session exceeds the profile limit?

    A. A warning is issued to the user.

    B. An ORA-600 message is created in the alert log.

    C. The transaction is rolled back.

    D. The user ID is suspended.

10. What utility is used to create a password file for a database?

    A. Server Manager

    B. ORAPWD

    C. instance_password_mgr

    D. Enterprise Manager

11. What level of the audit command will record an audit entry in the audit record every time the command that's being audited occurs?

    A. Session

    B. Access

    C. Whenever successful

    D. Whenever not successful

12. What level of the audit command will record only one audit entry in the audit record?

    A. Session

    B. Access

    C. Whenever successful

    D. Whenever not successful

13. What file must modified before you can run the audit facility in an Oracle database?

    A. Control file

    B. System file

    C. init.ora file

    D. Audit file

14. What user can't be audited?

    A. SYS

    B. Any user with the DBA role

    C. SYSTEM

    D. All users can be audited

APPLY YOUR KNOWLEDGE

Answers to Review Questions

1. **D.** You should make all of those decisions, but only the password is required. If the temporary and default tablespace isn't specified, the system tablespace is used. (This question deals with the objective, "Learn end-user management, including creating, altering, and dropping users.")

2. **C.** When external is specified, Oracle will identify only the user. The user must exist in the instance, but the operating system will authenticate the password. (This question deals with the objective, "Learn end-user management, including creating, altering, and dropping users.")

3. **A.** You use the ALTER USER command to modify parameters for a user, including a password. (This question deals with the objective, "Learn end-user management, including creating, altering, and dropping users.")

4. **C.** You must use the CASCADE option of the drop DCL command to remove a user from the database and its associated objects. (This question deals with the objective, "Learn end-user management, including creating, altering, and dropping users.")

5. **B.** The DBA role is included with all Oracle database installations and has complete authority in the database. (This question deals with the objective, "Learn how to implement a role-based security plan.")

6. **B.** The identified by clause is how you implement a password for a role. You can use it in the CREATE and ALTER commands for roles. (This question deals with the objective, "Learn how to implement a role-based security plan.")

7. **D.** You use the GRANT command to add a privilege to a role and a user. (This question deals with the objective, "Learn how to manage system and object privileges.")

8. **B.** You use the REVOKE command to remove a privilege from a role or a user. (This question deals with the objective, "Learn how to manage system and object privileges.")

9. **C.** The session activity is rolled back. (This question deals with the objective, "Create and maintain profiles to manage resource limits.")

10. **B.** You execute the ORAPWD utility at the operating-system level to create a password file for a database. (This question deals with the objective, "Create and maintain profiles to manage resource limits.")

11. **B.** The access option of the AUDIT command will record an entry every time the specified command is run. (This question deals with the objective, "Implement Oracle's auditing facility for objects and sessions.")

12. **C.** The session option of the AUDIT command will record an entry one time, no matter how many times the specified command was executed in a session. (This question deals with the objective, "Implement Oracle's auditing facility for objects and sessions.")

13. **C.** You must modify the init.ora file to tell Oracle where the Oracle audit trail will be stored, either in the operating system or the database. (This question deals with the objective, "Implement Oracle's auditing facility for objects and sessions.")

14. **A.** The SYS user can't be audited, nor can any Server Manager session that uses connect internal to connect to the database. (This question deals with the objective, "Implement Oracle's auditing facility for objects and sessions.")

ORACLE DATABASE ADMINISTRATION

This chapter helps you prepare for the exam by covering the following objectives:

Understand how an Oracle instance uses background processes and memory structures to handle database transactions.

▶ Oracle's background processes allow an instance to perform system and user requests. Some processes are required, whereas others are optional. The instance's memory structures manage the data, SQL, and PL/SQL and redo log transactions.

Understand the difference between a server process and a user process.

▶ Both processes work with a different part of the instance architecture.

Understand the different levels of starting an instance.

▶ The instance can be started in different states: NOMOUNT, MOUNT, and OPEN. Each state is used to perform database actions; the success of the database action depends on the state.

Understand the different levels of shutting down an instance.

▶ You can shut down the instance in normal, immediate, and abort mode. What has occurred on the instance determines how the instance is shut down.

CHAPTER 5

Oracle Database Architecture

OBJECTIVES

Understand the external files that support an Oracle instance.

▶ The datafiles, control files, and redo log files combine to make up the external files of a database. Each file type makes up the database file structure.

Understand the life cycle of an Oracle transaction.

▶ A transaction will weave its way through the Oracle instance memory structures and finally update the external files.

Know how to create an Oracle database with the CREATE DATABASE command.

▶ The CREATE DATABASE command is used to create a database and define system parameters for it. You must issue this command when the database is in NOMOUNT state.

Understand the architecture of Multithreaded Server (MTS).

▶ This architecture not only allows a large user base to share memory resources, but also creates a number of special background processes. Sometimes, you shouldn't use the MTS option, as discussed later in the chapter.

OUTLINE

STUDY STRATEGIES

▶ You can study the Oracle architecture by breaking it down to the Oracle instance, external structures, and the MTS option. The Oracle instance is configured by the init.ora file, which contains the parameters that define how much memory is used and whether any optional background processes are to be used. The external structures are redo logs, control files, and datafiles. Each structure has different characteristics that you need to understand. The alert file and trace files store system-level error information, such as important details about processes that have ended abnormally. The STARTUP command takes the Oracle instance through three levels: NOMOUNT, MOUNT, and OPEN. Each level can be used for specific database activities. The SHUTDOWN command also has three levels: NORMAL, IMMEDIATE, and ABORT. You issue the CREATE DATABASE command when the database is first created and when the database needs to be re-created due to a recovery operation. You use the MTS option to reduce memory and CPU usage when you have a large number of user processes connected to an Oracle instance.

INTRODUCTION

The Oracle database architecture consists of memory structures, external files, and processes. The memory structures are defined and the background processes begin when an Oracle server is started. Choosing the amount of memory and some of the optional background processes such as DBWR and CKPT determines how optimized the Oracle instance is. You configure these options in the init.ora file, and you can change them only by modifying the option and then stopping and restarting the Oracle instance.

The external files of the database include redo logs, control files, and datafiles. The redo logs are defined when the database is created, and you can also modify them later. The redo logs are defined as groups with datafiles as the members. Groups can have more than one member; Oracle recommends that each groups has at least two members defined on different disk devices. When the redo log group has two or more files on different disk devices, the redo logs are considered multiplexed. Control files contain information that is critical to starting an instance, and Oracle always recommends that an instance have more than one control file defined. The control files are defined in the init.ora file. The datafiles contain segments, which can be data, index, or rollback segments. These datafiles provide the physical structure of the logical structure tablespace.

MEMORY STRUCTURES

Oracle Server uses operating system memory for its System Global Area (SGA). The SGA belongs to only one database and consists of memory structures that Oracle uses to control and maintain the database (see Figure 5.1).

The other memory structures are shared pool, database buffer cache, redo log buffer, and program global area (PGA):

> NOTE
>
> **Oracle's Shared Memory Area.**
> Another name for the System Global Area is Shared Global Area because users on the same database server share the SGA.

◆ The shared pool is used to maintain and reuse SQL and PL/SQL statements. The area of the shared pool known as the *library cache* contains the text, parsed form, and execution plan of the SQL and PL/SQL statement. The application makes a parse call when a SQL statement is issued against an Oracle database. The parse call handles two tasks, verifying that the process has the appropriate security to issue the SQL statement and determining whether the statement has the correct syntax and semantics. The parse call creates a private SQL area for the statement, but when Oracle completes the parsing operation, the statement is placed in a shared SQL area. Once the statement is parsed, Oracle does not repeat the parse step for that statement. Because parsing is overhead, you should keep it to a minimum. Reusing SQL and PL/SQL happens only if the statements are identical (determined via a hashing algorithm). The dictionary cache contains information about database objects and their structure and the privileges for those objects.

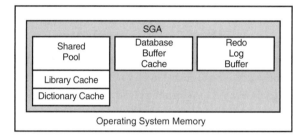

FIGURE 5.1
SGA memory structures.

◆ The database buffer cache contains the data blocks requested by database users. The first time the data blocks are requested, they're retrieved from the datafiles and placed in the cache. These data blocks are shared between users. When a user finds the data block in cache, it is called a *cache hit*; if the data block must be retrieved from the datafile, it is considered a *cache miss*. When a buffer is modified by a process, the buffer is considered "dirty," no longer usable. A buffer becomes clean when it is written to disk by the DBWR process. An LRU (least recently used) algorithm keeps only the most active data in the buffer pool. The LRU list contains dirty buffers (modified buffers), free buffers (buffers that have not been modified), and pinned buffers (buffers that are currently being used by a process).

◆ The redo log buffer contains all the changes made to the database except commands that don't generate redo log entries. Such commands, notably CREATE TABLE and CREATE INDEX, contain the UNRECOVERABLE option. The SQL*Load utility also contains an option to bypass the redo logs.

The redo log buffer is also used during a database recovery to re-create data modifications made to the database and rollback segments. The buffer is a circular buffer, so the oldest modifications are discarded first when the buffer fills.

◆ The PGA is an area of memory that is not shared. It contains stack space and user session data for only one user or a server process. The stack space contains session variables and arrays. The user session area contains data from the actual user session.

ORACLE BACKGROUND PROCESSES

Understand how an Oracle instance uses background processes and memory structures to handle database transactions.

Oracle has many background processes, each with an important task to do. Some processes are mandatory for a functioning Oracle environment. Table 5.1 lists the processes and their abbreviations.

TABLE 5.1

ORACLE'S BACKGROUND PROCESSES

Process Name	Abbreviation	Required?
Database Writer	DBWR	Yes
Log Writer	LGWR	Yes
System Monitor	SMON	Yes
Process Monitor	PMON	Yes
Checkpoint	CKPT	No
Recoverer	RECO	No
Lock	LCKn	No
Archiver	ARCH	No
Parallel Query	Pnnn	No
Dispatcher	Dnnn	No
Shared Server	Snnn	No
Snapshot Refresh	SNPn	No

When an Oracle server is started, background processes spring to life to perform their intended functions. Some processes are indicated by init.ora file parameters; other processes are required by the database server. Figure 5.2 shows how Oracle's background processes interrelate.

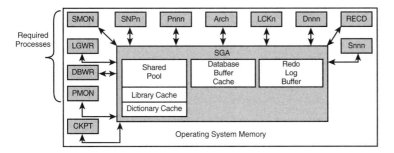

FIGURE 5.2
An Oracle instance running many processes.

Oracle's Required Processes

The following processes are created automatically when the instance is first created. The database server will crash if the Database Writer, Log Writer, System Monitor, and Process Monitor aren't available:

◆ **Database Writer (DBWR).** This process manages the database buffer cache and dictionary cache of the SGA. It reads the data blocks from the external files and places them in the database buffer cache. DBWR writes the changes out to the datafiles when any of the following occurs:

  • Every three seconds, DBWR takes a timeout.

  • A checkpoint occurs on the database.

  • The LRU is searched by a process and it does not find a free buffer.

  • The dirty buffer list has become full.

◆ **Log Writer (LGWR).** This process manages the redo log buffer contents of the SGA. It reads from this buffer and writes to the sequential online redo logs. The write occurs under the following conditions:

  • A LGWR timeout happens in the instance.

  • A commit occurs in a transaction.

- The redo log buffer pool becomes one-third full.
- The DBWR finishes cleaning dirty buffers after a checkpoint occurs.

◆ **System Monitor (SMON).** This process serves two purposes: automatic instance recovery and space management. If an Oracle Server crashes, this process performs instance recovery automatically when it's restarted by reading the redo logs. This process also coalesces free space in datafiles and temporary segments.

◆ **Process Monitor (PMON).** This process frees the resources used by a process that's no longer valid.

Processes Used by Add-On Options

Add-on processes are created to either enhance performance or support advanced database options that may require additional software licenses. The CKPT process frees the LGWR process from having to update all the datafile headers when a checkpoint occurs in the control file. Checkpoints are discussed later in this chapter. You enable the CKPT by setting the init.ora parameter CHECKPOINT_PROCESS=TRUE. The archiver process will copy the filled online redo logs to an archive destination. This destination can be another directory or tape device. The archiver is only active when an redo log switch occurs.

Pnnn, SNPn, LCKn, and RECO are processes that support tasks for add-on options to the Oracle database. The Pnnn process is used by the Parallel Query option, an additional licensed product. This process performs the parallelism for queries, index builds, data loads, and the create table as select DML. SNPn executes the automatic refresh of snapshots and manages the server job queues and replicated queues. You use SNPn with the distributed database option. LCKn performs the inner instance locking for Oracle's Parallel Server option. RECO manages the distributed transaction resources that fail.

Server and User Processes

Understand the difference between a server process and a user process.

The server process uses the shared pool to process SQL statements and retrieves data from the datafiles. The "parse" phase of the SQL statement checks for syntax, privilege security domain, and valid objects and creates the parse tree for data retrieval. The "execution" phase uses the parse tree as its map to the data and reads or updates the data, depending on the statement issued. The "fetch" phase happens during a SELECT statement and returns data to users.

The user process will communicate with the server process through SQL and PL/SQL. This process performs the transaction database work for the client in the client/server computer model shown in Figure 5.3.

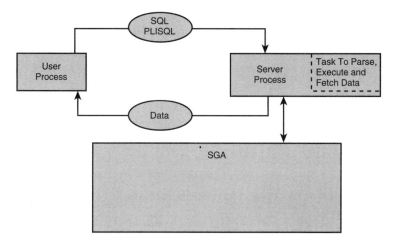

FIGURE 5.3
User and server processes.

CHARACTERISTICS OF AN ORACLE INSTANCE

The Oracle instance consists of the SGA memory structure and Oracle background processes. The init.ora initialization parameter file contains reserved words and associated values that determine the size of the SGA as well as which optional background processes are started. The initialization parameter is also used to specify rollback segments and control files.

Starting an Instance

Understand the different levels of starting an instance.

Server Manager and Instance Manager are the two Oracle tools that start an Oracle instance. The three startup states are NOMOUNT, MOUNT, and OPEN. You can issue the STARTUP command (see Listing 5.1) with the MOUNT or NOMOUNT option. If no option is specified, the database will MOUNT and OPEN the database by default, which is the normal state of an Oracle instance.

LISTING 5.1

SYNTAX FOR THE STARTUP COMMAND

```
STARTUP [FORCE] [RESTRICT] [PFILE=file_name]
OPEN MOUNT_options
MOUNT [RECOVER] [database]
NOMOUNT
MOUNT_options (EXCLUSIVE¦PARALLEL¦SHARED [RETRY])
```

You use the FORCE option when a database is already running. FORCE shuts down the database and then starts it.

The RESTRICT option prevents normal access to the database but allows any user with the restricted session system privilege to connect. To change the database from a restricted session to give all users access to the database, issue the ALTER SYSTEM command:

```
ALTER SYSTEM DISABLE RESTRICTED SESSION
```

The PFILE option starts the instance from a non-standard parameter file.

You use the NOMOUNT option when you first create a database; you use the MOUNT option for media recovery or special maintenance activities to the database or redo log files.

You use MOUNT to change the way the database performs the logging of redo logs. The modes ARCHIVELOG and NOARCHIVELOG indicate whether the database archives redo logs. To change from one type of archive log mode to another, you must mount the database without opening it. The instance is created and the control file is opened at the mount startup state. The RECOVER option begins media recovery.

The MOUNT command default is EXCLUSIVE, which allows only one instance to access the database. The PARALLEL option allows the database to be shared among multiple instances.

OPEN allows normal database operations with all files open. The ALTER DATABASE command is how you move a database from mounted to open:

```
ALTER DATABASE OPEN
```

Shutting Down an Instance

Understand the different levels of shutting down an instance.

Server Manager and Instance Manager are the two tools that can issue the SHUTDOWN command:

```
SHUTDOWN [NORMAL|IMMEDIATE|ABORT]
```

SHUTDOWN NORMAL or SHUTDOWN IMMEDIATE are how you typically shut down an instance. You use the ABORT option only in severe circumstances when the two other options are unsuccessful.

How the database is shut down determines whether the SMON process must perform automatic instance recovery when the database is started:

◆ Shutting down an instance as NORMAL prevents new sessions from being established, and the instance won't shut down until all current sessions are complete. The current users of the database can continue to work, which can present a problem because the database won't complete the shutdown until all current sessions are logged off.

◆ SHUTDOWN IMMEDIATE terminates all user sessions and rolls back all transactions not committed to the database.

◆ SHUTDOWN ABORT shuts down the instance but doesn't close and dismount the database. This type of shutdown requires that the SMON process perform automatic recovery.

ORACLE'S EXTERNAL FILES

Understand the external files that support an Oracle instance.

The external files are created by different Oracle commands and reside at the operating-system level of the database server. The redo logs are created for the first time with the CREATE database command, but you can modify them later. The control files are also defined when the database is created, but the init.ora file for the instance controls how they are written to and read from. When a tablespace is created, a datafile is created to support the contents. The tablespace is considered the logical structure and the datafile the physical structure. You can also add datafiles to a tablespace with the ALTER tablespace command using the add datafiles option. You usually apply this option when the segment that resides in the tablespace needs more space.

Redo Log Files

The redo logs are created in groups. An Oracle database must have at least two redo log groups. The redo log members are the actual datafiles. When a group has more than one member, the redo logs are considered multiplexed. A multiplexed redo log group writes to each member at the same time. This provides a way of mirroring the redo logs, and Oracle strongly recommends this procedure. You should place the group members on different disk devices and disk controllers to prevent problems from occurring due to disk or controller failure. The Backup Manager and Server Manager are the tools you use to create redo log groups and add or remove members. Once a group has a member, all subsequent new members must be the same size. For performance reasons, you might add redo log groups due to high levels of transaction activity. The alert log contains how often a redo log fills and whether a wait occurred for the database while the instance was switching from one redo group to another.

The Control File

The control file is a small binary file required to mount and open an Oracle database. The instance must be able to write to this file when the database is open. The database name and the location of all external files (database files and redo logs) associated with an instance are contained in the control file. When recovering a database, you use the control file to determine which datafiles must be recovered.

The control file name is specified in the init.ora file with the control_files parameter. Oracle recommends that you define at least three control files for one instance.

The Alert File

All Oracle instances have an alert log, a text file that contains messages about important events that occur to an instance or database (such as starting and stopping an instance), along with any modified init.ora parameters, administrative operations (DDL), and major error messages. Listing 5.2 shows an alert file with startup information (not the nondefault init.ora parameters), and Listing 5.3 shows shutdown information.

LISTING 5.2

ALERT FILE SHOWING MESSAGES FOR STARTUP COMMAND

```
Starting ORACLE instance (normal)
LICENSE_MAX_SESSION = 0
LICENSE_SESSIONS_WARNING = 0
LICENSE_MAX_USERS = 0
Starting up ORACLE RDBMS Version: 7.3.2.2.0.
System parameters with non-default values:
  processes              = 50
  control_files          =
/usr1/oracle/dbs/oradata/tst1/control01.ctl,
  /usr2/oracle/dbs/oradata/tst1/control02.ctl,
  /usr3/oracle/dbs/oradata/tst1/control03.ctl
  log_buffer             = 8192
  log_checkpoint_interval = 10000
  db_files               = 20
  rollback_segments      = r01, r02, r03, r04
  sequence_cache_hash_buckets= 10
  remote_login_passwordfile = NONE
  mts_service            = tst1
  mts_servers            = 1
  mts_max_servers        = 10
  mts_dispatchers        = ipc,1
  mts_max_dispatchers    = 10
  mts_listener_address   =
  (ADDRESS=(PROTOCOL=ipc)(KEY=tst1))
  audit_trail            = NONE
  sort_area_retained_size = 65536
  sort_direct_writes     = AUTO
  db_name                = tst1
  ifile        = /oracle/admin/tst1/pfile/configtst1.ora
```

continues

LISTING 5.2 | *continued*

**ALERT FILE SHOWING MESSAGES
FOR STARTUP COMMAND**

```
     background_dump_dest    = /oracle/admin/tst1/bdump
     user_dump_dest          = /oracle/admin/tst1/udump
     core_dump_dest          = /oracle/admin/tst1/cdump
     PMON started
     DBWR started
     LGWR started
     Wed Nov  5 15:01:35 1999
     starting up 1 shared server(s) ...
     starting up 1 dispatcher(s) for network protocol
      'ipc'...
     Wed Nov  5 15:01:35 1999
     alter database  mount exclusive
     Wed Nov  5 15:01:35 1999
     Successful mount of redo thread 1.
Wed Nov  5 15:01:35 1999
Completed: alter database  mount exclusive
Wed Nov  5 15:01:35 1999
alter database open
Wed Nov  5 15:01:35 1999
Thread 1 opened at log sequence 82
 Current log# 1 seq# 82 mem#
0:/oracle/dbs/oradata/tst1/redotst101.log
Successful open of redo thread 1.
Wed Nov  5 15:01:35 1999
SMON: enabling cache recovery
SMON: enabling tx recovery
Wed Nov  5 15:01:36 1999
Completed: alter database open
Wed Nov  5 15:01:39 1999
Thread 1 advanced to log sequence 83
 Current log# 2 seq# 83 mem# 0:
/oracle/dbs/oradata/tst1/redotst102.log
```

LISTING 5.3

ALERT FILE MESSAGES FOR SHUTDOWN COMMAND

```
Wed Nov  5 15:01:44 1999
Shutting down instance (immediate)
License high water mark = 1
Wed Nov  5 15:01:46 1999
ALTER DATABASE CLOSE NORMAL
Wed Nov  5 15:01:46 1999
SMON: disabling tx recovery
SMON: disabling cache recovery
Wed Nov  5 15:01:46 1999
Thread 1 closed at log sequence 83
 Current log# 2 seq# 83 mem# 0:
```

LISTING 5.3

ALERT FILE MESSAGES FOR SHUTDOWN COMMAND

```
/oracle/dbs/oradata/tst1/redotst102.log
Wed Nov  5 15:01:46 1999
Completed: ALTER DATABASE CLOSE NORMAL
Wed Nov  5 15:01:46 1999
ALTER DATABASE DISMOUNT
Completed: ALTER DATABASE DISMOUNT
```

The messages in the alert file are kept in chronological order. The alert file is placed in the location specified in the BACKGROUND_DUMP_DEST parameter in the init.ora file.

Trace Files

You can capture additional information in a trace file if the error was generated by a server process or a background process. A trace file is generated automatically at the database level if the init.ora parameter SQL_TRACE is set to true. Alternatively, you can set up a trace file at the session level by using the command:

```
ALTER SESSION SET sql_trace = TRUE
```

Trace files are kept in the directory specified in the init.ora parameter BACKGROUND_DUMP_DEST or USER_DUMP_DEST.

If an error is reported in the alert file (such as ORA-600 Internal Error, ORA-1578 Block corruption, or ORA-060 Deadlock errors), a trace file is created to contain additional information about the error.

> **NOTE**
>
> **The Alert File Can Contain Error Messages** You should review the alert file daily for error messages. The ORA-600 message is a catch-all message that can indicate a quite serious or moderately serious problem.

TRANSACTION PROCESSING

Understand the life cycle of an Oracle transaction.

A transaction is a logical unit of work on an Oracle database that uses SQL statements and has a begin point and end point. The end point can be the normal end of processing or a commit, such as an implicit commit made by a SQL statement (DDL or DCL). An end point can also be an unsuccessful termination of a transaction, which could occur for the following reasons:

◆ The SQL command ROLLBACK was issued.

◆ The user chose not to commit the transaction.

◆ A hardware failure occurred on the computer.

◆ An error in the user program caused the transaction to not finish successfully.

SELECT Statement

The SELECT statement retrieves data. If the data is found in memory, the read is considered logical; if the data must be retrieved from disk, the read is physical. The SELECT statement does not generate an entry in the rollback segment.

UPDATE Statement

The UPDATE statement retrieves the data to be modified into the database buffer cache. Rollback segment blocks are also placed in the database buffer cache. In the first step of the update process, exclusive row locks are placed on each row that will be updated. The original data is kept in the rollback segment block. In the last step of the process, the data blocks are updated.

Commits

When a commit happens in a transaction, it is parsed by Oracle and a commit record is placed in the redo log buffer. A system change number (SCN) is also assigned to the transaction. The LGWR writes the redo log buffer to the active redo log group. The transaction process is notified that the commit was successful. All resources held by that transaction, such as locks and rollback entries, are released. Finally, the DBWR writes the database blocks to disk.

Rollbacks

A rollback ends a transaction by undoing all of changes made by all SQL statements and releasing all locks.

Savepoints

If a rollback is issued after a savepoint, the transaction remains
active, but all other characteristics of the rollback statement apply:
The changes are removed and the data locks released.

Checkpoints

A checkpoint modifies the file headers of all datafiles and the control
file with the checkpoint sequence number. On database startup,
Oracle determines whether a datafile needs recovery by determining
whether the sequence numbers between the control file and file
header are in sync. Two init.ora parameters can force a checkpoint,
`LOG_CHECKPOINT_TIMEOUT` and `LOG_CHECK_POINT_INTERVAL`.
`LOG_CHECKPOINT_TIMEOUT` specifies how often in time a checkpoint
can occur. `LOG_CHECK_POINT_INTERVAL` is the number of filled redo
log blocks that must be filled before a checkpoint can occur. A DBA
can manually issue a checkpoint by using the `ALTER SYSTEM CHECK-
POINT` command. A checkpoint also occurs automatically if a table-
space is taken offline. Whenever you shut down the database with
the normal or immediate option, a checkpoint takes place. When
the instance is shut down with the abort option, a checkpoint cannot occur.

Locking Model

Oracle uses a multiversion consistency model that provides for
statement- and transaction-level read consistency. Locks are never
escalated. Reader processes do not have to wait for writer processes,
and writer processes do not wait for reader processes. Rollback
segments ensure read consistency for a given point in time.

CREATING A DATABASE

Know how to create an Oracle database with the
`CREATE DATABASE` command.

The `CREATE DATABASE` command allows you to define a database
datafile and the redo logs for the system tablespace. You must use

a new init.ora file to specify the control files. You must define the Oracle system ID (SID) for the new database. The instance must be started with the NOMOUNT option when you give the CREATE DATABASE command.

You create a database by using the CREATE DATABASE command at a Server Manager prompt:

```
CREATE DATABASE database_name
    [CONTROLFILE REUSE]
LOGFILE
        GROUP integer_for_group filespec_for_member
    MAXLOGFILES total_log_files
    MAXLOGMEMBERS max_number_log_members
    MAXLOGHISTORY max_number_logs_for_Parallel_Server
    DATAFILE filespec_for_system_tablespace_datafile
    MAXDATAFILES max_number_datafiles
    MAXINSTANCES max_number_instances
    ARCHIVELOG
    [NOARCHIVELOG]
    EXCLUSIVE
    CHARACTER SET charset
```

You must define a name (system identifier) for the Oracle instance at the operating-system level by using the environment variable ORACLE_SID. The software location for Oracle must be specified with the ORACLE_HOME variable.

You should specify the value of the ORA_NLS environmental variable before the database is created. This shows Oracle where to find the language object files. The database could become corrupt if the database is started later with a different ORA_NLS than originally specified during creation.

The init.ora parameter file, found in the ORACLE_HOME/rdbms directory (where the Oracle software is installed), should be copied to a file called init*sid*.ora, where *sid* is the name of the instance. Table 5.2 lists parameters that you should change in this file.

WARNING

CREATE DATABASE Command Problems Running the CREATE DATABASE command without changing the ORACLE_SID environment variable will destroy the database that ORACLE_SID points to. Running the CREATE DATABASE command with control file reuse when there isn't a control file to reuse (meaning this is the first time the instance is created) will cause the CREATE DATABASE command to fail. If a database was created with only one control file, the following steps allow you to create a mirrored file:

1. Shut down the database.

2. Copy the existing control file to another directory on another disk.

3. Alter the init.ora file's control_file parameter by placing a comma at the end of the first control file and naming the new control file.

4. Start the database.

TABLE 5.2

PARAMETERS THAT SHOULD BE CHANGED ON DATABASE CREATION

Parameter	Definition
DB_BLOCK_SIZE	Size of the data block for this instance (multiple of operating system file block size); default is 2KB.
DB_NAME	Required when the database is first created; usually the same name as the instance.

TABLE 5.2	
PARAMETERS THAT SHOULD BE CHANGED ON DATABASE CREATION	
CONTROL_FILES	Specifies the names of control files, including the directories; specifying more than one control file creates mirrored control files.
SHARED_POOL_SIZE	Number of bytes that make up the shared pool.
DB_BLOCK_BUFFERS	Amount of block size memory used to hold data.
COMPATIBLE	Allows this instance to be compatible with other instances of different Oracle releases.
BACKGROUND_DUMP_DEST	Specifies a directory for the alert files and trace files of background processes.
USER_DUMP_DEST	Specifies a directory for user trace files.

The user can connect to the database as internal or SYSDBA. (See Chapter 4, "Security," for more information on this special role.) When the CREATE DATABASE command completes successfully, statement processed is the output.

Two scripts will create data dictionary views and install database options such as the procedural option. You can find these scripts in ORACLE_HOME/rdbms/admin/catalog:

◆ catalog.sql creates the base data dictionary views.

◆ catproc.sql runs the scripts needed to use PL/SQL.

The views created by catalog.sql have four categories: USER, ALL, DBA, and ANSI-compatible. These views are owned by the SYS user:

◆ The USER view category shows all objects owned by the user who's now logged on to Oracle.

◆ The ALL view category shows information available to any user.

◆ The DBA view category shows information only to DBAs, including any information on any object in the database.

◆ The ANSI-compatible category lists synonyms used for ANSI compatibility.

MULTITHREADED SERVER (MTS)

Understand the architecture of Multithreaded
Server (MTS).

Oracle databases can run in dedicated server mode and MTS mode.
In dedicated server mode, user processes and server processes are
separate and have a one-to-one relationship (see Figure 5.4).

FIGURE 5.4
Dedicated server mode.

MTS reduces the amount of memory needed for every process that
connects to the Oracle database (see Figure 5.5). You must have
SQL*Net 2 installed to use MTS.

FIGURE 5.5
MTS architecture.

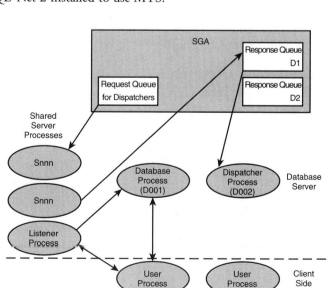

In MTS, a network process known as a *listener* gives the address of a dispatcher to the client process, unless the process requests a dedicated connection. The dispatcher uses a shared server process to make its request from a request queue in the SGA. The server process responds to the database request through the same request queue. The client then receives the response from the dispatcher. Oracle balances the shared server and dispatcher processes.

> **NOTE**
>
> **MTS Shouldn't Be Used for Recovery**
> When you're starting and stopping an instance and doing database recovery, Oracle recommends that the database be in dedicated server mode. MTS reduces memory usage and the number of server processes and performs load balancing of the database requests.

CHAPTER SUMMARY

The Oracle instance is configured by the init.ora file that is used to start it. The instance consists of background processes and different memory structures that allow Oracle to manage transactions which take place against the database. The database consists of external files, datafiles, redo log files, and control files. You can mirror the redo log and control file using Oracle's built-in software options. (Mirroring these files is highly recommended by Oracle.) The redo logs contain transactions that have been used to update the database, and the control file contains the critical information about the database and the current SCNs for all the datafiles. This information is used for both automatic and manual recovery.

KEY TERMS

Before you take the exam, make sure that you're comfortable with the definitions and concepts of the following key terms:

- SGA
- STARTUP NOMOUNT
- STARTUP MOUNT
- STARTUP OPEN
- STARTUP FORCE
- MTS
- SHUTDOWN NORMAL
- SHUTDOWN IMMEDIATE
- SHUTDOWN ABORT
- Background process
- External files
- Instance
- Database

APPLY YOUR KNOWLEDGE

This section allows you to assess how well you understand the material in the chapter. Review questions test your knowledge of the tasks and concepts specified in the objectives. The exercises provide you with opportunities to engage in the sorts of tasks that compose the skill sets the objectives reflect.

Exercises

5.1 Create a Database

Time Estimate: One hour

1. Choose an Oracle system identifier (SID) such as tst1.

2. Create an init.ora file for the new instance by copying the init.ora in the ORACLE_HOME/ dbs directory and calling the file inittst1.ora.

3. Modify the following parameters:

   DB_NAME "make equal to the SID"

4. Modify the CONTROL_FILES parameter to have a minimum of two files, each with different names:

   CONTROL_FILES=(/usr/local/oracle/ctltst1_01. ctl,/usr2/local/oracle/ctltst1_02.ctl)

5. Modify the BACKGRUND_DUMP_DEST to a directory that will contain the alert log for the instance.

6. Modify the USER_DUMP_DEST to a directory that will contain the user trace files.

7. Create a file with CREATE DATABASE command, and change the database name, logfile group member parameter, and system datafile parameter. The database name should be the same name as the instance name. The logfile and the system datafile will include the directory, file name, and size of file:

```
create database "tst1"
  maxinstances 1
  maxlogfiles  16
  character set "US7ASCII"
  maxdatafiles 255
  datafile
   '/oracle/disk1/tst1/system/system01.dbf'
size  60m
  logfile
GROUP 1 (
'/oracle/disk4/tst1/system/redo01a.log, /
➥oracle/
disk2/tst1/system/redo01b' size 500k,
GROUP 2 (
'/oracle/disk3/tst1/system/redo02a.log, /
➥oracle/
disk5/tst1/system/redo02b' size 500k;
```

8. At the operating system prompt, set the ORACLE_SID parameter to the new SID.

9. Start a SVRMGR session and connect as internal.

10. Issue the STARTUP command for the new instance in the NOMOUNT state:

    ```
    startup nomount
    pfile=/ORACLE_HOME/dbs/inittst1.ora
    ```

11. Issue the CREATE DATABASE command. If the command is successful, you see statement processed.

12. Create the system tables and install the procedural option by running the catalog.sql and the catproc.sql scripts.

5.2 Remove a Database

The following steps will remove a database from a database server. (Proceed with extreme caution; the following steps will remove *any* database.)

Time Estimate: 10 minutes

1. Shut down the instance. (This is the one time you can use the ABORT option without fear.)

2. Remove all the external files (control files, redo logs, and datafiles).

APPLY YOUR KNOWLEDGE

The instance and database are removed from the database server.

Review Questions

1. What four background processes are required for an instance?

   A. PMON, DBWR, SMON, LGWR

   B. PMON, RECO, SMON, LGWR

   C. PMON, LGWR, CKPT, DBWR

   D. PMON, LGWR, LCKn, DBWR

2. What does the optional process CKPT do?

   A. It updates the redo logs with checkpoint information

   B. It updates the datafiles and control files with checkpoint information

   C. It updates the control file only with check-point information

   D. It updates the rollback segments with check-point information

3. What two external files can be mirrored by Oracle?

   A. Datafiles and redo log files

   B. Control files and rollback segments

   C. Control files and redo log files

   D. No external file can be mirrored by Oracle

4. Where are control files specified for an instance?

   A. In the CREATE DATABASE command

   B. In the SGA

   C. In init.ora

   D. In group 1 of the redo logs

5. What two times do you start a database in the NOMOUNT state?

   A. To recover a database

   B. To create a new rollback segment

   C. To create a new redo log

   D. To create a database or a control file

6. What important procedure that aids in recovery doesn't happen during a SHUTDOWN ABORT?

   A. The RECO process for the distributive database option

   B. The MTS option server process cleanup doesn't happen automatically

   C. The checkpoint procedure

   D. The crash recovery for the instance isn't executed

7. What command releases all resources used by a transaction and allows normal processing to continue?

   A. Rollback

   B. Commit

   C. Savepoint

   D. Finish

8. Which of the following statements concerning the Oracle SGA is false?

   A. The SGA contains the data block buffer cache

B. The SGA is limited by the amount of disk storage space available on the machine

C. The SGA contains the redo log buffer

D. The SGA contains the shared SQL pool

9. Choose which statement concerning Oracle background processes is false.

   A. The SMON process will perform instance recovery if needed

   B. The PMON process will clean up behind failed user processes

   C. An Oracle instance can have more then one DBWR process

   D. All are true

10. The control file for an Oracle instance should always be

    A. Sized appropriately

    B. Mirrored across two disk devices

    C. Shared with another instance, if possible

    D. Placed offline when you perform backups

11. The redo logs for an Oracle instance should

    A. Be sized at 500KB

    B. Have more than one redo log group, with the members of the group mirrored

    C. Not be needed for every Oracle instance

    D. Be used with the archived log mode option

12. To increase the memory used by Oracle, which of the following files do you modify?

A. init.ora

B. The control file

C. The memory file

D. The system file

13. Which of the following options allows users to use fewer computing resources when connecting to an Oracle instance?

    A. Oracle's Distributive Database option

    B. Oracle's Parallel Server option

    C. Oracle's Multithreaded Server option

    D. Oracle's Enterprise Server option

Answers to Review Questions

1. **A.** SMON, DBWR, PMON, and LGWR are required background processes and will be started every time an instance is started. You can indicate optional background processes to start in the init.ora file. For more information, see the section "Oracle's Required Processes."

2. **B.** CKPT updates the datafiles and control files with checkpoint information. For more information, see "Oracle Background Processes."

3. **C.** You can mirror redo logs files by creating a redo log group with multiple members. You can mirror control files by specifying more than one in the init.ora file. For more details, see "Oracle's External Files."

4. **C.** The init.ora file contains all the parameters that are unique to an instance. For more information, see "Oracle Background Processes."

APPLY YOUR KNOWLEDGE

5. **D.** The NOMOUNT startup state is used to create a database and a control file as soon as a database is created. For more information, see "Starting an Instance."

6. **C.** The checkpoint procedure that updates the control file and datafiles with checkpoint information doesn't get executed.

7. **B.** A commit releases all resources for a transaction and allows it to continue normal processing. For more information on this topic, see "Transaction Processing."

8. **B.** SGA uses the operating system memory to configure memory structures for an Oracle instance. At no time does it use physical disk space. For more details, see "Oracle Background Processes."

9. **D.** All are true. For more information, see "Oracle Background Processes" and "Memory Structures."

10. **B.** Mirrored across two disk devices in case of media failure on one of the devices. For more information, see "Oracle's External Files."

11. **B.** Have more than one redo log group, with the members of the group mirrored. This multiplexing redo logs is recommended by Oracle. For more details, see "Oracle's External Files."

12. **A.** The init.ora file contains the configurable parameters that control the size of the memory structures for an Oracle instance. For more information, see "Oracle Background Processes."

13. **C.** The MTS option uses fewer resources. For more information on this option, see "Multithreaded Server (MTS)."

This chapter helps you prepare for the exam by covering the following objectives:

Manage the database structure.

▶ This objective is necessary because someone certified in Oracle database administration must understand structure components of a database, including tablespaces, segments, extents, and blocks. Each component fulfills fundamental and unique functions and requires a clear understanding for administrators.

Manage storage allocation.

▶ This objective is necessary because you need to understand how smaller structure elements are contained by larger elements. With a strong conceptual understanding of storage settings for tablespaces and segments, you can better manage the allocation of space in extents and blocks.

Manage table and index segments.

▶ This objective is necessary because you should clearly understand the structure of tables and indexes. Successful allocation of tables and indexes within tablespaces produces easily maintained data and reasonable performing queries.

CHAPTER 6

Managing Database Structures

Manage cluster segments.

▶ This objective is necessary because you need to understand the purpose and value of clustered data segments. The ability to create and manage clusters can pay big performance benefits, and a certified administrator will recognize when a cluster will be of value.

Manage constraints.

▶ This objective is necessary because you must understand referential integrity capabilities available at the database server. By applying constraints and managing their storage, you can ensure that the information in the tables is complete while improving response time on some queries.

Manage rollback segments.

▶ This objective is necessary because you must understand data concurrency and consistency in a multiuser database via rollback segments. Successful creation and management of rollbacks is vital to a smooth-running database server.

STUDY STRATEGIES

▶ Test 2 of the Oracle DBA certification exams focuses on the administration of an Oracle database. Much of this exam tests your knowledge of database structure elements. Some questions attempt to decipher whether you understand the differences between structure elements. Some questions will determine whether you understand the syntax of commands to manage structure elements. Other questions focus on your applied understanding of database structure components.

Before you begin to prepare for the test, note what you don't have to know yet. Focus on documentation for server release 7.3. The Oracle database certification test doesn't yet cover version 8.*x*, so avoid any books discussing Oracle8 to avoid confusion with newer database constructs.

As you prepare yourself, focus first on the conceptual understanding of each structure component: tablespaces, segments, extents, and blocks. Categorize in your mind the different types of segments and how each type functions uniquely in a database. Understand the common aspects of each segment type. Although you will read a brief conceptual explanation of structures in this chapter, you may want to review the *Oracle Concepts Guide* in your Oracle documentation set; much of the text in this chapter augments that guide. This chapter highlights differences and similarities between database structure elements.

Next, review syntax by performing the step-by-step instructions for each objective. (In this chapter, you will find abbreviated syntax for commands. You may want to refer to Oracle's *SQL Reference Manual* for complete syntax diagrams.) At a SQL prompt on a database, type the commands listed in this chapter. Mistype the commands and note the error message you receive. (Some exam questions list an error message, and ask you to determine the cause or the solution for the error.) After you review the syntax with the step-by-step commands, perform the exercises at the end of the chapter. (They repeat the step-by-step commands in the chapter.) Try to perform the exercises from memory. This will help you isolate areas you will want to review further.

Next, try the review questions in the back of the chapter. They are a sampling of the types of questions you might encounter on the test. The answers can be found in the back of the chapter, also.

Finally, go over the "Suggested Readings and References" section at the back of the chapter. If you find an area where your knowledge is a little thin, one of these references will help you shore up your understanding. You might find the review questions an especially good resource. By taking the practice exams, you can gain confidence in areas where your knowledge is deep. You will also become aware of subject areas where you can use some review.

INTRODUCTION

As a database administrator, you are responsible for the structure of an Oracle database. The certification exam tests your understanding of these structures and your ability to manage them effectively. Managing database structures is one of the more common tasks you will perform. These database structures are the foundation of the database for vendor applications and application developers.

You will be tested on your understanding of creating and managing basic database structures including tablespaces, segments, extents, and blocks. You will need to brush up on the different types of tablespaces and segments, because these will be covered on your certification exam to make sure that you have a practical on-the-job understanding of these structures. The test questions cover some of the lesser-known, but highly useful nuances you come to understand as your DBA experiences mount up. By digging through this chapter and working through the exercises, you will be better prepared for the test questions pertaining to database structure and you will better understand structures and apply them to your day-to-day administrative responsibilities.

When you manage database structures as an Oracle DBA, you have a choice of tools and methods to issue database commands. You can create and manage tablespaces by using Oracle Enterprise Manager's Storage Manager, for example. This GUI tool assists you in issuing database commands that report on tablespace status and instruct the database to modify tablespace configurations. With a database management tool such as OEM's Schema Manager, you can create a table.

The exam also focuses on your understanding of Oracle Dynamic Definition Language (DDL) and command syntax.

One other note: The Oracle database has matured through many years of industry application. The database is now in release 8 and has changed some through the years. Database structure management has changed in that new features and commands have been added. The certification test questions cover up to server release 7.3.*x* only and focus on the common functionality of structures across database versions up to this release.

ORACLE STRUCTURE FUNDAMENTALS

Before going into the specifics of Oracle database storage, you need to review some fundamentals of storage structure in an Oracle database. Having a good understanding of terminology and definitions will help you as you review the command specifics and nuances of managing storage structures for your exam. This section reviews the concepts and levels of storage from the largest storage structure through the most granular structure:

◆ Tablespaces

◆ Segments

◆ Extents

◆ Blocks

You will also touch on storage owners called *schemas* as they relate to the management of storage structures.

To help lay a foundation, let's draw a word picture that may help you grasp database storage concepts and definitions. Imagine that your company placed you in charge of managing the company library. Your responsibility is to manage the books, periodicals, and manual sets. You must create an organized means of storing these objects on shelves so that the volumes can be easily accessed and maintained. You will have three coworkers reporting to you. You will set up the shelves, and your coworkers will place the volumes on the shelves. The shelf size is adjustable and the manuals are comprised of 8 ½-by-11-inch sheets of paper stored in adjustable binders. Figure 6.1 portrays library shelves and contents that correlate to Oracle database structure elements.

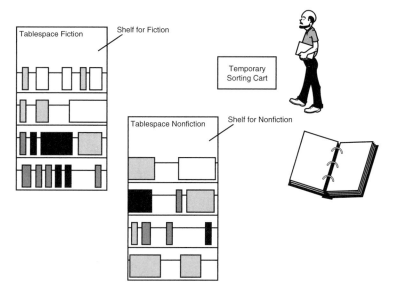

FIGURE 6.1
Oracle database structures can be compared to library shelves and contents.

Tablespaces

Databases hold data and provide capabilities to access, manage, and maintain that data. The fundamental logical storage unit of an Oracle database is a *tablespace*, which stores data in tables and clusters. A tablespace might also be called an *index space* because tablespaces store indexes, also. Rollback and temporary sorting information is stored in tablespaces. In fact, a tablespace is the basic storage container for all data and data objects in an Oracle database.

A tablespace is comprised of *data files*. A data file is just a file on a disk that the Oracle database uses to store information. These files have a fixed size that you control. A tablespace can expand as needed by extending the size of the data files comprising the tablespace.

As a DBA, you have a large range of control over tablespaces. You can create and drop tablespaces; add, size, resize, and move the data files that comprise a tablespace; and define a tablespace as read-only, read-write, temporary, or permanent. You also can bring them offline or bring them online. You can't remove a data file from a tablespace, however.

Refer to the library analogy. When you go to your company library to check out a manual, you find the binders on a shelf. The shelf is analogous to a tablespace. The tablespace (shelf) holds collections of tables (manuals).

By managing tablespaces, you can do the following:

- ◆ Allocate storage space on computer disks

- ◆ Spread access across disks for better performance

- ◆ Set user database storage allotments

- ◆ Manage data availability of data

- ◆ Back up and recover parts of the database

A tablespace can either permanently store database objects or be used to temporarily sort data within the database. A tablespace can therefore be PERMANENT or TEMPORARY.

In the company library, most of your shelves permanently store manuals. Occasionally, library members gather information from any number of manuals. To get this information, the member may require many pages from a manual or from sets of manuals. To temporarily summarize and organize this information, a library member needs a special shelf to sort, group, or summarize the information. This special kind of shelf (TEMPORARY tablespace) is used temporarily, and your library doesn't need many of these shelves.

Segments

The storage component of an Oracle database is a tablespace. The object component of an Oracle database is a *segment*. Tablespaces contain segments. Segments belong to a tablespace. A segment comes in five flavors: a table, an index, a rollback, a temporary, and a cluster. A segment must be one of these five types.

In the company library, you have shelves, which hold manuals in binders. A shelf is like a tablespace; a manual is a segment.

The following are some important rules for segments in tablespaces:

- ◆ A segment can't belong to more than one tablespace.

- ◆ A segment name must be unique for the database owner of the segment.

- ◆ A segment name must follow naming conventions.

Each segment type provides a unique database functionality. Table segments store data in rows and columns. Cluster segments store table data in a prejoined fashion for optimized and predictable data retrieval. Index segments provide fast access to data in table segments and cluster segments. Rollback segments temporarily retain a copy of modified data for data consistency and concurrency among multiple users. Temporary segments provide a location for data summarizing, sorting, and grouping.

Extents

Segments within a tablespace grow with use and must extend as needed. Each time a segment requires space beyond its current capacity, it must extend. Each such extension of a segment is named an *extent*. Extents comprise a segment in a tablespace and must have at least one initial extent.

Back to the library example. On a shelf, you will find manuals. Some manuals may be contained in a single binder, but other manuals span several binders. The binders comprising a manual can have different but individually predetermined widths because the binders can't change, expand, or contract. A manual (segment) is comprised of one or more physical binders (extents). So the shelf (tablespace) contains manuals (segments). Each manual is contained in binders (extents).

The following are some important rules for an extent:

◆ After an extent size is allocated within a tablespace, you can't change its size.

◆ An extent belongs to only one segment.

◆ Rollback segment extents behave differently than table, index, and cluster segments and have a minimum of two extents.

Blocks

All database objects within a tablespace are contained in segments. Segments are made up of extents. Extents are filled with blocks. A block is the smallest granular database storage unit. Determined at database creation, the block size can't be changed for a database. All data stored in tablespaces and moved through database instance memory is contained in a database block. Typically, the database block size will be a multiple of 2,000 bytes.

At your company library, all manual pages in the binders are exactly the same size—8 ½-by-11 inches. When you read, update, insert, and remove information from manuals, you always handle 8 ½-by-11-inch sheets of paper. The shelf (tablespace) contains manuals (segments) comprised of binders (extents) containing pages (blocks).

The following rules for blocks apply:

◆ Every block in the whole database has the same number of bytes. This value can't be changed; it is determined when the database is created.

◆ Blocks are filled with segment data and block header information.

◆ As blocks are filled with data; some room within the block is reserved for future updates to rows within the block.

◆ Data for a data segment row can span blocks. This is called a *chained row.*

Understanding the structure of blocks, extents, segments, and tablespaces is important as you prepare for your certification test on database administration. The test covers the various aspects of how data is stored on disk and within your tablespaces.

Although Oracle stores information in different types segments, managing the segment types varies as the purpose of the segment type varies. Let's look at each segment type and the specifics of how to manage each.

Schemas

Every database object in an Oracle database has an owner. The owner is a database user and the objects owned by this user are referred to as a *database schema.* Schemas relate to database structure in that the default settings for a schema relate to a tablespace in which a created object is placed and a user query is sorted.

In your library, the coworkers responsible for manuals have shelves they typically put books onto (DEFAULT tablespace) unless otherwise instructed. When they get sizable information from the manuals, they may at times have to make copies of the papers in the manuals, sort them, or summarize the contents (UNION, SORT, GROUP BY, and so on) on a temporary cart defined for them (TEMPORARY tablespace).

MANAGING DATABASE STRUCTURES

Understand structure components of a database, including tablespaces, segments, extents, and blocks. Understand each component's fundamental and unique functions.

Now that you have briefly reviewed the fundamentals of database structure in an Oracle database, look at the specific structures in detail. As you look at each structure category and variation, you will see how to manage the structure in four steps: creation, analysis, modification, and removal. These management steps are analogous to the SQL language data manipulation commands that enable you to manage and manipulate data within these Oracle structures: insert, select, update, and delete. You will review the nuances and specifics of each structure. You will see some of the commands you can use and explore special considerations you will want to be familiar with at test time.

Tablespace Management

The primary goal of a database administrator is to provide an efficient, highly available database with no data loss. Tablespace management skills are critical to keeping the data intact and available for your users.

All database objects are stored in tablespaces. Tablespaces can have different states and characteristics. The characteristics pertain to the tablespace use and management.

Tablespace Status

A tablespace can be online or offline. An *online tablespace* is available for use and is the default for any Oracle tablespace.

When a tablespace is online, users can make use of all objects within the tablespace. A tablespace can be placed *offline* for maintenance. Placing the tablespace offline can be done on database startup or while the database is open for users. When a tablespace is offline, the objects within the tablespace aren't available to users.

A tablespace can be placed in *read-only mode*, meaning that its contents can be seen by the user community but not changed. Read-only tablespaces secure their contents from user manipulation and, as a result, improve performance by reducing the overhead associated with updating the tablespace contents.

Tablespace Purpose

A tablespace can serve two primary purposes: store permanent data segments or provide a temporary storage location for sorting, grouping, and summarizing. A tablespace can't serve both purposes at the same time.

When creating a tablespace with the CREATE TABLESPACE command, you can specify the PERMANENT or TEMPORARY parameter. If you don't specify either, the tablespace created will be permanent.

The sizing and storage parameters of a tablespace define the characteristics of the extents within that tablespace. A user doesn't have control of the segments or segment extensions within a temporary tablespace.

TEMPORARY TABLESPACES

A database requires a disk area for sorting and grouping data when the amount of data is too large to manipulate in memory. Create at least one temporary tablespace specifically dedicated to temporary data functions. Include the letters TMP or TEMP in the tablespace name, reminding you and others that this tablespace serves as a sort area for database operations. SQL statements on big data sets will use this area to combine, sort, and group table rows. Index creation uses temporary disk space, too.

A temporary tablespace allocates extents as defined in the tablespace storage definition as needed. These extents hold the data for temporary operations. After the server finishes its use of these segments, they are released. This deallocated space can be reused by other subsequent temporary operations.

The SYSTEM tablespace has temporary area that can be used for these sorting operations. Be sure to set the temporary tablespace parameter for each nonsystem user to a dedicated temporary tablespace, to help prevent fragmentation of the SYSTEM tablespace.

Tablespace Rules

In a nutshell, here are some important aspects of a tablespace:

◆ An Oracle database must have one tablespace named SYSTEM and at least one data file for that tablespace. The name and location of this data file is your choice.

◆ A tablespace can be made up of many files.

◆ A single data file can't span tablespaces.

◆ Every tablespace name must be unique.

◆ You can add data files to a tablespace.

◆ You can enlarge or shrink a tablespace's data files.

◆ You can't delete a single file from a tablespace. After you add a data file, it can't be removed for this tablespace.

◆ You can rename a tablespace data file.

◆ Tablespaces aren't owned by a schema.

Designing and Planning

Before setting up a database, you must first allocate enough room for database objects. This usually involves some analysis of the purpose and scope of the database, the size of the data you will initially load, and some projections of data growth. To find out this information, you may need to interview users and database vendors and perform some transactional analysis. Basically, you are looking at allocating an appropriate amount of space for your data and group the data in an organized way.

Although you can adjust the amount of storage space allocated after your database is built, you will want to preallocate tablespace sizes when you set them up. You can do this in various ways, typically after you make a pass at the logical grouping of your data.

As you create tables and indexes for your tablespaces, you want to organize database objects together logically. In your local library, you have books on shelves that are stored in some related way. Fiction novels are stored with fiction novels; children's books are stored together; and periodicals, magazines, and reference books are grouped together on shelves that make information easier to find and manage. Likewise, you will want to group your data together in some logical fashion. Methods of grouping database objects include the following:

◆ Place objects together that have a common content theme—invoice information in one tablespace, factory information in another.

◆ Place objects together with a common function—staging tables for loading data in one tablespace, vendor application data in another.

◆ Place object types together in tablespaces—tables in one tablespace, indexes in another.

◆ Place application objects together—objects from the human resources application in one tablespace, objects from the accounts payable application in another.

NOTE

Vendor Application Tablespace Specifications   Many application vendors provide suggested tablespace names and sizing instructions in their documentation. Generally, you will want to follow their directions and sizing recommendations or formulae.

Optimal Flexible Architecture

Although you are involved with the workings of the database, some understanding of the operating system disks and file systems will help you manage your database well. Tablespaces are comprised of data files, which are stored in the operating system's directories. You will save yourself a lot of headaches if you name your data files well and place them in the directories in a way that's easily understood and managed.

Oracle recommends a standard for the architecture of an Oracle database. This standard, Optimal Flexible Architecture (OFA), provides direction for installing Oracle software and databases so that maintenance and flexibility is achieved. Within these guidelines, directory structure and filenames for data files prescribe that data files should be as follows:

◆ Named by using the tablespace name

◆ Placed in a directory named for the database instance

Storage Settings

Parameters for a tablespace define the storage definition of segments and blocks contained therein. These storage definitions can be over-ridden by the express storage definition at creation time of the database object.

Some important storage rules are as follows:

◆ A segment created in a schema will adopt the storage settings of that schema's default tablespace unless specified in the create statement.

◆ If the segments within a tablespace don't have specific storage characteristics defined at segment creation, the segment adopts the default storage setting values of the tablespace.

Keywords and Syntax

You must have the CREATE TABLESPACE system privilege to create a tablespace. To create a tablespace, use the following command:

```
CREATE TABLESPACE tablespace_name
    DATAFILE file_specification
    DEFAULT STORAGE storage clause;
```

The CREATE TABLESPACE command uses the following parameters:

Parameter	Description
TABLESPACE	The tablespace name must follow nonschema object naming conventions. Name the tablespace according to OFA guidelines and make the name reflect the purpose of the tablespace. This parameter is required.
DATAFILE	Specifies the data file or files to comprise the tablespace. You can have several files listed in a tablespace creation statement. This parameter is required.

continues

Parameter	*Description* *continued*
AUTOEXTEND	An optional parameter that enables (ON, the default) or disables (OFF) the automatic extension of data file. If you use this parameter, be sure to specify the value for NEXT and MAXSIZE later with an ALTER TABLESPACE command. This way, the tablespace will extend as you prescribe rather than grow at an unspecified rate.
NEXT	An optional parameter that specifies the extension amount in bytes to allocate to the data file when more tablespace space is required.
MAXSIZE	An optional parameter that specifies the maximum disk space (in bytes) allowed for allocation to the data file (used with the UNLIMITED parameter).
UNLIMITED	An optional parameter, used with MAXSIZE, that specifies an unlimited amount of disk space can be allocated disk space to the data file.
DEFAULT STORAGE	An optional parameter that specifies the default storage parameters for all objects created in the tablespace. These settings apply to data, index, and rollback segments unless specified for the segment specifically if the segment resides in this tablespace. Temporary segments will use these settings.
ONLINE	An optional keyword that makes the tablespace available immediately after creation to users who have been granted access to the tablespace. (This is the default.)
OFFLINE	An optional keyword that makes the tablespace unavailable immediately after creation.
PERMANENT	An optional keyword that indicates that the tablespace will be used to hold permanent objects. (This is the default.)

Parameter	*Description* *continued*
TEMPORARY	An optional keyword that indicates that the tablespace will be used only to hold temporary objects

WORKING WITH TABLESPACE REPORTS

After you create tablespaces, you can determine information about them in the data dictionary. Several dictionary views provide information about existing tablespaces. DBA_TABLESPACES and DBA_DATA_FILES provide tablespace information that you will need to review. Other data dictionary views contain information about tablespace configuration:

◆ DBA_USERS provides information about users in the database, including default tablespace settings:

View Column	*Description*
USERNAME	Name of the user/schema
DEFAULT_TABLESPACE	Tablespace holding this user's objects unless specified otherwise at object creation
TEMPORARY_TABLESPACE	Tablespace used for sorting, grouping, and other temporary SQL functions

◆ DBA_TS_QUOTAS lists tablespace quotas for all users/schemas:

View Column	*Description*
TABLESPACE_NAME	Tablespace name
USERNAME	User with resource rights on the tablespace
MAX_BYTES	User's quota in bytes (–1 if the quota is unlimited)

◆ DBA_FREE_SPACE lists the free extents in all tablespaces:

continues

View Column	*Description* continued
TABLESPACE_NAME	Name of the tablespace containing the extent
BYTES	Size of the extent in bytes

◆ DBA_TABLESPACES lists the key settings and status of tablespaces:

View Column	*Description*
INITIAL_EXTENT	Initial extent default size
NEXT_EXTENT	Next incremental extent default size
MIN_EXTENTS	Default minimum number of extents
MAX_EXTENTS	Default maximum number of extents
PCT_INCREASE	Default percent increase for extent size
STATUS	Tablespace status: ONLINE, OFFLINE, or READ ONLY

◆ DBA_DATA_FILES provides information about database files comprising the tablespaces:

View Column	*Description*
FILE_NAME	Name of the database file on the host operating system.
FILE_ID	Each database file has a unique numeric identifier.
TABLESPACE_NAME	Tablespace owning the file.
BYTES	Size of the file in bytes.
STATUS	File status: AVAILABLE or INVALID (INVALID typically indicates that a tablespace was dropped).

◆ V$DATAFILE lists tablespace data file information from the current control file:

View Column	Description
FILE#	File identification number
STATUS	System or user file and its status: OFFLINE, ONLINE, SYSTEM, RECOVER, or SYSOFF (an offline file from the SYSTEM tablespace)
NAME	Operating system name of the file

Altering a Tablespace

After a database is built and in use, your storage needs may change as the data grows and shrinks. (Very rarely does the data amount shrink—usually it grows.) Much of your tablespace effort as a DBA will be to ensure that your tablespaces have adequate storage space for your database. You will need to do the following:

◆ Reorganize your tablespace contents

◆ Add a tablespace

◆ Grow a tablespace

◆ Delete a tablespace

You can add a tablespace to an existing database, even while the database is in use. You also can add files to a tablespace while it is in use.

You can adjust the size of the tablespace by adjusting the size of the data files that comprise this tablespace. Or you can tell the tablespace to autoextend, a feature that allows the database to enlarge the size of the data files to accommodate tablespace growth.

You can change an existing tablespace by

◆ Adding data file(s)

◆ Renaming data file(s)

◆ Changing default storage parameters

◆ Taking the tablespace online or offline

◆ Beginning or ending a backup

◆ Controlling writing to a tablespace

◆ Coalescing extents

Keywords and Syntax

You change an existing tablespace with the following command (you must have ALTER TABLESPACE privilege):

```
ALTER TABLESPACE tablespace_name
   ADD DATAFILE datafile_name
   RENAME DATAFILE datafile_name
   DEFAULT STORAGE storage_clause
   ONLINE | OFFLINE [NORMAL | TEMPORARY | IMMEDIATE]
   change_backup_statement;
```

The following table lists the keywords and parameters available:

Parameter	Description
TABLESPACE	The tablespace name to be altered. (You can change the name of a tablespace.) This parameter is required.
ADD DATAFILE	An optional parameter that specifies the data file or files to add to the tablespace. You can have several files listed in a tablespace ALTER statement. You can add a data file while the tablespace is online or offline (make sure that the data file isn't already in use by another database).
AUTOEXTEND	An optional parameter that enables (ON) or disables (OFF) the automatic extension of data file. Be sure to specify a value for NEXT and MAXSIZE later with an ALTER TABLESPACE command.
NEXT	An optional parameter that indicates the extension amount in bytes to allocate to the data file when more tablespace space is required.
MAXSIZE	An optional parameter that specifies the maximum disk space in bytes allowed for allocation to the data file.
UNLIMITED	An optional keyword that indicates that an unlimited amount of disk space can be allocated disk space to the data file.
DEFAULT STORAGE	Optional keywords that specify the default storage parameters for all objects created in the tablespace. These settings apply to future data, index, and rollback segments unless

Parameter	*Description* *continued*
	specified for a segment residing in this tablespace. Temporary segments will use these settings.
ONLINE	An optional keyword that indicates that the tablespace is available immediately after creation to users who have been granted access to the tablespace.
OFFLINE	An optional keyword that indicates that the tablespace is unavailable immediately after creation.
PERMANENT	An optional keyword that indicates that the tablespace will be used to hold permanent objects.
TEMPORARY	An optional keyword that indicates that the tablespace will be used only to hold temporary objects.
RENAME DATAFILE	An optional parameter that renames one or more of the tablespace's data files. Take the tablespace offline before renaming the data file. You must rename the file on the operating system file directories with this command.
COALESCE	An optional keyword that brings together the adjacent free extents within a tablespace into larger free contiguous extents. COALESCE can't be specified with any other command option.
NORMAL	An optional keyword, used with the OFFLINE keyword, that forces a checkpoint for all online data files in the tablespace. Use this option if the database is in NOARCHIVELOG mode.
TEMPORARY	An optional keyword, used with the OFFLINE keyword, that forces a checkpoint for all online data files in the tablespace.
IMMEDIATE	An optional keyword, used with the OFFLINE keyword, that doesn't ensure that tablespace files are available and doesn't force a checkpoint.

NOTE

Moving a Data File You may need to change the disk location or filename of a tablespace data file. By using the ALTER DATABASE RENAME DATAFILE command, you can change the location and name of one or more tablespace files. Note that this command changes only the Oracle database internal record of the filename(s) and location(s); you must perform the operating system command to move the file. To move a file, follow these steps:

1. Take the affected tablespaces offline or place the database in mount status.

2. Move the file into an operating system directory.

3. Execute ALTER DATABASE RENAME DATAFILE, specifying a new filename(s).

4. Bring the offline tablespaces online or open the database.

Dropping a Tablespace

You must have the DROP TABLESPACE system privilege to use the DROP TABLESPACE command:

```
DROP TABLESPACE tablespace_name
    INCLUDING CONTENTS CASCADE CONSTRAINTS;
```

The following table lists the keywords and parameters available for this command:

Parameter	Description
tablespace	Name of the tablespace to be dropped.
INCLUDING CONTENTS	Drops all the contents of the tablespace. This option is required if the table contains database objects.
CASCADE CONSTRAINTS	Drops all referential integrity constraints from tables outside the tablespace that refer to primary and unique keys in the tables of the tablespace. This option is required if such constraints exist.

Consider the following when dropping a tablespace:

◆ You can drop a tablespace regardless of whether it is online or offline.

◆ Take the tablespace offline before dropping it to ensure that no SQL statements in currently running transactions access any of the objects in the tablespace.

◆ You may want to alter any users (use the ALTER USER command) that have been assigned the tablespace as default or temporary.

◆ You can't drop the SYSTEM tablespace.

STEP BY STEP

6.1 Time to Put Your Tablespace Knowledge to Work

1. By using a practice database that already contains a system tablespace, create a tablespace named

OCP_TRAINING. To do so, connect in SQL*Plus or
SQL Worksheet as user SYS and issue this command:

```
Create tablespace OCP_TRAINING
DATAFILE 'c:\orant\database\ocp_training_1.dbf' SIZE 2M
   DEFAULT STORAGE (INITIAL 100K NEXT 100K MINEXTENTS
➡2 MAXEXTENTS 50) OFFLINE;
```

This command creates a file on the operating system of
2MB named ocp_training_1.dbf in the c:\orant\database
directory. (The file directory structure may be different if
your database is on another operating system than
Windows NT.)

2. Confirm that the tablespace was created by executing this
command:

```
SELECT  file_name, bytes, tablespace_name, status
    FROM sys.dba_data_files;
FILE_NAME                                BYTES     TABLESPACE_NAME
-------------------------------------- --------- ---------------
c:\orant\database\system.dbf             10240000  SYSTEM
c:\orant\database\ocp_training_1.dbf     10240000  OCP_TRAINING
```

3. To list the names, sizes, and associated tablespaces of a
database, use the DBA_DATA_FILES view. View the tablespace storage settings and status like this:

```
SELECT tablespace_name "TABLESPACE",
initial_extent "INITIAL_EXT",
next_extent "NEXT_EXT",
min_extents "MIN_EXT",
max_extents "MAX_EXT",
pct_increase,
status
    FROM sys.dba_tablespaces;
TABLESPACE INITIAL_EXT NEXT_EXT MIN_EXT MAX_EXT PCT_INCREASE STATUS
---------- ----------- -------- ------- ------- ------------ -------
SYSTEM       10240000 10240000       1      99                50 ONLINE
OCP_TRAINI    1024000  1024000       2      50                50 OFFLINE
```

Note that the names and default storage parameters of all
tablespaces in a database can be found in the
DBA_TABLESPACES view.

4. Alter the tablespace to bring it online:

```
Alter tablespace OCP_TRAINING ONLINE;
```

5. Alter the tablespace and add another data file:

```
Alter tablespace OCP_TRAINING add datafile
➡'c:\orant\database\ocp_training_2.dbf'
➡SIZE 2M REUSE;
```

continues

continued

6. Alter the tablespace to change the default object parameters for PCTINCREASE and MAX_EXTENTS:

```
Alter tablespace OCP_TRAINING storage
➥(pctincrease 0 max_extents 200);
```

7. Requery the database as in step 2 and note the difference in the output. You should see an additional data file in the output.

8. Requery the database as in step 3 and note the difference in the output. You will see an online status and changed parameters for the OCP_TRAINING tablespace.

9. To see the amount of space available in the free extents of each tablespace in the database, select from the DBA_FREE_SPACE view:

```
SELECT tablespace_name, file_id,
    COUNT(*)    "PIECES",
    MAX(blocks) "MAXIMUM",
    MIN(blocks) "MINIMUM",
    AVG(blocks) "AVERAGE",
    SUM(blocks) "TOTAL"
    FROM sys.dba_free_space
WHERE tablespace_name in ('SYSTEM', 'OCP_TRAINING')
GROUP BY tablespace_name, file_id;
```

TABLESPACE	FILE_ID	PIECES	MAXIMUM	MINIMUM	AVERAGE	SUM
SYSTEM	1	2	2928	115	1521.5	3043
OCP_TRAINI	5	4	1023	4	927.2	2232

SUM shows the amount of free space in each tablespace, PIECES shows the amount of fragmentation in the data files of the tablespace, and MAXIMUM shows the largest contiguous area of space. This query is useful when you are going to create a new object or know that a segment is about to extend, and you want to make sure that enough space is in the containing tablespace.

10. Drop the OCP_TRAINING tablespace with the DROP TABLESPACE command:

```
DROP TABLESPACE OCP_TRAINING including contents;
```

The including contents keywords are necessary only if the tablespace contains schema objects.

11. Remove the tablespace data files from the operating system disk directory. From the operating system prompt in the c:\orant\database directory, remove the two data files:

```
Delete ocp_training_1.dbf
Delete ocp_training_2.dbf
```

12. Rerun queries in steps 2 and 3 and note the differences between current and preceding output.

MANAGING STORAGE ALLOCATION

Understand the relationship between larger and smaller storage components. Manage storage settings that control database structure elements.

Before discussing segments in an Oracle database, let's review the storage parameters that determine how segments fill a tablespace. For the sake of this discussion, I will discuss a table segment as an example, but most storage parameters apply to other segment types, also. At the end of the section, you review which parameters apply to each segment type specifically. Storage parameters—sometimes referred to as the *storage clause*—control object storage configuration at the tablespace, extent, and block levels.

Tablespace-Level Storage Parameters

Every segment must reside in a tablespace. On creation of a segment, you can use the `tablespace` parameter to define the tablespace to contain the segment.

When you create a segment, you can specify where and how a table is stored in one of two ways. You can define the storage parameters of the segment within the segment creation command, or you can allow the default storage parameters of the segment owner's tablespace to define the segment storage definition. Whichever storage parameters you specify at segment creation will override default parameters for the segment's tablespace. Whichever storage parameters you don't specify are defined by the tablespace's default parameters. Note that you can't change the tablespace location of a segment after the table is created without dropping the segment and re-creating it.

Extent-Level Storage Parameters

You can specify the size, number, and growth of extents a table uses with the INITIAL, NEXT, and PCTINCREASE parameters. The unit of measure for these settings is bytes; use K to specify kilobytes or M to denote megabytes. The size you specify is rounded up to the nearest block size multiple.

◆ To specify the size of the first extent allocated when a segment is created, use the INITIAL parameter. After the table is created, the INITIAL extent is allocated, and this first segment extent size can't be changed.

◆ To specify the size of the next incremental extent to be allocated for a segment, use NEXT. The second extent is equal to the original setting for NEXT. From there forward, NEXT is set to the previous size of NEXT multiplied by (1 + PCTINCREASE/100).

◆ To specify the percent that each incremental extent grows over the last incremental extent allocated for a segment, use PCTINCREASE. If PCTINCREASE is 0, all incremental extents are the same size. If PCTINCREASE is greater than zero, each time NEXT is calculated, it grows by PCTINCREASE. PCTINCREASE can't be negative.

You can control the segment's extent limits by using MINEXTENTS and MAXEXTENTS:

◆ To set an upper extent limit, use MAXEXTENTS, the total number of extents, including the first, that can ever be allocated for the segment.

◆ To set the number of extents at creation time, use MINEXTENTS. Set this value to allocate a large amount of space at creation time, even if contiguous space isn't available. If MINEXTENTS is greater than 1, the specified number of incremental extents are allocated at creation time by using the values of INITIAL, NEXT, and PCTINCREASE.

Block-Level Storage Parameters

Define how the data block space will be used by specifying the PCTFREE and PCTUSED parameters during table creation. These settings affect the efficiency of space utilization and amount of space reserved for updates for this table.

By including the INITRANS and MAXTRANS parameters during the creation of each table, you specify how much space is allocated for transaction entries for the table's data blocks.

Storage Reports

As you manage segment storage, you query from data dictionary views to find out about your current storage settings. Use DBA_SEGMENTS to find out about segment information and DBA_EXTENTS to examine extent information.

The following query returns the name of each rollback segment, the tablespace that contains each, and the size of each rollback segment:

```
SELECT segment_name, tablespace_name, bytes, blocks, extents
    FROM sys.dba_segments
    WHERE segment_type = 'ROLLBACK';
```

SEGMENT_NAME	TABLESPACE_NAME	BYTES	BLOCKS	EXTENTS
RS1	SYSTEM	20480	10	2
RS2	TS1	40960	20	3
SYSTEM	SYSTEM	184320	90	3

General information about the currently allocated extents in a database is stored in the DBA_EXTENTS data dictionary view. For example, the following query identifies the extents associated with rollback segments and the size of each extent:

```
SELECT segment_name, bytes, blocks
    FROM sys.dba_extents
    WHERE segment_type = 'ROLLBACK';
```

SEGMENT_NAME	BYTES	BLOCKS
RS1	10240	5
RS1	10240	5
SYSTEM	51200	25
SYSTEM	51200	25
SYSTEM	51200	25

Notice that the RS1 rollback segment is comprised of two extents, both 10KB, whereas the SYSTEM rollback segment is comprised of three equally sized extents of 50KB.

Two very useful data dictionary views for understanding segment storage information are DBA_SEGMENTS, which has one row for each database segment, and DBA_EXTENTS, which has one row for each extent for every database segment. The following are some of the more useful columns for the DBA_SEGMENTS view:

View Column	Description
TABLESPACE_NAME	The tablespace containing the segment
BYTES	Size of the segment in bytes
BLOCKS	Size of the segment in blocks
OWNER	Owner of the segment
NEXT	Size of the next extent

The following are some of the more useful columns for the DBA_EXTENTS view:

View Column	Description
TABLESPACE	The tablespace containing the segment
BYTES	Bytes allocated to this segment extent

Change-Storage Parameters

Storage parameters for segments are defined when the object is created from the creation command or from the default tablespace. After the parameters are set, many of them can be changed. To change a storage parameter, use the ALTER command. Storage parameters can't be dropped, but can only be reset.

Some storage parameters can be changed after table creation and others can't. After you set a parameter and the parameter is used, resetting the parameter affects storage for the segment from this point forward. The following table describes each segment storage parameter:

Parameter	Changes
INITIAL	No effect on existing table
NEXT	The size of NEXT from this point forward
MAXEXTENTS	The maximum number of extents from this point forward

Parameter	Changes *continued*
MINEXTENTS	Because initial extents have been allocated, has no effect
INITRANS	The initial number of transaction entries allocated to the segment
MAXTRANS	The maximum number of transaction entries allocated to the segment
PCTINCREASE	Percent allocation changes for subsequent extents
PCTFREE	Percent free in data blocks from this point forward
PCTUSED	Percent used in data blocks from this point forward

STEP BY STEP

6.2 Alter a Table to Note Changes to Segment Parameters

1. Create a tablespace to contain some practice tables:

```
Create tablespace OCP_TRAINING
DATAFILE 'c:\orant\database\ocp_training_1.dbf' SIZE 2M
    DEFAULT STORAGE (INITIAL 100K NEXT 100K
    ➡MINEXTENTS 2 MAXEXTENTS 50);
```

2. Create a table named EMPLOYEE in the OCP_TRAINING tablespace. Specify the OCP_TRAINING tablespace for the employee table by using the TABLESPACE clause:

```
CREATE TABLE employee (
    employee_id    NUMBER(5),
    employee_name  VARCHAR2(15)
)
TABLESPACE OCP_TRAINING;
```

3. Select data dictionary information to reveal the storage information about this table:

```
SELECT segment_name, tablespace_name, blocks,
➡extents, initial, next, pctincrease
   FROM sys.dba_segments
   WHERE segment_name = 'EMPLOYEE'
   AND tablespace_name = 'OCP_TRAINING';
   SEGMENT_NAME TABLESPACE_NAME     BYTES   BLOCKS EXTENTS
   ------------ --------------- --------- -------- -------
   EMPLOYEE     OCP_TRAINING      102400       63       2
```

continues

continued

4. Display the extent for the employee table by selecting from the DBA_EXTENTS view:

```
SELECT segment_name, bytes, blocks
   FROM sys.dba_extents
   WHERE segment_name = 'EMPLOYEE';
```

SEGMENT_NAME	BYTES	BLOCKS
EMPLOYEE	51200	25
EMPLOYEE	51200	25
EMPLOYEE	51200	25

5. Alter the table to change some of the storage parameters:

```
ALTER TABLE employee storage (pctincrease 0
➥next 50k, PCTFREE 20);
```

6. Alter the table to change the tablespace containing the employee table:

```
ALTER TABLE employee storage (tablespace SYSTEM);
```

This step will produce an error because you can't change the tablespace of an existing segment.

7. Select data dictionary information again as in step 3 to display the current storage parameters for the EMPLOYEE table. Note the difference in PCTINCREASE and NEXT for this table.

8. Drop the table and re-create it by specifying storage parameters to override tablespace parameters:

```
CREATE TABLE employee (
    employee_id     NUMBER(5),
    employee_name   VARCHAR2(15)
)
TABLESPACE OCP_TRAINING storage (initial 10K
➥next 20K minextents 10 pctincrease 10
➥maxtrans 8);
```

9. Select data dictionary information again as in step 3 to display the current storage parameters for the EMPLOYEE table. Note that the parameters specified in the CREATE TABLE statement appear in the output.

10. Requery the database as in step 4 to see the new segment sizes. Notice the growth of each extent based on the PCTINCREASE parameter in the CREATE TABLE statement. Note that NEXT is set to the previous size of NEXT multiplied by (1 + PCTINCREASE/100).

You can set default storage parameters for each tablespace of a database. Any storage parameter that you don't explicitly set when creating or subsequently altering a segment in a tablespace assumes the default storage parameter for the tablespace where the segment resides.

MANAGING TABLE AND INDEX SEGMENTS

Understand the structure of tables and indexes. Successfully manage and allocate storage for tables and indexes in tablespaces.

One stated objective of the certification test is to manage table and index segments. In this section, you review tables and indexes that prepare you for the questions on the exam.

Database Tables

Table segments—sometimes called *data segments*—are unique among the segment types. These segments contain user data. The data in an Oracle database is stored in rows and columns. You want to be very comfortable with concepts and details of table management.

A relational table contains data in two dimensions. A table contains rows and each row has columns. Each row will have the same number of columns. These rows are placed in database blocks within table extents in a table segment within a tablespace.

Creating a Table Segment

You create a table with the CREATE TABLE command. When you create a table, you must specify a tablename and at least one column. You also have the option of specifying many columns with unique names. A simple TABLE CREATION command is as follows:

```
CREATE TABLE employee (
    employee_id     NUMBER(5),
    employee_name   VARCHAR2(15)
);
```

Tables and their columns follow specific naming rules:

◆ The names of tables and columns must begin with a letter, not a number.

◆ Table and column names will be uppercase unless you enclose the name in quotation marks.

◆ Table and column names can't contain any other nonalphanumeric characters except _, -, or $.

◆ A table name must be unique for the table owner in the database.

◆ A column name can't be repeated within a table.

You can rename a table in an Oracle database by issuing a RENAME command. If you rename a table, all associated indexes and constraints remain with the newly named table.

OTHER WAYS TO CREATE A TABLE

You can create tables from a select statement. You can copy data from an existing table into a new table. To create a table named young_employees from an existing table named employee, for example, you could issue this command:

```
Create table young_employees as
Select employee_id, employee_name, birth_date
From employee
Where birth_date > '01-JAN-60';
```

On completion of this command, a new table is created and filled with employees born since January 1, 1960. The storage of this table will be the default settings for the default tablespace for the user who owns the table.

You can also use the SQL*Plus copy command unique to Oracle's SQL*Plus utility.

Notes on table segment creation commands: The order of the command clauses doesn't matter. The capitalization doesn't matter except if double quotation marks are used.

Table Reports

As mentioned earlier, storage information about a table can be found in the DBA_SEGMENTS and DBA_EXTENTS dictionary views. To examine specific table and column information for database tables, query from DBA_TABLES and DBA_TAB_COLUMNS:

◆ The DBA_TABLES data dictionary view describes tables in the database. It is similar to DBA_SEGMENTS in that the segment type is 'TABLE'. DBA_TABLES contains storage parameter settings for the tables and can also be found DBA_SEGMENTS. (DBA_SEGMENTS also provides information about other segments, such as indexes and rollbacks.) The DBA_TABLES view has the following columns:

View Column	Description
OWNER	Schema/owner of the table
TABLE_NAME	Name of the table
TABLESPACE_NAME	Name of the tablespace containing the table
BACKED_UP	Indicates whether table has been backed up since last modification

◆ The DBA_TAB_COLUMNS data dictionary view describes columns of tables, views, and clusters:

View Column	Description
OWNER	Owner of the table, view, or cluster
TABLE_NAME	Table, view, or cluster name
COLUMN_NAME	Column name in the table, view, or cluster
DATA_TYPE	Data type of the column (that is, NUMBER, CHAR, VARCHAR2, and so on)
DATA_LENGTH	Length of the column in bytes
DATA_PRECISION	Decimal precision for the NUMBER data type, binary precision for the FLOAT data type, and empty for all other data types
DATA_SCALE	Digits to right of decimal point in a numeric column, empty for other data types

continues

NOTE **A Quick Look at Tables** To see the tables you own, select from the TAB view. This view lists tables and other objects in your schema. To view a quick listing of the columns and data types for a table, use the DESCRIBE command. Either query can be done from a SQL prompt utility.

View Column	*Description* continued
NULLABLE	Indicates whether this column allows NULL values
COLUMN_ID	Order in which the column was created

> **The ANALYZE Command** The ANALYZE command collects statistics on tables that can be queried from the DBA_TABLES and DBA_TAB_COLUMNS views. The statistics help you understand block storage characteristics, table size, and column density for your table. Also, the cost-based optimizer requires these statistics for accurate query optimization. To analyze a table, use the ANALYZE TABLE command. The server gathers the range of table rows you specify, and then calculates and stores the statistics for query. Some things you can learn about a table are the number and average length of rows, the number of blocks, empty blocks and average free space in the blocks, and the number of chained rows. Some things you can learn about a table column are the lowest and highest value, the number of distinct values, and the uniqueness of column values.

Changing a Table

You can modify many aspects of a table, such as the following:

◆ Modify storage parameters (NEXT, PCTINCREASE, MAXEXTENTS)

◆ Modify data block space usage parameters (PCTFREE, PCTUSED)

◆ Modify transaction entry settings (INITRANS, MAXTRANS)

◆ Add one or more new columns

◆ Modify an existing column's definition (data type, length, default value, and NOT NULL integrity constraint)

◆ Add one or more integrity constraints

◆ Enable or disable integrity constraints or triggers associated with the table

◆ Drop integrity constraints associated with the table

You also can rename a table in an Oracle database by issuing a RENAME command. If you rename a table, all associated indexes and constraints remain with the newly named table.

You can't modify a table in some ways:

◆ You can't remove a column.

◆ You can't rename a column.

◆ You can't alter the size of an existing table extent.

As tables grow, you may need to change the storage of the table to manage its growth. The upper limit in extents for a table (MAXEXTENTS) can be changed:

```
Alter table employee storage (MAXEXTENTS 200);
```

If the table is growing faster than anticipated, you can change the size of the next extent with the NEXT parameter:

```
Alter table employee storage (NEXT 100K);
```

You can change the percentage growth in incremental extents by modifying a table's PCTINCREASE setting:

```
Alter table employee storage (PCTINCREASE 60);
```

As a table is used by a system, you may note that the storage of table data in the blocks can be improved by modifying the PCTFREE and PCTUSED parameters. If a table will be updated often and you want to increase the amount of room reserved for column updates, you can increase PCTFREE to 60%:

```
Alter table employee storage (PCTFREE 60);
```

You might find that a table has too much space allocated for data that's not being used when rows are inserted. You can decrease the PCTUSED parameter for this table:

```
Alter table employee storage (PCTUSED 30);
```

You can add columns to a table after the table is created. By using the ALTER TABLE command, specify the details of the new columns. To add a Social Security number and birth date to the employee table, you could issue a command like this:

```
Alter table employee add (social_security_num VARCHAR2(9),
➥birth_date date);
```

You can modify several column definitions, such as column length, a column's default value, or that a column have data in each row:

```
Alter table employee modify (social_security_num
➥VARCHAR2(11));
```

```
Alter table employee modify (social_security_num
➥VARCHAR2(7));
```

```
Alter table employee modify (social_security_num CHAR(11));
```

```
Alter table employee modify (social_security_num NOT
NULL));
```

```
Alter table employee modify (social_security_num
➥DEFAULT '999-99-999');
```

As you can see, you have a great deal of flexibility with the changes you can make to a column. The order of the modification of the column characteristics doesn't matter.

Dropping a Table

To remove a table from the database, you issue the DROP TABLE command. This command removes the table and all related objects and
segments for the database. If you drop a table, all associated indexes,
triggers, and constraints are also removed. If foreign-key constraints
to other tables exist on the table, a DROP command will fail. You
must remove the constraints from the table or add the CASCADE parameter to remove this table and any related data.

WORKING WITH DATABASE INDEXES

Data is stored in tables and is uniquely identified with a hidden column called a *rowid*. The fastest way to access an Oracle table row is
through the rowid, which labels each row by tablespace file, block
within the file, and row within the block. An index provides a means
of accessing rows via the rowid. Simply put, indexes are lists of
column values and their related table rowids.

Indexes serve two purposes in an Oracle database: They provide fast
access to specific database rows and ensure database data integrity.
This section focuses on indexes as access tools. Later, you will see
how constraints are actually indexes that enforce business rules.

The three index types are table indexes, cluster indexes, and bitmap
indexes. Cluster indexes provide access to the cluster key in cluster
segments, table indexes provide access to table segments, and bitmap
indexes provide access to table segments.

Table and cluster indexes follow a b*tree indexing scheme, which
provides fast access to a single row. A bitmap index is smaller and
quicker to build than a table index. Bitmap indexes are best used on
static data columns with only a few distinct values.

When considering which columns to index and how, keep in mind
that indexes must be updated when the data in the table is changed.
You can have as many indexes on a table as column permutations
exist. But every additional index increases server workload when data
is changed.

Note the following about indexes:

◆ An index is a segment and can be stored on a tablespace of
your choosing.

◆ An index can be stored with parameters that you specify.

◆ If you don't specify a storage parameter for an index, the index segment will use the parameter for the index owner's default tablespace.

◆ You can't create an index on the table until the table exists.

◆ An index doesn't change the data in the table or cluster.

◆ An index can exist on more than one column. A multicolumn index is called a *concatenated index*.

◆ A table or cluster can be in one schema, and the index on that table or cluster can be in another schema.

◆ A column with a null value isn't indexed.

◆ When loading large amounts of data, create the table, load the data, and then create the indexes to save processing time as the data is loaded.

Creating an Index Segment

To create an index, use the CREATE INDEX command. You must either own the table or cluster for the index, have the INDEX privilege on the table or cluster, or have the CREATE ANY INDEX system privilege. The command looks like this:

```
CREATE INDEX index_name [ON table_or_cluster_name]
   column(s)
   storage_information;
```

The parameters and settings to use when creating an index include the following:

Parameter	Description
UNIQUE	Optional. Defines that the column(s) indexed must be unique. Oracle recommends that you use unique constraints rather than unique indexes for future compatibility.
schema	Optional. Specifies the owner of the index. If omitted, the owner is the connect user issuing the command.

continues

Parameter	*Description* *continued*
`index_name`	Required. The name of the index must follow accepted naming guidelines.
`table_or_ cluster_name`	Optional. The table containing the columns to be indexed.
`column(s)`	Required. Column(s) to be indexed, up to 16 columns. The column data types can be any except LONG or LONG RAW.
`cluster`	Optional. The cluster for which the index is being created.
`tablespace`	Optional. The tablespace to store the index in. If omitted, the owner is the connected user issuing the command.
`NOSORT`	Optional. When creating the index, don't sort because the rows are already sorted as stored in the table.
`RECOVERABLE`	Optional. By default, the index creation is logged in the redo log file.
`UNRECOVERABLE`	Optional. The index creation isn't logged in the redo log file.
`PARALLEL`	Optional. Defines the degree of parallelism when creating the index.

The storage clause parameters apply to index segments as described in the storage section.

Index Reports

You can use the DBA_INDEXES view to find specific index characteristics, such as the average number of leaf blocks and data blocks per key. Like with other segments, you can query the DBA_SEGMENT and DBA_EXTENTS views to find storage information for an index within a tablespace.

Also, the DBA_IND_COLUMNS view enables you to see which columns are indexed on a table; this proves very helpful when tuning SQL statements. It has the following columns:

View Column	*Description*
INDEX_OWNER	Index owner. Note that the index schema can be different than the indexed table schema.
INDEX_NAME	Index name.
TABLE_OWNER	Table or cluster owner.
TABLE_NAME	Table or cluster name.
COLUMN_NAME	Column name.
COLUMN_POSITION	Position of the column within the index.
COLUMN_LENGTH	Indexed length of the column.

If key values in an index are inserted, updated, and deleted frequently, the index may or may not use its acquired space efficiently over time. Monitor an index's efficiency of space usage at regular intervals by first analyzing the index's structure and then querying the INDEX_STATS view:

```
SELECT pct_used FROM sys.index_stats
➥WHERE name = 'indexname';
```

Changing an Index

After an index exists on a table or cluster, you can modify the index with the ALTER INDEX command to modify storage parameters or to reduce fragmentation. The index must be in your schema or you must have ALTER ANY INDEX system privilege.

The ALTER INDEX REBUILD command uses the index as its source for the rebuild. Therefore, you must have enough room for both indexes to complete the command.

The syntax of the command looks like this:

```
ALTER INDEX index_name
    storage_information
    allocate_parameters
    deallocate_parameters
    rebuild_parameters;
```

The following table lists parameters for this command.

Parameter	Description
`tablespace`	Specifies the tablespace where the rebuilt index will be stored—by default, the tablespace of the user issuing the command.
`schema`	The schema containing the index. If you omit the schema, Oracle7 assumes that the index is in your own schema.
`index`	The name of the index to be altered.
ALLOCATE EXTENT	Explicitly allocates a new extent for the index.
SIZE	The size of the extent in bytes. You can use K or M to specify the extent size in kilobytes or megabytes. If you omit this parameter, Oracle7 determines the size based on the values of the index's STORAGE parameters.
DATAFILE	One of the data files in the index's tablespace to contain the new extent. If you omit this parameter, Oracle7 chooses the data file.
DEALLOCATE UNUSED	Explicitly deallocates unused space at the end of the index and makes the freed space available for other segments. Only unused space above the high-water mark can be freed. If KEEP is omitted, all unused space is freed.
KEEP	Specifies the number of bytes above the high-water mark that the index will have after deallocation. If the number of remaining extents is less than MINEXTENTS, MINEXTENTS is set to the current number of extents. If the initial extent becomes smaller than INITIAL, INITIAL is set to the value of the current initial extent.
REBUILD	Re-creates the index by using the existing index.

Parameter	Description *continued*
PARALLEL	Uses parallel processes to build the new index
NOPARALLEL	Uses one process to build the new index (default).
RECOVERABLE	The index rebuild will be logged in the redo log file (default).
UNRECOVERABLE	The index rebuild won't be logged in the redo log file.

Dropping an Index

You can remove an index with the DROP INDEX command. No data will be affected by this command. When the index is dropped, the segment extents are free for other extents in the tablespace where the index segment resided.

STEP BY STEP

6.3 Walk Through the Table-Creation Process

1. Create a table named EMPLOYEE in the OCP_TRAINING table-space. Specify the OCP_TRAINING tablespace for the employee table by using the TABLESPACE clause:

```
CREATE TABLE employee (
    employee_id      NUMBER(5),
    employee_name    VARCHAR2(15),
    ssn              VARCHAR2(9),
    gender           CHAR,
    hire_date        DATE,
    salary           Number(10,2)
)
TABLESPACE OCP_TRAINING;
```

2. Create an index on this table named employee_name_idx on employee_name:

```
CREATE INDEX employee_name_idx on employee
(employee_name);
```

3. Create a concatenated index on this table named employee_ssn_hire_date_idx on ssn and hire_date.

continues

continued

Put this index in the TOOLS tablespace with an initial extent of 10KB, a percentage increase of 10, and a maximum number of extents as 10:

```
CREATE INDEX employee_ssn_hire_date_idx on employee
➥(ssn, hire_date) TABLESPACE OCP_TRAINING STORAGE
➥(INITIAL 10K PCTINCREASE 10 MAXEXTENTS 10);
```

4. Rebuild the employee_name_idx index:

```
ALTER INDEX employee_name_idx REBUILD;
```

5. Drop both indexes:

```
DROP INDEX employee_name_idx;
DROP INDEX employee_ssn_hire_date_idx;
```

MANAGING CLUSTER SEGMENTS

Manage structure and storage allocation of clustered tables. Understand the difference between a table and a cluster of tables.

Tables store data in extents and blocks such that all the extent and block belonging to the table contains data for this table only. If a table contains a column or columns common with one or more other tables, you can choose to place these tables together in a *cluster*. A cluster stores data from one or more columns in the same database blocks. You might think of a cluster as prejoined tables stored together in database blocks. Creating a cluster has the following benefits:

◆ Reduced disk I/O when select tables are joined in the cluster

◆ Reduced storage because the common column(s) in the cluster are stored only once

The best tables to place into a cluster are those selected based on a common data column. The common columns (called a *cluster key*) must be chosen such that the rows in the cluster fill up a database block. A cluster key such as phone_number will leave too much of the block empty, whereas a key such as gender will span too many blocks.

Creating a Cluster Segment

After you create the cluster, you then create the cluster's tables and finally the cluster's index.

First, issue is the CREATE CLUSTER command, to establish the cluster name, the storage definition, and cluster key value. Use the SIZE parameter to estimate the number of bytes required by an average cluster key and its associated rows. Oracle will use this parameter to estimate the number of cluster keys (and associated rows) that can fit in a clustered data block and limit the number of cluster keys placed in a clustered data block.

Next, create the table or tables belonging to the table. Be sure to add the CLUSTER option on the column(s) participating in the cluster key. This instructs the server to place this table in the cluster you have created.

Finally, specify the cluster index for the cluster to speed access to the data blocks containing the cluster key in the cluster. A cluster index must be created before any rows can be inserted into any clustered table.

Cluster Reports

You will find cluster information in DBA_CLUSTERS. You can determine cluster storage parameters, cluster key information, block usage, and other columns similar to DBA_TABLES. Also, look at DBA_CLU_COLUMNS to find the mappings of table columns to cluster columns.

Changing a Cluster

You can alter an existing cluster to change several storage parameters:

◆ The SIZE parameter—the average cluster key size

◆ Data block space usage parameters (PCTFREE, PCTUSED)

◆ Transaction entry settings (INITRANS, MAXTRANS)

◆ Storage parameters (NEXT, PCTINCREASE)

You can't change the minimum number of extents or the initial size of a cluster extent because they already exist.

You can use the ALTER TABLE command to add or modify columns, or to add, drop, enable, or disable integrity constraints or triggers for a clustered table. You can't change storage setting for a table belonging to a cluster because the storage settings apply to the cluster and not the tables within the cluster.

You can add or drop indexes to columns of tables belonging to a cluster.

Dropping a Cluster

You can drop the cluster index, a table or tables within a cluster, or the whole cluster. If you drop a table within a cluster, each table row is deleted within the cluster blocks, which may take a long time. You can drop the cluster index without affecting the cluster or its clustered tables. However, clustered tables are unusable until you re-create the cluster index to allow access to the cluster. You may want to re-create a cluster indexes when it becomes fragmented.

To drop the cluster, use the DROP CLUSTER command. Use the including tables option if the cluster contains tables. If those tables have foreign keys referencing them from tables outside the cluster, you can also add the CASCADE CONSTRAINTS option.

STEP BY STEP

6.4 Create, Alter, and Change a Cluster

1. Create a cluster named emp_addr. This cluster will have a cluster key of employee_id.

```
CREATE CLUSTER emp_addr (employee_id NUMBER(8))
    PCTUSED 80
    PCTFREE 10
    SIZE 800
    TABLESPACE ocp_training
    STORAGE (INITIAL 200k
        NEXT 200K
        MINEXTENTS 2
        MAXEXTENTS 20
        PCTINCREASE 10);
```

2. Add two tables to the cluster—EMPLOYEE and ADDRESS:

```
CREATE TABLE employee (
    employee_id NUMBER(8) PRIMARY KEY,
    name        Varchar2(20))
    CLUSTER emp_addr (employee_id);

CREATE TABLE address (
    address_id   NUMBER(8) PRIMARY KEY,
    employee_id NUMBER(8),
    street        Varchar2(20)),
    city          Varchar2(20)))
    CLUSTER emp_addr (employee_id);
```

3. Build the cluster index on emp_addr:

```
CREATE INDEX emp_addr_index
    ON CLUSTER emp_addr
    INITRANS 2
    MAXTRANS 5
    TABLESPACE ocp_training
    STORAGE (INITIAL 50K
        NEXT 50K
        MINEXTENTS 2
        MAXEXTENTS 10
        PCTFREE 5;
        PCTINCREASE 33)
```

4. Drop the cluster and the tables:

```
DROP CLUSTER emp_addr INCLUDING TABLES;
```

MANAGING CONSTRAINTS

Manage constraints on a table and between tables. Understand different types of constraints and how they relate to tables and indexes.

With Oracle databases, you can store rules about data in the database tables and enforce those rules from the database. Data integrity—the rules about database data—are enforced by database constraints. The integrity constraint options that you can use to impose data restrictions on the input of column values are as follows:

Constraint	Description
NOT NULL	Requires that every row have a value. The NULL value isn't allowed in this column.

continues

Constraint	*Description* *continued*
UNIQUE KEY	Requires that no two rows of a table have duplicate values in a specified column or set of columns.
PRIMARY KEY	Denote the column or set of columns that uniquely identify a table row. The column(s) must be unique and have values in each row. A table can have only one primary key.
FOREIGN KEY (referential)	The column or set of columns included in the definition of the referential integrity constraint. The foreign key column(s) can't be inserted or changed unless the primary key on the referenced table has these same key values.
CHECK	Requires that a specified condition be true or unknown for every row of the table. The condition of a CHECK constraint must be a Boolean expression evaluated by using the values in the row being inserted or updated. The condition also can't contain subqueries; sequences; the SYSDATE, UID, USER, or USERENV SQL functions; or the pseudocolumns LEVEL and ROWNUM.

NOTE

Disable Constraints for Performance
To improve performance, you can temporarily disable a constraint when working with large amounts of table data. Try disabling constraints when loading large amounts of data into a table by using SQL*Loader, when manipulating large numbers of table rows, or when exporting/importing individual database tables. When you are done with your data manipulation, you can re-enable table constraints.

An integrity constraint is a statement about the data in a database. After a table constraint is created, the definition of the constraint is stored in the data dictionary. However, the constraint may or may not be enforcing data values. An integrity constraint defined on a table can enable or disabled. When a constraint is enabled, the rule defined by the constraint is enforced on the data values in the columns that define the constraint. When a constraint is disabled, the rule defined by the constraint isn't enforced on the data values in the columns included in the constraint, but the definition of the constraint is retained in the data dictionary.

Two constraint types use indexes to enforce table data integrity: PRIMARY KEY and UNIQUE KEY. The server will create an index for the constraint after you enable the constraint. When you disable the constraint, its definition remains in the data dictionary but the index is dropped. You can define the index name and storage parameters for the `PRIMARY` and `UNIQUE KEY` constraints on constraint creation. This way, you can separate the index tablespace from the table tablespace, add an intuitive index name rather than a system-generated one, and control the storage of the index segment extents.

Creating a Constraint

You can add, drop, enable, or disable constraints at table creation or after the table is created and has rows. All this can be done to tables that exist on a database while it is in use.

To place a constraint on a table at table creation, use this command:

```
CREATE TABLE employee (
    employee_id     NUMBER(5) PRIMARY KEY
    employee_name   VARCHAR2(15)
)
TABLESPACE OCP_TRAINING;
```

To alter a table to create a primary key after the table is created, use this command:

```
ALTER TABLE employee
ADD CONSTRAINT EMPLOYEE_PK PRIMARY KEY (EMPLOYEE_ID);
```

You also can add a check constraint with an `ALTER TABLE` command:

```
ALTER TABLE employee
ADD CONSTRAINT EMP_STATUS CHECK ((status_flag in
➥('U','N','E','M','A','F'))) ;
```

You might temporarily disable a constraint to load data, and then enable it after the table is loaded:

```
ALTER TABLE employee DISABLE CONSTRAINT EMPLOYEE_PK;
```

After this command is completed, the constraint remains on the table and within the data dictionary, but the table data may or may not be enforced by this constraint. To re-enable the constraint, you alter the table again and change this command by replacing the word `DISABLE` with `ENABLE`.

Constraint Reports

To inquire about constraints on database tables, use the `DBA_CONSTRAINTS` and `DBA_CONS_COLUMNS` data dictionary views. Both views have these columns in common:

View Column	*Description*
CONSTRAINT_NAME	If you don't define a constraint name, the server will name it for you (something like SYS_12345).
TABLE_NAME	The table name where the constraint is placed.

The DBA_CONSTRAINTS data dictionary view contains table constraint definitions. It has the following columns:

View Column	*Description*
OWNER	The table owner where the constraint is placed.
CONSTRAINT_TYPE	P = primary, R = referential, C = check, U = unique. Null constraints are contained in the table definition and aren't listed in this view.
SEARCH_CONDITION	A SQL condition for a check constraint, empty for others.
R_OWNER	For foreign-key constraints, the owner of table referenced by this constraint.
R_CONSTRAINT_NAME	For foreign-key constraints, the constraint name referenced by this constraint.
DELETE_RULE	The delete rule for a referential constraint: RESTRICTED or CASCADE.
STATUS	Enforcement status of constraint: ENABLED or DISABLED.

The DBA_CONS_COLUMNS view contains information about accessible columns in constraint definitions. It uses the following columns:

View Column	*Description*
COLUMN_NAME	The column name where the constraint is placed
POSITION	The order of the column where the constraint is placed

To see the constraints on the EMPLOYEE table, you could query DBA_CONSTRAINTS as follows:

```
SELECT constraint_name, constraint_type,
➥search_condition, status
FROM DBA_CONSTRAINTS
WHERE table_name = 'EMPLOYEE';
```

Changing a Constraint

The constraint on a table can be enabled (enforced) or disabled with the ALTER TABLE command. You can't change the definition of a constraint in the data dictionary; instead, you must drop or re-create the constraint.

CONSTRAINTS AND EXCEPTIONS

One trick you might be asked about is the EXCEPTIONS clause on the ENABLE CONSTRAINT clause of the ALTER TABLE command. When you enable a constraint and the data doesn't meet the conditions of the constraint, you can find out the rows that fail to meet the constraint condition. In the ALTER TABLE command with the EXCEPTIONS clause, you direct that failed records be written to a table you specify. If you wanted to write the constraint-offending rows to a table named EXCEPTIONS, you might issue the following:

```
ALTER TABLE employee
➥DISABLE CONSTRAINT EMPLOYEE_PK
➥exceptions into EXCEPTIONS;
```

If enabling the constraint isn't successful, you can examine the contents of the EXCEPTIONS table to find the records that don't fit the constraint criteria.

Dropping a Constraint

When a constraint is dropped from the database, it no longer exists in the database. To drop a constraint, use ALTER TABLE as follows:

```
ALTER TABLE employee DROP PRIMARY KEY;
```

STEP BY STEP

6.5 **Create and Alter Constraints**

1. Create a table named EMPLOYEE in the OCP_
   TRAINING tablespaces. (You might need to drop this
   table if it already exists from a previous step-by-step exercise.) Include a check constraint to the column gender,
   confirming that all employees are M for male or F for
   female:

   ```
   CREATE TABLE employee (
       employee_id          NUMBER(8),
       employee_name        VARCHAR2(15),
       ssn                  VARCHAR2(9),
       gender               CHAR,
       hire_date            DATE,
       phone_number_id      NUMBER(8),
       salary               Number(10,2)
   )
   TABLESPACE OCP_TRAINING;
   ```

2. Add a phone number table to hold employee phone numbers with phone_number_id as the primary key:

   ```
   CREATE TABLE phone_number (
       phone_number_id      NUMBER(8) primary key,
       home_phone           VARCHAR2(9),
       work_phone           VARCHAR2(9)
   )
   TABLESPACE OCP_TRAINING;
   ```

3. Add a primary key to the table on employee_id by using
   an index named employee_id_pk. Place this index in the
   OCP_TRAINING_INDEX tablespace rather than in
   OCP_TRAINING.

   ```
   ALTER TABLE employee
   add constraint employee_pk Primary Key (employee_id)
   Using index employee_id_pk
   Tablespace OCP_TRAINING_INDEX
   (Storage initial 10k next 10k minextents 2);
   ```

4. Add a foreign-key constraint on table employee referencing the primary key on phone_number. Add a delete cascade rule.

   ```
   ALTER TABLE employee add constraint phone_number_fk
   foreign key (phone_number_id)
   references phone_number
   (phone_number_id) on delete cascade;
   ```

5. Add a unique key on column Social Security number by
using an index named `employee_ssn_uk`:

```
ALTER TABLE employee add unique constraint
➥employee_ssn_uk
using index Tablespace OCP_TRAINING_INDEX
(Storage initial 10k next 10k minextents 2);
```

6. Add a check constraint named `employee_gender_chk` on
the gender column of employee so that all values are
M or F:

```
ALTER TABLE employee add constraint
➥employee_gender_chk check (gender in ('M','F');
```

7. Use the data dictionary view to see important information
about these constraints:

```
SELECT owner, table_name, constraint_name,
➥constraint_type, status
FROM dba_constraints
WHERE table_name in ('EMPLOYEE','PHONE_NUMBER');
```

8. Disable the foreign-key constraint on employee:

```
ALTER TABLE employee disable constraint
➥phone_number_fk;
```

9. Drop the check constraint on the gender column of
`EMPLOYEE`:

```
ALTER TABLE employee drop constraint
➥employee_gender_chk;
```

10. Repeat step 7 to note the differences in output.

MANAGING ROLLBACK SEGMENTS

Understand the workings of a rollback segment. Manage rollbacks
on a database instances.

A very unique but critical Oracle segment type is the *rollback segment*. A rollback's job is to provide a place for a copy of data that's
now being changed. This role allows data concurrency in an Oracle
database and enables users manipulating data to undo their work.

As a quick review, here's how it works: A user changes data in the
EMPLOYEE table while connected to the Oracle database. He updates

a phone number, adds a new employee, and deletes another employee row. His session makes these changes to data stored in database block buffers stored in the server's memory. With each change made to the database table, a copy of that data is placed in a single rollback. While the user is changing this information, other connected users see a copy of the way the EMPLOYEE table was before he began his changes—they are looking at the rows of the EMPLOYEE table temporarily stored in the server-assigned rollback. When the user updating the employee table commits his changes, other users will see his changes committed to the EMPLOYEE table. If he decides to undo his changes (perform a rollback), the original data temporarily copied by the server to the rollback is copied back to the EMPLOYEE table. After this undo process is completed, other users will see the original EMPLOYEE table as before.

As a DBA managing the structure of the database, you are responsible for managing rollbacks for the database. All rollback work is handled by the server processes, and users have little control over rollback activity. Therefore, you must understand how to appropriately create, monitor, and manage rollbacks.

Rollback segments are much like table, cluster, and index segments in many ways. They hold data in extents and blocks. Many of the storage parameters apply and can be modified. Rollbacks are most similar to temporary segments because both segments

♦ Aren't owned by a schema

♦ Are managed completely by the server

♦ Typically reside in their own tablespace

Rollback segments have the following characteristics:

♦ Must have at least one rollback segment in the SYSTEM tablespace dedicated to the system user

♦ Must have another rollback segment created initially in the SYSTEM tablespace when creating a database and adding a second tablespace

♦ Must have a PCTINCREASE storage parameter of 0 (you can't modify it otherwise)

A rollback segment can be private or public. A private rollback is used by only this database instance. Public rollbacks can be used by this instance and other instances.

When setting up rollbacks for your database, you want to appropriately size and locate those rollbacks so that user transactions use the rollbacks optimally. For each rollback, you can control the number for segments, the size and number of the extents, and the optimal rollback size. Transactions that use your rollbacks must find a place for temporary storage.

Note these points as you prepare for your test:

◆ A database with smaller transactions performs better with many smaller rollback segments.

◆ Set your OPTIMAL parameter for the rollback to minimize the server workload.

◆ Set a uniform size for your rollbacks, with the exception of a possible large rollback or two for long running batch jobs.

◆ Create one tablespace specifically to hold all rollback segments, in addition to the two required in the SYSTEM tablespace.

You have some degree of control over the server's use of rollbacks. Setting the following database initialization parameters establishes rollback parameters at instance startup:

Parameter	*Description*
TRANSACTIONS	The number of concurrent transactions you expect for the instance
TRANSACTIONS_PER_ ROLLBACK_SEGMENT	The number of transactions you expect each rollback segment to have to handle
ROLLBACK_SEGMENTS	The names of the rollbacks brought online at instance startup

Creating a Rollback Segment

To make a rollback available for users, you create it with the CREATE ROLLBACK command and then bring it online.

The CREATE ROLLBACK command is very similar to the CREATE TABLE command, with these exceptions:

◆ You don't specify column names.

◆ You can't specify PCTINCREASE—the default value is zero.

◆ You can specify the OPTIMAL parameter to indicate the size (in bytes) you believe is best for this rollback.

◆ You want to have equal extent sizes to reduce fragmentation in your rollback. Set INITIAL and NEXT to the same number.

◆ You usually want to set MINEXTENTS to a value that, when multiplied by the extent size, will equal the OPTIMAL size.

◆ You want to specify the tablespace you have set up for rollbacks.

After you create the rollback, bring it online with the ALTER ROLLBACK SEGMENT command. To bring this rollback online at system startup, add this rollback to the list of rollbacks specified by the ROLLBACK_SEGMENT parameter in the database parameter file.

Rollback Reports

Several database views provide you with information about current rollback configuration and usage. In addition to DBA_SEGMENTS, you have DBA_ROLLBACK_SEGS, V$ROLLNAME, and V$ROLLSTAT.

◆ DBA_ROLLBACK_SEGS provides you with the structural details of your rollbacks:

View Column	Description
SEGMENT_NAME	Name of the rollback segment
OWNER	Owner of the rollback segment
TABLESPACE_NAME	Name of the tablespace containing the rollback segment
SEGMENT_ID	ID number of the rollback segment
FILE_ID	ID number of the file containing the segment head

View Column	Description *continued*
BLOCK_ID	ID number of the block containing the segment header
INITIAL_EXTENT	Initial extent size in bytes
NEXT_EXTENT	Secondary extent size in bytes
MIN_EXTENTS	Minimum number of extents
MAX_EXTENTS	Maximum number of extents
PCT_INCREASE	Percent increase for extent size
STATUS	Rollback segment status
INSTANCE_NUM	Rollback segment owning parallel server instance number

◆ The V$ROLLNAME dynamic view lists the names of all online rollback segments. This view can be accessed only when the database is open:

View Column	Description
USN	Rollback (undo) segment number
NAME	Rollback segment name

◆ The V$ROLLSTAT dynamic view contains rollback segment statistics useful to monitoring current rollback activity:

View Column	Description
USN	Rollback segment number
EXTENTS	Number of rollback extents
RSSIZE	Size in bytes of rollback segment
WRITES	Number of bytes written to rollback segment
XACTS	Number of active transactions
GETS	Number of header gets
WAITS	Number of header waits
OPTSIZE	Optimal size of rollback segment
HWMSIZE	High-water mark of rollback segment size
SHRINKS	Number of times the size of a rollback segment decreases

continues

View Column	*Description* *continued*
EXTENDS	Number of times the rollback segment size is extended
AVESHRINK	Average shrink size
AVEACTIVE	Current size of active extents, averaged over time
STATUS	Rollback segment status
CUREXT	Current extent
CURBLK	Current block

Changing a Rollback

After you create a rollback segment, you can modify it in several ways:

◆ Take it offline or online

◆ Change the storage parameters

◆ Alter the rollback format

◆ Shrink the size of the rollback

A rollback is available to users if it is online. A rollback can have several states:

◆ *Online* means that it is available for users.

◆ *Offline* means that it is unavailable for users, but is available for maintenance.

◆ *Pending offline* means that the rollback has been placed offline, but still has active transactions.

◆ *Partly available* contains data for an in-doubt or recovered distributed transaction, and yet-to-be recovered transactions.

◆ *Need recovery* means that data in the rollback must be applied to recover a database.

◆ *Invalid* means that the rollback has been dropped and another one hasn't been added in its place.

Change the storage parameters of a rollback as you would a data segment. By using the `ALTER ROLLBACK SEGMENT` command, supply the storage clause parameter you would like to change.

A rollback can have a limited or unlimited format. Change the format by using `ALTER ROLLBACK SEGMENT` to a rollback that has been taken offline.

You can also shrink a rollback to a size you specify with `ALTER ROLLBACK SEGMENT`. This capability enables you to do manually what the `OPTIMAL` setting provides for you via server background process. The rollback must be online to perform this function.

SPECIFY A ROLLBACK SEGMENT

When you must run a very large transaction, such as a batch job, you can choose to specify the rollback segment for this transaction. You can create a very large rollback segment for large batch jobs, bring it online as needed, and then take it offline when your large transaction is completed.

Perhaps weekly you must move all invoices in the invoice table that are more than one month old to the invoice audit table. You can bring a large rollback segment online, issue a commit statement, issue a `SET TRANSACTION USE ROLLBACK SEGMENT` statement, insert and delete rows, commit, and then take your large rollback segment offline again.

Dropping a Rollback

You may want to drop a rollback for two primary reasons: The segment has become fragmented over time, or you need to move the rollback segment to a different location. To drop a rollback, issue the `DROP ROLLBACK SEGMENT` command. This command will work only if the rollback is offline. If the state of the rollback is anything other than `OFFLINE`, take the necessary action to get it offline.

After you bring the rollback offline, its status will be `INVALID` in the `DBA_ROLLBACK_SEGS` view. The `INVALID` state will remain until another rollback segment is added to take its place on the list.

Be sure to remove this rollback from the database parameter file. Otherwise, at the next database startup, the startup will fail because the instance tries to bring online an invalid rollback.

STEP BY STEP

6.6 Create and Manage a Rollback Segment

1. Create a rollback segment named RBS_TRAIN1 in the OCP_TRAINING tablespace:

```
CREATE PUBLIC ROLLBACK SEGMENT RBS_TRAIN1
➡TABLESPACE OCP_TRAINING;
```

2. Create a second rollback segment named RBS_TRAIN2 in the OCP_TRAINING tablespace, but this time specify the storage parameters:

```
CREATE PUBLIC ROLLBACK SEGMENT RBS_TRAIN2
➡TABLESPACE OCP_TRAINING;
STORAGE (
        INITIAL 10K
        NEXT 10K
        OPTIMAL 50K
        MINEXTENTS 5
        MAXEXTENTS 20);
```

3. Select from the data dictionary to see the storage parameters for the new rollback segments:

```
SELECT segment_name, initial_extent, next_extent,
➡pct_increase, status
    FROM sys.DBA_ROLLBACK_SEGS
    WHERE TABLESPACE_NAME = 'OCP_TRAINING';

SELECT segment_name, tablespace_name, bytes,
➡blocks, extents
    FROM sys.dba_segments
    WHERE segment_type = 'ROLLBACK';

SELECT segment_name, bytes, blocks
    FROM sys.dba_extents
    WHERE segment_type = 'ROLLBACK';
```

4. Change the maximum extents on RBS_TRAIN1 to 20:

```
ALTER PUBLIC ROLLBACK SEGMENT RBS_TRAIN1
    STORAGE (MAXEXTENTS 20);
```

5. Bring both rollbacks offline:

```
ALTER PUBLIC ROLLBACK SEGMENT RBS_TRAIN1 Offline;
ALTER PUBLIC ROLLBACK SEGMENT RBS_TRAIN2 Offline;
```

6. Select again from `DBA_ROLLBACK_SEGS` and note the status difference and `MAX_EXTENTS` change.

7. Drop both rollback segments:

```
DROP PUBLIC ROLLBACK SEGMENT RBS_TRAIN1;
DROP PUBLIC ROLLBACK SEGMENT RBS_TRAIN2;
```

CHAPTER SUMMARY

This chapter discussed key database structure topics that you will encounter on the Oracle exam. These topics revolve around two primary goals: understanding database structures and functions, and understanding management of those structures.

◆ All information in a database is stored in tablespaces. Tablespaces are comprised of segments. Segments expand into extents and contain database blocks.

◆ Data in a database is stored in table segments. Faster access to that data is provided by index segments.

◆ Specially grouped data tables at a database block level are called *cluster segments*.

◆ Data integrity is governed by constraints. Some constraints use indexes to validate data.

◆ Data concurrency on a multiuser database is managed by the server in rollback segments.

KEY TERMS

Before you take the exam, make sure that you are comfortable with the definitions and concepts for each of the following key terms:

- tablespace
- segment
- extent
- block
- table
- index
- cluster
- constraint
- rollback

APPLY YOUR KNOWLEDGE

This section enables you to assess how well you understood the material in the chapter. Review questions test your knowledge of the tasks and concepts specified in the objectives. The exercises provide you with opportunities to engage in the sorts of tasks that comprise the skill sets the objects reflect.

Exercises

6.1 Create a Tablespace with Two Tables

Go through the process of creating a tablespace and putting two tables in that tablespace. This exercise will help you review for managing database structures and managing tables and indexes objectives.

Time Estimate: Less than 5 minutes

1. Logged on as system in SQL*Plus or SQL Worksheet, create a tablespace named OCP_TRAINING. Make the tablespace 1MB.

2. Create a second tablespace named OCP_TRAINING_IDX. Make this tablespace 500KB.

3. Alter the OCP_TRAINING_IDX tablespace and set the default initial extent to 25KB, the next extent to 25KB, and PCTINCREASE to 40%.

4. Change the default storage settings for the OCP_TRAINING tablespace. Set the initial extent size to 10KB, the subsequent extent size to be 20KB, and the percentage increase of extents to be 10%.

5. Alter the OCP_TRAINING_IDX tablespace and set the default initial extent to 50KB, the next extent to 50KB, and PCTINCREASE to 25%.

6. Create a table named EMPLOYEE with four columns: employee_id (number 9), employee_name (variable character length 20), department_id (number 4), and birth_date (date).

7. Create a second table named DEPARTMENT with these columns: department_id (number 4) and department_name (variable character length 10).

8. Use the database data dictionary view to confirm that the tables and columns are created correctly for these two tables.

9. Use the database data dictionary view to confirm that the tables created are placed in the correct tablespace, have the correct storage settings, and have columns created correctly.

6.2 Create and Maintain Constraints

This exercise walks you through the creation and maintenance of constraints and helps you review for the managing constraints objective. You can use the tables created in Exercise 6.1.

Time Estimate: About 5 minutes

1. The unique identification of rows in the DEPARTMENT table is the department_id. Create a primary key constraint on this column by using an index named department_pk. This index must reside in the OCP_TRAINING_IDX tablespace with an initial extent of 10KB, next extent of 10KB, percentage increase of 10%, and maximum extents of 100.

2. The business analyst informs you that no one in the company will be born before January 1, 1900. The database needs a check constraint on the EMPLOYEE table to prevent any really old people in the database. Add a check constraint with a server message Birth date out of range.

3. For every employee in the database, the department must be entered and must be validated. Add a foreign-key constraint to the EMPLOYEE table.

APPLY YOUR KNOWLEDGE

4. The application developers need to load some data into the EMPLOYEE and DEPARTMENT tables. Disable the constraints and confirm that they're disabled. Re-enable the constraints and confirm that they're re-enabled.

Review Questions

1. Given the following SQL statement on a database with a 2KB block size,

```
CREATE TABLE emp (
    empno     NUMBER(5) PRIMARY KEY,
    ename     VARCHAR2(15) NOT NULL,
    job       VARCHAR2(10),
    mgr       NUMBER(5),
    hiredate  DATE DEFAULT (sysdate),
    sal       NUMBER(7,2),
    comm      NUMBER(7,2),
    deptno    NUMBER(3) NOT NULL
              CONSTRAINT dept_fkey REFERENCES
➡dept)
    PCTFREE 10
    PCTUSED 40
    TABLESPACE users
    STORAGE ( INITIAL 50K
              NEXT 50K
              MAXEXTENTS 10
              PCTINCREASE 25 );
```

what will be the size of the second extent of this table?

A. 50KB

B. 75KB

C. 100KB

D. 125KB

2. The EMPLOYEE table is having more-than-expected to heavy update activity. To ensure that your data blocks have plenty of room for update activity,

A. Increase the NEXT extent setting with the ALTER TABLE command.

B. Decrease the PCTUSED setting with the ALTER TABLE command.

C. Increase the PCTFREE setting with the ALTER TABLE command.

D. Decrease the PCTINCREASE setting with the ALTER TABLE command.

3. Which segment type is used for implicit sorts and allocates space as needed?

A. Rollback

B. Index

C. Temporary

D. Cluster

4. What data dictionary view would you use to find out the check constraint definitions for a column on a table?

A. DBA_CONS_COLUMNS

B. DBA_CONSTRAINTS

C. DBA_CONS_ENABLES

D. DBA_TABLES

5. What system privilege is required to create a rollback segment?

A. ALTER ROLLBACK SEGMENT

B. CREATE ROLLBACK SEGMENT

C. MANAGE ROLLBACK SEGMENT

D. DBA

APPLY YOUR KNOWLEDGE

6. Suppose that you have a table that won't require many updates to existing rows. If you want to maximize space usage, what block-level parameter would you set, and how?

    A. Increase PCTFREE

    B. Decrease PCTFREE

    C. Increase PCTUSED

    D. Decrease PCTUSED

7. A user named John creates a table named JOHNS_DATA. He will create the table without specifying the tablespace in the storage clause. What tablespace will the table be created in?

    A. The default tablespace for user John

    B. The system tablespace

    C. The table won't be created.

    D. A temporary tablespace

8. To determine the allocated size of an index, you can query from which data dictionary view?

    A. DBA_INDEXES

    B. DBA_IND_COLUMNS

    C. DBA_SEGMENTS

    D. DBA_EXTENTS

9. The structure of an Oracle database is composed of which of the following (from largest to smallest)?

    A. Table, extent, segment, rowid

    B. Tablespace, segment, extent, block

    C. Tablespace, extent, segment, block

    D. Segment, block, extent, data file

10. When moving a data file, you issue the ALTER TABLESPACE command. Remember that you must do what? (Choose two.)

    A. Alter the tablespace and make it temporary first

    B. Shut down the database first

    C. Move the file at the operating system level, also

    D. Bring the tablespace offline

Answers to Review Questions

1. **A.** The second extent of the table is defined by the NEXT statement in the storage clause. Future extents will be 25% bigger because of the setting of PCTINCREASE.

2. **C.** Increasing PCTFREE allows for more room in the EMPLOYEE table for future updates.

3. **C.** When the database needs disk space for implicit sorts and summarization, it uses temporary segments in a temporary tablespace. All allocation and deallocation is handled automatically by the server processes based on default tablespace parameters.

4. **B.** The check constraints for a table are listed in the DBA_CONSTRAINTS data dictionary view.

5. **B.** To create a rollback segment, you need to have the CREATE ROLLBACK SEGMENT privilege. The DBA role contains this privilege, but DBA is a role, not a specific system privilege.

6. **B.** A lower value for PCTFREE means that a small percentage of each block remains for future row updates. Because you don't anticipate updates,

APPLY YOUR KNOWLEDGE

make PCTFREE lower so that more of the block can be filled with inserted rows.

7. **A**. Each user has a default tablespace. All objects created by this user or owned by this user are placed in the default tablespace for this user unless specified in the storage clause at creation time.

8. **D**. Because an index is a segment containing extents, you can select the sum of the bytes column of DBA_EXTENTS for an individual index.

9. **B**. Tablespaces contain segments that contain extents comprised of blocks.

10. **C** and **D**. When altering a data file to change its location, the tablespace must be offline. Also, when the tablespace is altered, the control file(s) is modified, indicating that the filename is different. You must ensure that the file is moved on the operating system.

Suggested Readings and Resources

We recommend the following resources for further study in the area of database structures:

1. *Oracle7™ Server Concepts, Release 7.3* (Part No. A32534-1)

   • Database Structures

2. *Oracle7™ Server Administrator's Guide, Release 7.3* (Part No. A32535-1)

   • Database Storage

3. *Oracle7™ Server Reference, Release 7.3* (Part No. A32589-1)

4. *Oracle7™ SQL Reference Manual, Release 7.3* (Part No. A32538-1)

This chapter helps you prepare for the exam by covering the following objectives:

Understand the different components of the SQL*Loader utility.

▶ SQL*Loader uses a DDL to control its data load function and can create a log and a bad file as output for its data load.

Know the difference between using the SQL*Loader conventional data load and using the direct load option.

▶ The direct load option can speed up the loads by sometimes as much as 50 percent, but you must understand the restrictions to know when this option is a good choice.

Understand how the Oracle Export utility works.

▶ This utility will allow you to back up objects, data, and even the entire database, including the security privileges. The database must be open for this utility to function. Export creates a binary file that is used by Import.

Recognize the different Export parameters.

▶ You must understand how to use the vast array of Export options. Some options don't work together, and others can be used to tune the Export process.

Understand how the Oracle Import utility works.

▶ This utility uses the binary output file from the Export utility. It can rebuild objects and entire databases. Import can move data from one platform to another.

Recognize the different Import parameters.

▶ Import's parameters are important because they affect the performance and the success of the run. They can be entered interactively or kept in a parameter file.

CHAPTER 7

Utilities

STUDY STRATEGIES

▶ The SQL*Loader utility is a powerful tool for loading data into an Oracle database. What makes it so powerful is its ability to load data from a flat file into the Oracle database by using parameters kept in the control file. The data in the file can be different formats, and SQL*Loader can "map" the data to the format stored in the database.

SQL*Loader has two modes of operation, direct and conventional. The direct mode is designed to load data in the fastest possible manner while maintaining the ability to do normal data recovery. The Unrecoverable option runs even faster because no redo log entries are made, but you cannot restore the data from the archived redo logs. It's important to understand the restrictions on the direct mode.

The Export utility will allow you to back up and place both the data and structure in a binary file that can be read only by the Import utility. Export has three levels: database, owner, and table. How the data is exported affects the parameters used when the data is imported. Using the parameter file also lets you repeat exports without rekeying the Export keywords. The parameters are important to know because they can affect how fast Export will run. Some of the parameters are the same for both the Export and Import utility, but some are unique to each utility.

Export has a direct option that will bypass the evaluation buffer; the data is already in the Export format, so no data conversion occurs.

The Import utility loads the data into an Oracle database, but the parameters determine the speed and success of the import. The parameters critical to the success of the Import are buffer and commit.

INTRODUCTION

Oracle provides three utilities to help you move and manipulate data: SQL*Loader, Export, and Import. SQL*Loader reads from an external file and loads data into an existing table while the Oracle database is open by mapping the data into Oracle format. The Export utility unloads data to a file that can be read only by the Import utility. You can use Export to reorganize a database and move data from one Oracle database to another. It is not platform specific. Export is the only way to back up the objects of the database so that they can be restored. A normal database recovery occurs at the database, tablespace, or datafile level. The Import utility reads the file made by Export and loads the data into the database. The Import utility will only load data, but it can create database objects and then load the data. System-level data can even re-create the database.

WHAT YOU CAN DO WITH SQL*LOADER

With SQL*Loader, you can specify multiple datafiles in the control file and load records of different formats (such as fixed, delimited, and variable length). You also can use SQL functions to modify data before it's inserted. You can load multiple tables during the same SQL*Loader run. You can use multiple physical records to create one or more than one logical record. You can put conditions on the incoming data to select which records will be inserted. (This is called filtering the data.)

Figure 7.1 shows all the components of the SQL*Loader process.

SQL*Loader's Files

SQL*Loader is controlled by its own data definition language (DDL), which is kept in the control file. The control file will control the SQL*Loader run, telling it where to find the input files and where to place the log file and the bad file. Data mapping can also occur in the control file.

FIGURE 7.1
The components of SQL*Loader.

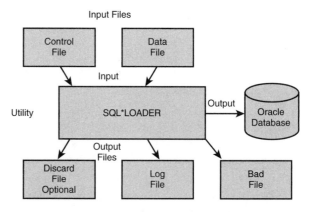

SQL*Loader Control File

The control file contains all the options for the SQL*Loader run and can even include data. The options are specified in the control file using a DDL.

These options are reserved words. They include the name and format of the datafiles, the character set, and the data types contained in the datafiles. The following list contains the reserved words in SQL*Loader:

AND	APPEND	BADFILE
BDDN	BEGINDATA	BLANKS
BLOCKSIZE	BY	CHAR
CONCATENATE	CONSTANT	CONTINUE_LOAD
CONTINUEIF	COUNT	DATA
DATE	DECIMAL	DEFAULTIF
DISCARDDN	DISCARDFILE	DISCARDMAX
DISCARDS	DOUBLE	ENCLOSED
EXTERNAL	FIELDS	FIXED
FLOAT	FORMAT	GENERATED
GRAPHIC	INDDN	INDEXES
INFILE	INSERT	INTEGER
INTO	LAST	LOAD
LOG	MAX	NEXT
NO	NULLCOLS	NULLIF
OPTIONALLY	OPTIONS	PARALLEL
PART	PIECED	POSITION
PRESERVE	RAW	RECLEN
RECNUM	RECORD	REPLACE
RESUME	SEQUENCE	SKIP
SMALLINT	SORTDEVT	SORTED
SORTNUM	SQL/DS	STREAM
SYSDATE	TABLE	TERMINATED
THIS	TRAILING	UNLOAD
VARCHAR	VARGRAPHIC	VARIABLE
WHEN	WHITESPACE	WORKDDM
YES	ZONED	

The control file contains required and optional keywords. The control file isn't case sensitive, so you can use both uppercase and lowercase for reserved words; however, the standard convention is to present reserved words in uppercase.

The control file will specify the load type:

- INSERT requires the table to not have any data; if data is found, an error is returned.

- APPEND adds rows to a table that already has data.

- REPLACE removes the table's current data and then loads new data. This option uses the SQL delete command, which lets you maintain referential integrity constraints, but the rollback segments for the database must be large enough to hold all the undo entries for the table.

- TRUNCATE removes the data in the table and then loads the new data. This option requires you to disable the table's referential integrity constraints.

NOTE **Comments in the Control File** To place comments in a control file, precede them with two hyphens. You can't put comments in the data section if the data is included in the control file. It's always a good policy to include comments in the control file.

SQL*Loader Datafile

Every line in the datafile is considered a physical record by SQL*Loader. It's possible for tables with many columns to have many physical records for one row of a table. That row is called a *logical record.*

The format for the data records can be fixed or variable:

- Fixed format requires that a column of data be the same size for all loaded records and that the columns be delimited by position and length.

- The variable format for a record requires the column to be delimited in two ways: terminated and enclosed. Terminating requires a termination delimiter, a character such as a comma or period (as in Monday,Tuesday). An enclosed delimited field has a special character in front of the field and after the field (as in "Monday").

SQL*Loader Bad File

The bad file contains records that weren't loaded into the target table. These records could have been rejected by SQL*Loader due to an invalid format. They also could have been rejected by the Oracle database if they violated an integrity constraint or had an invalid data type for the target table.

SQL*Loader Log File

The log file must be available during the entire run of the SQL*Loader. It will contain detailed information about the run and any errors found while parsing the control file.

SQL*Loader Discard File

The discard file is created only if specified by the control file. It will contain records that didn't meet the conditional selection DDL specified in the control file.

Mapping Data

A SQL INSERT statement is created from the field specification of the control file. SQL*Loader then stores the data in the database by finding the field in the datafile, mapping the data, and passing it on to the Oracle server. The database will accept or reject the record.

Two Methods of Loading Data

During a conventional load of the database, the SQL*Loader acts as a normal background process, using all the Oracle database resources. The direct mode works faster than the conventional load but has certain restrictions that might preclude it as an alternative for normal day-to-day processing.

Conventional Load

The conventional load competes with other Oracle processes and allows certain other transactions against the table being loaded. This method uses an INSERT statement with a bind-array buffer for processing.

You should use a conventional load in the following situations:

◆ When loading a table that needs to be available for other processing. If the table is indexed, all processing is still valid while the table is being loaded. A table without an index can have inserts and updates performed only while it's being loaded.

◆ When a load is done over SQL*Net.

◆ When a load is done on a clustered table.

◆ Whenever a small number of rows is inserted.

◆ When SQL functions must be used on data fields. The rows parameter specified in the control file will control how many rows are added before a commit can occur. The redo logs record SQL*Loader activity. The INSERT statement uses a bind array that stores multiple rows and issues a commit after all the rows in the array are loaded.

◆ When you want to use partially filled data blocks.

The table must exist before SQL*Loader can load data into it.

The table may be clustered or indexed; it can even be a view. The user ID specified in the control file must have the insert privilege for the table being loaded. If you use the replace option, the user ID specified in the control file must have the delete privilege as well as the insert privilege.

Direct Load

The direct load option is highly optimized and can be significantly faster than the conventional method. It's faster because the data is loaded not by an INSERT statement, but by formatting the data in Oracle data block configuration and then loading it directly into the database file. This bypasses the SGA buffer cache, although a few calls are made to the Oracle database at the beginning and end of the direct load.

You can make the direct load even faster by using the unrecoverable option. This option will not log redo entries into the redo log. The only problem with this option is that the transaction is not recorded in the redo logs, so you have to repeat the load process if the database must be recovered.

Referential integrity isn't checked during the data load, but after the load is complete. This means that the referential integrity constraints are disabled during the load and re-enabled after the load.

It's possible to load invalid data to your database. Default data values specified at the column level aren't used during a direct load.

You should use a direct load in the following situations:

◆ When a table can be locked for the duration of a load.

◆ When the table being loaded isn't a cluster table.

◆ When the table to be loaded doesn't have any active transactions right before the load occurs.

The direct load option uses asynchronous I/O, when it's available.

The table must exist before SQL*Loader can use a direct load.

The user ID specified in the control file must have the insert privilege for the table being loaded. If you use the replace option, the user ID specified in the control file must have the delete privilege as well as insert privilege. If the direct path load is unsuccessful, the indexes assume a "direct load state," rendering them unusable. To change an index from direct load state to a usable state, you have to drop and re-create the index.

The logical backup (Oracle's Export utility) will create a file in an Oracle binary format that has the information to re-create all database entities and database data. The Import utility, which can read the binary file created by the Export utility, is what you use to re-create the objects and data. The information can be stored on a disk device or tape media. The logical backup will take longer and may require additional work in preparing the database for recovery. There are three Export modes:

◆ User mode, which will back up all objects owned by a user

◆ Table mode, which will back up specific tables owned by a user

◆ Full database, which will back up all objects of the database

USING ORACLE'S EXPORT UTILITY

The Export utility has many options controlled by keywords. You can put these keywords in a parameter file to perform custom backups of the database or enter them interactively at an operating system command prompt. Keywords aren't case sensitive. The syntax is *KEYWORD=value.*

You can perform an export at three levels of data collection:

◆ **An incremental export** will back up only data that has changed since the last incremental export.

◆ **A cumulative export** will export only data from tables that have changed since the last cumulative export. This export type is used to condense incremental exports.

◆ **A complete export** will export all the data contained in a database. You should use the complete export only on a limited basis due to the volume of data collected.

The Export utility is very flexible. A good schedule for using Export might include performing a full export on the first day of the month (exporting all the data takes the longest amount of time). Every day after, perform an incremental export, which should take the shortest amount of time. On the weekend, run a cumulative export. This schedule follows:

Day One: Full export

Day Two: Incremental export

Day Three: Incremental export

Day Four: Incremental export

Day Five: Incremental export

Day Six: Cumulative export

If a recovery situation occurs on Day Three before the incremental export, you use the full export file created on Day One and the incremental export file of Day Two for recovery. If a recovery situation occurs on Day Seven, you use the full export file from Day One and the cumulative export file from Day Six for recovery.

Oracle's Export and Import Keywords

Oracle's Export utility creates as output a binary file that is read as input by the Import utility. The two utilities share many of the same keywords, noted in Table 7.1. Some keywords are unique to each utility.

TABLE 7.1

EXPORT AND IMPORT KEYWORDS

Keyword	Export	Import
USERID	×	×
BUFFER	×	×
FILE	×	×
GRANTS	×	×
INDEXES	×	×
ROWS	×	×
FULL	×	×
TABLES	×	×
RECORDLENGTH	×	×
INCTYPE	×	×
LOG	×	×
OWNER	×	
RECORD	×	
HELP	×	×
FEEDBACK	×	
CONSTRAINTS	×	
COMPRESS	×	
CONSISTENT	×	
STATISTICS	×	
PARFILE	×	
DIRECT	×	

The following keywords are available when you use Oracle's Export utility:

- ◆ USERID specifies the name and password of the user who will do the export:

```
USERID=smith/password
```

Valid values are any Oracle user IDs that have the create session privilege. The user must have the role `EXP_FULL_DATABASE` to export objects other than their own or all the system privileges contained in that role.

◆ `BUFFER` specifies the size in bytes of the data buffer for the export run:

```
BUFFER=20000000
```

The larger the buffer, the faster the export, all other things remaining equal. Ten percent of the total operating system's memory is an optimal setting.

◆ `FILE` specifies the name of the output file and can contain a directory path to tell Export where to place the file:

```
FILE=/usr/data/prd1_user_one.dmp
```

If a path isn't specified, the file is placed in the current directory where the export was executed. The default filename is expdat.dmp.

If the output file is placed on tape, the device name is specified:

```
FILE=/dev/rmt/0m
```

◆ `COMPRESS` takes segments in multiple extents and compresses them into one initial extent (if set to `Y`) or keeps them in multiple extents (if set to `N`). After you use this option, the initial segment might have problems if the tablespace doesn't have enough contiguous blocks. This could happen if the tablespace is heavily fragmented.

◆ `GRANTS` exports the grants on exported entities if `Y` is specified:

```
GRANTS=Y
```

◆ `INDEXES` controls whether indexes are exported:

```
INDEXES=n
```

◆ `ROWS` controls whether any data for the segments is exported:

```
ROWS=y
```

◆ `CONSISTENT`, when set to `Y`, ensures that the export data is consistent at a single point in time. Export does this by using the

SET TRANSACTION READ ONLY command. This method requires large rollback segments and slows down the export process because it has to scan the rollback segment for uncommitted transactions for every table exported. The CONSTRAINTS keyword, when set to Y, also exports the constraints:

CONSTRAINTS=y

◆ When DIRECT is set to Y, the export of the data speeds up considerably:

DIRECT=y

This performance increase occurs by minimizing the steps the data has to take from the Oracle database to the Oracle export file. DIRECT takes the data from the database to the buffer cache and then to the dump file. The data is already in export format, which eliminates a data conversion step.

◆ When set to Y, FULL exports the entire database, with the exception of the SYS user objects. FULL set to N results in a user-level export if the keyword table isn't used. The syntax follows:

FULL=y

◆ FEEDBACK, when specified with a number other than zero, displays a dot whenever the number of rows exported is equal to that number. This feedback is for the entire export run, not just the table level. The syntax for this option follows:

FEEDBACK=100

◆ LOG specifies the name of the file that contains all the messages pertaining to the export:

log=/usr/log/prd1_Export.log

It can contain a directory path to tell Export where to place the log file. If a path isn't specified, the file is placed in the current directory.

◆ OWNER, when specified, creates a user-level export for all the user IDs specified:

OWNER=smith,jones
OWNER=smith

◆ RECORD, when set to Y, records whether the export was incremental or cumulative:

RECORD=y

Parameters That Don't Work Together   Certain parameters are incompatible with each other. The TABLES and OWNER parameters shouldn't be used together.

NOTE

◆ HELP, when set to Y, shows all valid keywords for the export:

```
HELP=y
```

◆ PARFILE is the name of the parameter file. This keyword can contain a directory path to tell Export where to find the file. If a path isn't specified, Export expects to find the file in the directory where the export was executed. The syntax follows:

```
PARFILE=/usr/parfile/prd1_parfile
```

◆ STATISTICS has three valid values: estimate, compute, and none. These database-optimizer statistics are created when the data is imported. The syntax follows:

```
STATISTICS=estimate¦compute¦none
```

◆ TABLES, when specified, creates a table-level export for all tables specified:

```
TABLES=customer_tbl,payroll_tbl
TABLES=customer_tbl
```

◆ INCTYPE can be one of three values: complete, cumulative, and incremental.

> **NOTE**
>
> **Sequence-Number Things to Watch for When Exporting Sequences**
> When a sequence is exported, any sequences created using the cache option are lost if the sequence is re-created by using the Import utility.

STEP BY STEP

7.1 Doing an Interactive Export

1. Invoke the Export utility by issuing the exp command:

```
SERVER_PROMT:> exp
```

2. The current release of the Oracle database is indicated, and you are prompted for a user name:

```
Export: Release 7.3.3.0.0 - Production on Sat Jun 27
➥ 13:30:08 1998

Copyright (c) Oracle Corporation 1979, 1994.  All
➥ rights reserved.
Username: system
Password:
```

3. The next direction prompts you for the size of the buffer. It is important to keep in mind the memory situation on the server. If the server is not fully utilizing its memory, you can dramatically increase the speed of the Export by increasing the size of this parameter. The default is set very low:

```
Connected to: Oracle7 Server Release 7.3.3.0.0 -
Production Release
With the distributed option
PL/SQL Release 2.3.3.0.0 - Production
Enter array fetch buffer size: 4096 >
```

4. Specify the filename. If you do not indicate a full path, the export information is placed in the current directory where the user gave the exp command. If you want the export file to go to a tape device, provide the device name here, such as /dev/rmt/0m:

```
Export file: expdat.dmp > test
```

5. The next option prompts you for the type of export—either database, users, or table:

```
(1)E(ntire database), (2)U(sers), or (3)T(ables):
➥(2)U > E
```

6. Next, you are prompted to back up the security of the tables being exported:

```
Export grants (yes/no): yes >
```

7. For a backup, you must indicate whether to back up only the structure of the object or the data and the structure:

```
Export table data (yes/no): yes >
```

8. The next option compresses all objects with multiple extents into one extent, thereby increasing the size of the initial extent to the sum of all extents allocated:

```
Compress extents (yes/no): yes >
```

9. The next information shows the progress of the database export; the last line declares whether the export completed successfully.

STEP BY STEP

7.2 Performing an Export by Using Parfiles

1. Invoke the Export utility by issuing the exp command with the keyword parfile and then specifying a parameter file:

```
SERVER_PROMT:> exp parfile=parfile_for_export
```

2. If the parfile doesn't contain a user ID and password, the user ID will be prompted in an interactive manner:

```
contents of the parfile_for_export
userid=system/manager
full=y
file=/usr/local/full_export.dmp
log=/usr/local/full_export.log

buffer=10000000
```

RECOVERING FROM A LOGICAL BACKUP WITH ORACLE'S IMPORT UTILITY

Oracle's Import utility uses the logical backup file created by the Export utility to re-create database structures and then insert rows of data into the structures. (If the database structures already exist, only the data is added.) The Import utility uses the output of the Export utility as its input file (see Figure 7.2).

The Import utility can use any level of export to re-create objects and data. If the export occurred at the database level, the import can be used to create objects at the database, user, or table level. A database-level import will import all entities except those owned by the SYS user. This means that you can re-create a database with this option and export all entities at the database level.

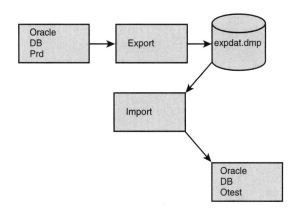

FIGURE 7.2
How Export creates a file that's used by Import.

Keywords of special interest are FROMUSER, TOUSER, DESTROY, INDEXFILE, INCTYPE, and IGNORE.

Oracle's Import Keywords

The Import utility, like the Export utility, uses keywords to control its behavior:

◆ USERID specifies the name and password of the user who will do the import. Valid values are any Oracle user IDs that have the create session privilege. The syntax follows:

USERID=smith/*password*

◆ BUFFER specifies the size in bytes of the data buffer for the import:

BUFFER=20000000

The larger the buffer, the faster the import, all other things remaining equal. Ten percent of the total operating system's memory is an optimal setting.

◆ FILE specifies the name of the input file and can contain a directory path to tell Import where to find the file. If a path isn't specified, Import expects the file to be in the directory where the import was executed:

FILE=/usr/data/prd1_user_one.dmp

If the input file is on tape, the device name is specified:

FILE=/dev/rmt/0m

◆ GRANTS imports the grants on imported entities if Y is specified:

GRANTS=Y

◆ INDEXES controls whether indexes are imported:

INDEXES=n

◆ ROWS controls whether any data for the segments is imported:

ROWS=y

◆ FULL specifies whether to import the entire database (with the exception of the SYS user objects):

FULL=y

If you specify N, the import will be a user-level import if the keyword table isn't used.

◆ FEEDBACK, when specified with a number other than zero, displays a dot whenever the number of rows imported equals that number. This feedback is for the entire import, not just the table level. The syntax follows:

```
FEEDBACK=100
```

◆ LOG specifies the name of the file that will contain all the messages pertaining to the import. You can provide a directory path to tell Import where to place the log file. If you do not indicate a path, the file is placed in the current directory:

```
LOG=/usr/log/prd1_Import.log
```

◆ HELP, when set to Y, shows all the valid keywords for Import:

```
HELP=y
```

◆ PARFILE is the name of the file that contains all the keywords for an import. It can contain a directory path to tell Import where to find the file:

```
PARFILE=/usr/parfile/prd1_parfile
```

If a path isn't specified, Import expects the file to be in the directory where the export was executed.

◆ TABLES, when specified, performs a table-level import for all tables specified:

```
TABLES=(customer_tbl,payroll_tbl)
TABLES=customer_tbl
```

◆ SHOW, when specified, doesn't execute an import but does show the contents of the export file:

```
SHOW=y
```

◆ IGNORE, when set to Y, ignores creation errors on objects that already exist before the import and loads the objects with data:

```
IGNORE=y
```

If IGNORE is set to N, Import creates an object. If the object already exists, an error occurs, and Import skips the object without importing any data to it.

◆ FROMUSER, when specified, causes Import to create and load the data to the user ID specified. If the user ID doesn't exist in the database, the objects are created and loaded to the user ID specified by the USERID keyword. The syntax follows:

```
imp USERID=smith/password FROMUSER=jones FILE=expdat.dmp
```

If jones doesn't exist on the database, all the objects and data are created under the smith schema. If jones does exist, the objects and data are created under the jones schema.

- ◆ TOUSER, when specified, causes an object exported by one user to be imported to another user. Whoever uses this option must have a special security role, IMP_FULL_DATABASE. The syntax follows:

```
imp USERID=smith/password FROMUSER=jones TOUSER=barnes
➥ FILE=expdat.dmp
```

The Import utility checks user smith's security privileges. If they're valid, jones's objects and data are created in user barnes's schema.

- ◆ INDEXFILE, when specified, creates a file with index-creation commands generated by the Import utility.

- ◆ DESTROY, when set to Y, creates the tablespace with reuse specified for the datafile. This process re-creates all the tablespaces and removes all the segments that reside in them.

- ◆ INCTYPE is used with incremental export files. Valid values are SYSTEM, which imports the most recent version of system objects but no other objects or data. The other value, RESTORE, imports the user objects and data that has changed since the last incremental export.

Real-World Experiences

When importing large objects with a large amount of rows, you should set the COMMIT option to Y. Even if you set the import to commit after every insert array, you might still experience problems if the buffer parameter is set high because that determines the array size. When importing at the database level, it's better to use COMMIT with a recently created database that requires all the entities to be created.

Managing Storage Parameters When Using Import

You can perform a user-level import to migrate a user's objects from one database to another. If you want different storage parameters on the segments, you should create them before running the import.

How Triggers Are Affected by Import

An import is actually performing an insert on a table, so any triggers that fire on insert will execute when the import occurs. In some cases, you should disable those triggers.

Managing Integrity Constraints with Import

Referential integrity constraints can cause problems on a user-level import because children tables may be loaded before parent tables. You might want to drop those constraints before importing if you set up the export to capture constraints.

Handling Sequences with Import

Sequences can pose a special problem when you import them into a database where they already existed. Sequences are closely tied to the data on the database, and the Export utility performs a backup of the data and its sequences at a certain point in time. When Import finishes the load of the data, if it can't re-create the sequences that correspond to the data, they may become out of sync.

In Figure 7.3, a user-level Export was done on Monday for the Oracle database PRD1DB. On Tuesday, the DBA was asked to restore cust_tbl, which uses a sequence to generate a number for its primary key, which means that the sequence also has to be restored. To restore a sequence, you drop it from the database so it is re-created by Import.

One advantage of a table-level import is that you can specify which tables will be imported first. This feature lets you first load the parent tables and then the child tables for all tables that have referential integrity.

You still may want to disable triggers before running the Import utility. To achieve the fastest load times, you should build indexes after the import is finished. Disable or drop the indexes and use the keyword and value INDEXES=n. You can create the indexes' DDL by using the keyword INDEXFILE and then using the file generated to create all the indexes.

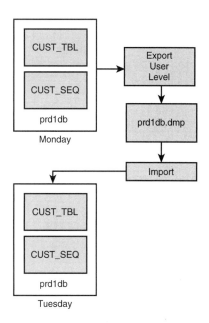

FIGURE 7.3
Potential problems with sequences.

CHAPTER SUMMARY

KEY TERMS

Before you take the exam, make sure that you are comfortable with the definitions and concepts of each of the following key terms:

- Parameter file (parfile)

- Import keywords: FROMUSER, TOUSER, DESTROY, INDEXFILE, INCTYPE, IGNORE

- Export keywords: OWNER, GRANTS, INDEXES, ROWS, FULL

- SQL*Loader keywords: APPEND, INSERT, REPLACE, TRUNCATE, DIRECT

SQL*Loader lets you load data from a flat file into an Oracle database. The data can be formatted, or mapped, to provide compatibility for data from other DBMSs. The control file contains a DDL that controls SQL*Loader. The tool includes a direct mode that optimizes the load process but has some restrictions. For the fastest load, you can use unrecoverable option that does not generate any redo log entries.

The Export utility lets you back up the entire database, an entire schema, or selected tables. It generates a binary file that can be read only by the Import utility. It supports incremental runs that work effectively even on large databases. This tool has a direct mode that will optimize processing and provide the fastest export possible.

The Import utility allows you to restore data that was backed up by using the Export utility. You can use the Import utility at a more restrictive level than what was used for the Export utility that generated the file. For example, you can use an export file that contains the entire database to import just one table. You must consider referential integrity when importing data at anything but the table level. Because you can specify at the table level which table is to be loaded first, you might load the parent tables before the children tables. Another option is to disable referential integrity and re-enable it after the import. To keep synchronized sequences during the process, you must drop the sequence and allow Import to re-create it from the export file.

APPLY YOUR KNOWLEDGE

This section allows you to assess how well you understand the material in the chapter. Review questions test your knowledge of the tasks and concepts specified in the objectives. The exercises provide you with opportunities to engage in the sorts of tasks that compose the skill sets the objectives reflect.

Exercises

7.1   Use SQL*Loader to Load Variable-Length Data

Create a control file to load a table with two columns. The table belongs to the schema scott; the table name is states and has the following definition:

```
(state_id number(2) NOT NULL,
state      VARCHAR2(25))
```

Also, the data should be in the control file. Columns should be terminated by commas. This exercise will show you how to load data by using SQL*Loader.

Time Estimate: Less than 15 minutes

1. Use any text editor to create the following control file, and save the file as test.ctl:

```
LOAD DATA
INFILE *
INTO TABLE states
FIELDS TERMINATED BY ',' OPTIONALLY ENCLOSED
BY '"'
(state_id,state)
BEGINDATA
      21,"FLORIDA"
      22,"CALIFORNIA"
      36,"ALASKA"
      41,"TEXAS"
      50,"ALABAMA"
      31,"NEVADA"
```

2. Invoke SQL*Loader from the command prompt with the following command to load the data:

```
C:>sqlldr userid=scott/tiger
➡ control=test.ctl log=test.log
```

7.2   Using Export with Different Parameters

Export the entire database for a given Oracle database, specifying a file called *sid*_database (where *sid* is the system identifier of the Oracle database). Modify the buffer to 1MB and export only the structure, not the data. This exercise will help you accomplish the objective of understanding the Export utility.

Time Estimate: Less than 10 minutes

1. Invoke the Export utility by issuing the exp command:

```
SERVER_PROMT:> exp
```

2. Enter a user name:

```
Username: system
Password:
```

3. Specify the buffer to be 1000000:

```
Connected to: Oracle7 Server Release
➡ 7.3.3.0.0 - Production Release
With the distributed option
PL/SQL Release 2.3.3.0.0 - Production
Enter array fetch buffer size: 4096 >
➡ 1000000
```

4. Specify the filename:

```
Export file: expdat.dmp > tst1_database
```

5. Indicate E for the entire database:

```
(1)E(ntire database), (2)U(sers), or
➡ (3)T(ables): (2)U > E
```

6. Accept the default yes:

```
Export grants (yes/no): yes >
```

7. By specifying no here, you export only the structure:

```
Export table data (yes/no): yes > no
```

8. Set the next option to no because you're exporting only the structure:

```
Compress extents (yes/no): yes > no
```

APPLY YOUR KNOWLEDGE

You should see the following message if the export is successful:

```
Export completed successfully.
```

7.3   Perform a Database Import

Import using a parameter file, a single table from an export file, using the export file that was created in Exercise 7.2. This will help you accomplish the objective of understanding the Import utility.

Time Estimate: 10 minutes

1. Use a text editor to create a file with the following keywords and call the file imp_parfile:

```
userid=system/manager
file=sid_database
log=sid_database_imp
buffer=500000
tables=(table_name)
```

2. Execute the import at the server prompt:

```
imp parfile=imp_parfile
```

The message should indicate that the import was successful without warnings.

Review Questions

1. When using SQL*Loader in direct mode, what does the unrecoverable option mean in terms of database recovery?

   A. Rollback segments won't be used.

   B. Temporary segments won't be used.

   C. Redo log entries won't be used, and if the database is recovered, you will have to repeat the SQL*Loader run.

   D. Recovery won't be affected.

2. In what file is the DDL for SQL*Loader kept?

   A. Control file

   B. Bad file

   C. Log file

   D. Error file

3. What are the three levels at which a database can be exported?

   A. User, index, table

   B. Database, owner, table

   C. Owner, table, column

   D. Database, user, index

4. What one parameter can speed up a full conventional database export running on a server with extra memory available?

   A. BUFFER

   B. LOGFILE

   C. UNRECOVERABLE

   D. CONSISTENT

5. What two import parameters will control how much of a rollback segment is used?

   A. UNRECOVERABLE and COMMIT

   B. FILE and BUFFER

   C. COMMIT and BUFFER

   D. LOGFILE and UNRECOVERABLE

6. What import parameter is used to load data into existing objects?

   A. FROMUSER

   B. USERID

C. COMMIT

D. IGNORE

7. How do you re-create a sequence by using the Import utility?

   A. Import cannot re-create a sequence.

   B. Drop the sequence before importing.

   C. Drop the sequence after importing.

   D. Nothing has to be done.

8. Select a method to restore tables that have referential integrity defined for them by using Import.

   A. Load the parent table first and then load the child table.

   B. Disable the foreign key between the parent and the child table before importing.

   C. Nothing has to be done; Import can handle it without intervention.

   D. A and B.

Answers to Review Questions

1. **C.** The unrecoverable option will allow SQL*Loader to run against the database without generating any redo log entries. If the database must be recovered and archived redo logs applied, you would have to repeat the SQL*Loader run.

2. **A.** The control file contains the DDL for SQL*Loader.

3. **B.** The database level will export the entire database, including all entities defined to the database. The user-level export will export all objects and data owned by the user. The table-level export will export all entities related to the table.

4. **A.** Increasing the buffer size can speed up the export by increasing the array size for the fetch of the data.

5. **C.** Commit will cause Import to commit when the buffer is full. If you do not specify the keyword COMMIT, commits will occur on a table-by-table basis. If the buffer size is larger than the existing rollback segment, you'll still run out of rollback segment space.

6. **D.** Ignore=y won't generate an error message if the object already exists in the database.

7. **B.** If the sequence already exists on the target database, drop it first and then run the import.

8. **D.** There are two ways to do this. One is by disabling the integrity constraints and importing the data. The other is to use the table parameter to specify that the parent table is loaded before the child table.

BACKUP AND RECOVERY

This chapter helps you prepare for the exam by covering the following objectives:

Plan to back up your DBMS.

▶ As a certified professional, you need to understand what parts of the Oracle architecture you need to back up. These components are referred to as the backup file set, which consists of the external files that are backed up.

Choose what type of backup is best for the database application.

▶ The three different backup types are cold (offline), hot (online), and logical. Each backup type backs up the data in different ways with different requirements from the DBMS. As a certified professional, you need to know when to implement a particular backup scheme.

CHAPTER 8

Backing Up a Database

STUDY STRATEGIES

▶ To prepare for the exam, you should begin by understanding the external files and their different characteristics. You might want to review Chapter 5, "Oracle Database Architecture," to fully understand the datafile, redo log, archive redo logs, and the control file. Pay special attention to the control file and the redo logs. You can back up the control file in two different ways.

An offline backup is the more straightforward of the backup schemes. You need to be aware of how the database is shut down and make sure that all external files are backed up. This is done best with SQL reading dynamic views from the database; you should be familiar with those views.

An online backup requires special attention. You should be familiar with the checkpoint process because it plays a key role in how you use an online backup for recovery.

INTRODUCTION

You must be able to restore or reconstruct your Oracle database in case of a minor or catastrophic failure. To restore a database, you must have a good backup of its external files. This chapter will show you how you use physical backups to prepare for the time when a database needs recovering. The chapter discusses principles of good backup techniques, as well as implementing online (hot) backups and offline (cold) backups. Logical backups or exports are discussed more fully in Chapter 7, "Utilities," but are contrasted to a physical backup in this chapter.

WHY BACK UP A DATABASE?

Plan to back up your DBMS.

Backing up a database can be time-consuming and costly in hardware and software. You back up the database files so that they can be restored in case of any kind of failure, either procedural or hardware.

Procedural failures can fall into four categories: DBA error, application error, operation personnel error, or environmental.

◆ DBAs might drop an object, such as a tablespace, from a production database when they meant to drop it from a test database.

◆ An application program might run out of sequence or fail to check database error codes, logically corrupting a database.

◆ Operations personnel might shut down the operating system without shutting down the database first or remove a directory that contained a database file.

◆ Environmental factors include fire, electrical problems, and man-made or natural disasters.

Hardware failure can occur any time and usually will result in a database failure that requires a database recovery. The most common hardware failure is disk failure, but motherboards and disk controllers can fail as well.

A database failure is disruption from normal activity that is so significant it requires you to restore the database. You should restore the database only if you cannot resolve the problem any other way.

What to Back Up

Different databases have different backup needs. A database backup includes all external datafiles for an instance and the Oracle home software directory.

A test database may need a weekly backup, whereas a production database may need a daily backup. A database backup consists of all the external files associated with a given instance, as shown in Table 8.1.

TABLE 8.1

EXTERNAL FILES FOR BACKUP

File	Description
Control file	Keeps track of the database schema; should be mirrored
Redo log file	Keeps track of all transactions that update the database; should be mirrored by using Oracle's multiplex feature
Archive log file	Redo logs that have been archived
init.ora	Contains tuning parameters used to configure the instance SGA
Password file	Optional file generated by the ORAPWD utility
Config file	Contains tuning parameters for an instance

You also need to consider backing up the Oracle software, which contains all the tools needed to run an Oracle database. Each tool will have its own subdirectory in the main ORACLE_HOME directory. The software should change only when an upgrade of the software occurs or a software patch is applied. You should back up this directory once and exclude it from the normal backup operation, unless an upgrade or patch of the software occurs.

ORACLE SEGMENTS ARE STORED IN TABLESPACES, BUT GET BACKED UP VIA DATAFILES

Oracle stores its data, index, and rollback segments in table-spaces. Each tablespace can have one or many datafiles. Good Oracle design practice will keep data segments in data table-spaces, index segments in index tablespaces, and rollback segments in rollback segment tablespaces.

An external datafile can contain a data, index, or rollback segment (see Figure 8.1). Critical to the Oracle database is the system tablespace, which contains all the data dictionary tables and system rollback segments.

Index segments can be rebuilt from the segment data that they were created by the first time. To rebuild an index segment, you must have the DDL to re-create it. You can also rebuild rollback segments that aren't being used by transactions.

Rollback segments (also referred to as *undo*) are associated with an instance via the init.ora file.

Redo log files record all transaction activity that caused a change to occur to the database. A database running in ARCHIVELOG mode will generate archives of the current online redo log; you should back up these archives.

The control file is the brains of the Oracle instance. It maintains the blueprint of the database and keeps track of the states of all the datafiles and redo log files. Each datafile has a system control number (SCN); when a checkpoint occurs and data is written to disk, the SCN is updated at the datafile level and in the control file. Oracle will know how many control files to write to via the CONTROL_FILES parameter in init.ora. Oracle will write all control files listed in the parameter but will read only the first one in the list.

Where to Find the External Files

You can retrieve the datafile names by using the name column on the view V$DATAFILE:

```
*SELECT name FROM v$datafile
output
NAME
------------------------------
/usr1/oracle/tdb/system01.dbf
/usr2/oracle/tdb/rbs01.dbf
/usr3/oracle/tdb/temp01.dbf
/usr4/oracle/tdb/tools01.dbf
```

FIGURE 8.1
External datafiles support tablespaces that can contain three types of segments.

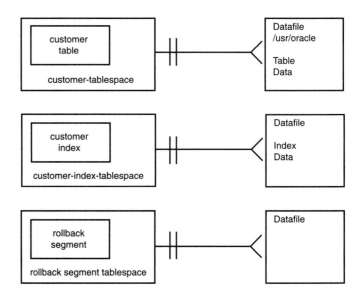

You can determine the redo log member files by using the column member on the view V$LOGFILE:

```
SELECT member FROM v$logfile
output
MEMBER
------------------------------
/usr1/oracle/tdb/redotdb01a.log
/usr2/oracle/tdb/redotdb01b.log
```

You can find the control file locations by using the column name on the view V$CONTROLFILE:

```
SELECT name FROM v$controlfile
output
NAME
------------------------------
/usr1/oracle/tdb/control01.ctl
/usr2/oracle/tdb/control02.ctl
/usr3/oracle/tdb/control03.ctl
```

Each command should produce a list containing the external files that make up a database. If the database was built by using the Optimal Flexible Architecture (OFA), as shown in Figure 8.2, generating the backup file list becomes a lot easier. OFA is designed to provide a way of logically defining all the files that support an Oracle database. It uses directory structures to help compartmentalize the different datafiles. The system identifier (SID) is used as part of the directory structure to provide an easy way of determining which files are associated with a given database.

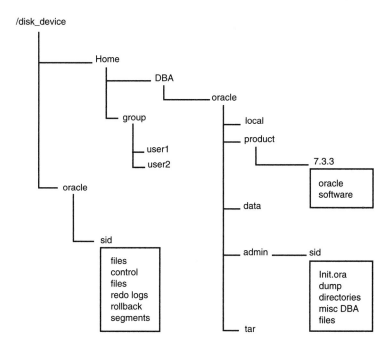

FIGURE 8.2
Optimal Flexible Architecture.

If the database is OFA-compliant, the backup software can follow the directory path to the external files without trying to generate them from system views. OFA will provide a structured approach to storing Oracle software and external files for an Oracle instance on one or many disk devices. The Oracle software is kept in the Oracle product directory, and all external files that relate to an Oracle instance are placed in the directory with Oracle and the corresponding Oracle system identifier (SID) that they belong to.

The goal of the backup operation is to copy all the files needed in the event that the database must be restored. Oracle can restore at the datafile, tablespace, or database level, but recovery is discussed in further detail in Chapter 9, "Database Recovery."

BACKING UP TO ANOTHER DEVICE

When backing up the external files, you can copy them to another device such as a disk, optical disk, or tape drive. If you use the backup software, it can take the many external files and place them in one backup file (see Figure 8.3). After a file is backed up, you should verify the integrity of the backup file and, if possible, store the backup offsite for disaster recovery. Backup media should be replaced in accordance with the manufacturers' guidelines and your own experience. You should keep a backup log to show when the backup was completed and by whom.

FIGURE 8.3
Copying datafiles to other devices.

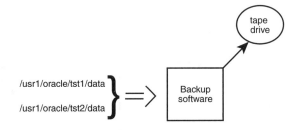

ARCHIVELOG Versus NOARCHIVELOG Mode

The Oracle database redo logs record all the transaction activity on the database. These logs are written in a circular fashion, meaning that when the log writer (LGWR, the background process that writes to these logs) comes to the end, it will begin writing at the beginning of the next redo log if the database is in NOARCHIVELOG mode (see Figure 8.4). When the database is in NOARCHIVELOG mode, the only physical backup option is an offline (cold) backup.

When the database is in ARCHIVELOG mode, when the redo log fills up, the archiver (ARCH) background process will read the full redo log and write its contents to an archived redo log (see Figure 8.5).

When the full redo log is completely archived, the LGWR can write to it again.

If the disk device for the archived redo logs runs out of free space, Oracle will stop all processing and wait until the ARCH process can finish archiving the redo logs. The error shows up in the init.ora file, and an ARCH*nnn*.trc file is generated.

If the database is run in NOARCHIVELOG mode and a tablespace becomes unavailable, normal operations can't continue until it's fixed or restored. If the database is recovered to a prior point in time, transactions are lost because the redo logs weren't archived, so they can't be reapplied. The data can be recovered only partially.

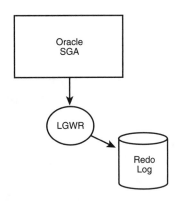

FIGURE 8.4
Database in NOARCHIVELOG mode.

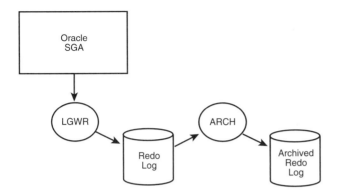

FIGURE 8.5
Oracle instance in ARCHIVELOG mode.

Setting up your database to run in ARCHIVELOG mode involves using the Server Manager utility.

STEP BY STEP

8.1 Setting Up a Database to Run in ARCHIVELOG or NOARCHIVELOG Mode

1. Shut down the database in normal or immediate mode.

2. Edit init.ora to add three new parameters:

```
log_archive_start = true
log_archive_dest =/disk_device/arch_sid_
log_archive_format=%s.log
```

- The first parameter will cause all redo log archiving to happen automatically. Set LOG_ARCHIVE_START to true.

- The destination of the archived redo logs is controlled by the LOG_ARCHIVE_DEST parameter.

- To format the archived redo log file name, place the sequence number of the redo log in the name by specifying %s for a nonpadded sequence number or %S for a padded sequence number. Oracle Parallel Server (OPS) can use the option %t for a nonpadded thread number and %T for a left-zero-padded thread number.

The archive redo logs for the Oracle instance with the SID of tst1 reside in the directory /disk_device/arch_tst1. The filename is arch_tst1_3930.log.

N O T E

Taking a Database from ARCHIVELOG Mode—When you're reorganizing a database, it's a good idea to take the instance out of ARCHIVELOG mode, due to the increase in overhead in writing to the archive area. When the database maintenance is complete, you can put the instance back in ARCHIVELOG mode.

3. Shut down the instance in normal or immediate mode.

4. Restart the database with the STARTUP MOUNT command.

5. Place the database in archived log mode:
ALTER DATABASE ARCHIVELOG;

6. Open the database for normal processing by issuing
ALTER DATABASE OPEN;

To change the database from ARCHIVELOG to NOARCHIVELOG mode, repeat Step by Step 8.1, except use the ALTER DATABASE NOARCHIVELOG; command for Step 5.

You can place the database in ARCHIVELOG or NOARCHIVELOG mode when you create the database; the CREATE DATABASE command has ARCHIVELOG and NOARCHIVELOG options.

With the database in ARCHIVELOG mode, you next need to decide whether to allow the redo logs to be archived automatically or manually. The LOG_ARCHIVE_START parameter, if set to true, automatically archives all filled redo logs. If this parameter is set to false, you must do manual archiving of the redo logs. To start automatic archiving without shutting down the instance, issue the following command:

ALTER SYSTEM ARCHIVE LOG START;

To stop automatic archiving of the redo logs, issue the following command:

ALTER SYSTEM ARCHIVE LOG STOP;

These commands don't change the archive log mode of the instance; they just indicate whether the redo logs are archived automatically.

Operating System Disk Capacity

When an Oracle database is set up to run in ARCHIVELOG mode, you must have enough operating system disk capacity to hold the archived redo logs. When Oracle switches from one redo log to another, the alert file for the instances records the event.

Multiply the size of the redo logs by how many times they fill up during the day to get a good idea of the size needed for the archive directory. For example, a system generates 10 redo logs a day, and each redo log is 5MB. The archive log destination must be at least 50MB. After a redo log is archived, it can be moved from the archive destination directory to maintain control over capacity.

The Log History View

The V$LOGHIST view shows the sequence number of the archive redo log and the time it was generated:

```
select sequence#,first_time from v$loghist;
--OUTPUT ----
SEQUENCE# FIRST_TIME
------ --------------------
3862 06/07/98 09:42:51
3861 06/06/98 17:53:45
3860 06/06/98 07:33:28
3859 06/06/98 06:49:04
3858 06/05/98 23:25:16
3857 06/05/98 15:52:52
3856 06/05/98 12:38:37
3855 06/05/98 10:47:59
```

Determining the Log Mode of an Instance

Use Server Manager to issue the archive log list command:

```
SVRMGR> archive log list
--OUTPUT OF COMMAND---
Database log mode              Archive Mode
Automatic archival             Enabled
Archive destination
/disk_device/tst1db/archive/arch_tst1_
Oldest online log sequence     3861
Next log sequence to archive   3863
Current log sequence           3863
```

The output of this command shows the following:

◆ The database log mode of the instance (archive or noarchive)

◆ Whether automatic archiving is being used

◆ The destination of the archive redo logs

◆ The oldest online log sequence

◆ The next log sequence to archive

Physical Offline Backup (Cold Backup)

Choose what type of backup is best for the database application.

A physical offline backup is considered a consistent backup because all blocks of data within the database correspond to a specific point in time.

You should generate a list of external files from the database to back up before shutting it down.

The database must be shut down before an offline backup can begin. The shutdown command has three options: normal, immediate, and abort. (See Chapter 5 for details on the shutdown options.)

You should back up databases only when a normal or immediate shutdown has been issued. The SHUTDOWN ABORT option requires the system monitor (SMON) process to perform automatic recovery when the database is started again. Because automatic recovery isn't guaranteed to work every time, a database backup after a SHUTDOWN ABORT may not be a good one.

Control File

Oracle uses the control file to keep track of all database structures at a particular point in time. The control file maintains checkpoint information, names of log files and datafiles, file header information, and log sequence numbers. Because the control file information changes whenever a database changes, a database backup should include the control file.

With SQL*Plus, you can copy the control file to a text file, which you can use to re-create a control file or a binary file. At the SQL*Plus prompt, connect as the SYSTEM user and enter the following statement:

```
ALTER DATABASE BACKUP CONTROLFILE TO TRACE;
```

This statement produces a text file that allows you to re-create the control file (if it's damaged) and gives a list of datafiles used by the database, with the exception of init.ora. The created file will be placed wherever the user dump destination is set in the init.ora file.

You should back up the control file whenever the structure of the database changes by adding or removing a datafile. The following statement will back up a control file in a binary format for use in recovery:

```
ALTER DATABASE BACKUP CONTROLFILE TO /disk_device;
```

You should mirror the control file across disk devices and note the different locations. The mirroring technique creates redundant control files that you can use in case of a disk failure that contains a control file.

Physical Online Backups (Hot Backups)

The online backup type is considered by Oracle an inconsistent backup. An offline backup is considered a consistent backup because all database blocks are consistent at the point in time the database was backed up. An online backup requires the backup of the datafile, the control file, and the archived redo logs generated at the time of the backup.

Online backups require the coordination of the operating-system-level backup software and Oracle tablespace commands. The database can be open and performing transaction processing during this type of backup. The backup from the Oracle perspective occurs at a tablespace-to-tablespace level. The operating system is backing up the datafiles associated with a tablespace.

Online backups can occur only on a database running in ARCHIVELOG mode. An online backup cycle will begin with the ARCHIVE LOG LIST command. This will tell you the current online redo log and can be referenced later in the first redo log of this backup cycle. The cycle must have all the redo logs generated during the backup cycle, so you should give the archived log command at the end to show the last redo log of the backup cycle.

An online backup cycle must back up all tablespaces for a given backup run, but not all tablespaces will be backed up at the same time. The steps of an online backup require that Oracle knows when a tablespace is being backed up. The operating system software can then back up the datafiles associated with the tablespace being backed up. When the operating system is done backing up the datafiles, Oracle is told that the tablespace backup has ended (see Table 8.2).

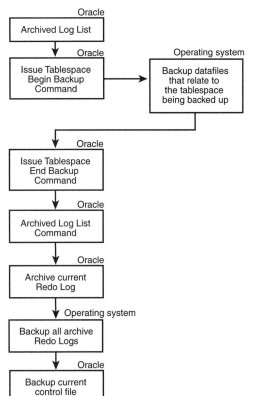

TABLE 8.2	

COMMANDS USED TO BACK UP ALL TABLESPACES IN
AN ONLINE BACKUP CYCLE

Step Number	*Task*
1. Oracle commands to begin a tablespace backup	Tell Oracle to begin backup of tablespace: `ALTER TABLESPACE tablespace_name begin backup;`
2. Operating system commands	Back up all datafiles associated with that tablespace
3. Oracle commands to end a tablespace backup	Tell Oracle that the backup of the tablespace has ended: `ALTER TABLESPACE tablespace_name end backup;`

You must repeat the three steps in Table 8.2 for all the tablespaces in an instance. When all tablespaces have a backup copy of their datafiles, you can issue the `ARCHIVE LOG LIST` command to determine the current redo log sequence number. This is the last redo log associated with this online backup cycle.

The next step of the cycle is to force the archiving of the current redo log by issuing the command

```
ALTER SYSTEM SWITCH LOGFILE;
```

You should back up all archived redo logs to form the archived redo log piece of the online backup cycle.

The last step of the cycle should include backing up the control file:

```
ALTER DATABASE BACKUP CONTROLFILE to 'file_spec';
```

The online backup cycle should contain all the datafiles for the instance, all archived redo logs that occurred during the backup cycle, and a copy of the control file (see Figure 8.6).

Online Backup Internals

The `ALTER TABLESPACE BEGIN BACKUP` command tells all files related to the tablespace that an online backup has begun on the tablespace. If the file backup occurs before this command is issued, the backup is no good. Oracle will flush to disk all the data buffers that belong

FIGURE 8.6
The online backup cycle.

to the datafiles being backed up, and the system control number (SCN) will be affected. The SCN for the file header is set to the SCN at the beginning of the online backup and won't change until the backup has ended.

The redo logs will have entire blocks written to them for the duration of the online backup. This process protects you from copying only a partial data block to the operating system.

Oracle works with the operating system to store rows of data within a block, and depending on how the operating system copies the block, it might create a split block of data. This could be a problem during recovery, so Oracle avoids the problem altogether by storing at the block level during an online backup. ALTER TABLESPACE END BACKUP will make an entry in the redo log with the same checkpoint SCN as the begin backup. The SCN is also stored in the header of the online backup datafiles.

Read-Only Tablespaces

A read-only tablespace won't allow any modifications to the segment blocks contained in it. After a read-only tablespace is physically backed up, there's no need to back it up again. The control file is updated to record which tablespaces and datafiles have been placed in read-only mode. If the instance becomes unavailable and automatic recovery is required, the read-only tablespace will be bypassed.

A tablespace is a good candidate for read-only if the data is static and doesn't contain rollback segments. The following commands place a tablespace in read-only and read/write mode:

```
ALTER TABLESPACE tablespace_name READ ONLY;

ALTER TABLESPACE tablespace_name READ WRITE;
```

When a tablespace changes modes from read-only to read-write, you should back up the control file for recovery purposes. To determine which tablespaces, if any, are in read-only mode, query the V$DATAFILE view:

```
SELECT name, enabled FROM V$DATAFILE;
---OUTPUT---
NAME                    enabled

/disk_device/datafile_1    READ WRITE
/disk_device/datafile_2    READ
```

> **NOTE**
>
> **System Overhead When Doing Online Backups**—Online backups should back up tablespaces during the lightest load time on the system. You should back up tablespaces only one at time due to the overhead of the block writes on the redo logs. It's your responsibility to manage the coordination of the Oracle tablespace commands and actual operating system backup of the datafiles. The database won't shut down with the normal or immediate option if the database is in hot backup mode; you must use the shutdown abort option.

This output shows that `datafile_2` is in read-only mode and wouldn't have to be included in the backup file set.

Doing an Export (Logical Backup)

The Export utility, covered in detail in Chapter 7, is another tool you can use to perform backups. Export requires that the database be online while it's running.

Export backs up at three levels: database, user, and table. It backs up not only the data, but also the actual SQL commands needed to rebuild the objects.

This type of backup has the most granularity for recovery. It allows you to recover a single table, whereas the other backup types require that you recover the whole database or a datafile or tablespace. Database recovery is discussed in Chapter 9.

CHAPTER SUMMARY

KEY TERMS

Before you take the exam, make sure that you're comfortable with the definitions and concepts for each of the following key terms:

- Cold (offline) backup
- Hot (online) backup
- Datafile
- Control file
- Redo logs
- Archived redo logs
- Tablespace
- Export
- OFA

The Oracle external file architecture is controlled best by OFA. When you're doing cold backups, the external file structure is all that concerns you as soon as the database is shut down. An online backup requires the database to be in ARCHIVELOG mode, and backing up the database is done with Oracle commands and operating system commands. Recovery occurs the same way, whether the backup was done using the online or offline technique. The online technique is more complex and therefore harder to administrate. The Export utility is the most flexible of the backup types but is limited in speed of recovery, which may make it a bad choice for large database environments.

APPLY YOUR KNOWLEDGE

This section allows you to assess how well you understand the material in the chapter. Review questions test your knowledge of the tasks and concepts specified in the objectives. The exercises provide you with opportunities to engage in the sorts of tasks that compose the skill sets the objectives reflect.

Exercises

8.1 Finding the External Files to Back Up

The following steps will help you develop a complete list of external files to back up. Use Server Manager to perform these steps.

Time Estimate: Less than 10 minutes

1. List all the datafiles by using the V$DATAFILE view:

   ```
   SELECT name FROM v$datafile
   ```

2. List all the online redo logs by using the V$LOGFILE view:

   ```
   SELECT member FROM v$logfile
   ```

3. List all the control files by using the V$CONTROLFILE view:

   ```
   SELECT name FROM v$controlfile
   ```

8.2 Determine Whether an Oracle Instance Is Running in ARCHIVELOG Mode

To find out whether an Oracle instance is in ARCHIVELOG mode, issue the command archive log list in Server Manager. The output will show whether the database is in ARCHIVELOG mode and indicate the archive destination for the archived logs.

Time Estimate: Less than 10 minutes

Review Questions

1. What dynamic view will show all the datafiles for an instance?

   A. V$LOGFILE

   B. V$DATAFILE

   C. V$TABLESPACE

   D. V$CONTROLFILE

2. An offline backup requires the database to be

   A. Closed (shut down)

   B. Open

   C. Running in ARCHIVELOG mode

   D. Doesn't matter

3. An online backup requires the database to be

   A. Closed (shut down)

   B. Running in NOARCHIVELOG mode

   C. Open

   D. Doesn't matter

4. An online backup requires which of the following?

   A. The database needs to be running in ARCHIVELOG mode.

   B. The database needs to be mounted but not open.

   C. The online backup has no special requirements.

   D. The database needs to be in single-user mode.

5. What does OFA stands for?

   A. Oracle Flexible Architecture

   B. Oracle File Architecture

   C. Optimal File Architecture

   D. Optimal Flexible Architecture

6. Which dynamic view will show redo log history?

   A. V$REDOHIST

   B. V$LOGHIST

   C. V$LOGHISTORY

   D. V$HISTORY

7. What command will allow you to see what archive log mode your database is running?

   A. Query the dynamic view V$ARCHIVE.

   B. Archive log list.

   C. Check the init.ora file.

   D. There's no way to check.

8. What command will back up the control file so that you can re-create it using Server Manager?

   A. BACKUP controlfile

   B. Issue an operating system copy command to back up the control file to another disk device.

   C. ALTER database BACKUP controlfile to trace;

   D. Use create controlfile with the backup option.

9. The Export utility allows you to back up what on an Oracle database?

   A. Database, tablespace, and tables

   B. Operating system, database, and tablespaces

   C. Tablespace, users, and tables

   D. Database, users, and their objects and tables

10. How often should you back up a read-only tablespace?

    A. Every time the system is backed up

    B. On Saturday nights

    C. Only upon creation

    D. They don't need to be backed up

Answers to Review Questions

1. **B**. The V$DATAFILE view will show all the datafiles associated with an instance. (This question deals with the objective "Plan to back up your DBMS.")

2. **A**. You must shut down the database for an offline backup to have any integrity. (This question deals with the objective "Choose what type of backup is best for the database application.")

3. **C**. The database must be open so that you can give the ALTER tablespace commands to back up the tablespaces. (This question deals with the objective "Choose what type of backup is best for the database application.")

4. **A**. The database must be running in ARCHIVELOG mode. The archived redo logs will contain all the transactions that occurred during the backup and will be needed for recovery. (This question deals with the objective "Choose what type of backup is best for the database application.")

5. **D**. Optimal Flexible Architecture allows you to manage the external files through the Oracle system identifier (SID). (This question deals with the objective "Plan to back up your DBMS.")

APPLY YOUR KNOWLEDGE

6. **B**. The V$LOGHIST view will show redo log history for a given instance. This is useful for online backups and recovery. (This question deals with the objective "Plan to back up your DBMS.")

7. **B**. The archive log list will show you what redo log mode you're in and the destination of the archive redo logs. (This question deals with the objective "Plan to back up your DBMS.")

8. **C**. The ALTER database BACKUP controlfile to trace; command will back up the control file to an operating system file in text format. (This question deals with the objective "Plan to back up your DBMS.")

9. **D**. The Export utility will back up the entire database, a user and its objects, a table, or list of tables. (This question deals with the objective "Choose what type of backup is best for the database application.")

10. **C**. You should back up the read-only tablespace when it's created; after that, there's no reason to continue to back up its files. (This question deals with the objective "Choose what type of backup is best for the database application.")

This chapter helps you prepare for the exam by covering the following objectives:

Understand how a transaction weaves its way through the instance memory structures and the database external structures.

▶ This is the only way to plan a successful recovery, due to the many facets of the recovery process. The exam will contain specific questions to the life cycle of the transaction.

Which option to use to start up the database.

▶ This is critical to implement the different types of recovery. Some recovery scenarios will require the database to not be open; others will allow the database to be open and functioning.

Understand the checkpoint event within a database.

▶ Several actions can cause a checkpoint to occur, and it is part of the core transaction management for Oracle.

Understand the recovery options of running an instance in ARCHIVELOG or NOARCHIVELOG mode.

▶ By running an instance in NOARCHIVELOG mode, the recovery types are limited but also simplified. For most database environments, the business will require the most robust recovery scheme available, and that will require archiving the redo logs.

CHAPTER 9

Database Recovery

Understand the differences between complete recovery and incomplete recovery.

▶ Sometimes when recovering a database, data is lost; this is an incomplete recovery. A complete recovery restores all data to the database.

Understand the RECOVER command.

▶ The RECOVER command can be issued at three levels: database, tablespace, and data file. This is where the complexity begins, and you must understand which RECOVER command is appropriate for the recovery scenario.

STUDY STRATEGIES

▶ Read this chapter closely to understand how Oracle manages a transaction in the database to truly understand automatic and manual recovery. The test can contain scenario-type questions to test your knowledge of recovery.

The system control number (SCN) is a key part of the recovery, and you must understand how it is used in the redo logs, data files, and the control file to pass the test.

Pay special attention to the checkpoint event. It is very important to understand not only what can trigger a checkpoint, but also how it affects the redo logs' data files and the control files. When you understand this process, it is easier to decide which recovery option to use.

The redo logs are critical to the recovery process and the use of ARCHIVELOG mode enables Oracle to perform advance recovery features. You should understand what recoveries are possible when you are running in the different log modes.

The RECOVERY command can be used at three levels: database, tablespace, and data file. The question is at what level does the recovery have to occur. The database recovery will enable you to do a time-based recovery, but the database can't be open. The tablespace- and data-file–level recovery can be performed with the database open. Also, two advance features of the recovery process must be understood: the resetting of the redo logs and recovering with a backup control file.

INTRODUCTION

Database recovery is a complicated process of restoring data that has become corrupt or damaged. The data could be physically or logically corrupt. The process is considered complex because of the many options and decisions you have to make.

First, you have to understand how Oracle manages a transaction within the different database structures. This will help in recovery planning. The database structures that come into play for a recovery are tablespace, data files, redo logs, archived redo logs (optional), and control files. When performing a recovery, you should recover only what was damaged. Because Oracle enables you to recover at three levels (database, tablespace, and data file), you must choose which level is the best fit for your given circumstances.

The RECOVERY command has three options: cancel, time, and change. Each option may require the database to be in a different startup state and will depend on what level of recovery you are trying to do (database, tablespace, or data file). Depending on the recovery scenario, the process will depend on the type or level of the recovery. You always want to recover the least amount of data required.

SOME COMMON ERRORS AND FAILURES

An user error can cause a database to become logically corrupt—for example, month-end processing was done in the middle of the month, but the problem wasn't caught for several days.

A statement-failure error can occur when a SQL statement fails, but this usually will recover automatically. The best example is an INSERT command trying to add data to a table that has reached maxextents and is full. The statement will continue to fail until the table is expanded.

A process failure can occur for a user, server, or background process. PMON will clean up after the user or server process; if a background process fails, however, the instance will have to be restarted.

An instance failure can occur when the SGA or background processes are prevented from continuing normal execution. This can occur due to operating system problems or hardware problems.

EXPLANATIONS OF STRUCTURES

Understand how a transaction weaves its way through the instance memory structures and the database external structures.

The recovery of any database begins with the repair of what was broken. In a database, the structures that may need to be recovered are data files, control files, redo logs, and archived redo logs (if the database was in ARCHIVELOG mode). Those are the physical structures, but the logical structure of the tablespace can also be recovered.

Tablespaces

A *tablespace* is a logical structure that contains segments. Rollback, data, and index are the three types of segments created inside a tablespace. Each segment is made up of extents, and the extents are comprised of data blocks (see Figure 9.1).

The system tablespace contains the data dictionary for the Oracle database. Therefore, neither the system tablespace nor the data file used by the system tablespace can be taken offline. If the system tablespace or data file must be recovered, the database will have to be in the mounted-and-not-open state for recovery.

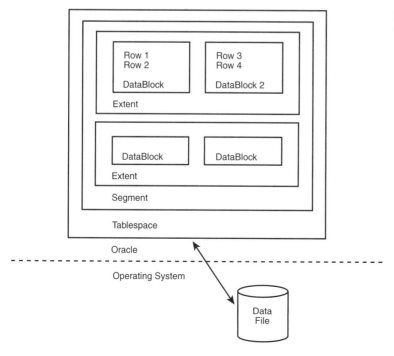

FIGURE 9.1
Components that support a row of data.

Index segments can be rebuilt and may not require a recovery in the traditional sense of the word. The tablespace that contains the index segment could be rebuilt and the indexes re-created, for example. This would require the DDL for the indexes.

The rollback segments are created to manage the rollback of a transaction if needed and provide read consistency for the database. A transaction modifies a row or rows of data in the data block that is part of the extent of a tablespace that uses a data file for the physical storage.

The rollback segment contains the before image of that row or rows changed in the data block (see Table 9.1). These before images are called *undo information*. If a row is inserted into a block, the undo information will include the rowid. This rowid could be used to remove the row, which would be the undo of an insert. A delete would require all the information of the rowid. An update transaction will contain all the before images of the updated rows plus the rowid. Modified index entries will follow the same rules as the data segments.

TABLE 9.1

CONTENTS OF A ROLLBACK SEGMENT

Transaction	*Rollback Segment Contents*
Insert	Rowid
Update	All modified columns plus rowid
Delete	All columns plus rowid
All txns	Rollback transaction table; all index modifications are treated in the same manner as data transactions

The modified data block will contain the rollback segment that has the undo information for the transaction. The structure of the rollback transaction table includes the address of the changed data block, transaction state active or committed, and where the undo information is stored within the rollback segment (see Figure 9.2).

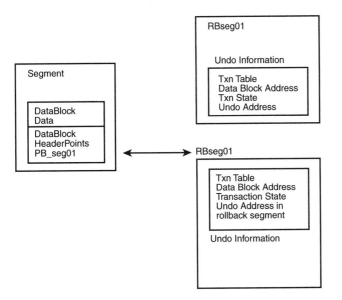

FIGURE 9.2
Internals of the rollback segment.

You must take tablespaces offline to recover them. For the exam, it is important to understand the three options of taking a tablespace offline: normal, temporary, and immediate.

```
ALTER TABLESPACE tablespace_name
normal¦temporary¦immediate;
```

◆ The normal option allows a checkpoint to occur before the tablespace is taken offline. (Checkpoints are covered later in this chapter.)

◆ The normal option won't work if a data file for the tablespace is damaged and Oracle is getting a write error for the data file. In that case, the temporary option should be used. Oracle will checkpoint all the data files it can and then take the database offline.

◆ The immediate option can be issued only in a database that is running in ARCHIVELOG mode and won't checkpoint any data files.

You can use the DBA_TABLESPACES view to determine what state the tablespaces are now in, under the columns tablespace_name and status. The status column will show whether the tablespace is online or offline.

DATA FILES

Data files are allocated through the CREATE and ALTER TABLESPACE commands. When you issue the DROP TABLESPACE command, the data file still exists at the operating system level and has to be removed with an operating system command.

The first block of the data file is reserved for the file header. This is where the SCN is stored for the file, and the control file has a corresponding entry for the data file with an SCN. When the control file's SCN for a data file doesn't agree with the SCN in the data file, Oracle will ask for recovery of the data file.

The system data file that belongs to the system tablespace will require special handling if it needs to be recovered. All other data files can be recovered with the database open.

A data file should be taken offline only if recovery needs to be done to it. The recover data file command (discussed later in this chapter) would be used. If the database isn't being run in ARCHIVELOG mode, the ALTER DATABASE command used to take the data file offline must include the drop option. If the database is in ARCHIVELOG mode, the command can just be offline:

```
ALTER DATABASE DATAFILE 'datafile_name' OFFLINE;
ALTER DATABASE DATAFILE 'datafile_name' OFFLINE DROP;
```

The V$DATAFILE view can be used to determine the status of data files on a database, using the name and status columns:

```
SELECT name,status FROM V$DATAFILE;
```

The name will be the name of the data file and the status will be ONLINE (normal), OFFLINE (probably needs recovery), or SYSTEM (the file for the system tablespace).

CONTROL FILES

The control file is the most important file in the database, because it contains the database schema. This includes all the database's data filenames and the latest SCNs for each and what state they are in. The states of the data file are online, offline, or needs media recovery. It also contains the log sequence number and the low and high SCN for the redo log group. When the database is being started, it is in the mount stage that the control file is open and read. All control files listed in init.ora's `control_file` parameter are written to, but only the first one in the list is read.

If a control file is lost due to media failure, the database must be shut down with the `abort` option. When the database is down, you must update the `control_file` parameter by removing the name of the damaged control file. The database can now be started. If the only control file is lost due to media damage, a database recovery will have to be done, as covered later in this chapter.

> **NOTE**
>
> **Adding a Control File** To add a control file to your current control file set, do a normal shutdown of the database. Copy a current control file to a new location. Edit the `control_file` parameter in init.ora to include the new file and start up the database.

REDO LOGS

Two log file groups are required by Oracle to maintain an instance. The group can have only one member, but Oracle strongly recommends having two members, each on different disk devices. This is how Oracle mirrors or multiplexes the redo logs.

Each redo log member in a group must be the same size. The `LGWR` background process will write the same information to all members of a redo log group. If one member can't be written to, it will have a status of `STALE`. `LGWR` will continue to try to write the member four times; after that, the member won't be written to anymore. If all members of the redo log group become unavailable, the `LGWR` process will stop working and the database will have to be shut down.

Archived Redo Logs

The database must be in `ARCHIVELOG` mode to have the filled online redo log information saved so that it can be used for database recovery later. The `ARCH` background process will read the full redo log and create an archive log of that redo log. Each redo log block will be verified by the `ARCH` process before it is written to the archive log. If the database isn't running in `ARCHIVELOG` mode, the redo log will be written over and the contents will be lost.

KEY RECOVERY PRINCIPLES

If a database needs to be recovered, you first need to determine what area of the database needs to be recovered and what state the instance was in when the problem occurred. The instance may have to be shut down and restarted to perform the recovery.

Using the `abort` option to shut down the instance could cause a recovery to be needed. The checkpoint is used to keep the database in sync to a particular point in time and will update the control file with the latest SCNs for the data files.

Startup Options

Which option to use to start up the database.

When the database is being started, it is easy to take for granted that it will always mount and open successfully. You can specify different options at startup. (All of these options are covered in Chapter 8, "Backing Up a Database.")

Sometimes during a recovery, you will want to start up the database and stop the process at the mount stage. You do so by issuing the `STARTUP MOUNT` command. The database can't be open to perform recovery at the database level, but it must be started and mounted. You can use the `RECOVER` and `ALTER DATABASE` commands when the database is mounted. A tablespace or data file recovery can be done with the instance mounted or opened.

`STARTUP NOMOUNT` will read the init.ora file for the instance, configure the SGA, and start the background processes. When the database is mounted, the control file is read. When the database is open, it reads the online redo logs, performs a roll forward of the transactions, rolls back all uncommitted transactions, and releases any held resources. If any distributive transactions are waiting for a two-phase commit, they are resolved at this time. The `SMON` process will synchronize the database files and control files' SCN.

Shutdown Options

When the database is shut down with the `abort` option, a checkpoint doesn't occur and crash recovery will be needed when the instance is started. Crash recovery will perform a roll forward of all transactions in the redo log and a roll back for all uncommitted transactions at the time of the instance crash. This is accomplished by using the SCN numbers contained in the control file and data file header. When a shutdown abort occurs, the stop SCN in the control file for all data files is set to infinity. This is the clue Oracle uses to perform crash recovery.

CHECKPOINTS

Understand the checkpoint event within a database.

A *checkpoint* in the database will write data buffers that have been changed (also called *dirty buffers*) to disk and update the control file and file headers with the new SCN information. There are fast and slow checkpoints, and it depends on what triggered the checkpoint as to what type it is. If the DBWR process is writing a large number of buffers due to a checkpoint occurring on the database, this is called a *fast checkpoint*. Fast checkpoints are triggered by the following:

```
ALTER SYSTEM CHECKPOINT (LOCAL OR GLOBAL)
INSTANCE SHUTDOWN (NORMAL¦IMMEDIATE)
ALTER TABLESPACE BEGIN BACKUP
ALTER TABLESPACE OFFLINE (NORMAL ¦TEMPORARY)
LOG FILE SWITCH STUCK
```

If the DBWR writes only a small amount of buffers due to a checkpoint, it is considered slow. The following are examples of slow checkpoints:

```
INIT.ORA parameter LOG_CHECKPOINT_INTERVAL,
➡LOG_CHECKPOINT_TIMEOUT
log file switch normal
ALTER SYSTEM SWITCH LOGFILE command
```

The DBWR will write the dirty buffers to disk via the least recently used (LRU) algorithm, but a very active buffer might not get written to disk for quite some time. A checkpoint isn't triggered by an LRU. The three types of checkpoints are local, global, and file:

◆ A *local checkpoint* will occur if you issue the ALTER SYSTEM CHECKPOINT LOCAL; command. This command will flush all modified buffers for an instance to disk and cause a checkpoint to occur.

◆ A *global checkpoint* is used only when the Oracle database is in Parallel Server configuration. The global checkpoint will cause all instances to perform a checkpoint. The command is this:

```
ALTER SYSTEM CHECKPOINT GLOBAL;
```

◆ A *file checkpoint* will occur on data files that support a tablespace that has issued on it the ALTER TABLESPACE command to begin backup.

Triggering Events for Checkpoints

When a redo log group is switched, a checkpoint will occur. This checkpoint will override any currently running checkpoint.

The following two init.ora parameters control when a checkpoint can occur:

◆ The LOG_CHECKPOINT_TIMEOUT will set the number of seconds to go between checkpoints.

◆ The LOG_CHECKPOINT_INTERVAL can be set to the number of redo log blocks that get written to disk. When that number is reached, a checkpoint will occur.

These parameters are used to force a checkpoint in databases that have very large redo log files. The checkpoint will speed instance recovery, because there will be less transaction activity to roll back.

Two ALTER TABLESPACE commands will trigger a checkpoint: the ALTER tablespace begin backup command (discussed in Chapter 8, "Backing Up a Database,"), and whenever a tablespace is taken offline with a normal or temporary setting.

Checkpoints are overhead intensive and can cause quite a lot of physical I/O.

Understand the recovery options of running an instance in ARCHIVELOG or NOARCHIVELOG mode.

When a database is running in ARCHIVELOG mode, the online redo logs are archived to be used for complete database recovery (see Figure 9.3). The actual archiving can be done manually by using an ALTER SYSTEM command or automatically by setting init.ora parameters.

Three init.ora parameters affect the archiving process:

◆ The LOG_ARCHIVE_START parameter, when set to TRUE, starts the ARCH background process, which automatically archives the online redo logs.

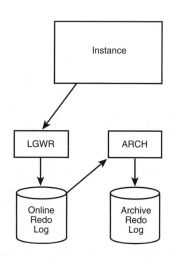

FIGURE 9.3
An instance in ARCHIVELOG mode.

◆ The LOG_ARCHIVE_DEST parameter determines where to store the archived redo logs. This is also the destination directory where Oracle will look for the archived redo logs when applying them in a database recovery.

◆ The LOG_ARCHIVE_FORMAT parameter enables you to customize the name of the archived redo logs. The options include a redo thread number for databases that use the Oracle Parallel Server option with the parameter %t (non-zero padded) or %T (zero padded), and the log sequence number %s (non-zero padded) or %S (zero padded) for all other database options. The statement

```
LOG_ARCHIVE_FORMAT=arch%s.log
```

will create archived redo logs named with arch as a prefix, the sequence number in the middle, and log as a suffix.

STEP BY STEP

9.1 Place a Database That Is in NOARCHIVELOG Mode into ARCHIVELOG Mode

1. Modify the init.ora file to include the new archive log parameters.

2. Shut down the database with the normal or immediate option.

3. Back up the database.

4. Start up and mount a new instance, but don't open it. Issue the STARTUP MOUNT command from Server Manager to do this.

5. Issue this command:
   ```
   ALTER DATABASE ARCHIVELOG;
   ```

6. Open this database:
   ```
   ALTER DATABASE OPEN;
   ```

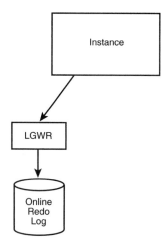

FIGURE 9.4
Instance in NOARCHIVELOG mode.

If the database is running in NOARCHIVELOG mode, the online redo logs will be overwritten and the transactions they contained won't be available for recovery purposes (see Figure 9.4).

Archived and online redo logs can contain committed and uncommitted transactions. When the redo logs are applied in a recovery scenario, this is the roll-forward phase of the recovery; when the uncommitted transactions occur, this becomes the rollback phase.

DATABASE RECOVERY OPTIONS

Understand the differences between complete recovery and incomplete recovery.

Understand the RECOVER command.

The recovery process has three phases: the restoration of files, the roll-forward phase, and the rollback phase. The roll-forward and rollback phases occur with the application of archived redo logs and are used only in complete recovery.

The reasons to recover a database can include everything from complete instance failure to hardware failure at the data file level to a user error that logically corrupts the database. If a user process fails for whatever reason, the PMON background process will roll back the transaction automatically and release all resources. When an instance fails, it, too, can be restarted, and the SMON background process will perform all needed recovery automatically. Instance failure can occur due to operating system problems, hardware problems involving the computer's motherboard, and failure of background processes. The alert log of the instance will contain the cause of the instance failure.

Complete recovery of a database means that no data was lost during the recovery operation; *incomplete recovery* means that data was lost. A complete recovery will require the database to be in ARCHIVELOG mode if the database supports transactions and isn't a read-only database; recovery options are limited if the database isn't running in ARCHIVELOG mode. Online recovery is done with the database open and able to accept transactions; you can recover only tablespaces and data files with the database in this state. The RECOVER DATABASE command is considered an offline recovery, because the database is mounted but not open.

If the database isn't running in ARCHIVELOG mode, the user has agreed to lose data or has another way of restoring the transactions that occur on the database. The only choice of recovery for a database running in this mode is to restore all the data files, control files, and online redo logs from a prior backup file set. This is an incomplete recovery, however, because data has been lost. If the database is recovered to an incomplete state, it must be open with the reset logs option. This will reset the log sequence number to one and clear the current online redo logs. It will also update the current control file and all data file headers to reflect the new redo log sequence number. This will prevent the archived logs from being applied to the database in the future.

Figure 9.5 shows the components of recovery. Listing 9.1 shows the RECOVER DATABASE command with all its options.

LISTING 9.1

THE RECOVER DATABASE COMMAND

```
RECOVER [AUTOMATIC] [FROM 'archive_file_location']
¦[STANDBY] DATABASE [UNTIL CANCEL]  ¦ [UNTIL TIME time]
     ¦ [UNTIL CHANGE integer]
     [USING BACKUP CONTROLFILE]
TABLESPACE 'tablespace_name'
DATAFILE   'datafile_name'
CONTINUE
CANCEL
PARALLEL parallel_clause ;
```

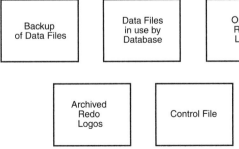

FIGURE 9.5
Components of recovery.

You can recover Oracle databases at three different levels: database, tablespace, and data file. The database level must be used when recovering the system tablespace or a data file that supports the system tablespace. It also must be used when you know the recovery will be incomplete. The options for database recovery that will cause the database to be incomplete are cancel, time, and change.

RECOVERING AT THE DATABASE LEVEL

Recovery must be done at the database level if you are recovering the system tablespace or a data file used by the system tablespace, or performing an incomplete recovery.

When a database needs to be recovered, you need to know what has to be recovered. Never recover more than what you need to recover. If the recovery is due to media failure, the hardware problem must be fixed and the necessary data files restored. If the media can't be fixed, you can restore the data files to another disk and use the ALTER DATABASE RENAME command to alter the control file to recognize the new location for the data file.

Using the Cancel Option (Incomplete and Closed Recovery)

Use the UNTIL CANCEL option when an archived redo log is damaged.

STEP BY STEP

9.2 Performing a Cancel-Based Recovery

1. Back up the database in its current state.

2. Restore the data files and archived redo logs from the backup.

3. Start up and mount the database with the STARTUP MOUNT command in Server Manager.

4. Issue the RECOVER DATABASE command with the UNTIL CANCEL option. This will begin recovering the database by applying the first redo log in sequence, and give you the opportunity to cancel the recovery before applying the next redo log.

5. Issue the CANCEL RECOVER DATABASE command to stop the recovery process.

6. Open the database and reset the redo logs with the ALTER DATABASE OPEN RESETLOGS command.

The database should now be backed up, because the RESETLOGS command was issued, and now the archived redo logs can't be applied.

Using the TIME Option (Incomplete and Closed Recovery)

The UNTIL TIME option is used when the database is to be restored to a specific time. One example may be that a user error occurred at 2 p.m. during the day and logically corrupted the data. The database could then be restored to 1:59 p.m.

STEP BY STEP

9.3 Recovering to a Point in Time

1. Back up the database in its current state.

2. Restore the data files and archived redo logs from the backup.

3. Start up and mount the database by using the STARTUP MOUNT command in Server Manager.

4. Issue the RECOVER DATABASE command with the UNTIL TIME option.

5. Open the database and reset the redo logs by issuing the ALTER DATABASE OPEN RESETLOGS command.

> **NOTE**
> **Using the AUTOMATIC Option** When you specify the AUTOMATIC option, the redo log filenames will be generated without user intervention. This will begin the database recovery and apply all the required archived redo logs until the time specified.

The database should now be backed up because the reset log command was issued and now the archived redo logs can't be applied.

Using the CHANGE Option (Incomplete and Closed Recovery)

The UNTIL CHANGE option is used in a database environment that requires the recovery to stop on a specific SCN. The SCN is updated when a database transaction is committed. The recovery will continue applying transactions that were committed *before* the specified SCN.

STEP BY STEP

9.4 Using the UNTIL CHANGE Option

1. Back up the database in its current state.

2. Restore the data files and archived redo logs from the backup.

3. Start up and mount the database by using the STARTUP MOUNT command in Server Manager.

4. Issue the RECOVER DATABASE command with the UNTIL CHANGE option.

5. Open the database and reset the redo logs by issuing the ALTER DATABASE OPEN RESETLOGS command.

> **NOTE**
>
> **Using the AUTOMATIC Option** When you specify the AUTOMATIC option, the redo log filenames will be generated without user intervention. This will begin the database recovery and apply all the required archived redo logs until the SCN specified.

The database should now be backed up because the reset log command was issued and now the archived redo logs can't be applied.

Using a Backup Control File

Recovering the database requires a control file. You perform a recovery with a backup control file on a closed database. The control file must contain the database's current structure.

The RECOVER command (refer to Listing 9.1) should be used with the USING BACKUP CONTROLFILE option in two situations:

◆ When the existing control file isn't available for recovery purposes. In a typical recovery, only the data files and archived redo logs are restored from the backup file set. If the current control file isn't available and wasn't mirrored, it must also be restored from the backup file set.

◆ When the current control file doesn't reflect the current physical structure of the database.

STEP BY STEP

9.5 Recovering with a Backup Control File

1. Back up the database in its current state.

2. Restore the data files and archived redo logs and control file from backups.

3. Start up and mount the database by using the STARTUP MOUNT command in Server Manager.

4. Issue the RECOVER DATABASE command with any of the options—UNTIL CANCEL, UNTIL CHANGE, or UNTIL TIME—or do a complete recovery. Remember also to issue the command with the USING BACKUP CONTROLFILE option.

5. Open the database and reset the redo logs by issuing the ALTER DATABASE OPEN RESETLOGS command.

The database should now be backed up because the reset log command was issued and now the archived redo logs can't be applied.

Re-Creating a Control File

You can re-create the control file by using the CREATE CONTROLFILE command. To issue this command, you must know the names of all the data files and online redo logs. The loss of a nonmirrored control file requires either restoring the control file from a backup or re-creating the control file.

STEP BY STEP

9.6 Creating a New Control File

1. Back up the database in its current state.

2. Start up with the NOMOUNT option in Server Manager.

3. Issue the CREATE CONTROLFILE command:

```
CREATE CONTROLFILE [REUSE] [SET DATABASE]
database_name
LOGFILE GROUP group_number 'redo_log_member'
     RESETLOGS|NORESETLOGS
DATAFILE 'datafile_path_and_name'
     MAXLOGFILES integer
     MAXLOGMEMBERS integer
     MAXDATAFILES integer
     MAXINSTANCES integer
     ARCHIVELOG |NOARCHIVELOG;
```

4. Mount the database by issuing the ALTER DATABASE MOUNT command.

5. The database can now be recovered. If the control file was created with the RESETLOGS option, recover by using the RECOVER command's BACKUP CONTROLFILE option. If the CREATE CONTROLFILE command was done with the NORESETLOGS option, a complete recovery is possible without using the BACKUP CONTROLFILE option.

6. Open the database and reset the redo logs only if the control file was created with RESETLOGS option; otherwise, you can just open the database.

> **NOTE**
>
> **Using the NORESETLOGS Option** If the current online redo logs haven't been damaged, it is *very* important to create the new control file with the NORESETLOGS option. Then you can open the database without specifying the RESETLOGS option.

The database should be backed up if the RESETLOGS command was issued, because now the archived redo logs can't be applied.

Doing a Tablespace-Level Recovery

During a tablespace-level recovery, the database doesn't have to be mounted, but the tablespace must be offline while the recovery is being done. This is considered a complete recovery, because all archived redo logs must be applied. If all archived redo logs aren't available, a database-level recovery must be done.

STEP BY STEP

9.7 Performing a Tablespace Recovery

1. Back up the database in its current state.

2. Take the tablespace offline by using the ALTER TABLESPACE command.

3. Restore the data files associated with the tablespace and archived redo logs from the backup.

4. Issue the RECOVER DATABASE command with the TABLESPACE option.

5. Place the tablespace online by using the ALTER TABLESPACE command.

Doing a Data File Recovery

The capability to recover a data file is considered an open database recovery, because the database doesn't have to be mounted. The data file must be placed offline while the recovery is being done, but the tablespace may be kept online if it has other data files. A data file recovery is considered a complete recovery, because all archived redo logs must be applied. If all archived redo logs aren't available, a database-level recovery must be done.

STEP BY STEP

9.8 Performing a Data File Recovery

1. Back up the database in its current state.

2. Take the data file offline by using the ALTER DATAFILE command.

3. Restore the data file being recovered and archived redo logs from the backup.

> **NOTE**
>
> **Using the AUTOMATIC Option** When specifying the RECOVER DATABASE command with the AUTOMATIC option, the redo log filenames will be generated without user intervention. This will begin the database recovery and apply all the required archived redo logs until all the redo information has been applied.

continues

continued

4. Issue the RECOVER DATABASE command with the DATAFILE option.

5. Place the data file online by using the ALTER DATAFILE command.

CHAPTER SUMMARY

KEY TERMS

Before you take the exam, make sure that you are comfortable with the definitions and concepts for each of the following key terms:

- SCN
- checkpoint
- archive log
- recover
- backup control file
- reset logs
- tablespace
- data file
- rowid
- undo
- control file
- redo log
- shutdown
- startup
- DBWR
- PMON
- SMON

The recovery process is complex due to the many options available to perform the recovery. You must understand how Oracle manages a transaction from beginning to end. The guiding rule should always be *recover only what is needed*, which usually means that you will be recovering at the tablespace or data file level. When you are given a scenario where you have to recover an entire database, be careful and look at all the details. Do you have all the archived log files? Are you being asked to recover to a point in time, or do you know the SCN to recover to?

If you are dealing with a damaged control file, first check to see whether it was mirrored. If it wasn't mirrored, is there any other damage to the other data files? If not, can it be re-created?

APPLY YOUR KNOWLEDGE

This section enables you to assess how well you understood the material in the chapter. Review questions test your knowledge of the tasks and concepts specified in the objectives. The exercises provide you with opportunities to engage in the sorts of tasks that comprise the skill sets that the objectives reflect.

Exercise

9.1 Restore a Data File That Was Removed by User Error

This exercise will help you understand how to use the RECOVER command objective.

Time Estimate: 20 minutes

1. Back up the database in its current state.

2. Take the data file /usr/data1.dbf offline by using the ALTER DATAFILE command.

3. Restore the data file /usr/data1.dbf being recovered and archived redo logs from the backup file set.

4. Issue the RECOVER DATABASE command with the DATAFILE option to begin recovering the database.

5. Place the data file /usr/data1.dbf online by using the ALTER DATAFILE command.

Review Questions

1. What important function isn't done when the database is shut down with the abort option?

   A. Checkpoint

   B. All files aren't closed properly.

   C. The SGA doesn't release its memory resources.

   D. The control file stays open.

2. What are the levels of database recovery?

   A. Table, index, cluster

   B. Owner, table, index

   C. Database, tablespace, data file

   D. Database, tablespace, table

3. When doing an incomplete recovery, what three options stop the recovery?

   A. Cancel, time, change

   B. Rollback number, cancel, stop

   C. Time, redo log stop number, cancel

   D. Time, change, control number

4. What process performs user-process recovery?

   A. SMON

   B. DBWR

   C. CKPT

   D. PMON

5. What two files does Oracle recommend mirroring?

   A. The control file and redo logs files

   B. Rollback segment files and redo logs

   C. System data files and the control file

   D. All files should be mirrored.

APPLY YOUR KNOWLEDGE

6. What file contains configurable parameters for running a database in ARCHIVELOG mode?

   A. Control file

   B. Redo log file

   C. init.ora file

   D. System data file

7. What parameter will format the name of the archived redo logs?

   A. LOG_ARCHIVED_FORMAT

   B. LOG_ARCHIVED_NAME

   C. LOG_NAME

   D. ARCHIVED_LOG_FORMAT

8. When will the init.ora file be read and the SGA be configured when an Oracle instance is started?

   A. When the database is open

   B. When the database is mounted

   C. When the database is in NOMOUNT state

   D. To start an instance, you must have the init.ora file.

9. When you create a control file, what startup state must the Oracle instance be in?

   A. Open

   B. MOUNTED

   C. NOMOUNT

   D. Can be created in any mount state

10. What file can you configure parameters in to control a checkpoint?

    A. None

    B. Control file

    C. init.ora

    D. System data file

11. What parameter will place a time limit on checkpoints?

    A. TIME_FOR_CHECKPOINT

    B. LOG_CHECKPOINT_TIMEOUT

    C. CHECKPOINT_TIMER

    D. This can't be done.

12. If a control file is lost, what shutdown command must be used to shut down an instance?

    A. SHUTDOWN ABORT

    B. SHUTDOWN IMMEDIATE

    C. SHUTDOWN

    D. Any shutdown command will work.

13. When do you open the database with the RESETLOGS option?

    A. Whenever incomplete recovery is done on a database

    B. Whenever a tablespace is recovered

    C. Whenever a data file is recovered

    D. Whenever a new control file is created

APPLY YOUR KNOWLEDGE

Answers to Review Questions

1. **A.** A checkpoint of the data files won't be done when the SHUTDOWN ABORT command is issued. (This question deals with the objective "Understand the checkpoint event within a database.")

2. **C.** The RECOVER command can recover at the database, tablespace, and data file levels. (This question deals with the objective "Understand the RECOVER command.")

3. **A.** The capability to stop a recovery from applying all the archived logs is called incomplete recovery. Cancel, time, and change are the three ways it can be stopped. (This question deals with the objective "Understand the RECOVER command.")

4. **D.** The PMON process will manage the cleaning up of the user process, if it fails. (This question deals with the objective "Understand how a transaction weaves its way through the instance memory structures and the database external structures.")

5. **A.** The control file and the redo logs files can be software mirrored by using Oracle architecture. (This question deals with the objective "Understand how a transaction weaves its way through the instance memory structures and the database external structures.")

6. **C.** The init.ora file contains the parameters that can configure the destination and name of the archived redo logs. (This question deals with the objective "Understand the recovery options of running an instance in ARCHIVELOG or NOARCHIVELOG mode.")

7. **A.** LOG_ARCHIVED_FORMAT will format the name of the archived redo logs. (This question deals with the objective "Understand the recovery options of running an instance in ARCHIVELOG or NOARCHIVELOG mode.")

8. **D.** The instance can't be started without an init.ora file. (This question deals with the objective "Which option to use to start up the database.")

9. **C.** The instance must be in the NOMOUNT state, using the STARTUP NOMOUNT command. (This question deals with the objective "Which option to use to start up the database.")

10. **C.** The init.ora file contains parameters that will control when a checkpoint will be done on the database. (This question deals with the objective "Understand the checkpoint event within a database.")

11. **B.** The LOG_CHECKPOINT_TIMEOUT will set the number of seconds to go between checkpoints. (This question deals with the objective "Understand the checkpoint event within a database.")

12. **A.** The SHUTDOWN ABORT command must be used. (This question deals with the objective "Understand the RECOVER command."

13. **A.** The database must be open with the RESETLOGS option whenever incomplete recovery is performed. Tablespace and data file recoveries are always complete recoveries. A new control file can be created with the NORESETLOGS option. (This question deals with the objective "Understand the RECOVER command.")

TUNING

TUNING

This chapter helps you prepare for the exam by covering the following objectives:

Working and setup of dedicated server and multithreaded configurations.

▶ This objective is necessary in order to understand the differences between the working of two important types of Oracle Server configurations. Because no single tuning formula can work for all configuration types, it is important that you know the differences and working of different configurations so that you can tune accordingly.

Working and setup of Oracle Parallel Query option.

▶ This objective is necessary to understand the working of the Oracle Parallel Query option. Oracle Parallel Query plays an important role in tuning when it comes to data-intensive operations.

Working and setup of Oracle Parallel Server option and Oracle Distributed Systems.

▶ This objective is necessary to understand the setup of the Parallel Server option and Oracle Distributed Systems. To tune the system, you must understand its working and setup.

Types of contentions and methods of detecting and reducing them.

▶ This objective is necessary to understand the most important factor of poor performance—that is, contentions. To minimize contentions, you must know the methods for detecting and reducing them.

CHAPTER 10

Database Tuning

Issues in database design, when and how to denormalize database design for data warehousing.

▶ This objective is necessary to understand when denormalization is the solution for improving the performance and how to denormalize a system.

How to use different database objects to improve application performance.

▶ This objective helps you understand how to use database objects to improve application performance. No matter how well the application is written, if the right database objects aren't used to support the application, optimized performance can't be achieved.

STUDY STRATEGIES

▶ Because this chapter contains theoretical concepts about different configurations, contentions, and the working of database objects, it doesn't require that you be in front of a computer. What's more, even if you want to practice the examples given in this chapter for performing various tasks—such as setting up particular configuration, detecting and reducing contentions, and using database objects with an application—you need to have Oracle Server installed on the computer as well as a medium-size database and application ready for use. As most of you are expected to have Personal Oracle installed on your PC, most of the examples in this chapter can be practiced.

As you are reading the chapter, it is recommended that you take your own notes on features of different configurations discussed, procedures for setting up a particular configuration, methods for detecting and reducing the contentions, and when to use different database objects. Revise these notes and the figures included in this chapter before going to the exam. These notes and the figures will summarize all the theoretical concepts about database tuning that you need to know before going to the exam.

INTRODUCTION

Database applications vary in terms of the nature of tasks they perform. Online Transaction Processing (OLTP) applications, for example, manipulate data often. On the other hand, data warehousing applications perform complex queries on very large tables but very little manipulation. Oracle Server is a very tunable and flexible software that enables you to make small adjustments to affect database performance depending on the nature of the applications running on it.

Keep in mind that performance tuning measures have been taken since the beginning stages of the application development cycle. Special design considerations are taken into account, for example, and suitable database objects are created to speed up the application's performance. In other words, the performance must be built in. Optimal performance tuning can't be performed after the system is put into production.

Your goal for tuning varies depending on the application's need. OLTP applications need best throughput, for example, whereas data warehousing applications need best response time. There must be some performance targets that you should try to achieve by your tuning attempts. Suppose that you are given the target of reducing the response time to two seconds. You first step should be to identify the bottleneck or contentions that are slowing down the system, determine the cause, and take corrective action. You should never tune just for the sake of tuning, without any target in mind.

Database tuning is not only a responsibility of the DBA, but also demands cooperation of database designers and developers. No matter how efficiently the application is written, if the designers haven't taken performance issues into account while developing the database model, the application's overall performance can't be optimized. Similarly, developers must optimize the data-flow model of the application and tune the SQL.

This chapter discusses database-tuning issues. The beginning section familiarizes you with different types of configurations an Oracle Server can have and which types of applications each configuration is suitable for. When you understand the working of several configuration types, you will learn how several types of contentions can arise in the system and how to monitor and reduce them. The chapter ends with a discussion on database and application design considerations that can help reduce the application performance problems that have been around since the development stage.

This chapter assumes that you have the basic knowledge of database architecture and structures that is covered in Chapter 5, "Oracle Database Architecture," and Chapter 6, "Managing Database Structures."

OPTIMAL CONFIGURATION

The following sections detail several ways in which you can configure an Oracle Server. The first section discusses the working and setup of two configuration options—Dedicated Server process and Multithreaded Server process—that are available for connecting user processes to the Oracle memory areas. Then the configuration and working of Parallel Query processes is explained. The last two sections explain the setup and working of the Oracle Parallel Server option and the Oracle Distributed option.

Configuring Oracle Server

Working and setup of dedicated server and multithreaded configurations.

In a multiprocess system, processes can be divided into two categories: *user processes* and *Oracle processes*. The combination of Oracle processes and memory allocated by Oracle for its use is called an *Oracle instance*.

When users run an application program such as Pro*C or an Oracle tool such as Server Manager or Developer/2000, they have some Oracle server code executing on their behalf, which interprets and processes the SQL statements of the application. Oracle creates a user process to execute this code.

Oracle processes can be divided further into two groups: server processes and background processes. Oracle creates the server processes to handle the requests of user processes connected to the Oracle instance. Server processes created on behalf of each user's application performs many functions, such as parsing and executing

SQL statements issued by the application, reading data blocks from the disks into memory buffer (SGA), and returning results to the application.

To accommodate many users, a multiprocess Oracle system uses a few additional processes known as *background processes*. These processes are in the memory to manage different tasks such as writing data to the datafiles and redo log files, performing recovery in case of a process failure, resolving failures in distributed transactions, archiving data, providing inter-instance locking, and refreshing snapshots. Figure 10.1 illustrates the concept of several types of processes.

FIGURE 10.1

The relationship between Oracle processes and user processes.

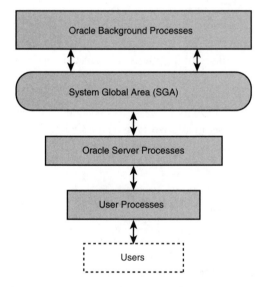

In a multiprocess instance, users can connect to one of two different types of Oracle Server processes to manipulate data in an Oracle database:

- ◆ Dedicated Server process
- ◆ Multithreaded Server process

Dedicated Server Process

Consider a system in which many users are using applications on different computers and are connected to one Oracle server. Oracle will create as many user processes as the number of users. In a Dedicated Server configuration, Oracle will also create as many server processes as the number of user processes to serve the users' requests.

There's a one-to-one relationship between the number of user processes and the number of server processes. The server processes keep running in the server's memory. When a user process requests any information from the database, its corresponding server process handles the request and returns the desired data to the user process. Figure 10.2 illustrates the concept of Dedicated Server processes.

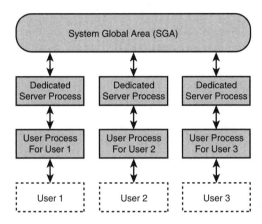

FIGURE 10.2
Oracle Dedicated Server configuration.

In a Dedicated Server configuration when a user isn't requesting any information from the database, the user process is idle; but its corresponding server process is still running in the memory, resulting in inefficient memory usage.

When Oracle is installed, Dedicated Server configuration is the default setting. These initialization parameters may to be set to "null" or omitted from the initialization file in order to run Oracle in this configuration:

◆ MTS_DISPATCHER

◆ MTS_SERVICE

◆ MTS_SERVERS

◆ MTS_LISTENER_ADDRESS

When the number of users is high, it is impractical to devote a separate process to each user in memory. Therefore, if possible, users shouldn't connect to Oracle with a Dedicated Server process; instead, they should use Multithreaded Server processes, which eliminate inefficient memory usage. In some situations, however, users or database administrators should explicitly connect to an instance with a Dedicated Server process. For example, activities such as submitting a batch job, using Server Manager to start up and shut down, and performing media recovery on a database should be conducted using Dedicated Server process because they don't allow much idle time to server processes.

Multithreaded Server Process

Dedicated Server processes result in an inefficient memory usage because user process is idle most of the time and isn't requesting any information. Oracle designed Multithreaded Server (MTS) to remove this inefficiency.

MTS configuration allows many user processes to share a small number of server processes. There's not a one-to-one relationship between user processes and server process. Without the multithreaded configuration, each user requires its own dedicated server process (as discussed earlier). For a small number of server processes to serve many user processes, a dispatcher processes is used. Each client's user process is connected to a dispatcher process that routes a client's request to the next available server process. Thus, server processes are shared among many user processes via dispatcher processes and are therefore called *Shared Server processes*. Multithreaded configuration reduces system overhead and increases the number of users who could be connected to an instance. Figure 10.3 shows how many user processes can share a few server processes through dispatcher.

When a user tries to connect to an instance, a network listener process determines whether a user process can use Shared Server processes. If it can, the listener gives the user process the address of a dispatcher process. When a user process makes a request on behalf of the application, its dispatcher process places the request in the request queue common for all dispatchers in the SGA. The request is picked up from this queue by the next available Shared Server process. The shared server process brings the desired results by making calls to the database and places them to the dispatcher's response queue. The dispatcher picks up the results from its response queue and hands it over to the user process that requested the data.

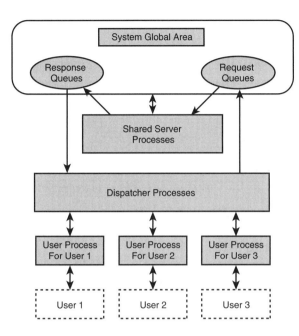

FIGURE 10.3
Oracle MTS configuration.

To set the MTS configuration, these parameters must be assigned values: SHARED_POOL_SIZE, MTS_LISTENER_ADDRESS, MTS_SERVICE, MTS_DISPATCHERS, MTS_MAX_DISPATCHERS, MTS_SERVERS, and MTS_MAX_SERVERS. After setting up these parameters, you must restart the instance. Instance will be started in multithreaded configuration.

SHARED_POOL_SIZE

The SHARED_POOL_SIZE parameter specifies the size of the shared pool in bytes. The shared pool is a part of SGA memory and contains the data dictionary cache, library cache, and session information. When users connect through MTS, Oracle needs to allocate more space in the shared pool to store information about the connections between user processes, dispatcher processes, and shared servers. Add 1KB to the value of SHARED_POOL_SIZE for each user who will connect to the instance using MTS.

MTS_LISTENER_ADDRESS

As mentioned earlier, the network listener process waits for an incoming connection request and gives the user process the address of a dispatcher process. The MTS_LISTENER_ADDRESS parameter specifies the address at which the listener process will listen for connection requests for a specific protocol. The parameter file may contain multiple addresses, as follows:

```
MTS_LISTENER_ADDRESS="(ADDRESS=(PROTOCOL=tcp)
➥(HOST=hostname)(PORT=6000))"
MTS_LISTENER_ADDRESS="(ADDRESS=(PROTOCOL=decnet)
➥(OBJECT=objectname)(NODE=nodename))"
```

MTS_SERVICE

The MTS_SERVICE parameter specifies the name of the service associated with dispatchers. A user requests MTS by specifying this service name in the connect string. A service name must be unique. If this parameter isn't set, its value defaults to the value of the DB_NAME parameter. If DB_NAME also isn't set, an error is returned.

```
MTS_SERVICE = "dispatcher_sevice_name"
```

MTS_DISPATCHERS

The MTS_DISPATCHERS parameter specifies the number of dispatchers processes started at instance startup for each network protocol. Each network protocol requires a separate specification—for example,

```
MTS_DISPATCHERS = "decnet, 3"
MTS_DISPATCHERS = "tcp, 2"
MTS_DISPATCHERS = "ipx, 3"
```

Before specifying the value to MTS_DISPATCHER parameters, you have to estimate the number of dispatchers to start for each network protocol at instance startup. The number of dispatchers for each protocol can be calculated as follows:

```
Number of dispatcher = CEIL(maximum number of concurrent
➥sessions / connections per dispatcher)
```

The CEIL function is very similar to the ROUND function. It returns an integer greater than or equal to the value passed into the function. The following examples clarify the difference between CEIL and ROUND:

	15.35	*15.50*	*15.74*
CEIL	16.00	16.00	16.00
ROUND	15.00	16.00	16.00

The numerator specifies the number of concurrent sessions that you are expecting on the particular network protocol. The denominator specifies the number of session connections per dispatcher process. The host operating system limits the number sessions that could be connected to one dispatcher process. The more dispatchers you have, the better database performance users will experience, because they won't have to wait as long for dispatcher service.

You can change the number of dispatcher processes for a specific protocol while the instance is running by the ALTER SYSTEM command as follows:

```
ALTER SYSTEM SET MTS_DISPATCHERS = "decnet, 1"
```

After the instance starts, you can change the number of dispatcher processes only for those protocols mentioned in the MTS_LISTENER_ ADDRESS parameter. To start dispatcher processes for the protocols for which there are now no dispatchers, you have to shut down the database, change the parameter file, and restart the database.

MTS_MAX_DISPATCHERS

The MTS_MAX_DISPATHCHER parameter specifies the maximum number of total dispatcher processes that can be started on an instance for all protocols combined. You can estimate the maximum number of dispatcher processes an instance will require as follows:

```
Max dispatchers = maximum number of concurrent sessions on
➥all protocols / connections per dispatcher
```

MTS_SERVERS

The MTS_SERVERS parameter determines the number of Shared Server processes that will start at instance startup. The value for this parameter depends on the number of users connected to an instance and the level of processing each user requires. If 100 users are connected to an instance and no single user is doing heavy processing, for example, one Shared Server process can server 10 to 20 users. If the processing level required by users is high, the ratio of users to Shared Server processes will be small because the Shared Server process will increase.

If the current number of Shared Server processes is small as specified by MTS_SERVERS, and the amount of processing required by the users is high, Oracle can create more Shared Server process automatically. When the load of processing comes down again, the extra Shared Server processes are eliminated by Oracle until the number of shared processes comes back to the value of MTS_SERVERS.

On the other hand, consider the situation where the value specified by the MTS_SERVERS parameter is high. High numbers of Shared

Server processes have been started at instance startup. If users aren't performing any tasks that require heavy processing or the number of users connected to an instance is small, most of the Shared Server processes will be idle. Oracle can't remove the idle processes in this situation because the minimum number of Shared Server processes present in the memory can't go below the value of MTS_SERVERS. The idle Shared Server processes will be an extra burden on the memory. Therefore, it is best to estimate fewer initial Shared Server processes. Additional processes are automatically created by Oracle, if needed, and deallocated when they become idle, but the number of Shared Server processes can't go below the value of MTS_SERVERS.

Oracle will use Shared Server processes if MTS_SERVERS is set to at least 1. If this parameter is set to 0 or omitted, Oracle won't start any shared server process at all. You can change the number of minimum server processes that could be started while the instance is running by using the ALTER SYSTEM command:

```
ALTER SYSTEM SET MTS_SERVERS = 4;
```

See the later section "Reducing Contentions" for more details on this topic.

MTS_MAX_SERVERS

The maximum number of Shared Server processes that can be started at any time is determined by the MTS_MAX_SERVERS parameter. If the processing load increases or the number of user increases, Oracle can create additional server processes until the number of processes present in memory is equal to the value of MTS_MAX_SERVERS. Set this parameter to allow an appropriate number of Shared Server processes at times of highest activity. By experimenting with this limit and by monitoring Shared Server processes, you can determine the ideal setting for this parameter. See the later section "Reducing Contentions" for more details.

Parallel Query Option

Working and setup of Oracle Parallel Query option.

One of Oracle's most exciting features is its capability to partition a SQL query into subqueries and concurrently process these subqueries. This feature is known as *Parallel Query processing*. Without the Parallel Query option, a SQL statement is always processed by a single server process; with the Parallel Query option, multiple processes can work together simultaneously to process a single SQL statement. The Parallel Query feature results in much faster performance. At this time, Parallel Query is useful only for queries that perform full-table scans.

For most queries, the time spent to read the data from disk is far more than the actual time spent on processing that data. With the Parallel Query option, you can compensate for the I/O delay by using several query processes. To be most effective, the table should be placed on separate disks by striping its tablespace across many disks, so that each process can perform I/O against its segment of table without interfering with the other concurrent query processes. Parallel Query works best on Symmetric Multiprocessor (SMP) machines and Massively Parallel Processing (MPP) machines.

When a SQL statement is executed without a Parallel Query option, a single query server process does the necessary work of processing. In Parallel Query processing, a query coordinator process divides the work into several pieces and assigns each piece to different query servers to process. The number of query servers, which are given a single task to perform in pieces, is called the *degree of parallelism*. These query servers perform simultaneous small table scans on the table, which appear to users as fast full-table scans. When all query servers return the results to the query coordinator, the query coordinator puts together all the results and returns the final result to the user process (or to the dispatcher in case of multithreaded configuration). Figure 10.4 shows the working of the Parallel Query option.

An instance starts with the number of query servers equal to the value of the PARALLEL_MIN_SERVERS parameter. If the number of query servers in the pool isn't enough to handle the load, Oracle can create more query server processes up to the maximum limit of PARALLEL_MAX_SERVERS. If a query server is idle for time equal to the value of PARALLEL_SERVER_IDLE_TIME, Oracle automatically terminates this process. The number of query server processes can't go below the value given in PARALLEL_MIN_SERVERS.

FIGURE 10.4
How the Parallel Query option executes a query.

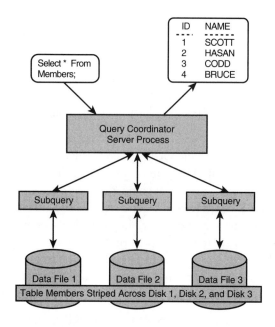

The Oracle Server can process the following statements in parallel with Parallel Query option:

- ◆ SELECT statements
- ◆ Subqueries in UPDATE, INSERT, and DELETE statements
- ◆ CREATE TABLE AS SELECT statements

The following operations in these statements can be made parallel by the Oracle server:

- ◆ Joins
- ◆ Sorts
- ◆ Table scans

The working of a Parallel Query process can be divided into sequential five steps:

1. The optimizer determines the statement execution plan.

2. The operation to be performed in parallel is determined by the query coordinator.

3. Degree of parallelism, or the number of query servers to use, is determined by the query coordinator.

4. The query servers are given their portion of work to do by the query coordinator.

5. On receiving the individual results from the query servers, the query coordinator reassembles the data and returns it to the user process.

The query coordinator process determines the degree of parallelism by using the following precedence:

◆ Hints included in the SQL statement

◆ The default degree of parallelism defined in the CREATE TABLE statement

◆ Degree of parallelism defined in initialization parameters

Degree of parallelism can be mentioned in the hint. For example, the following SQL statement will use five query servers to process the request:

```
SELECT /*+ FULL(MEMBERS) PARALLEL (MEMBERS, 5)*/
id, name, address
FROM members
WHERE phone like '416%' and upper(address) like
➥'%TORONTO%';
```

Degree of parallelism can also be mentioned in the PARALLEL clause of the CREATE TABLE statement. For example, five query servers will populate the following new table:

```
CREATE TABLE member_analyses
PARALLEL (degree 5)
AS SELECT id, name, address
FROM members
WHERE phone like '416%' and upper(address) like
➥'%TORONTO%';
```

If the degree of parallelism isn't mentioned in the hint or in the PARALLEL clause, it is determined by the initialization parameter PARALLEL_DEFAULT_SCANSIZE as follows:

```
Degree of parallelism = size of the table /
➥PARALLEL_DEFAULT_SCANSIZE
(up to PARALLEL_DEFAULT_MAX_SIZE)
```

The Parallel Query option dramatically improves the performance of data warehousing applications, in which SQL statements involve very large table scans. As mentioned earlier, for Parallel Query processing to be effective, the table should be striped on many separate disks so that multiple processes can read the data at the same time.

The number and capacity of CPUs also affect Parallel Query processing. If your CPU is already running at 100% capacity, however, the degree of parallelism won't have much effect. Therefore, the Parallel Query option works best on multiple CPU machines such as SMP and MPP.

In addition to Parallel Query processing, the Parallel Query option offers parallel index creation, parallel loading, and parallel recovery:

◆ When creating an index with the Parallel Query option, a coordinator process dispatches two sets of query servers. One set scans the table to be indexed and obtains the rowids and column values, whereas the other set performs the sorting on these values and forwards the results to the coordinator process. The coordinator process then assembles the b*tree index from the sorted data items. Creating an index with the Parallel Query option can greatly reduce the time of index creation.

◆ Loading can be done in parallel by having multiple simultaneous sessions perform a direct path load into the same table. Each direct loader process uses the PARALLEL=TRUE and DIRECT=TRUE options. When PARALLEL=TRUE is specified, the loader doesn't place a lock on the table being loaded; instead, it creates a temporary segment for each concurrent process and merges them on completion. Best performance is achieved when each temporary file is located on separate disks.

◆ Parallel recovery can reduce recovery time dramatically. In traditional recovery, one process reads from the redo log file and then applies the changes to the datafiles. In parallel recovery, one process reads the redo log file and passes the entries onto the many recovery processes, which in turn simultaneously apply the changes to the datafiles (see Figure 10.5). Best performance is achieved when the data is striped into many datafiles, because recovery processes then write changes concurrently to the datafiles.

The following initialization parameters affect the operation of the Parallel Query option.

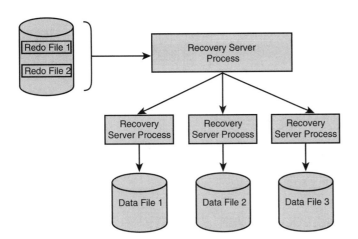

FIGURE 10.5
Parallel recovery.

PARALLEL_DEFAULT_MAX_SCANS

The PARALLEL_DEFAULT_MAX_SCANS parameter specifies the maximum number of query servers to be used by default for a query. This value is used when no value is given by the hint or by the table's PARALLEL clause.

PARALLEL_DEFAULT_SCANSIZE

The PARALLEL_DEFAULT_SCANSIZE parameter is used to determine the number of query servers to be used for a particular table. The number of query servers used for a table is determined by the following formula:

Number of servers =
size of the table / PARALLEL_DEFAULT_SCANSIZE
up to PARALLEL_DEFAULT_MAX_SIZE

As mentioned earlier, the query coordinator first tries to determine the degree of parallelism by the hint, and then by the default value given in the PARALLEL definition clause of the table. If no information is given in either of them, this formula is used.

RECOVERY_PARALLELISM

The RECOVERY_PARALLELISM parameter determines the number of processes to be used for recovery. If a value of 0 or 1 is given, recovery will be performed in serial rather than parallel.

PARALLEL_MAX_SERVERS

The PARALLEL_MAX_SERVERS parameter specifies the maximum number of query servers or parallel recovery processes an instance can use.

PARALLEL_MIN_SERVERS

The PARALLEL_MAX_SERVERS parameter specifies the minimum number of query servers or parallel recovery processes an instance can use.

PARALLEL_SERVER_IDLE_TIME

If a query server process is idle for the time equal to the value of PARALLEL_SERVER_IDLE_TIME, Oracle terminates this process. The number of Parallel Query servers can't be reduced below the value of PARALLEL_MIN_SERVERS.

Parallel Server Option

The Parallel Server option enables you to link several computers to form one large RDBMS. The Oracle parallel system is made up of several nodes, each running an Oracle instance that accesses a common database through a shared disk system.

Two important reasons for using Oracle Parallel Server is fault tolerance and performance. Better performance results from more memory resources available because more than one machine is being used.

The shared disk system also contains redo log files and rollback segments; therefore, it is possible for a node to perform instance recovery on another node in the event of a failure. If one node fails, other member nodes aren't affected. Fault tolerance increases with the addition of nodes in the system.

Communication between nodes is performed by a server interconnect, which consists of one or more high-speed network devices. Two important functions performed by the server interconnect are communicating locking information and providing system heartbeat, which is actually the message to other systems in the cluster that this system is still operational. Figure 10.6 shows the working of Oracle Parallel Server option.

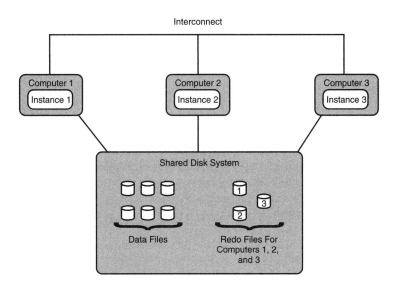

FIGURE 10.6
Oracle Parallel Server architecture.

To allow multiple instances to access the same data, the Oracle Parallel Server option uses a sophisticated locking mechanism performed through a process called the Distributed Lock Manager (DLM). The locks are referred to as Parallel Cache Management (PCM) locks. DLM is responsible for locking data that is being modified by an instance so that it can't be modified by any other instance during the time it is locked. Locking enables the data integrity across the Parallel Server system, or cluster. A group of blocks is locked by an instance until another instance needs that data. Because locks are held on a group of data blocks until another instance requests to use this group, dividing the users in such a manner that all the users accessing a set of data blocks use the same instance can reduce the contention among instances. Properly partitioning the data is very important to enhancing the performance.

When the instance starts, a number of PCM locks are created. Depending on the configuration of the instance, the number of data blocks under one lock varies. PCM locks can be acquired in one of the two different modes by an instance:

♦ Exclusive lock mode

♦ Read lock mode

When a lock is acquired in exclusive lock mode, the instance is allowed to update the blocks locked by its PCM lock. If some other instance is already using the blocks, the DLM will request that instance to release its lock, before the blocks can be locked by the requesting instance. After receiving the request from the DLM, the instance already holding the lock writes the data to the share disk before the lock is released. This process is called *pinging*. Now the requesting instance can lock the data blocks.

When a lock is acquired in read lock mode, during the time the instance has a lock on the data blocks, the data can't be changed. Many instances can acquire locks in read lock mode on the same data blocks, which isn't possible in exclusive lock mode. Using read-only tablespaces can reduce contention among instances. Oracle doesn't allocate PCM locks for the tables created in read-only tablespaces because these tables can't be updated.

PCM locks are allocated to the datafiles. The number of blocks each PCM lock can lock depends on the size of the datafile and the number of locks allocated to this file. The greater the number of PCM locks allocated to one datafile, the smaller the number of data blocks locked by one PCM lock. Because overhead is associated with PCM locks, it is not advisable to overconfigure PCM locks. If a PCM lock covers many data blocks, you may be unnecessarily pinging data blocks that aren't needed by the requesting instance. Therefore, it is advisable to put many locks on hot data blocks and a small number of locks on cold data blocks, which aren't modified much.

Oracle Parallel Server provides the framework for the Parallel Query option to work between nodes. Nodes are interconnected computers, each of which can be a client or a server depending on whether it is sending requests to other computers or responding to requests from other computers. It enables Parallel Query to ship queries between nodes so that multiple nodes can execute multiple subqueries on behalf of a single query. As a result, Oracle Parallel Query option works best in Oracle Parallel Server configuration.

The Oracle Parallel Server option is suitable for certain types of applications. The applications that will achieve the most benefits from Oracle Parallel Server option should have certain characteristics. They should have very little update activity, which reduces the amount of locking involved. Applications should be partitioned in such a way that one set of users who update a particular set of tables can use one server while other users who update a different set of tables can use a different server. This reduces the contention between servers. Very large applications that have small cache hit ratios benefit from the Oracle Parallel Server option. The smaller the chance that data is in the cache, the smaller the chance that the data is locked by the node and the smaller the contention between servers. Applications that perform large queries benefit from the Oracle Parallel Server option, as well as from the Oracle Parallel Query option.

An appropriate configuration of an Oracle parallel system is important to achieve high performance. The applications should be appropriately partitioned so that users of one instance aren't using the same data blocks as users of other instances. Many PCM locks should be put on the tables with heavy updates, and a small number of locks should be put on tables used for read-only purposes. If possible, read-only tablespaces should be used for read-only tables. PCTFREE and PCTUSED should be used to cause fewer rows per block on high-contention tables. This will reduce the contention by reducing the number of locks per block. The FREELIST GROUPS storage parameter allows different instances to maintain separate free lists. This parameter should be used to cause inserts to occur on different parts of the datafiles, thus reducing contention.

The following dynamic performance views contain information about the frequency of PCM lock contention:

- ◆ V$LOCK_ACTIVITY
- ◆ V$BH
- ◆ V$CACHE
- ◆ V$PING

The FREQUENCY column in these tables gives you an idea about the number of times lock conversion is taking place due to the contention among instances. You can use the following parameters to properly configure PCM locks in an Oracle parallel system.

GC_FILES_TO_LOCKS

The GC_FILES_TO_LOCKS parameter specifies the list of filenames with the number of PCM locks allocated to them. You can also specify the number of data blocks covered by a PCM lock. It is important to set this parameter to cover as many files as possible. To avoid performance problems, you should change it when the size of datafiles changes or when new datafiles are added. This requires you to shut down and restart your parallel server.

GC_DB_LOCKS

The GC_DB_LOCKS parameter specifies the total number of PCM locks covering data blocks cached in the multiple SGAs of a parallel server. The value of GC_DB_LOCKS must be at least one greater than the sum of the locks specified with the GC_FILES_TO_LOCKS initialization parameter of each node.

GC_LCK_PROCS

The GC_LCK_PROCS parameter specifies the number of lock processes to create for the instance. If unusually high numbers of locks are occurring, the value for this parameter could be increased. The default value is 1, which, in most cases, is sufficient. However, add 1 for each new LCKn process created.

GC_ROLLBACK_LOCKS

The GC_ROLLBACK_LOCKS parameter specifies the number of locks available for the rollback segment.

Distributed Systems

Working and setup of Oracle Parallel Server option and Oracle Distributed Systems.

A *distributed database system* is a set of two or more Oracle database servers that appears to users as a single database server. The data on each server can be concurrently accessed and modified via a network. Each server is controlled by its local DBA and cooperates to maintain the consistency of the global database. Every computer in a distributed system is a node. A node can be a client, a server, or both. Figure 10.7 shows an Oracle distributed system.

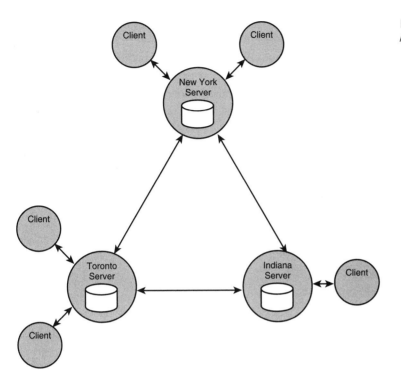

FIGURE 10.7
A typical Oracle distributed system.

Ensuring reliable data replication is important in a distributed system. Data replication means that a given data object of any database can have several stored copies, also called *replicas*, at several different databases in a distributed system. If the object is updatable, there must be a mechanism for ensuring that all the copies of this object at other databases also reflect the changes. Oracle Server provides various mechanisms for replicating the data. The type of the application you are using may dictate which method to use. Two methods are available for replicating data:

◆ Read-only snapshots

◆ Oracle's symmetric replication facility

Read-only snapshots are used if you just want to view the object or data at multiple sites without updating it. Oracle's symmetric replication is used when multiple copies of the object at different databases have to reflect the changes made to the original object.

Each server participating in a distributed system is administered independently from the other servers by their DBAs. Although all the servers can work together, each is a distinct repository of data and is administered separately. Each administrator's area of responsibility is more manageable because he controls and manages only local data. Failure recovery is usually performed on an individual-node basis. A distributed system is less likely to be disrupted by a node's failure. The global database is partially available as long as one database and the network are available. No single database failure will halt all global operations of a distributed database.

An efficient system must guarantee that all statements in a transaction are committed or rolled back as a unit, so that the data in the logical database can be kept consistent. This should be true for transactions that include any type of operation, including queries, updates, or remote procedure calls. In a distributed system, Oracle must maintain data consistency, even if a network or system failure occurs. Transaction recovery management guarantees that the database servers participating in a distributed transaction either all commit or all roll back the transaction statements.

A distributed system also provides facilities to transparently copy data among the nodes of the system. Copies of a table are maintained across the databases in a distributed system. Tables can be accessed faster by local user sessions because no network communication is involved. If a database that contains a critical table experiences a prolonged failure, replicas of the table in other databases can still be accessed. A database server that manages a distributed system makes table replication transparent to users working with the replicated tables.

An object has a unique name within a schema, and a schema has a unique name within a database. Therefore, within a database it is guaranteed that an object will be identified uniquely, even if more than one schema has objects with the same names. Suppose that two schemas in a database—SCHEMA1 and SCHEMA2—have tables called MEMBERS. Both tables can be uniquely identified as SCHEMA1.MEMBERS and SCHEMA2.MEMBERS. In a distributed system, an object of a database has to be uniquely identified by any other database. This is possible only when the names of all the databases are unique. To achieve this purpose, the databases are arranged in a hierarchical manner so that they can be given distinct names. Suppose that a private public library has branches in many cities in North America, and all the branches have their own databases. In a distributed system, the library can arrange its database hierarchy (see Figure 10.8).

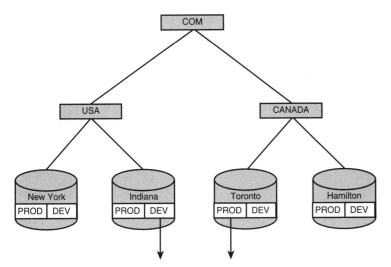

FIGURE 10.8
Global database names: The Oracle naming scheme in a distributed system.

Suppose that each database has two schemas, PROD and DEV, and each schema has a table called MEMBERS. Table MEMBERS of any database can be uniquely identified:

```
prod.members@toronto.canada.com
dev.members@indiana.usa.com
```

In a distributed system, a query can be local, remote, or distributed. A query retrieving data from a local database is a local query:

```
SELECT * FROM members;
```

If the query is retrieving information from another database, it is a remote query:

```
SELECT * FROM prod.members@toronto.canada.com
```

If it is retrieving information from more than one database, it would be a distributed query:

```
SELECT * FROM prod.members@toronto.canada.com a
    WHERE a.name in
        (SELECT b.name FROM
        prod.members@indiana.usa.com b);
```

Synonyms can be created for the object that resides on different databases:

```
CREATE SYNONYM toronto_members FOR
➥prod.members@toronto.canada.com;
```

Now users can use this table without knowing the name of database in which it resides:

```
SELECT * from toronto_members;
```

The term *location transparency* is used to describe the functionality of hiding location information from users.

REDUCING CONTENTIONS

Types of contentions and methods of detecting and reducing them.

The term *contention* describes the situation that occurs when more than one Oracle process attempts to obtain the same resource simultaneously. Some processes have to wait until the other process frees the resource.

The V$SYSTEM_EVENT dynamic performance view is a good source of information about resource contention symptoms. It can reveal various system problems that may affect performance. I/O contention, buffer contention, and latch contention are a few examples of such problems.

Start the investigation of contention problems by checking V$SYSTEM_EVENT. Look for the events with the highest average wait time and then take necessary actions on each. Action can be taken in the Oracle database or in applications to solve the problem. Sometimes problems can't be solved without changing the application.

Contentions can be of the following types:

- ◆ Disk contention
- ◆ Rollback segment contention
- ◆ Multithreaded Server process contention
- ◆ Query server contention
- ◆ Redo log buffer latches contention
- ◆ LRU (least recently used) latch contention
- ◆ Free list contention

Disk (I/O) Contention

A fixed number of I/Os can occur on disk in a unit time. Disk contention can occur when multiple processes try to access the same disk simultaneously. Disk contention or I/O per disk can be reduced by spreading the datafiles to many disks or by caching data blocks in the SGA. If the desired data is already in the SGA, the disk won't be accessed, and hence I/Os will be reduced.

The main idea in designing the physical layout of a system with heavy I/O, as in an online transaction processing system (OLTP) system, is to spread the datafiles and redo log files evenly across disks and to provide balanced I/Os across them. This can be achieved by placing one or more heavily accessed files on a less active disk. Apply this principle to each disk until the I/O is uniformly distributed. Files unrelated to Oracle should not be stored on the same disk that contains Oracle datafiles. This is important to reduce disk contention.

Similarly, place each set of redo log files on a separate disk with no other activity. The LGWR process writes information of redo log files sequentially when the transaction is committed. If no other files are on disk other than redo log files, LGWR can write smoothly. If you are maintaining multiple copies of redo log files, place each set on a separate disk. Mirroring won't affect the performance of LGWR because it writes on each set of redo log files in parallel.

If you are running Oracle in ARCHIVELOG mode, placing the whole set of redo log files on a separate disk will create an LGWR-ARCH contention. LGWR will try to write data on one redo log file, and ARCH will try to read data from another redo log file on the same disk. Therefore, when ARCHIVELOG mode is on, each set of redo log files should be distributed across more than one disk drive.

Using separate disks for each set of redo log files and datafiles is a good practice—if one disk fails, you have data on the other one. Mirroring redo log files is also an important safety measure—if one redo log disk fails, you have the other one.

A table containing large data can be placed on more than one disk. This practice is known as *striping*. A large table's data is broken into small portions and stored into separate datafiles. These datafiles are then placed on separate disks. This permits concurrent access to different portions of the table by different processes, and hence reduces disk contention. Striping can be done manually or with the help of operating system striping utilities.

In manual striping, you create a tablespace and assign more than one datafile to it. Then you create a table in this tablespace and set the minimum number of extents for the table equal to the number of datafiles and the size of the extents equal to the size of the datafile. All extents are immediately allocated in separate datafiles, so the data for this table is written evenly on each datafile. Figure 10.9 shows the advantage of striping a table across many datafiles.

FIGURE 10.9
Table striping and its performance benefits.

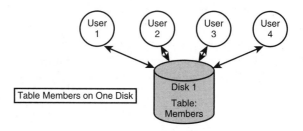

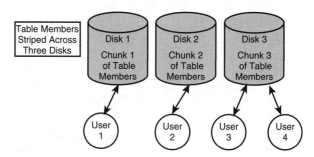

Suppose that you have a table that's taking 10GB in an Oracle datafile. You have an option of placing the data of this table evenly on five different disks of 2GB each. Create a tablespace and assign five datafiles to it as follows:

```
CREATE TABLESPACE my_striped_tablespace
DATAFILE 'data_file_1' SIZE 2 GB,
'data_file_2' SIZE 2GB,
'data_file_3' SIZE 2GB,
'data_file_4' SIZE 2GB,
'data_file_5' SIZE 2GB;
```

Now you can create a striped table. Specify the size of an extent equal to the size of a datafile (2GB) and the number of extents equal to the number of datafiles (five) in the storage clause of the CREATE TABLE statement:

```
CREATE TABLE my_striped_table      (
                    EMPNO      number,
                    ENAME      varchar2(20))
                    TABLESPACE my_striped_tablespace
     STORAGE   ( INITIAL 2046 MB NEXT 2046 MB
                    MINEXTENTS 5 PCTINCREASE 0 );
```

It could be difficult to manage the striping of hundreds of datafiles across hundreds of disks and to balance the load across these disks. Therefore, hot tables should be striped across many disks, and cold tables should be striped across fewer disks or not striped at all.

Alternatively, operating system striping can be used with the help of striping software such as Logical Storage Manager for UNIX. Operating system disk striping is done by taking two or more disks and creating one large logical disk. In sequence, stripes appear on the first disk, and then on the second disk, and so on. The size of each stripe depends on the operating system and striping software. To figure out which disk has the desired piece of data, the operating system keeps track of where the data is located. In the process of maintaining this information, a certain amount of CPU time is spent.

Advances in disk technology have made some traditional database recovery methods obsolete. Disk memory schemes such as redundant arrays of inexpensive disks (RAID) offer a very high degree of reliability and availability. RAID consists of three components: an array of small disk devices, a controller to manage the I/O against the disks, and software to distribute the data across the disk array and to manage recovery. Different vendors offer array management software with different algorithms of array management. In case of disk failure, the RAID software redirects any new write operations to temporary storage. After the bad disk is replaced, the software automatically resynchronizes the new disk. Figure 10.10 shows the working of RAID.

RAID can be used for striping the data. Because its main advantage is that it automatically distributes all the data evenly across many disks, you don't have to create hundreds of datafiles and place them into hundreds of separate disks yourself. All the available datafiles will be distributed evenly across the disks by the array management software. You also don't have to worry about striping hot tables across many disks and cold tables across fewer disks because all the data is evenly distributed and the striping size is small. Disk arrays are sometimes preferred on operating system striping, because hardware striping doesn't incur any additional load on the CPU.

NOTE **Note** Although the size of a 2GB datafile is really 1024 * 2 = 2048MB, the size of an extent is specified here to be 2046MB because table extents should be slightly smaller than the datafiles to allow for overhead.

FIGURE 10.10
A simplified diagram of RAID architecture.

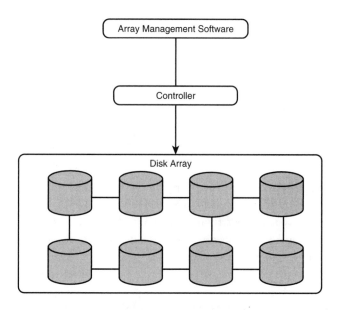

Rollback Segment Contention

Rollback segments are constantly used during transaction processing. Delays caused by rollback segment contention can affect performance. Rollback segments record information about the transactions that may be used in the event of a rollback. Rollback segments are also used to provide read consistency and database recovery. It is important to size the rollback segments correctly, to create an appropriate number of rollback segments, and to distribute them properly according to the number of user processes that require them.

When the transaction is being performed, the information about which blocks are modified and what the values were before the modification is written to the rollback segment. When the transaction begins, it is assigned a rollback segment automatically, or an application can manually specify a rollback segment with the SET TRANSACTION command's USE ROLLBACK SEGMENT parameter. At the end of the transaction, when a commit occurs, the rollback information is released from the rollback segment and isn't deleted to provide read-consistent views for other queries that started before the transaction was committed. For this reason, rollback segments are written as a circular buffer.

A rollback segment must have at least two extents. When one extent is full, the information is written on the second extent. When the second extent is full, the information is written on the first extent. But if the first extent isn't free and is being used to provide read-consistent view to other queries, another extent is created and the information is written to this new extent. If the number of extents is more than the optimal size of the rollback segments (two in this example), the extra extents are dropped from the rollback segments as soon as they become free. Figure 10.11 shows the process of allocating extents in a rollback segment.

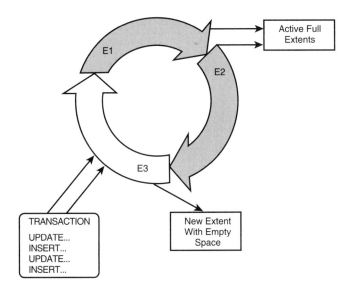

FIGURE 10.11
Allocating extents in a rollback segment.

Rollback contention occurs when many concurrent transactions attempt to use the same rollback segment. As a rule of thumb, most users create one rollback segment for every four concurrent transactions.

Two dynamic performance views are important to identify the rollback segment contention:

◆ V$WAITSTAT (CLASS, COUNT, TIME)

◆ V$SYSSTAT (STATISTIC#, NAME, CLASS, VALUE)

Four rows of V$WAITSTAT are relevant, where the value for the CLASS column is as follows:

Value	*Meaning*
'undo header'	Number of waits for buffers containing header blocks of the SYSTEM rollback segment

continues

continued

Value	Meaning
'undo block'	Number of waits for buffers containing blocks other than header blocks of the SYSTEM rollback segment
'system undo header'	Number of waits for buffers containing header blocks of rollback segments other than the SYSTEM rollback segment
'system undo block'	Number of waits for buffers containing blocks other than header blocks of rollback segments other than the SYSTEM rollback segment

When the database is created, the only rollback segment present is the SYSTEM rollback segment. It is also used when other rollback segments aren't available.

Use the following query to monitor these statistics over a period of time while your application is running:

```
SELECT class, count
FROM v$waitstat
WHERE class IN ('system undo header', 'system undo block',
➡'undo header', 'undo block');


CLASS               COUNT
- - - - - - - - - - - - - - - - - - - - - - - - - -
system undo header   3023
system undo block     523
undo header          1345
undo block            871
```

Compare these values with the total number of requests for data over the same period of time. The number of requests for data is equal to the sum of the values of 'db buffer gets' and 'consistent gets', which you can get from the V$SYSSTAT view. The following query brings this information:

```
SELECT SUM(value) 'TOTAL DATA REQUEST'
FROM v$sysstat
WHERE name IN ('db block gets', 'consistent gets');


TOTAL DATA REQUEST
- - - - - - - - - - - - - - - - -
          926212
```

If the number of waits from any rollback segment blocks or header is greater than 1% of the total number of data requests, you should consider creating more rollback segments to reduce contention. When creating rollback segments, two things are important: size and number of rollback segments. Values of these variables depend on the type and length of the transaction and the nature of the application. Several different sizes of rollback segments should be created and used for different purposes. If OLTP is using the system, there should be many small rollback segments about 10KB to 20KB in size and with two to four extents. In an OLTP system, many concurrent transactions may occur, each affecting a small portion of data. Performance is improved, because small size of the segments provides for the better chance of being cached in the SGA. For transactions that update large amounts of data, you should use a larger rollback segment. As a rule of thumb, the size of the rollback segment should be about 10% of the size of the largest table. Most SQL statements affect only 10% of the data in a table. Similarly, if there are large queries in the system, larger rollback segments should also be used about 10% of the size of the largest table. Long queries need quite a bit of rollback information to maintain read consistency.

You have seen that the size of rollback segments should be approximately 10% of the size of the largest table, except in the case of OLTP systems. Best performance can be achieved when there are about 10 to 20 same-size extents per rollback segments. Therefore, the size of each extent would be the size of the rollback segment divided by the number of extents.

When using these rules, performance may still be lost if dynamic growth occurs in rollback segments. To determine whether this is a problem, look in the dynamic performance views V$ROLLSTAT and V$ROLLNAME. Relevant columns of the table V$ROLLSTAT are as follows:

Column	Meaning
AVEACTIVE	The current average size of active extents (extents with uncommitted transactions).
EXTENDS	The number of times the rollback segment added an extent.
SHRINKS	The number of times the rollback segment shrank; each shrink may drop one or more extents at a time from the rollback segment.

The V$ROLLNAME view is used to get names of the rollback segments. Use the following query to fetch the desired rows:

```
SELECT a.name, b.aveactive "average size", b.extends,
➡b.shrinks
FROM v$rollname a, v$rollstat b;
```

NAME	AVERAGE	SIZE	EXTENDS	SHRINKS
SYSTEM	0	0	0	0
SYSTEM	0	0	0	0
RB1	0	0	0	0
RB1	0	0	0	0
RB2	0	0	0	0
RB2	0	0	0	0

If the average size is close to the optimal size of the rollback segment, the optimal size is correct. Otherwise, more segments have to be created. A high value of extends or shrinks also suggests the creation of more segments. A rollback segment can be created by the following command:

```
CREATE PUBLIC ROLLBACK SEGMENT my_rollback_segment
TABLESPACE my_tablespace
STORAGE (
    INITIAL 150K
    NEXT 50K
    OPTIMAL 500K
    MINEXTENTS 10
    MAXEXTENTS 100
    );
```

MTS Process Contention

In a Multithreaded Server configuration, many user processes can share very few server processes, unlike a Dedicated Server configuration, in which there's one server process for every user process. With a Multithreaded Server (MTS) configuration, many user processes connect to a dispatcher process, which routes client requests to the next available Shared Server process. A Multithreaded Server configuration offers many advantages, such as reduced system overhead and increased number of users that can be supported.

Three main types of processes are involved in an MTS architecture: listener process, dispatcher process, and Shared Server processes. The listener process waits for incoming connection requests and gives the user process the address of a dispatcher process. The dispatcher process places the request on the request queue in the SGA, where it is picked up by the next available Shared Server process. The Shared Server process completes each user process's request by making calls to the database. The Shared Server process then returns the result to the dispatcher's response queue. The dispatcher then returns the result to the user process. Figure 10.3 earlier in this chapter shows the working of a Multithreaded Server.

In a Multithreaded Server configuration, contention can occur in dispatcher and Shared Server processes.

Contention in Dispatcher Processes

The symptoms that indicate contention in dispatcher process are high busy rates for existing dispatcher processes and a steady rise in waiting time for responses in the response queues of dispatcher processes.

The V$DISPATCHER dynamic performance view shows the idle and busy rates for the dispatcher processes. Relevant columns for this table are as follows:

Column	Meaning
IDLE	Idle time for the dispatcher process in hundredths of a second
BUSY	Busy time for the dispatcher process in hundredths of a second

Over a period of time, you can monitor the statistics by using the following query:

```
SELECT network, sum(busy) / (sum(busy) + sum(idle)) "busy
➡rate"
FROM v$dispatcher
GROUP BY network;

NETWORK   BUSY RATE
-------   ---------
decnet    .008283817
tcp       .041222051
```

The query will give you the total busy rate for the dispatcher processes of each protocol. The decnet process has been in use about .08% of the time since the instance was started, and tcp has been in use for about 4% of the time. If a dispatcher process is busy for more than 50% of the time, the performance of the user connected to the protocol through this dispatcher may be increased by adding a new dispatcher process to that protocol. You should measure these statistics for the time database is in use, not since when the instance was started. The statistic given by the table shows the idle and busy rates since the instance was started.

The V$QUEUE dynamic performance view shows the response queue activity for the dispatcher processes. Relevant columns of this table are as follows:

Column	Meaning
WAIT	Total waiting time for all responses that have been in the queue in hundredths of a second
TOTALQ	Total number of responses that have been in the queue

Over a period of time, use the following query to monitor the statistics:

```
SELECT network, SUM(wait)/SUM(totalq) "average wait time
➥per response"
FROM v$queue a, dispatcher b
WHERE a.type='DISPATCHER'
AND a.paddr=b.paddr
GROUP BY network;

NETWORK   AVERAGE WAIT TIME PER RESPONSE
- - - - - - - - - - - - - - - - - - - - - - - - - - - - - - - - - - -
decnet                          .2184930
tcp                                    0
```

You can see that a response in the queue for decnet dispatcher processes waits an average of 0.21 second. There have been no responses in the queue for tcp dispatcher processes. If the average wait time for a specific network protocol continues to increase with time as the application runs, adding dispatcher processes may improve performance of those user processes connected to servers using that protocol. Dispatcher processes can be added by using the MTS_DISPATCHERS parameter of the ALTER SYSTEM command while Oracle is running. Or you can change this parameter in the initialization file, which will then be effective when a new instance is started.

Contention in Shared Server Processes

A steady increase in waiting time for requests in the request queue identifies contention in Shared Server processes. The dynamic performance view V$QUEUE contains relevant statistics in this regard. Relevant columns of this table are as follows:

Column	Meaning
WAIT	Total waiting time for all requests that have been in the queue, in hundredths of a second
TOTALQ	Total number of requests that have ever been in the queue

Over a period of time, use the following query to monitor the statistics:

```
SELECT DECODE (totalq,0,0,wait/totalq) "average wait time
➥per requests"
FROM v$queue
WHERE type = 'COMMON';

AVERAGE WAIT TIME PER REQUEST
-----------------------------
                     .081231
```

Note that, like the preceding query, the data hasn't been grouped by the networks because only one request queue is shared by all dispatchers. Each dispatcher has its own response queue in the SGA. Also notice that the DECODE function is used to prevent division by 0.

You can see that the average wait time per request is .09 second. If the average wait time rises with time as the application is running, increasing the number of share servers may improve performance. You can find out the currently running shared servers from the dynamic performance view V$SHARED_SERVERS:

```
SELECT COUNT(*)
FROM v$shared_servers
WHERE status != 'QUIT'

COUNT(*)
--------
       8
```

If the load on existing shared servers increases drastically, Oracle automatically adds Shared Server processes. You may not be able to improve performance just by adding more Shared Server processes by yourself. If, however, the number of Shared Server processes has reached the limit given by the initialization parameter MTS_MAX_ SERVERS and the average wait time in the requests queue is still increasing, you may be able to improve performance by increasing the MTS_MAX_SERVERS value. The default value is 20; the maximum value depends on the operating system. You can add Shared Server processes by using the MTS_SERVERS parameters of the ALTER SYSTEM command while Oracle is running. Or you can change this parameter in the initialization file, which will then be effective only when a new instance is started.

Query Server Contention

Let's look at the summary of how the Parallel Query option works. The Parallel Query option is one of the most exciting features of Oracle, first introduced in Oracle7.3. The Parallel Query option can partition SQL queries into subqueries and dedicate separate processes to simultaneously service each query. These separate processes can simultaneously read different portions of the table if they are located on datafiles at separate disks, and simultaneously sort these fetched portions in the memory. Therefore, a considerable portion of the time wasted in I/O can be saved by using this option. Now, this option is available only for queries that perform full-table scans. You may like to review Figure 10.4, which shows the workings of the Parallel Query option.

When an instance is started, Oracle creates a pool of query server processes available for the query coordinator. The PARALLEL_MIN_SERVERS initialization parameter determines this minimum number of Parallel Query processes. If the volume of SQL statements processed simultaneously increases and the current number of Parallel Query processes can't handle this load, Oracle automatically creates additional query processes. The maximum number of query processes Oracle can create is specified by the initialization parameter PARALLEL_MAX_SERVERS. When the query load comes back to normal and there are query processes in the memory that have been idle for the time specified by the PARALLEL_SERVER_IDLE_TIME initialization parameter, Oracle terminates those processes. Oracle can't reduce the number of processes below the value of the initialization parameter PARALLEL_MIN_SERVERS, even if some query processes have been idle for the time specified in PARALLEL_SERVER_IDLE_TIME.

In an attempt to improve the performance, you can't set the value of PARALLEL_MAX_SERVERS too high, because it depends on the CPU and I/O bandwidth. You should set this value equal to the highest number of processes your machine can manage. You can increase the value for PARALLEL_MIN_SERVERS, however, if the query processes are continuously starting and shutting down. You should try to set this value equal to the highest degree of parallelism you can expect from the queries executed simultaneously.

Four queries will be executed concurrently, for example, each with an average degree of parallelism equal to 10. This implies that at any given time, 80 query servers could be busy in the instance. Therefore, the PARALLEL_MIN_SERVERS parameter should be set to 80. Now your job is to verify this value—whether it is correct or needs to be changed—by using the dynamic performance view V$PQ_SYSSTAT. You can use the following query to view the number of busy Parallel Query processes at any moment:

```
SELECT * FROM v$pq_sysstat
WHERE statistic = 'Servers Busy';

STATISTIC        VALUE
--------------------
Servers Busy      30
```

It is a good idea to issue this query many times over a period of time, because Parallel Query processes are constantly accepting work or returning to the idle status. If you find over a period of time that fewer processes are busy than specified by PARALLEL_MIN_SERVERS, your idle query processes are an additional overhead on the system and you should consider decreasing the value of PARALLEL_MIN_SERVERS. If, on the other hand, you find that over a period of time more query servers are active than the value of PARALLEL_MIN_SERVERS and the Servers Started statistic is continuously growing, consider increasing the parameter's value.

Redo Log Buffer and Redo Log Latches Contention

When a transaction is processed, first the information of the affected rows is written in the redo log buffer, and then the LGWR process writes these transactions to the mirrored groups of redo log files. LGWR writes these entries into the redo log files fast enough to make sure that enough room is available in the redo log buffer to hold information of the new transactions. Therefore, the redo log buffer works in a circular manner. After the entries in the buffer are copied to disk, new entries could be written over them by the user process as the transactions continue to take place in the application.

Normally, LGWR works efficiently enough even when the system is under a heavy load, and space is always available in the redo buffer for the user process to write new transactions in the memory. You can see whether this is the case in your system or whether user processes are sometimes waiting to find space in the redo buffer before they could write information there. Use the V$SYSSTAT dynamic performance view to see this information. The following query will bring the number of times the user process had to wait to find free space in the redo log buffer since the instance was started:

```
SELECT name, value
FROM v$sysstat
WHERE name =  aredo log space requests';

NAME                              VALUE
----------------------            -----
redo log space requests             0
```

You should get 0 in the result; otherwise, the redo log buffer might be too small. The size of the redo log buffer is specified by the LOG_BUFFER initialization parameter. The value of this parameter is expressed in bytes and must be a multiple of DB_BLOCK_SIZE. Try to increase the value of this parameter by 5% to 10% until your system runs with redo log space requests close to 0.

So far we have discussed the contention in redo log buffer. Another type of contention can occur related to redo log activity—contention in redo log buffer latches. Two latch types control the access of user processes to redo log buffer: redo allocation latch and redo copy latch. The redo allocation latch controls the writing of redo entries to the redo log buffer. The user process must obtain the redo allocation latch to write information to the redo log buffer. The redo allocation latch allocates the space in the redo log buffer, and then copies the entry into the buffer. After the user process is finished copying the transaction information into the redo log buffer, it releases the latch, making it available to other user processes. Only one user process can write information into the buffer because only one redo allocation latch exists. The LOG_SMALL_ENTRY_MAX_SIZE parameter specifies the amount of information that can be written through this latch.

If the amount of information that has to be copied exceeds the value specified by the initialization parameter, the user process has to obtain a redo copy latch before copying the large information. After the redo copy latch is obtained, the user process can write into the buffer. In multi-CPU machines, you could have many redo copy latches that can allow simultaneous entries into the redo log buffer. In a single-CPU machine, there's no redo copy latch and all accesses to the redo buffer is through the redo allocation latch. The LOG_ SIMULTANEOUS_COPIES initialization parameter specifies the number of redo copy latches an instance would have. The default value is the number of CPUs for multi-CPU machines and 0 for single-CPU machines.

Processes can access both latches in two ways:

◆ **Willing to wait.** The process requests a latch. If the latch isn't available, it requests again after sleeping for a while. It continues requesting until the latch is available.

◆ **Immediate.** The process requests a latch. If it is not available, it continues processing.

The V$LATCH dynamic performance view has important symptoms for a larch contention. Relevant columns of this table are as follows:

Column	Meaning
GETS	The number of successful willing-to-wait requests
MISSES	The number of times the initial willing-to-wait request fails
SLEEPS	The number of times the subsequent willing-to-wait request fails
IMMEDIATE_GETS	The number of times the immediate request was successful
IMMEDIATE_MISSES	The number of times the immediate request failed

You can use the following query to see the desired results:

```
SELECT SUBSTR b.name, gets, misses, sleeps, immediate_gets
➥"IMM GETS", immediate_misses "IMM MISSES"
FROM v$latch a, v$latchname b
WHERE a.latch#=b.latch#
AND b.name in ( aredo allocation', aredo copy');

NAME         GETS MISSES SLEEP IMM GETS IMM MISSES
----------- ---- ------ ----- -------- ----------
redo all... 2660    60   110        0          0
redo cop...    0     0     0        0          0
```

Latch contention may be a performance problem if the ratio of MISSES to GETS exceeds 1%, or the ratio of IMMEDIATE_MISSES to the sum of IMMEDIATE_GETS and IMMEDIATE_MISSES exceeds 1%.

To reduce the contention for the redo allocation latch, you should minimize the time that any single process holds the latch. This can be done by reducing the value of the LOG_SMALL_ENTRY_MAX_SIZE initialization parameter. Decreasing this value will reduce the number and size of redo entries copied on the redo allocation latch, and the latch won't be busy for a long time before a user process can have access to it.

To reduce the contention for redo copy latches in a multi-CPU machine, you can increase the number of redo copy latches specified by the LOG_SIMULTANEOUS_COPIES parameter. Multiple redo copy latches allow multiple processes to copy entries to the redo log buffer concurrently. You can increase the value up to twice the number of CPUs available on the machine.

LRU Latch Contention

When a transaction requests any data from the database to manipulate it, Oracle first checks to see whether the data is already in the memory buffer. If it is there, the data is handed over to the user processes that requested it, without going to disk. If the data isn't in the buffer, it will be fetched from disk and brought into the buffer. To bring data from disk into the buffer, there must be enough space in the buffer. Oracle manages the data buffer very efficiently by using the least recently used (LRU) algorithm. The data in the most recently used buffer is kept there, and the least recently used data is written back to the disk after it is manipulated in the buffer. The incoming data in the data buffer can replace this LRU data after it is written back to disk. The idea is that most recently used data is likely to be requested by the user again, and if it is already in the buffer, it wouldn't have to be fetched from the disk and performance would be improved because of less I/O.

The LRU latch controls the least recently used algorithm and the replacement of buffers in the buffer cache. In a single-CPU machine, there's one LRU latch; in the multi-CPU machines such as symmetric multiprocessor (SMP) machines with a large number of CPUs, Oracle automatically sets the number of LRU latches to be half the number of CPUs. The DB_BLOCK_LRU_LATCHES initialization parameter specifies the maximum number of latches on the system.

In SMP machines, contention in the LRU latch can impede performance. The following dynamic performance views list symptoms of LRU latch contention:

◆ V$LATCH

◆ V$SESSION_EVENT

◆ V$SYSTEM_EVENT

Contention can be removed by setting the appropriate value for the
DB_BLOCK_LRU_LATCHES parameter. A system can have the number of
latches up to twice the number of CPUs. If the workload on the
instance is heavy, a higher number of latches should be used. If you
have 16 CPUs, for example, the number of latches specified should
be between half the number of CPUs (eight) and the actual number
of CPUs (16).

Each LRU latch controls a set of buffers. Oracle balances the allocation of replacement buffers among the sets. A latch should have no
fewer than 50 buffers in its set.

Free List Contention

Oracle keeps one free list for each table in memory. This free list is
used to determine which database block to use when an insert occurs
on the table. When a row is added, the free list is locked. If more
than one simultaneous process attempts to insert into a table, one
process might need to wait until the free list has been released by the
previous process. To find out whether adding a free list to a table will
improve the performance, you need to determine how frequently
Oracle has to wait for a free list. The V$WAITSTAT dynamic perfor-
mance view has the relevant information. You can use the following
query to determine the desired information:

```
SELECT class, count
FROM v$waitstat
WHERE class = 'free list';

CLASS         COUNT
----------------
free list     72
```

The output shows that Oracle had to wait 72 times for a table's free
list to become available. This could mean that Oracle had to wait
72 times on the same table or on different tables. 72 isn't a very large
number because Oracle can perform hundreds of I/Os each second.

If the COUNT column of the preceding query shows a value greater
than 1% of the total number of requests, you should increase the
number of free lists on tables. The total number of requests can be
found out by the following query:

```
SELECT sum(value) "Total Data Requests"
FROM v$systat
```

```
WHERE name in ('consistent gets','db block gets');

TOTAL DATA REQUESTS
-------------------
804
```

You can drop and re-create the suspected table with more free lists. If your application is performing many concurrent insertions into the MEMBERS table and the table was initially created with number of free lists set to 1, for example, you can create a temporary table with the same data as the MEMBERS table and set the number of free lists to 3:

```
CREATE TABLE temp
AS SELECT * FROM members
STORAGE (PCTFREE 10 PCTUSED 40 FREELISTS 3);
```

Now you can drop the MEMBERS table and rename the TEMP table to MEMBERS:

```
DROP TABLE members;
RENAME temp TO members;
```

Although extra free lists will consume more memory, they can help improve the throughput on tables that have many inserts.

DATABASE DESIGN

Optimal performance can't be achieved without an effective database design, no matter how much you tune the system. Several important topics discussed in this section will help you achieve an optimal database design:

- ◆ Denormalization
- ◆ Entities with nonkey attributes
- ◆ Storing RAW and LONG RAW datatypes
- ◆ Use of VARCHAR2 datatype
- ◆ Database design for data warehousing

Denormalization

A designer's task with a database is to sensibly represent entities and different types of relationships among them—that is, one-to-one,

one-to-many, many-to-many, and recursive—in the form of tables and constraints. Many designers try to design a normalized system in which there's almost no redundancy of data. This gives rise to major performance problems. For example, a designer has kept department names in one table and employee names in a different type. To show which employee works in which department, a department ID column has been included in the employee table (see Figure 10.12). Now if a user gives the query to fetch all the employee names and their department names, Oracle has to look in two separate tables.

NORMALIZED FORM

DEPARTMENTS

DEPT_ID	NAME
1	MARKETING
2	FINANCE
3	ACCOUNTING
4	PRODUCTION

EMPLOYEES

EMPNO	NAME	APT	STREET	ZIP_CODE	PHONE	SALARY	DEPT_ID
1	HASAN	1601	50 JEROME CRESCENT	L8E5K1	9055600541	6500	10
2	CODD	1200	100 MAIN ST	65123	7132354612	45000	10
3	SCOTT		120 KING ST	54786	7652435124	70000	20
4	PETER		105 QUEEN ST	12654	7659878331	35000	30
5	BRUCE	410	100 ST PAUL AVE	87678	4153563567	90000	40
6	ROBERT		15 MAIN ST	12365	7651245675	20000	20

DENORMALIZED FORM

EMPLOYEES

EMPNO	NAME	APT	STREET	ZIP_CODE	PHONE	SALARY	DEPT_NAME
1	HASAN	1601	50 JEROME CRESCENT	L8E5K1	9055600541	6500	MARKETING
2	CODD	1200	100 MAIN ST	65123	7132354612	45000	MARKETING
3	SCOTT		120 KING ST	54786	7652435124	70000	FINANCE
4	PETER		105 QUEEN ST	12654	7659878331	35000	ACCOUNTING
5	BRUCE	410	100 ST PAUL AVE	87678	4153563567	90000	PRODUCTION
6	ROBERT		15 MAIN ST	12365	7651245675	20000	FINANCE

FIGURE 10.12
A table in normalized and denormalized form.

Therefore, a purely logical design gives you performance cost and storage benefit. Because there's less data redundancy, data storage cost is reduced. For users, if performance is more important than the cost of storing data, they may decide to keep department names in the employee table rather than in a separate department table. In this case, more data has to be stored on disk, but performance will improve because to fetch the result for the same query, Oracle now has to look into only one table. This is called *denormalization*.

Adding redundancy or denormalizing poses two problems: Additional space is required for redundant data, and a technique has to be developed to update this redundant data. If the department name has changed, for example, you have to update more rows when the database is denormalized than in a normalized database.

Let's look at a more complex example of denormalization. Suppose that you have developed a model for a library management system as shown in Figure 10.13.

FIGURE 10.13

A normalized model for a library management system.

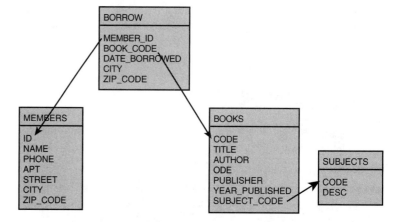

If you want to know which members have borrowed books on which subjects, you issue the following SQL statement:

```
SELECT distinct a.name, d.desc
FROM members a, borrow b, books c, subjects d
WHERE a.id = b.member.id
AND b.book_code = c.code
AND c.subject_code = d.code;
```

This query will result in joining of four tables. This type of complex join guarantees that at least one table is read front to back with a full-table scan. Full-table scans are very expensive in terms of performance.

Suppose that this type of query is often used in your application. You can improve the performance by reducing the number of tables and hence number of joins. Rather than keep the information of subjects in a separate table, for example, you decide to keep this information in the table BOOK as well. Figure 10.14 shows the new model.

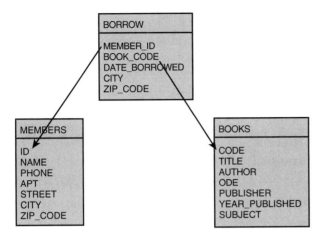

FIGURE 10.14
A denormalized model for a library management system.

The SELECT statement to bring the same data in this denormalized structure would become

```
SELECT distinct a.name, c.subject
FROM members a, borrow b, books c
WHERE a.id = b.member_id
AND b.book_code = c.code;
```

This SELECT statement will be executed much faster because it is joining three tables rather than four. A user can continue denormalizing the database by repeating this process on other tables until the additional redundancy cost resulting from the next step outweighs the additional performance benefit.

You always have to weigh the performance gains against the extra data maintenance needed because of denormalization. Sometimes it may not be worth it to denormalize if it will cost so many hours to maintain the data in the tables when something changes.

Entities with Nonkey Attributes

When designing a model, it is often tempting to look at the model from a purely logical point of view. This may result in some misleading relationships and some entities with no nonkey attributes. Let's look at the model shown in Figure 10.15 for managing addresses.

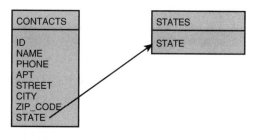

FIGURE 10.15
An entity with no nonkey attributes.

At first, it looks very reasonable that STATE and CITY are separate entities, because there's a one-to-many relationship between them. A city is in a state and a state can have many cities in it. Therefore, this one-to-many relationship is represented in the model as two different tables. However, the STATE entity lacks any key data item—in other words, it has no associated data items. Creating a database table with only one column wouldn't be very practical. If an entity has no attributes or a table has only one field, the presence of the entity is nothing more than an index to the foreign key in the child entity.

It would be practical to create a separate table for the entity STATE, if you also had to store the population of each state or some other information (such as tax rates) in that entity.

Storing RAW and LONG RAW Data Types

You can store pictures, sounds, and videos in Oracle database as binary data. LONG RAW and RAW data types are used for this purpose. If columns of LONG or LONG RAW data types are used in the database, they should be placed in a table separate from other data associated with it. Both tables can be related with a referential integrity constraint. In this way, SQL statements can access the associated data without reading through LONG or LONG RAW data. If you want to store the photos of the library members in your database with other information, for example, the database design shown in Figure 10.16 can be used.

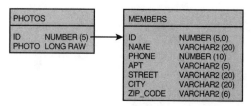

FIGURE 10.16
How to store RAW and LONG RAW datatypes.

Storing the VARCHAR2 Data Type

If you are storing string values in a column, you should use the VARCHAR2 data type rather than the CHAR data type. VARCHAR2 stores variable-length character strings, unlike CHAR, which stores fixed-length character strings. If you have declared a data type of a column as VARCHAR2(40) and insert a string of 20 single-byte characters in it, the column in the row piece stores only 20 characters (20 bytes), not 40. On the other hand, if you declare the column to be data type CHAR(40) and insert a string of 20 single-byte characters in it, Oracle will pad the string with blanks, and 40 characters (40 bytes) will be stored in the row piece for this column.

Database Design for Data Warehousing

Issues in database design, when and how to denormalize, and database design for data warehousing.

When it comes to data warehousing, performance is far more important than disk storage. Special designing techniques are used in data warehousing, including one known as *star schema* designing. In a star schema design, a large fact table resides at the center of the model, and various reference tables surround this star or fact table. The main idea behind this technique is the introduction of fast performance at the cost of highly redundant data.

Take the example of a library management system again. Suppose that the library management team wants to find out which member has borrowed books on which subjects. Based on the current normalized model, the following query will bring the desired information:

```
SELECT distinct a.name, d.desc
FROM members a, borrow b, books c, subjects d
WHERE a.id = b.member.id
AND b.book_code = c.code
AND c.subject_code = d.code;
```

Now suppose that there are 10,000 members in this library, and 100,000 books on 2,000 different subjects. This query will take a pretty long time before bringing results. While analyzing the information, management might also be asking other related questions. The normalized system may affect management's analysis due to the performance problems. Therefore, in a data warehousing environment, the following star table can be created that will return the results of the previous query and other related queries much more quickly:

```
CREATE TABLE analysis AS
SELECT a.id  "MEMBER_ID", a.name "MEMBER_NAME",
➥c.code "BOOK_CODE", d.desc "SUBJECT_DESC"
FROM members a, borrow b, books c, subjects d
WHERE a.id = b.member.id
AND b.book_code = c.code
AND c.subject_code = d.code;
```

Now the following query on the central fact table named ANALYSIS can bring the same results much more quickly:

```
SELECT a.name, b.subject_desc
FROM member a, analysis b
WHERE a.id = b.member_id;
```

Other related queries will also benefit from this new table. Management wants to know which subject is the most popular, for example. The following query on the fact tables will bring the answer:

```
SELECT subject_desc FROM analysis
GROUP BY subject_desc
HAVING count (subject_desc) =
( SELECT max ( count ( subject_desc ) )
FROM analysis );
```

Notice that the central fact table is surrounded by reference tables. The fact table can be joined with reference tables to provide extra information. Updating or inserting the data through the fact table is almost impossible due to high redundancy. The fact table is created only for analysis purposes and used as read-only in star schema designs.

APPLICATION PERFORMANCE DESIGN AND DATABASE OBJECTS

How to use different database objects to improve application performance.

After a data design is created, it is translated into Oracle database objects that can give optimal performance. These database objects—such as tables, views, indexes, packages, and triggers—are then used by the application code and hence are part of the application.

In the following sections, these database objects are discussed in the context of how they can improve the application performance:

- ◆ Indexes
- ◆ Table allocation (PCTFREE, PCTUSED, and FREELIST)
- ◆ Clusters
- ◆ Hash clusters
- ◆ Integrity constraints
- ◆ Triggers

◆ Procedures and packages

◆ Sequences

Indexes

As you know, full-table scans can be very expensive in terms of performance for two main reasons:

◆ Considerable amount of time is lost, because Oracle has to request every row into the buffer.

◆ Other activities suffer, too, because they have to incur additional I/O because they have been flushed from the buffer by the full-table scan.

Indexes are used to prevent the full-table scan. Oracle indexes use a b*tree data structure, in which each tree node can contain many sets of key values. Indexes consume extra space on disk, but provide performance benefits.

Indexes shouldn't be created on every column in the table. You have to select the right columns that will benefit from the creation of indexes. Because columns used in a SQL WHERE clause can be candidates for indexing, it is a good idea to collect the application's SQL and analyze the WHERE clauses. After all the candidate columns are selected, you have to see the selectivity and distribution of these columns.

Selectivity refers to the uniqueness of the values in the column. To be most effective, an index column should have many unique values. Columns with few unique values—for example, male/female, yes/no, or true/false—won't benefit from b*tree indexes. You can determine the percentage of unique values in a particular column as

```
SELECT COUNT (DISTINCT column_name) / COUNT (column_name)
FROM table_name;
```

If this percentage is greater than 10, a b*tree index can be created on this column. Otherwise, this column isn't a good candidate for Oracle b*tree indexing.

The term *distribution* refers to the distribution of unique values throughout the column. The SUBJECT column contains names of

100 different subjects, for example. If five of these subjects are used 95% of the time and the other 95 are used 5% of the time, the distribution isn't uniform and this column isn't a good candidate for indexing. The following query counts the number of times each unique value is used and then finds the standard deviation of these counts. If the result isn't a very high number, the column is a good candidate for indexing. The distribution is uniform if the value returned by the query is small or close to zero.

```
SELECT STDDEV(COUNT( column_name ))
FROM table_name
GROUP BY column_name;
```

If you are using Oracle's cost-based optimizer, ANALYZE TABLE will look at the selectivity and distribution of the column values. If they are out of reasonable limit, Oracle may decide not to use the index. The cost-based optimizer uses the DBA_HISTOGRAMS view to find information about the distribution of values within a column.

A column shouldn't be indexed if the application is updating its values or inserting new rows in the table frequently. When a column value is modified or a new row is added or deleted, Oracle must first make the changes in the table and then rearrange the index based on the new entries. Therefore, performance still is affected if frequently manipulated tables are indexed.

Oracle doesn't use an index if the column is used with a LIKE operator or in any of the available SQL functions except MIN and MAX, so such columns shouldn't be indexed at all. Columns with descriptive values such as MEMBERS_DESCRIPTION or COMMENTS also aren't good candidates for indexing, because of the length and because they will most likely be used in the application with a function such as UPPER, LOWER, SUBSTR, or LIKE.

Consider indexing foreign keys of a table that has a large number of concurrent INSERT, UPDATE, and DELETE statements accessing the parent and child tables. Such an index allows Oracle to modify data in the child table without locking the parent table.

Any table is a candidate for indexing if its columns satisfy the discussed criteria. The only exception is a very small table that occupies fewer than two blocks on the disk. When an index is used on any table, Oracle must perform at least two I/Os — one for reading the index and one for reading the desired table data. If a table is already occupying two blocks or fewer, creating an index won't do any better. Even without an index, Oracle will perform at most two I/Os, one for each block, to read the table data in a full-table scan.

You can also create multicolumn indexes in Oracle. You should create multicolumn indexes on columns when most of these columns are used together in the WHERE clause of the application's SQL. It is important to understand the concept of *leading portion* here. Oracle will use a multicolumn index only if the column(s) used in the WHERE clause form the leading portion of the multicolumn index. For example, you have created an index on the columns ID, FIRST_NAME, and LAST_NAME of the table MEMBER:

```
CREATE INDEX member_index ON MEMBER (ID, FIRST_NAME,
LAST_NAME);
```

The leading portions of these three columns are as follows:

◆ ID, FIRST_NAME, LAST_NAME

◆ ID, FIRST_NAME

◆ ID

If one set is used in a WHERE clause, the index member_index will be used; otherwise, Oracle will perform a full-table scan. The following SELECT statement will use the index member_index, for example:

```
SELECT * FROM member
WHERE id >10 AND first_name = "HASAN";
```

The following SELECT statement won't use the index because the columns stated in the WHERE clause aren't in the leading portion of the index:

```
SELECT * FROM member
WHERE first_name = "HASAN" and last_name = "MIR";
```

Column order is very important when creating multicolumn indexes. Try to maintain an order so that most SQL statements can use the index. Oracle creates indexes to enforce primary key and unique key constraints. The column order in a composite primary key becomes the column order of the index that enforces this key. Therefore, it is also important to choose the column order in a composite primary key carefully.

Another important use of indexing is for selecting the values of the column in an order. Consider the following query, for example:

```
SELECT member_id, first_name
FROM member
ORDER by member_id, first_name;
```

If your application is using this type of query quite frequently, you can improve the performance by creating an index on the two columns. Oracle always creates ascending indexes:

```
CREATE INDEX member_index
ON member (member_id, first_name);
```

Now, the following SELECT statement will bring the same results much more quickly. Also note that the WHERE clause is used to make Oracle use the index you just created:

```
SELECT member_id, first_name
FROM member
WHERE member_id >= 0;
```

Columns with low selectivity are the best candidates for bitmap indexes. In a bitmap index, a bitmap for each key value is used rather than a list of rowids. A mapping function is used to convert the bit position to an actual rowid. Therefore, the same functionality is provided by the bitmap index as a regular index, even though it uses a different representation internally. If the number of different key values is small, bitmaps could be very space efficient. Because bitmap indexes can seriously slow the execution of update and insert operations, they are used more often in data warehousing applications than in online transaction processing (OLTP) applications. Bitmap indexes consume less space than b*tree indexes if they are used on the column with low selectivity. Consider using bitmap indexes for the columns such as GENDER (male/female), GRADE (A/B/C), and APPROVED (yes/no).

If you are using Oracle's Parallel Query option, all tables in the SQL query must cause a full-table scan. If an index exists, you should use the cost-based optimizer to invalidate the index to access the Parallel Query option.

Table Allocation

When you are creating tables to be used by an application, three parameters are crucial: PCTFREE, PCTUSED, and FREELIST. These parameters are set depending on the type of manipulation on the table—that is, insert, update, or delete.

When a data is inserted into the table, Oracle keeps on adding the new rows into the database block until the block has a percentage of free space equal to the value specified in the PCTFREE parameter. When new rows can't be added into the block without making the percentage of free space less than the value of PCTFREE, this block has reached its limit and new rows for the tables are added into the new block. When a block has reached its limit once and rows are deleted from the block later, new rows won't be added into this block until the percentage of used space reaches the value specified in the PCTUSED parameter. Consider the following table, for example:

```
CREATE TABLE member (id number, name varchar2(20),
➥address varchar2(30), phone varchar2(11))
STORAGE (      PCTFREE 10
          PCTUSED 60
          FREELISTS 1      );
```

When rows are inserted into this table, Oracle will first add rows into the first block. When the block is 90% (1-PCTFREE) full, rows will then be added into the new block. This block will be kept 10% free to accommodate the expansion of rows due to the update operation. Suppose that the application is deleting some rows from the first block and the block is getting empty. The block won't be available to accept new rows until its used space is decreased to 60% (PCTUSED) or less of the total block space. The sum of PCTFREE and PCTUSED must be less than or equal to 100.

If you are expecting quite a bit of update activity on a table, you should use a higher value for PCFREE. Suppose that you are expecting the rows of the table MEMBERS to expand in the future due to update operations. The blocks of the MEMBER table have 10% free space to accommodate this expansion. If the rows expand further, Oracle must fragment the row and store some row information on the next block in the tablespace. In this way, long chains can be created if the blocks don't have enough room for the row expansion. This condition can lead to many unnecessary I/Os when the row is read from the disk, because Oracle has to read more than one block to read one row. Therefore, PCTFREE should be used to reserve the appropriate amount of space for the row expansion. For tables with high update activity, the value of PCTFREE could be set to 40; for read-only tables, it should be set to a lower value—about 5—to fully occupy each database block.

Oracle tries to keep the database block at least PCTUSED full. If frequent delete operations are expected on a table and performance is more important than efficient storage, PCTUSED should be set to a low value, like 40. In this way, Oracle won't constantly move the database block into the FREELIST as rows are deleted, until the block is less than 40% full. The default value of PCTUSED is also 40. On the other hand, if you want to use space efficiently, you should set PCTUSED to a high value, like 60. In this way, as soon as the block is less than 60% full, it will be moved to the FREELIST and Oracle will keep the database block full.

The FREELIST parameter specifies the number of free lists a table will have in memory. Free lists tell Oracle which database block should be used when an insert occurs on the table. If frequent inserts could occur on a table by concurrent processes, it is a good idea to have more than one free list for this table. A detailed discussion about this topic can be found earlier in the section "Reducing Contentions."

Clusters

Clustering plays an important role in improving application performance. The concept of clustering is very simple: Child table rows are stored in the same block as their parent table row, as shown in Figure 10.17. Two main advantages of using clusters are better performance and efficient storage.

FIGURE 10.17
A cluster of tables: books and subjects.

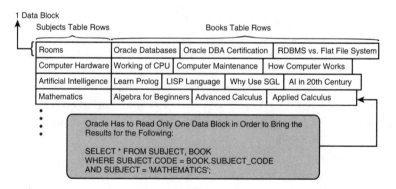

You should consider using clusters if your application frequently uses a join SELECT statement on parent/child tables linked with a foreign key. In a library management system, for example, there could be two tables—BOOK (ID, AUTHOR, PUBLISHER, SUBJECT_CODE) and SUBJECT (SUBJECT_CODE, DESCRIPTION)—with a one-to-many relationship between them. Many books may be written on one subject. You can cluster these tables together. All the child rows of BOOK will be stored close to their parent row of SUBJECT, possibly in the same block. Because the values for the cluster key column SUBJECT_CODE will be stored only once, disk storage is reduced. If your application queries the database to fetch all the books on a particular subject and all the child rows are stored in the same block with their parent row, Oracle can fetch the result in one I/O (in addition to an index I/O), which improves the performance.

In a many-to-many relationship, clustering can improve performance in one direction, whereas queries in another direction may suffer. For example, there's a many-to-many relationship between the tables MEMBERS (ID, NAME, ADDRESS) and BOOKS (ID, AUTHOR, PUBLISHER, SUBJECT_CODE). A member can borrow many books, and a book can be borrowed by many members. Table BORROW (MEMBER_ID, BOOK_ID, DATA_BORROWED) represents the association between them. If the application commonly traverses from MEMBERS to BOOKS, the junction table BORROW should be clustered with the table MEMBERS. On the other hand, if the application traverses from BOOKS to MEMBERS, the table BORROW should be clustered with the table BOOK. Otherwise, queries in the opposite direction would have to perform additional I/Os. Figure 10.18 shows this concept.

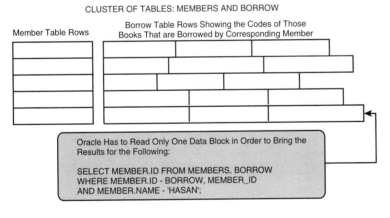

CLUSTER OF TABLES: MEMBERS AND BORROW

Member Table Rows

Borrow Table Rows Showing the Codes of Those Books That are Borrowed by Corresponding Member

Oracle Has to Read Only One Data Block in Order to Bring the Results for the Following:

SELECT MEMBER.ID FROM MEMBERS, BORROW
WHERE MEMBER.ID - BORROW, MEMBER_ID
AND MEMBER.NAME - 'HASAN';

CLUSTER OF TABLES: BOOK AND BORROW

Book Table Rows

Borrow Table Rows Showing the IDs of Those Members That Have Borrowed the Corresponding Book

Oracle Has to Read Only One Data Block in Order to Bring the Results for the Following:

SELECT BOOKS.CODE FROM BOOKS, BORROW
WHERE BOOKS.CODE - BORROW, BOOK_CODE
AND BOOKS.TITLE - 'ORACLE DBA';

FIGURE 10.18
Clustering tables in many-to-many relationship.

Clustering slows DML insert, delete, and update operations on a table, compared with storing the table separately with its index. Multiple tables share each block, hence a clustered table is scattered in more blocks. Oracle must visit more blocks to perform these operations.

Hash Clusters

An alternative to indexing, hash clusters can improve application performance if the application queries a table with an equality condition on its column. This column would be the hash cluster key. In this condition, hash clusters perform better than b*tree indexes because with a hashing algorithm Oracle converts the symbolic key into the rowid of the desired row. Therefore Oracle can bring the result just in one I/O, compared with minimum two I/Os in indexing.

Hash keys should be the columns with many unique values. Primary key columns are the best candidates. A hash function won't work if the hash key column is used in the WHERE clause without an equality condition.

Also, while creating a hash cluster, you should be able to predict how large the table will grow. If the table is growing constantly, it is not a good candidate for hash clusters. DML statements such as INSERT, DELETE, and UPDATE that change the value of hash cluster key column can cause serious performance problems, because Oracle's hashing algorithm will generate new locations for the changed hash cluster key values.

Integrity Constraints

Integrity constraints enable you to set certain requirements for the data that can be included in a table. No programming is required because they are included as part of the table definition. If you have enforced business rules with integrity constraints, all data in the table must conform to the rules specified by these constraints.

Without integrity constraints, an application must enforce the business rules programmatically. Oracle recommends that you use integrity constraints rather than enforce rules by the application wherever possible, for performance and security reasons.

Internal operations performed by Oracle to enforce the constraints are beneath the level of SQL statements and result in faster operation. Enforcing business rules programmatically can be very costly in a network environment because SQL statements must be transmitted over the network. Using Oracle integrity constraints can eliminate extra network overhead.

Suppose that you want to enforce a unique constraint on the column license number. You can define the license column to be a unique key while creating the table as follows:

```
CREATE TABLE member (
id number primary key,
name varchar2(30),
license varchar2(20),
constraints unique (license)
        );
```

Now Oracle won't accept any duplicates in this column, no matter which application tries to insert rows. Instead, if you choose to enforce this rule in your application, you first have to read all the already existing values in this column with the help of a cursor. Then you compare the value the user has entered with all the values the cursor has returned. Based on the comparison, the new entry of user will be inserted or an error will be raised. In this process, a cursor is taking a space in memory and creating a load on the network.

Another good reason for using Oracle integrity constraints instead of programmatically enforcing them is that if many applications are using the same database, business rules must be enforced by each application. If this isn't the case, the application that is not enforcing business rules can destroy data integrity, and users might see nonsense data in the applications enforcing business rules. Also, if database integrity constraints aren't there, ad hoc updates from SQL*Plus can ruin data easily.

In some cases, it is necessary to enforce rules in the application. Suppose that your application asks users to fill a form of about 10 entries. The application will try to insert this row into Oracle when the whole form is finished. At that time, Oracle may refuse to insert the row if one value isn't obeying the database business rule.

Therefore, it is a good idea to programmatically validate each value in your application at the time users enter it rather than validate all 10 values at one time.

Triggers

Complex business rules that can't be handled by the integrity constraints could be enforced with the help of triggers. Triggers are fired when a specific event (for example, an insert, update, or delete) occurs on the table. Database triggers can be used for diverse purposes such as performing auditing, maintaining derived data values, and enforcing complex security rules.

Again, it is better to enforce business rules with the help of triggers than by enforcing them programmatically by the application. If the rules are enforced with triggers, all the applications have to obey them and hence data is more secure. Performance is also improved due to less load on the network.

Oracle database triggers can call other stored procedures and functions. Oracle recommends that if a trigger's PL/SQL code takes more than 60 lines, the code should be stored in a stored procedure that's called by the trigger.

Stored Procedures, Functions, and Packages

Code is gradually moving from applications into databases, as objects such as procedures and functions are becoming popular. Oracle is encouraging this approach for many reasons, the main one being performance. Database code results in improved performance. Stored procedures are loaded into the SGA when they are called by the application, and remain there until they are paged out. Items are paged out of memory based on the least recently used algorithm. As in the case of database triggers and constraints, execution of database procedures and functions eliminates extra load from the network compared with the alternative of writing codes in the application itself. Stored procedures and functions also have the advantage of being stored in the library cache in an already parsed form, thereby reducing parsing time.

If code is written internally in the database, applications would become nothing more than a series of calls to the database code. It is easy to write an application when most of the code is already available from the database. It is also easy to swap out one database and swap in another.

Oracle also provides an object known as a *package*, which is a collection of related procedures and functions. With packages, modules can have specific functions that can be logically grouped. A package is created in a statement with two different parts: a declaration part and a package body part. The declaration part consists of the definitions of procedures and functions that are part of the package and are available to the users. The package body consists of actual PL/SQL code for these procedures and functions.

You can change a package body without requiring any change to the application as long as the package specification doesn't change. Because the package body is hidden from users, you can access tables from the PL/SQL of a package body that you may not want users to see. The best advantage of using packages is that the entire package is loaded into memory when the first component is accessed; additional calls to the package don't invoke disk I/O.

Oracle offers the option of pinning a package into the SGA. A pinned package remains in the SGA for the life of an instance, after its first component is accessed. You can also unpin a package from memory. The procedure DBMS_SHARED_POOL.KEEP is used to pin a package, and DBMS_SHARED_POOL.UNKEEP is used to unpin a package:

```
EXECUTE dbms_shared_pool.keep ('member.register');
```

You can look at the information about pinned packages and those frequently used by the application in the V$DB_OBJECT_CACHE dynamic performance view. The following columns are important:

Column	*Meaning*
NAME	Name of the object
KEPT	Whether it is pinned

Sequences

A *sequence* is a database object that can generate a unique number each time it is called. Your application can use database sequence numbers to automatically generate unique keys for the data and to coordinate keys across multiple rows or tables. This is a performance-efficient alternative to locking all currently existing values of the column in the database, and then programmatically generating a unique number that's not present in these lock values.

Moreover, you can keep a certain number of sequence values in the cache. Sequence numbers can be accessed more quickly in the sequence cache than they can be read from disk. The sequence cache consists of entries. Each entry can hold many sequence numbers for a single sequence. The number of entries in the sequence cache is determined by the initialization parameter SEQUENCE_CACHE_ENTRIES, the default value of which is 10 entries, meaning that values for 10 sequences can be stored in the cache. If the value specified by SEQUENCE_CACHE_ENTRIES is low, it is possible to skip sequence values. If this parameter is set to 5 and you have five cached sequences, for example, a sixth sequence will replace the least recently used sequence in the cache and all the remaining values in this displaced sequence are lost from the memory.

The number of sequence values for a particular sequence stored in the cache is specified by the CACHE parameter of the CREATE SEQUENCE statement. The default value is 20. The following statement creates a sequence named MEMBER_IDS. One hundred values of this sequence are stored in the cache. When the 101th value is used by the application, the next 100 values—101 to 200—will be read from the disk and stored in the cache.

```
CREATE SEQUENCE member_id CACHE 100;
```

SQL Statements

Applications communicate with Oracle through SQL and PL/SQL. Tuning SQL is crucial to achieve high performance. Chapter 11, "Tuning Memory Structures," discusses this topic in detail. You might also want to use the Parallel Query option to improve application performance. The Parallel Query option was discussed in detail earlier in the section "Optimal Configuration."

CHAPTER SUMMARY

Users can connect to an Oracle Server by using a Dedicated Server process or Multithreaded Server process. In a Dedicated Server option, a separate server process serves the request of each user and thus results in inefficient memory usage when most users aren't performing any tasks. In a Multithreaded Server environment, few Shared Server processes serve many users, so more users can be connected to the system with a limited number of server processes. An Oracle Server can also be configured for the Parallel Query option, one of the most powerful features offered by Oracle that divides a query into many small pieces. More than one query process simultaneously processes one piece each and brings the result much more quickly. It is important that the data is striped across more than one disk to take full advantage of the Parallel Query option. Parallel Query also offers other features, such as parallel loading, parallel recovery, and parallel indexing.

Depending on the type of application you are using, you can also take advantage of Oracle's Parallel Server option and Oracle Distributed System:

◆ A parallel server is a group of computers running separate instances and using a common shared database. Oracle's Parallel Server option requires special hardware considerations and offers the advantages of low fault tolerance and high performance. The Parallel Server option uses a locking mechanism to protect data integrity.

◆ An Oracle distributed system is a collection of many databases that appears to a user as one large database. Some prominent features of this type of configuration are data replication, location transparency, and localized database management.

KEY TERMS

Before you take the exam, be sure that you understand the following key terms described in this chapter. If necessary, go back and review them in the chapter.

- Oracle instance

- user processes, server processes, background processes

- dispatchers

- Shared Server processes

- Multithreaded Server, Dedicated Server

- degree of parallelism

- dynamic performance views

- distributed lock manager

- node (in the Parallel Server option and Distributed System)

- shared disk system

- replication, location transparency, transaction recovery manager

continues

continues

CHAPTER SUMMARY *continued*

Resource contention in a system occurs when more than one process tries to access the same resource. Other processes have to wait until the process using the resource frees it. Resource contention can seriously degrade performance. Examples of resource contentions are disk contention, rollback segment contention, Multithreaded Server process contention, query server contention, redo log buffer latches contention, LRU latch contention, and free list contention.

It is important to design databases efficiently from the beginning to prevent tuning issues later. It is necessary sometimes to denormalize a database to achieve better performance at the cost of data redundancy. Data duplication raises issues of disk space management and methods for updating redundant data. Data warehousing systems have high data redundancy to achieve fast performance.

In addition to designing a performance-efficient database design, it is important to use appropriate database objects to achieve optimal performance. Applications can take advantage of stored procedures, functions, packages, and triggers, which are executed much more quickly than the application code. Database triggers provide global database security against ad hoc queries from SQL*Plus and applications. An application can also take advantage of database sequences that can be pinned into the memory. Database constraints also protect data integrity without requiring you to write any application code. An application's query performance can be enhanced by using database objects such as indexes, clusters, and hash clusters.

This section enables you to assess how well you understood the material in the chapter. Review questions test
your knowledge of the tasks and concepts specified in
the objectives.

Review Questions

1. Which of the following two things combined are
   called an Oracle instance?

   A. Database files

   B. User processes

   C. Oracle processes

   D. Memory allocated by Oracle

   E. Network connection

2. Which two of the following types of processes
   are subcategories of Oracle processes?

   A. Background processes

   B. User processes

   C. Server processes

   D. Operating system processes

3. Which of the following are two main functions
   of a server process?

   A. Write unsaved data from memory to datafiles

   B. Read data from datafiles into memory

   C. Perform data recovery

   D. Communicate requests from users' applications to Oracle database

   E. Execute users' requests and return the results
   to user processes

4. Which of the following functions is not
   performed by background processes?

   A. Writing data to datafiles

   B. Writing data to redo log files

   C. Performing data recovery

   D. Refreshing snapshots

   E. Executing SQL

5. Which of the following statements is not true for
   multithreaded configuration?

   A. DBAs use it to start and shut down the
   instance.

   B. It results in a more efficient usage of resources
   than dedicated server processes.

   C. It allows an increased number of users to connect to Oracle as compared with Dedicated
   Server processes.

   D. It uses dispatcher processes.

6. Which two of the following initialization parameters define the limits for the number of Shared
   Server processes in a multithreaded configuration?

   A. MTS_DIPATCHER

   B. MTS_SERVERS

   C. MTS_MAX_DISPATCHERS

   D. MTS_MAX_SERVERS

   E. MTS_MIN_SERVERS

7. Which of the following systems is likely to take
   the most advantage of the Oracle Parallel Query
   option?

   A. Single-processor machine with database files
   striped across 20 disks

B. Multiprocessor machine with database files striped across 20 disks

C. Single-processor machine with database files stored in one hard disk

D. Multiprocessor machine with database files stored in one hard disk

8. Which of the following statements won't use the Oracle Parallel Query option?

   A. `CREATE TABLE ITEMS (ID NUMBER(3), DESC VARCHAR2(100));`

   B. `CREATE TABLE ITEMS AS SELECT * FROM TEST_ITEMS;`

   C. `SELECT * FROM ITEMS;`

   D. `INSERT INTO ITEMS SELECT * FROM TEST_ITEMS;`

   E. `DELETE FROM ITEMS;`

9. In what order does Oracle look for the degree of parallelism?

   A. Initialization parameter, `CREATE TABLE` clause, hints

   B. Hints, initialization parameter, `CREATE TABLE` clause

   C. Hints, `CREATE TABLE` clause, initialization parameter

   D. Initialization parameter, hints, `CREATE TABLE` clause

10. Which of the following features isn't provided by the Oracle Parallel Query option?

   A. Executing DCL in parallel

   B. Executing `SELECT` statements in parallel

C. Parallel Loading

D. Parallel Recovery

E. Creating index in parallel

11. Which of the following statements is false about Oracle Parallel Server?

   A. It allows better performance for Oracle Parallel Query option.

   B. One major disadvantage is that if one node fails, all the nodes stop working.

   C. One disk system that contains redo log files and database files is shared by all the nodes.

   D. Each node has a separate Oracle instance running.

   E. It uses a locking mechanism to maintain data integrity.

12. Which of the following systems is likely to take the most advantage of the Oracle Parallel Server option in terms of performance?

   A. Application is performing heavy data manipulation, and users on each node are using different sets of tables.

   B. Application is performing very little data manipulation, and users of all the nodes are using the same sets of tables.

   C. Application is performing heavy data manipulation, and users of all the nodes are using the same sets of tables.

   D. Application is performing very little data manipulation, and users on each node are using different sets of tables.

13. Which of the following systems best describes the Oracle Distributed System?

APPLY YOUR KNOWLEDGE

A. Each node is running an Oracle instance and is connected to a common database.

B. Each node has its own database and is connected to a common Oracle instance.

C. Each node has its own database and its own instance and is connected to other nodes through a network.

D. Some nodes have databases, and others are running Oracle instance, and nodes are connected through a network.

14. Which of the following best describes the characteristics of an Oracle Distributed System?

    A. Replication, Transaction Recovery Management, Location Transparency

    B. Distributed Lock Manager, Interconnect, Shared Database

    C. Parallel Query Execution, Parallel Recovery, Parallel Loading

    D. Distributed Lock Manager, Replication, Interconnect

15. Which of the following is not a method of striping?

    A. RAID technology

    B. Operating system striping

    C. Manual striping by assigning more than one tablespace to a table

    D. Manual striping by assigning more than one datafile to a tablespace

16. Which of the following views give you the information about rollback contentions?

A. V$QUEUE

B. V$WAITSTAT

C. V$LATCH

D. V$ROLLNAME

E. V$SYSSTAT

17. The total number of requests for data is equal to the sum of which of the following two values?

    A. Consistent changes

    B. Consistent gets

    C. db block changes

    D. db block gets

    E. Execute count

18. Which of the following views will give information on the total number of requests?

    A. V$SYSSTAT

    B. V$SESSION

    C. V$TRANSACTION

    D. V$RESOURCE

    E. V$QUEUE

19. Which of the following views will give information about dynamic growth of rollback segments?

    A. V$WAITSTAT

    B. V$SYSSTAT

    C. V$ROLLNAME

    D. V$QUEUE

    E. V$ROLLSTAT

APPLY YOUR KNOWLEDGE

20. Which of the following views are used to find information about contention in dispatchers?

    A. V$DISPATCHER

    B. V$QUEUE

    C. V$SHARED_SERVERS

    D. V$PQ_SYSSTAT

    E. V$SYSSTAT

21. Which of the following views are used to find information about contention in Shared Server processes?

    A. V$DISPATCHER

    B. V$QUEUE

    C. V$SHARED_SERVERS

    D. V$PQ_SYSSTAT

    E. V$SYSSTAT

22. Which of the following views are used to find information about query server contention?

    A. V$DISPATCHER

    B. V$QUEUE

    D. V$SHARED_POOL_RE

    C. V$PQ_SYSSTAT

    E. V$SYSSTAT

23. Which of the following views are used to find information about redo log buffer contention?

    A. V$DISPATCHER

    B. V$QUEUE

    C. V$SHARED_POOL_RE

D. V$PQ_SYSSTAT

E. V$SYSSTAT

24. Which of the following views give you the information about free list contention?

    A. V$QUEUE

    B. V$WAITSTAT

    C. V$LATCH

    D. V$ROLLNAME

    E. V$SYSSTAT

25. Which of the following statements about denormalization isn't true?

    A. It results in higher storage cost.

    B. It results in faster query performance.

    C. It results in purely logical design.

    D. It results in data duplications.

    E. It results in extra maintenance cost.

26. Which two of the following characteristics make the column a bad candidate for a b*tree index?

    A. High selectivity of column values

    B. Normal distribution of column values

    C. SELECT statements use the column in MIN function.

    D. SELECT statements use the column in UPPER function.

    E. There is heavy update activity in the column.

27. An index is created on the STUDENTS table as
    CREATE INDEX STD_INDEX ON STUDENTS (ID, FNAME, LNAME);

APPLY YOUR KNOWLEDGE

Which of the following queries will use the index?

A. `SELECT * FROM STUDENTS;`

B. `SELECT * FROM STUDENTS WHERE ID > 100;`

C. `SELECT * FROM STUDENTS WHERE FNAME='HASAN' AND ID < 100;`

D. `SELECT * FROM STUDENTS WHERE FNAME ='HASAN' AND LNAME = 'MIR';`

E. `SELECT * FROM STUDENTS WHERE ID < 200 AND FNAME LIKE 'H%';`

28. A table with high update activity is likely to have

    A. High `PCTFREE` value

    B. Low `PCTFREE` value

    C. High `PCTUSED` value

    D. Low `PCTUSED` value

    E. High `FREELIST` value

    F. Low `FREELIST` value

29. A table with high delete activity is likely to have

    A. High `PCTFREE` value

    B. Low `PCTFREE` value

    C. High `PCTUSED` value

    D. Low `PCTUSED` value

    E. High `FREELIST` value

    F. Low `FREELIST` value

30. A table with high insert activity is likely to have

    A. High `PCTFREE` value

    B. Low `PCTFREE` value

    C. High `PCTUSED` value

    D. Low `PCTUSED` value

    E. High `FREELIST` value

    F. Low `FREELIST` value

31. Which of the following characteristics should a column not have to become a candidate for a b*tree index?

    A. Used in a `WHERE` clause

    B. Used in a SQL function such as `UPPER` and `LOWER`

    C. Low update activity

    C. High selectivity

    E. Normal distribution of values

32. Which of the following tables aren't a good candidate for a cluster?

    A. `EMP` and `DEPT` tables. `DEPTNO` column of `DEPT` table is a primary key. `DEPTNO` column of `EMP` table is a foreign key of `DEPT(DEPTNO)`.

    B. `EMP` and `DEPT` tables. Both have `DEPTNO` columns, but no primary key/foreign key relationship.

    C. `EMP` and `CUSTOMERS` table. There is no relationship between them of any sort.

    D. `EMP` table. `MGR` column is a foreign key to `EMPNO` column of the same table.

33. A hash cluster algorithm will be used only when

    A. Hash cluster key is used in `WHERE` clause with equality condition.

    B. Hash cluster consists of more than one table.

454   **Chapter 10** DATABASE TUNING

APPLY YOUR KNOWLEDGE

C. Hash cluster tables are not growing rapidly.

D. Hash cluster tables have primary key foreign key relationship between them.

Answers to Review Questions

1. **C and D.** An Oracle instance consists of Oracle processes and memory allocated by Oracle for its use.

2. **A and C.** Oracle processes consist of background processes and server processes.

3. **B and E.** Two of the main functions performed by server processes are to read data from datafiles into memory and to execute user requests.

4. **E.** SQL is executed by server processes.

5. **A.** DBAs always use a dedicated server for shutting down and starting the instance.

6. **B and D.** The MTS_SERVER parameter defines the minimum number of servers that would be present in the system even if they aren't used. Oracle can increase the number of server processes when required, up to the limit specified by MTS_MAX_SERVERS.

7. **B.** The more CPUs a machine has, the better the performance for the Parallel Query option. Also, the more disks that data is striped across, the better the performance of the Parallel Query option.

8. **A.** This statement isn't using a subquery.

9. **C.** The first degree of parallelism is located in hints given in the SELECT statement, then in the CREATE TABLE clause, and finally in the initialization parameter.

10. **A.** The Parallel Query option provides the following features:
    - Parallel retrieval of data from a table
    - Parallel loading
    - Parallel recovery
    - Parallel index creation

11. **B.** Because all nodes are sharing a common disk system, failure of one node doesn't stop other nodes from using the database.

12. **D.** Two things can degrade the performance of the Oracle Parallel Server option:
    - Frequent data manipulation, because the table must be locked and isn't available to other nodes until it is unlocked by the node using it.
    - Tables used by one node are also needed by the users on other nodes. Again, other nodes have to request to unlock the table if it is not read-only.

13. **C.** Each node has its own database and instance and its own DBA. It can access data of other nodes and allows other nodes to access its data.

14. **A.** Data Replication, Transaction Recovery Manager, and Location Transparency are the features of the Oracle Distributed System.

15. **C.** A table can be assigned only one tablespace.

16. **B.** V$WAITSTAT gives you the information about rollback segment contention.

17. **B and D.** Total request = consistent gets + db block gets.

18. **A.** V$SYSSTAT gives you the information about the total number of requests.

19. **E.** V$ROLLSTAT gives you the information about the dynamic growth of rollback segments.

20. **A and B.** V$DISPATHER and V$QUEUE give you the information about dispatcher contention.

21. **B and C.** V$SHARED_SERVERS and V$QUEUE give you the information about Shared Server process contention.

22. **D.** V$PQ_SYSSTAT gives you information about query server contention.

23. **E.** V$SYSSTAT gives you information about redo log buffer contention.

24. **E.** V$SYSSTAT gives you information about free list contention.

25. **C.** Denormalization is a solution to the performance problems given by purely logical database design. Therefore, when you denormalize, you change the design from purely logical design to performance-efficient design and allow data duplication in it.

26. **D and E.** Index on a column isn't used at all if that column is used in the SELECT statement within any function other than MIN and MAX or with the LIKE operator. If an index is created on a column in which data values are heavily updated and inserted, performance becomes very slow because the index needs to be updated on each manipulation.

27. **B and C.** An composite index is used only when the WHERE clause contains its leading columns.

28. **A.** Performance is best when a table with high update activity has a high PCTFREE value.

29. **D.** Performance is best when a table with high delete activity has a low PCTUSED value.

30. **E.** Performance is best when a table with high insert activity has a high FREELIST value.

31. **B.** A column index isn't used at all if that column is used in the SELECT statement within any function other than MIN and MAX or with the LIKE operator.

32. **C.** Tables with primary key and foreign key relationships between them benefit most when stored in a cluster, because the common values are stored only once and related data is stored together.

33. **A.** Unlike indexes, hash clusters will improve performance only if the cluster key column is used in the WHERE clause with an equality condition.

This chapter helps you prepare for the exam by covering the following objectives:

Tune applications by using TKPROF.

▶ An Oracle certified professional must know how application tuning can be done to improve overall system performance. You should be familiar with the use of TKPROF for SQL tuning and also understand how the optimizer works.

Tune the shared pool.

▶ Tuning the shared pool includes tuning the library cache. To be an Oracle certified professional, you must know how to identify and reduce the contention for the library cache and how to tune the shared pool.

Tune the buffer cache.

▶ You can use several initialization parameters to tune the buffer cache. For the exam, you must know how to identify and reduce the contention for the buffer cache and also how to use the various initialization parameters to tune the buffer cache.

Tune the redo mechanisms.

▶ You can use several initialization parameters for tuning redo mechanisms. To pass the exam, you must know how to identify and reduce the contention for the redo and how to use the various initialization parameters to manage checkpoints.

CHAPTER 11

Tuning Memory Structures

▶ Tuning applications is an important part of tuning the overall system. For the exam, you should be familiar with the use of TKPROF for analyzing how the SQL statements are executed. You also should be familiar with the way the optimizer can be manipulated. You should be able to identify the possible causes of inefficient SQL statements.

The exam will test you on your understanding of the shared pool and how to identify and reduce the problems with incorrect shared pool sizes.

You will be tested on your understanding of the buffer cache and how to identify and reduce the problems with incorrect buffer cache sizes. Make sure that you understand the various initialization parameters that you can use to optimize the buffer cache.

Make sure that you understand the use of the redo logs and how to identify and reduce the problems with the redo log mechanism. Make sure that you understand the various initialization parameters that you can use to optimize the checkpoint process.

Make sure that you also understand the use of the rollback segment and the problems that arise from incorrect numbers and sizing of rollback segments. For the exam, understand the various commands that you can use to create, alter, and change the status of rollback segments.

The exam will require you to know the ways you can monitor locking activity for a database. Also, make sure that you understand the use of locks based on the types of transactions in the system. For the exam, you should be familiar with the different types of locks and understand the possible causes of contention.

You should be familiar with the use and interpretation of the report.txt generated from the utlbstat/utlestat scripts for the various tuning activities. Also, become familiar with the various v$ views, which you can use to monitor shared pool usage, buffer cache usage, rollback segment usage, and locking activity.

INTRODUCTION

Tuning memory structures usually means tuning the SGA. This includes monitoring and tuning the shared pool (data dictionary and library cache), database buffer cache, and redo log buffers. However, tuning memory is closely related to tuning the other components of the overall system. The biggest causes of contention are generally the database, application, operating system, and I/O. This chapter focuses on tuning the SGA, rollback segments, redo log buffers, and application. You'll also review how to monitor the database activity by using various tools, such as dynamic views and Oracle-provided scripts.

TUNING APPLICATIONS

Tune applications by using TKPROF.

The performance of your entire system depends on several components, such as the operating system, the Oracle server, the network, and the application. Optimize all these components. If an application is poorly designed and implemented, however, no matter what strategies you use to tune the other components, overall system performance will suffer.

It's not practical to tune each and every SQL statement that's part of your application; instead, focus on the statements that consume the most resources and on those executed most often in your application. You can identify these statements by running SQL*Trace and TKPROF on the parts of the application that don't perform adequately.

Using the Optimizer

You can use the Oracle optimizer in one of two modes:

◆ **Rule-based.** In this mode, the optimizer will examine the SQL statement and choose the access path based on a ranking system.

◆ **Cost-based.** In this mode, the optimizer examines each statement and determines all access paths to the data. It then chooses the access path with the least cost, based on the number of logical reads that will be required.

You can also manipulate the optimizer's behavior by providing hints in SQL statements. The optimizer will use these suggestions when it's trying to choose the execution plan to use for a particular statement. Per SQL statement, there can be only one comment containing hints, and this hint should follow the keyword SELECT, INSERT, UPDATE, or DELETE. (Refer to the Oracle SQL reference manual for a complete list of the hints you can use.) You can supply the hint by using one of the following two syntax lines:

```
{SELECT|INSERT|UPDATE|DELETE} /*+ hint [text]..... */.....

{SELECT|INSERT|UPDATE|DELETE} --+ hint [text].........
```

You can set the optimizer mode at various levels:

◆ At the instance level by using init.ora parameter OPTIMIZER_MODE. Set this to RULE for rule-based, ALL_ROWS for the cost-based optimizer (with the goal being the best throughput), FIRST_ROWS for the cost-based optimizer (with the goal being best response time), or CHOOSE. If you use the CHOOSE option, Oracle decides between rule-based and cost-based by using the statistics present on the table.

◆ At the session level by using the ALTER SESSION command with the OPTIMIZER_GOAL parameter:

```
SVRMGR> ALTER SESSION SET OPTIMIZER_GOAL = value;
```

◆ At the statement level by using hints:

```
SQL> SELECT /*+ CHOOSE */ * from products;
```

SQL Tuning with SQL Trace and TKPROF

When you have a SQL statement that doesn't perform satisfactorily, you gather performance statistics related to that statement and then rewrite it so that it runs more efficiently.

STEP BY STEP

11.1 Tuning a SQL Statement

1. Set the initialization parameters MAX_DUMP_FILE_SIZE (maximum size of the trace file), USER_DUMP_DEST (destination of the trace file), and TIMED_STATISTICS (display timing statistics) to TRUE.

2. Start SQL*Trace at the session or instance level. You can choose the instance level by setting SQL_TRACE in the init.ora file; the following is an example of setting SQL_TRACE at the session level:

   ```
   SVRMGR> ALTER SESSION SET SQL_TRACE = TRUE
   ```

3. Run the application.

4. Turn off SQL*Trace:

   ```
   SVRMGR> ALTER SESSION SET SQL_TRACE = FALSE
   ```

5. Use TKPROF to format the trace file.

6. Interpret the trace file and take appropriate action based on the cause of the performance problem.

NOTE

Have the Necessary Operating System Privileges The generated files can be owned by an operating system user other than you, so before using TKPROF on this trace file, you should get access permission to this file.

You can use SQL*Trace to provide performance information about individual SQL statements. For each statement, it generates the following output to a trace file (.trc):

◆ Parse, execute, and fetch counts

◆ CPU and elapsed times

◆ Physical and logical reads

◆ Number of rows processed

◆ Library cache misses

Using TKPROF

The TKPROF facility accepts a SQL trace file as input and produces a formatted output file. Refer to the Oracle server tuning manual for the complete syntax of TKPROF. The following table describes the most commonly used TKPROF options:

TKPROF *Option*	*Description*
TRACEFILE	Name of the trace file to be formatted.
OUTPUTFILE	Name of the formatted output file.
SORT=*option*	The order in which to sort the SQL statements.
EXPLAIN=*user/password*	Run EXPLAIN PLAN in the specified schema. TKPROF determines execution plans by issuing EXPLAIN PLAN after connecting to Oracle with the user and password specified in this parameter. The specified user must have CREATE SESSION privileges.
SYS=NO	Ignore recursive SQL run as user SYS.
TABLE=*schema.tablename*	Place the execution plan in the specified table rather than the default PLAN_TABLE. If this table doesn't exist, TKPROF creates, uses, and then drops it. The user specified in the EXPLAIN option must be able to issue INSERT, SELECT, and DELETE statements against the table. If the table doesn't already exist, the user must also be able to issue CREATE TABLE and DROP TABLE statements. With this option, multiple individuals can run TKPROF concurrently with the same user in the EXPLAIN value, specify different TABLE values, and avoid interfering with each other's information in the plan.

The following example shows TKPROF being run to format a trace file named megh_trace.trc and writing it to a formatted output file named megh_trace.out:

```
C:> TKPROF megh_trace.trc megh_trace.out SYS=NO
    ➥EXPLAIN=SCOTT/TIGER
```

In this example, TKPROF connects as user SCOTT and then uses the EXPLAIN PLAN command to generate the execution plan for each traced SQL statement. The SYS parameter set to NO causes TKPROF to omit recursive SQL statements from the output file.

Using TKPROF Options to Tune Inefficient SQL Statements

Use the sort functions on the TKPROF command line to identify the most resource-intensive SQL statements. You can access a huge number of sort options by simply typing **tkprof** at the command prompt. A good example is the sort option fchela, which orders the output by elapsed time fetching. The resultant output file will contain the most time-consuming SQL statement at the beginning of the file.

By using the SYS parameter on the TKPROF command line, you can prevent SQL statements run as user SYS from being displayed. The output file will be small and manageable.

Interpreting TKPROF Output

TKPROF prints the following statistics for each statement:

Statistics	Interpretation
Call	The activities of each cursor are divided into three areas: parse statistics from parsing the cursor, which includes information for plan generation and so on; execute statistics for the execution phase of a cursor; and fetch statistics for actually fetching the rows.
Count	The number of times the particular activity was performed on this cursor.
CPU	Time in seconds used to process each phase.
Elapsed	Elapsed time in seconds.
Disk	Physical block reads.
Query	Logical buffer reads for read consistency (usually for SELECT statements).
Current	Logical buffer reads for current mode (usually for DML statements).
Rows	Rows processed.

Look at the following output:

call	count	cpu	elapsed	disk	query	current	rows
Parse	9	109	4.52	401	621	27	0
Execute	9	0.02	0.09	0	0	0	0
Fetch	7	1.22	4.01	193	809	5	3

You can analyze this output as follows:

1. Check for overparsing. This example shows that 3 rows are returned for which you had to read 809 blocks and there are 9 parses. CPU utilization is high (109 seconds) compared to the execute figures of 0.02 and 0.09 seconds. The causes for the overparsing here can be that the application is doing some kind of preparsing or that the library cache needs tuning.

2. Determine the hit ratio:

   Logical Reads = Consistent Gets + DB Block Gets

   Logical Reads = query + current

   Logical Reads = (0+809) + (0+5)

   Logical Reads = 809 + 5

   Logical Reads = 814

   Hit Ratio = 1 – (Physical Reads / Logical Reads)

   Hit Ratio = 1 – (193 / 814)

   Hit Ratio = 1 – (0.237)

   Hit Ratio = 0.763 or 76%

In this case, you've done 621 fetches from the library cache.

TUNING THE SHARED POOL

Tune the shared pool.

The shared pool is an important component of the shared global area (SGA). The shared pool is public and accessible to all server processes. The structures can have a life span of the instance. You use the init.ora parameter SHARED_POOL_SIZE to set the shared pool size.

The shared pool contains shared cursors and PL/SQL objects, among other things. It consists primarily of two components:

◆ The *dictionary cache* contains an in-memory version of portions of the data dictionary.

◆ The *library cache* contains an in-memory collection of shared objects such as packages, procedures, shared cursors, tables, views, and other dependencies. You manage the library cache by using a least recently used (LRU) algorithm, which eliminates the reparsing of already cached statements.

Library Cache Tuning

Tuning the library cache involves making sure that the parsing of statements is kept to a minimum and that large objects can find continuous space in the pool. You can minimize parsing by preventing statements from being aged out of the cache and making sure that users can share statements. Using generic code and bind variables as much as possible can increase statement sharing.

You use the DBMS_SHARED_POOL package created with the dbmspool.sql script to pin large packages in the library cache so that they don't age out. You can use the dynamic view V$DB_OBJECT_CACHE, whose KEPT column you can query to verify that a package is pinned. Another strategy to minimize object aging is to set the init.ora parameter CURSOR_SPACE_FOR_TIME to TRUE; this will prevent shared SQL areas from aging out until the cursor referencing them is closed.

Use the following command to pin a package in the cache:

```
SQL> execute dbms_shared_pool.keep('large_package_name');
```

Use the following command to unpin the package:

```
SQL> execute dbms_shared_pool.unkeep('large_package_name');
```

The following table shows several dynamic views that you can use to obtain useful information about the library cache:

Dynamic View	Usage
V$SQLAREA- column "users_executing"	Statistics of the shared cursors and the first 80 characters of the SQL statements.
V$SQL	Information about the SQL statements.
V$SQLTEXT	The full SQL text.

Dynamic View	Usage
V$DB_OBJECT_CACHE	Cached database objects.
V$LIBRARYCACHEColumn "gethitratio"Column "reloads"	Library cache management statistics.
V$SGASTAT	Information about the SGA structures.

Identifying and Reducing Contention for the Library Cache

Because the shared pool is a shared component, latches, state objects, and enqueues are used to synchronize operations and recover from aborted processes. The library cache latches are required to prevent multiple access to a shared library cache entry.

You can use the following query to identify library cache latch contention:

```
SELECT count(*) number_of_waiters
FROM v$session_wait sw, v$latch l
WHERE sw.wait_time = 0
AND sw.event = 'latch free'
AND sw.p2 = l.latch#
AND l.name like 'library%';
```

> **NOTE** **Seeing Latch Information** V$LATCH shows values accumulated since the instance startup.

If the result of this query indicates a large number of waiters, you have contention.

Use the following suggestions to minimize contention for the library cache latch:

◆ You should minimize shared pool fragmentation by pinning large objects in the library cache.

◆ Minimize reloads by sharing more statements.

◆ Minimize parsing by using bind variables. You can use the following query to identify the SQL statements receiving many parse calls:

```
SELECT sql_text, parse_calls, executions
FROM v$sqlarea
WHERE parse_calls > 100
AND executions < 2*parse_calls;
```

◆ If reloads are consistently zero, you should set CURSOR_SPACE_FOR_TIME to TRUE.

◆ Use fully qualified names as much as possible.

TUNING THE BUFFER CACHE

Tune the buffer cache.

The buffer cache is one of the most important components of the SGA. It holds copies of data blocks that all users can share. You use the init.ora parameters DB_BLOCK_BUFFERS (number of database buffers) and DB_BLOCK_SIZE (size of database buffers) to determine the total size of the database buffer cache, as follows:

Size of the database buffer cache = DB_BLOCK_BUFFERS * DB_BLOCK_SIZE

Using Initialization Parameters to Manage the Buffer Cache

The buffer cache is generally managed by the server processes that read the required blocks from disk. All blocks are represented in a least recently used (LRU) list. The dirty blocks are written back to the disk by the DBWR background process, working from the LRU end of the list. When performing an index access, the server reads one block at a time; when performing a full table scan, however, the server process can read multiple blocks at a time into the buffer cache. You can use the init.ora parameter DB_FILE_MULTIBLOCK_READ_COUNT to set the batch size when performing full table scans.

In an optimally tuned system, users should be able to find the data in memory most of the time, and there shouldn't be any contention for the LRU latch. Setting the buffer cache too large can result in performance problems due to paging and swapping, whereas setting it too small can result in the application running too slowly. (However, the application won't generate any errors or hang.)

The LRU latch controls the replacement of buffers in the buffer cache. You can use the V$LATCH, V$SESSION_EVENT, and V$SYSTEM_EVENT dynamic views to determine whether there's contention for the LRU latch. From these views, you can focus on the following latches to tune the buffer cache:

> **NOTE**
>
> **Well-Designed Applications Can Improve Performance** Application design can have a significant influence on LRU contention. You can design applications to employ code reuse and sharing of SQL. Also, you should make proper use of indexes.

◆ **The cache buffers chains latch** is needed when user processes scan the SGA for database cache buffers. To reduce contention for this latch, adjust the DB_BLOCK_BUFFERS parameter.

◆ **The cache buffers LRU chain latch** is needed when user processes scan the LRU chain containing all the dirty blocks in the buffer cache. Increasing the DB_BLOCK_BUFFERS and DB_BLOCK_WRITE_BATCH parameters can reduce contention for this latch.

The DB_BLOCK_LRU_LATCHES initialization parameter specifies the maximum number of LRU latches on your system. Follow these guidelines when choosing the value for this parameter:

◆ There should be at least 50 buffers per latch.

◆ Oracle uses only one LRU latch in a single CPU machine.

◆ The maximum number of latches is twice the number of CPUs.

> **NOTE**
>
> **Changing DB_BLOCK_BUFFERS**
> You can change the DB_BLOCK_BUFFERS parameter in the init.ora file, but before the parameter becomes effective, you must shut down and restart the instance.

> **NOTE**
>
> **Choosing the Number of LRU Latches**
> For SMP machines, Oracle automatically sets the number of LRU latches to half the number of CPUs on the system. For non-SMP machines, one LRU latch is sufficient.

Identifying and Reducing Contention for the Buffer Cache

The *cache hit ratio* is a measure of the efficiency of the buffer cache. It determines the amount of time the requested data was found in the cache and the server process didn't have to go to the disk to get it. It should be at least 80 percent during normal processing. The cache hit ratio uses three statistics:

◆ db_block_gets lists accesses to current copies of the block.

◆ consistent_gets lists accesses to read-consistent copies of the block.

◆ physical_reads lists the number of disk reads.

You can obtain these statistics in various ways, such as by querying the V$SYSSTAT view or from the utlbstat/utlestat report. Calculate the cache hit ratio by using the following formula:

cache hit ratio = 100 * (db_block_gets + consistent_gets) / (db_block_gets + consistent_gets + physical_reads)

For example, the output of the following query:

```
SQL> SELECT  100* (dbg.value + cg.value) / (dbg.value
➥+ cg.value + pr.value)
2> "CACHE HIT RATIO"
3> FROM v$sysstat dbg, v$sysstat cg, v$sysstat pr
4> WHERE  dbg.name = 'db block gets' and
5> cg.name = 'consistent gets' and
6> pr.name = ' physical reads'
7> /
```

can be something like this:

```
CACHE HIT RATIO
    89.2957846
```

If your cache hit ratio is less than desired, use the following steps to determine the impact on the ratio of adding more db block buffers:

1. Set the DB_BLOCK_LRU_EXTENDED_STATISTICS parameter to the number or buffers you want to add.

2. Shut down the database.

3. Restart the database.

4. After a period of normal activity, query the virtual table X$KCBRBH, which contains two columns: INDX (an identifier for each new buffer) and COUNT (the number of additional cache hits that will be obtained by adding these buffers).

TUNING REDO LOGS

Tune the redo mechanisms.

Redo log files are organized in groups that consist of one or more members. All group members should have identical contents. You should place redo log files of the same group on separate devices because the LGWR is almost continuously writing to them. You should check for contention of the redo log buffers and redo log buffer latches because any redo contention can hurt the performance of all processes.

Using Initialization Parameters to Manage Checkpoints

During a checkpoint, the LGWR flushes the log buffer to disk, the DBWR writes all the dirty blocks to the data files, and the data file headers are updated by the LGWR or CKPT process. Usually during a checkpoint, you'll experience a lot of disk writes, and a slow DBWR can cause the LGWR to wait. You should reduce the waits for checkpoints by using larger redo log files and more redo log groups.

You can use the following init.ora parameters to control checkpoint frequency:

◆ LOG_CHECKPOINT_INTERVAL sets the number of operating system blocks between checkpoints. You can set this to a very large value if you want to perform checkpoints only on log switches.

◆ LOG_CHECKPOINT_TIMEOUT sets the number of seconds between checkpoints.

Identifying and Reducing Contention for Redo

You can identify contention for various resources by using the dynamic performance table V$SYSSTAT, which stores system-wide statistics. The statistic REDO BUFFER ALLOCATION RETRIES reflects the number of times a user process waits for space in the redo log buffer. If this statistic is continuously increasing, it indicates that the LGWR isn't fast enough. To reduce this problem, try the following:

◆ Increase the LOG_BUFFER parameter in the init.ora and thereby increase the space for the redo log buffer.

◆ Speed up the checkpointing process.

◆ Speed up the archiving process.

A process can request a latch in one of two ways:

◆ **Willing to wait.** The requesting process will go through a cycle of request-wait until the requested latch is available.

◆ **Immediate.** If the requested latch is unavailable, the requesting process doesn't wait but continues processing.

The V$LATCH dynamic view contains information that you can use to determine whether there's contention for latches. The following columns indicate such information:

GETS
: Number of successful willing-to-wait requests

MISSES
: Number of unsuccessful, initial willing-to-wait requests

SLEEPS
: Number of times a process waited and requested a latch after an initial request

IMMEDIATE GETS
: Number of successful immediate requests

IMMEDIATE MISSES
: Number of unsuccessful immediate requests

Use the following query to monitor contention of the redo allocation and redo copy latches:

```
SELECT ln.name, gets, misses, immediate_gets, immediate_misses
FROM V$LATCH l, V$LATCHNAME ln
WHERE ln.name IN (' redo allocation', 'redo copy')
AND ln.latch# = l.latch#;
```

The output of this query might look like this:

NAME	GETS	MISSES	IMMEDIATE_GETS	IMMEDIATE_MISSES
redo alloc...	14108	503	5	0
redo copy	10	0	1004	2

The following indicates latch contention:

◆ The ratio of MISSES to GETS exceeds 1 percent.

◆ The ratio of IMMEDIATE_MISSES to the sum of IMMEDIATE_MISSES and IMMEDIATE_GETS exceeds 1 percent.

In this example, the ratio of misses to gets is 3.5 percent for the redo allocation latch, indicating contention.

On a single-CPU machine, redo latch contention rarely occurs because only one process can be active at any given time. An Oracle process must obtain the redo allocation latch before it can allocate space in the redo log buffer because there's only one redo allocation latch; therefore, only one process can allocate space in the redo log buffer at a time. The LOG_SMALL_ENTRY_MAX_SIZE parameter determines the number and size of redo entries copied on the redo allocation latch; therefore, by decreasing this parameter, you'll minimize the copying on it, which in turn will reduce the amount of time for which the redo allocation latch is held by the process.

The redo copy latch is held for a longer amount of time because the user process first obtains the redo copy latch and then the redo allocation latch. The process then performs allocation and releases the allocation latch. The copy latch isn't released until after the copy is performed.

On multiple-CPU machines, you can increase the LOG_SIMULTANEOUS_COPIES parameter to reduce contention for redo copy latches. The default value of this parameter is the number of CPUs available to the instance; the maximum value is twice the number of CPUs.

Another strategy is to use the init.ora parameter LOG_ENTRY_PREBUILD_THRESHOLD, which, when set, prebuilds the redo entry before requesting the latch. The default value for this parameter is 0. When this parameter is set, any redo entry of a smaller size than this parameter must be prebuilt.

TUNING ROLLBACK SEGMENTS

Rollback segments maintain the undo information for transactions and during the following situations:

◆ Rollback of transactions

◆ Database recovery

◆ Read consistency

Get a good estimate of the number and size of rollback segments you might need. Underestimating can lead to performance problems, whereas overestimating can lead to a waste of space. You should tune rollback segments with the following in mind:

◆ Have enough rollback segments so that the transactions don't have to wait for rollback segments.

◆ Set rollback segments with OPTIMAL size so that they don't extend during normal processing.

◆ Transactions shouldn't run out of rollback space.

◆ Readers should be able to see read-consistent images when needed.

Identifying and Reducing Rollback Contention

Tune the rollback segments.

Rollback segments hold transaction tables in their headers. Undo header contention is caused by concurrent transactions contending for the same rollback segment.

Transactions can be assigned to rollback segments automatically (when the first DDL or DML statement is issued) or manually (by using the SET TRANSACTION command with the USE ROLLBACK SEGMENT parameter and manually specifying a rollback segment to use for a transaction).

The dynamic view V$WAITSTAT contains statistics for block contention. The following table shows the different classes of blocks tracked through this view for rollback information:

Block Class	*Description*
System undo header	Buffers containing header blocks of the SYSTEM rollback segment.
System undo block	Buffers containing blocks of the SYSTEM rollback segment other than header blocks.
Undo header	Buffers containing header blocks of the rollback segments other than the SYSTEM rollback segment.
Undo block	Buffers containing blocks other than header blocks of the rollback segments other than the SYSTEM rollback segment.

Use the following queries to determine the number of requests for data and the number of waits for each class of block over a period of time:

◆
```
SELECT SUM(value) "DATA REQUESTS"
FROM V$SYSSTAT
WHERE name IN ('db block gets', 'consistent gets');
```

The output of this query might look like this:

```
DATA REQUESTS
----------------------
       319856
```

◆ SELECT class, count
  FROM V$WAITSTAT
  WHERE class LIKE '%undo%'
  AND COUNT > 0;

The output of this query might look like this:

```
CLASS                   COUNT
------------------      -------
system undo header       1005
system undo block         109
undo header              6178
undo block                632
```

As you can see from these results, the number of waits for a system undo header is (1005 / 319856) * 100 = 0.3 percent, and the number of waits for an undo header is (6178 / 319856) * 100 = 1.9 percent. A number of waits for any blocks that is greater than 1 percent of the total requests indicates contention.

Contention is indicated by frequent occurrence of ORA-01555 or if transaction table wait events are much greater than zero. To reduce contention for rollback segments, you should increase the number of rollback segments. Follow these recommendations to reduce contention for rollback segments:

◆ Set NEXT to INITIAL.

◆ Set MINEXTENTS to at least 20.

◆ Set OPTIMAL to INITIAL times MINEXTENTS.

◆ Use the following query to determine the amount of undo generated by transactions:

  ```
  SELECT MAX(USED_UBLK)
  FROM v$transaction;
  ```

  and set INITIAL to be greater than or equal to MAX(USED_UBLK).

◆ By using V$ROLLNAME and V$ROLLSTAT, determine the average size of rollback segments and then set OPTIMAL close to this average.

TUNING SORTS

Oracle uses the temporary tablespace to temporarily store row information related to data sorts. Oracle will begin by sorting data in memory and allocating RAM up to the limit defined in init.ora by the SORT_AREA_SIZE parameter. If this limit is reached but the sort requires more space, Oracle will create a temporary segment in the tablespace designated in the data dictionary for the current user. The default storage parameters (INITIAL, NEXT, PCTINCREASE, MINEXTENTS, and so on) for that tablespace will be used for creating the segment.

Extents are allocated until the segment is large enough to hold the contents of SORT_AREA_SIZE, at which point SORT_AREA_SIZE is cleared and the process repeats. Oracle will continue filling SORT_AREA_SIZE and placing the sort runs into the temporary tablespace until all the data required by the sort is contained in the tablespace. Oracle will then merge the individual runs into a single set of sorted rows by using SORT_AREA_SIZE and allocating additional temporary space in the segment as needed.

After the sort finishes, the sort space can shrink to the size specified by SORT_AREA_RETAINED_SIZE. This sort space is part of the user's memory area and has no impact on the SGA unless you're using Multithreaded Server (MTS), in which case the sort space becomes part of the user global area (UGA) in the shared pool. As you can see, the efficiency of the sort will depend highly on how well SORT_AREA_SIZE and the temporary space in the segment are set up to work together.

The following operations will require sorting:

◆ Index creation

◆ Altering an index

◆ Queries using ORDER BY or GROUP BY clauses

◆ Queries using IN or NOT IN clauses

◆ The DISTINCT keyword

◆ The UNION, INTERSECT, and MINUS operation

The dynamic view V$SORT_SEGMENT contains several columns you can use to monitor sort segments:

Column	*Description*
CURRENT_USERS	Number of active users
TOTAL_EXTENTS	Total number of extents

Column	Description
USED_EXTENTS	Number of extents now allocated to sorts
MAX_USED_BLOCKS	Maximum number of used blocks
MAX_SORT_BLOCKS	Maximum number of blocks used by an individual sort

You can improve sort performance by setting the init.ora parameter SORT_DIRECT_WRITES to TRUE. This will bypass the buffer cache and write the sort runs directly to disk. With SORT_DIRECT_WRITES, each sort uses its own memory buffers. You can control the number and size of these memory buffers by setting the init.ora parameters SORT_WRITE_BUFFERS and SORT_WRITE_BUFFER_SIZE.

Applications that use a large amount of sorting shouldn't be using MTS. For multithreaded servers, set the SORT_AREA_RETAINED_SIZE much smaller than SORT_AREA_SIZE.

MONITORING DATABASES

Monitor database activity for lock contention.

Oracle server uses locks for concurrency control. Transactions hold locks until they commit or roll back. In general, locks are inexpensive and efficient but can cause contention for several reasons:

◆ Users not committing transactions appropriately

◆ Coding very long transactions

◆ Coding high locking levels

◆ Third-party applications that place high locking levels

With the growing complexity of applications, it has become a challenge for Oracle DBAs to properly diagnose and resolve locking (hanging) issues. I'll focus on a combination of three utilities: using SQL to query the V$LOCK dynamic view, using MONITORING FACILITY, and using Oracle's locking scripts to monitor the database activity.

Most locking issues are application specific. As a result, you need to take the appropriate steps to free the resource causing the lock contention. This can be done in several ways:

◆ Asking the user that holds the resource to commit or roll back.

◆ Killing the session that holds the lock:

    ALTER SESSION KILL SESSION sid, serial

◆ Using ROLLBACK FORCE or COMMIT FORCE if 2pc pending transaction.

You might encounter several unusual locking problems while running your applications:

◆ In your application, if you're using referential integrity and trying to modify the child table, Oracle will get a TABLE LEVEL SHARE LOCK on the parent table when there's *no* index on the foreign key.

◆ The shared lock might be requested by a DML if a table's PCTFREE is set too low, the block is full with data, and many concurrent DMLs are occurring on rows within the block. Instead of waiting for a lock, this process is waiting for some extra space or a release of an INITRANS slot.

The following matrix shows the compatibility between the various lock modes:

	NULL	SS	SX	S	SSX	X
NULL	Yes	Yes	Yes	Yes	Yes	Yes
SS	Yes	Yes	Yes	Yes	Yes	No
SX	Yes	Yes	Yes	No	No	No
S	Yes	Yes	No	Yes	No	No
SSX	Yes	Yes	No	No	No	No
X	Yes	No	No	No	No	No

This matrix uses the following notations:

◆ S represents the shared lock that's obtained when you read a record.

◆ X represents the exclusive lock, which is obtained when you try to perform a DML operation.

◆ SS represents the row-share lock, meaning that you get a share lock on the table and exclusive locks on the rows that you query. This can be obtained through the SELECT...FOR UPDATE statement.

◆ SX represents the row-exclusive lock used with referential integrity. You get a shared lock on the parent table, a shared lock on the child table, and exclusive locks on the rows being queried.

◆ SSX represents the share-row exclusive lock used with referential integrity. You need a share-row exclusive lock on the child table when you delete from the parent table, there's no index on the foreign-key columns of the child table, and the foreign-key constraint has an ON DELETE CASCADE condition. This table-level lock prevents DML and SELECT...FOR UPDATE statements on the table.

Using CATBLOCK.SQL and UTLLOCKT.SQL to Monitor Lock Activity

Oracle provides two useful scripts to monitor lock activity, cat-block.sql and utllockt.sql. First, run catblock.sql as SYS to create the data dictionary views, and then, run utllock.sql as SYS. Print out the result in a tree-structured fashion.

Here is some sample output:

```
waiting_session lock_type mode_requested mode_held lock_id1 lock_id2
--------------- --------- -------------- --------- -------- --------
    2 None
    7 Transaction Exclusive Exclusive 873901 90
   12 Transaction Exclusive Exclusive 873901 90
Sessions 7 and 12 are waiting on session 2
```

A deadlock occurs in a cyclic hold-and-wait situation in which two or more processes wait for data locked by each other. The Oracle server automatically detects and resolves deadlocks by rolling back the statement that detected the deadlock. When a deadlock is detected, a trace file is generated that contains the lock holders, lock waiters graph, and the ROWIDs of the rows holding the lock.

CHAPTER SUMMARY

KEY TERMS

Before taking the exam, make sure that you're familiar with the definitions and concepts for each of the following key terms:

- Bind variable
- Checkpoint
- Cursor
- Data dictionary
- Latch
- Parse
- Read consistency
- Redo log
- Rollback segment
- Shared Global Area (SGA)

This chapter discussed the tuning topics related to memory structures that you will be tested on in the fourth OCP exam. Tuning of any system should begin with tuning of the application because you can obtain most performance gains that way. Use TKPROF for SQL tuning and look at the execution plan to see whether indexes are being used. The shared pool consists of the library cache, data dictionary cache, and user global area (if you're using Multithreaded Server). Make sure that cursors are shared and that frequently accessed packages are pinned. Use the initialization parameters properly to tune the buffer cache and the redo mechanism. Use rollback segments properly by estimating their size and number based on the type of application environment. You should frequently monitor the database activity to make sure the configuration of the memory structures is giving you optimal performance.

APPLY YOUR KNOWLEDGE

This section allows you to assess how well you understand the material in the chapter. Review questions test your knowledge of the tasks and concepts specified in the objectives. The exercises provide you with opportunities to engage in the sorts of tasks that compose the skill sets the objectives reflect.

Exercises

11.1 Pinning Packages in Memory

This exercise gives you some practice with the objective "Tune the shared pool." The following steps show you how to pin packages—specifically the STANDARD and DBMS_STANDARD packages—and how to make sure that they've been pinned.

Time Estimate: Less than 15 minutes

1. Connect as internal using Server Manager:

   ```
   Svrmgr> connect internal
   ```

2. Execute the script dbmspool.sql:

   ```
   Svrmgr> @?/rdbms/admin/dbmspool
   ```

3. Execute the script prvtpool.plb:

   ```
   Svrmgr> @?/rdbms/admin/prvtpool.plb
   ```

4. Pin the packages by using dbms_shared_pool.keep:

   ```
   Svrmgr>execute dbms_shared_pool.keep('
   ➥STANDARD');
   Svrmgr>execute dbms_shared_pool.
   ➥keep('DBMS_STANDARD');
   ```

5. Verify that the packages are pinned:

   ```
   Svrmgr> select * from v$db_object_cache
   where kept = 'YES';
   ```

11.2 Determining Whether the Shared Pool Is Sized Properly

This exercise gives you some more practice with the objective "Tune the shared pool." The following steps generate and analyze the report obtained by running utlbstat and utlestat, check the hit ratio, and then reload to determine whether the shared pool should be increased.

Time Estimate: Less than 30 minutes

1. Edit the init.ora file and set the TIMED_STATISTICS parameter to TRUE.

2. Shut down the instance.

3. Restart the instance.

4. Connect as internal using Server Manager and execute the utlbstat.sql script:

   ```
   Svrmgr> connect internal
   Svrmgr> @?/rdbms/admin/utlbstat
   ```

5. Do your normal activity or execute your batch job that you want to test the system against.

6. Execute the utlestat.sql script:

   ```
   Svrmgr> @?/rdbms/admin/utlestat
   ```

7. Use any text editor to open the file report.txt that's generated in the current directory. Check the GETHITRATIO, RELOADS, and PINS statistics from the Library Cache Statistics section of the report.txt file. If the GETHITRATIO is less than 90 percent or the RELOADS to PINS ratio is more than 1 percent, you should increase the shared pool size.

APPLY YOUR KNOWLEDGE

Review Questions

1. If the parameter CURSOR_SPACE_FOR_TIME is set to TRUE, the shared SQL areas are aged out

   A. When the cursor times out

   B. When the cursor is removed by using the LRU algorithm

   C. When a second block of SQL is read into the area

   D. When the cursor referencing the area is closed

2. You can query the amount of sharable memory used by a cached object from which view?

   A. V$CIRCUIT

   B. V$LOADSTAT

   C. V$DB_OBJECT_CACHE

   D. V$PROCESS

   E. V$LIBRARYCACHE

3. If you see CPU contention on your machine, you should set the LOG_SIMULTANEOUS_COPIES parameter in init.ora to which value?

   A. 4

   B. 6

   C. 8

   D. 10

4. Which three of the following tasks use rollback segments?

   A. Archiving

   B. Recovery

   C. Read consistency

   D. Undo information for transactions

   E. Data analysis

   F. Store the after image of the data

5. What will happen if the SORT_AREA_SIZE value is smaller than the required sort?

   A. The sort won't occur.

   B. The sort won't occur and an error will be generated.

   C. The sort will ignore this parameter.

   D. The sort will be split into separate sort runs.

6. Which two views can you use to find out the statements being run by the users?

   A. V$SGASTAT

   B. V$INSTANCE

   C. V$SQLAREA

   D. V$SQLTEXT

   E. V$LIBRARYCACHE

7. Which of the following would you use to determine the number of rollback segments to allocate to an application?

   A. The number of users who will be logged in to the application

   B. The number of transactions expected to be active at any given time

   C. The number of database buffers

   D. The number of files in the tablespace

APPLY YOUR KNOWLEDGE

8. Oracle performs deadlock resolution at which level?

   A. Row

   B. Statement

   C. Transaction

   D. Database

9. A user complains that a large update is failing. Which two of the following are the likely causes?

   A. The rollback segment tablespace doesn't have room for expansion.

   B. The information in the rollback segment has been erased.

   C. Lock information has been lost.

   D. The MINEXTENTS parameter is set to 100.

   E. The MAXEXTENTS parameter is set too low.

   F. There are very few rollback segment extents.

10. The sort extent pool resides in which of the following?

    A. SGA

    B. PGA

    C. UGA

11. By using the OPTIMIZER_MODE parameter, you're setting the optimizer mode at which level?

    A. System

    B. Instance

    C. Session

    D. Statement

    E. Data

12. What will occur if the database buffer cache is sized too small?

    A. The application will generate errors.

    B. The application will run slowly.

    C. The application will hang.

    D. The application will continue to run unaffected by this setting.

13. You're on a multi-CPU system, and the utlbstat/utlestat report indicates contention for the redo copy latch. What action should you take to reduce this contention?

    A. Increase the number of redo log buffers.

    B. Decrease the number of redo log buffers.

    C. Increase the value of the LOG_SIMULTANEOUS_COPIES parameter.

    D. Decrease the value of the LOG_SMALL_ENTRY_MAX_SIZE parameter.

14. Which of the following is most important when determining the OPTIMAL size of a rollback segment?

    A. Number of rollback segments available

    B. Value of the MAXEXTENTS parameter

    C. Transaction activity during normal processing

    D. Transaction activity during periods of high activity

15. Which system are you using if most of your queries are accessing data through full table scans?

    A. Decision Support System

    B. Online Transaction Processing

C. Dedicated System

D. Shared System

16. Which SQL statement requires a sort operation?

    A. `Select * from products;`

    B. `Select product_id, product_name from` ➥`products;`

    C. `Select product_id, product_name from` ➥`products Order by product_id;`

    D. `Select product_id, product_name from` ➥`products`

    E. `Where product_name like '%oracle%';`

17. If you're running an application that uses many large sorts and you have limited physical memory, which parameter can you use to improve sort performance?

    A. `SORT_DIRECT_WRITES`

    B. `SORT_AREA_SIZE`

    C. `SORT_AREA_RETAINED_SIZE`

    D. `SORT_WRITE_BUFFERS`

18. Which type of lock is always requested in `NOWAIT` mode and won't cause contention?

    A. DML

    B. DDL

    C. Exclusive

    D. Nested

19. Which two of the following statistics combine to give the total number of logical reads from the database buffer cache?

    A. Physical reads

    B. Buffer busy waits

    C. db_block_gets

    D. Consistent gets

    E. Physical writes

20. Which two steps are necessary to determine the impact of reducing the buffer size?

    A. Query the `V$FILESTAT` view.

    B. Query the `X$KCBRBH` table.

    C. Set `DB_BLOCK_LRU_STATISTICS` to `TRUE`.

    D. Decrease the `DB_BLOCK_SIZE` parameter.

Answers to Review Questions

1. **D.** If the parameter `CURSOR_SPACE_FOR_TIME` is set to `TRUE`, the shared SQL areas are aged out when the cursor referencing the area is closed. You can get more information on this in the section "Tuning the Shared Pool."

2. **C.** The amount of sharable memory used by a cached object can be queried from the `V$DB_OBJECT_CACHE` view. You can get more information from the section "Tuning the Shared Pool."

3. **C.** Set `LOG_SIMULTANEOUS_COPIES` to 8 if you see CPU contention on your machine. For more information, refer to the section "Tuning Redo Logs."

4. **B, C,** and **D.** Recovery, read consistency, and undo information for transactions all use rollback segments. Refer to the section "Tuning Rollback Segments" for more information.

5. **D.** If the SORT_AREA_SIZE value is smaller than the required sort, the sort will be split into separate sort runs. The section "Tuning Sorts" provides more information.

6. **C** and **D.** You can use the V$SQLAREA and V$SQLTEXT views to find out which statements are being run by users. Refer to the section "Tuning the Shared Pool" for details.

7. **B.** Use the number of transactions expected to be active at any given time to determine the number of rollback segments to allocate to an application. Refer to the section "Tuning the Rollback Segments" for more information.

8. **B.** Oracle performs deadlock resolution at the statement level. The section "Monitoring Databases" provides more details.

9. **A** and **E.** If a large update is failing, the likely cause is that the information in the rollback segment has been erased or that the MAXEXTENTS parameter is set too low. You can find more information on this area in the section "Tuning the Rollback Segments."

10. **A.** The sort extent pool resides in the SGA. The section "Tuning Sorts" provides more information.

11. **B.** You're setting the optimizer mode at the instance level by using the OPTIMIZER_MODE parameter. For more information, refer to the section "Tuning Applications."

12. **B.** The application will run slowly if the database buffer cache is sized too small. Refer to the section "Tuning the Buffer Cache" for details.

13. **C.** To reduce contention for the redo copy latch, increase the value of the LOG_SIMULTANEOUS_COPIES parameter. You can find more

information on this in the section "Tuning the Redo Logs."

14. **C.** The transaction activity during normal processing is the most important statistic when determining the OPTIMAL size of a rollback segment. The section "Tuning the Rollback Segments" provides more information.

15. **A.** You're using the Decision Support System if most of your queries are accessing data through full table scans. Refer to the section "Tuning Applications" for more details.

16. **C.** The statement

```
Select product_id, product_name from
➥products
Order by product_id;
```

requires a sort operation. The section "Tuning Sorts" provides more information.

17. **A.** You can use the SORT_DIRECT_WRITES parameter to improve sort performance if you're running an application that uses many large sorts and has limited physical memory. Refer to the section "Tuning Sorts" for more information.

18. **B.** The DDL lock is always requested in NOWAIT mode and won't cause contention. For more details, refer to the section "Monitoring Databases."

19. **B** and **C.** Buffer busy waits and db_block_gets give the total number of logical reads from the database buffer cache. The section "Tuning the Buffer Cache" provides more detail.

20. **B** and **C.** To determine the impact of reducing the buffer size, you need to query the X$KCBRBH table and set DB_BLOCK_LRU_STATISTICS to TRUE. For more information, refer to the section "Tuning the Buffer Cache."

APPENDIXES

Glossary

A

ALTER   A SQL command that changes an existing data object or structure.

Anonymous block   The general name for a body of PL/SQL code that's not part of a function or procedure. It's submitted to the database server for immediate compilation and execution.

ARCHIVELOG   A mode that, when specified in the CREATE DATABASE command, uses a log file to store redo information when an archive is performed.

Audit   The process of recording activities on the database.

Authentication   The combination of a username and password that, when verified by the database security, allows users certain access rights to the database objects.

B

b*tree   An index structure that uses levels of branch blocks, each level containing pointers to the next lower level, with a set of leaf blocks at the lowest level. Oracle's b*tree indexes always have the same number of levels between the top of the index and a leaf block, regardless of the value of the index entry.

Background process   An Oracle process not associated with a client process. Background processes perform many functions at the operating system level to support an Oracle database.

Bad file   A file that contains records that were rejected from a SQL*Loader run.

Block   The smallest physical storage unit for a database. The maximum block size varies according to the operating system.

Buffer cache   A part of the SGA that holds copies of data blocks read from data files. The buffer cache is shared by all the processes.

C

Calling context   A block or program that calls another block or subprogram.

Checkpoint   An event that causes the Oracle DBWR process to write modified database buffers from the SGA to the data files. It will make the data files consistent with respect to the system change numbers. See *System change number (SCN)*.

Client process   The process with which the user interacts. It communicates with the Oracle server process by using the Oracle Call Interface (OCI) or the User Program Interface (UPI).

Cluster   A database structure that stores one or more tables in the same segment. These tables have one or more columns in common.

Cold backup   See *Offline backup*.

Collection   An ordered group of data elements, all having the same data type.

Collection methods   A set of procedures and functions used for manipulating collections. They have the syntax collection.method(optional_parameters). Method examples include ADD and REMOVE.

Comma-delimited   An ASCII file format that contains commas to separate columns and carriage returns/line feeds to separate rows.

Commit   A process in which data changes made by a transaction become permanent.

Conditional logic   Program logic that causes the path of execution to change based on certain conditions—for example, IF...THEN...ELSE.

Consistent read   A form of multiversioning done at the statement level. By using Set transaction readonly, it can be set across multiple statements.

Constraint   A restriction on a column or columns that defines allowable values, thus preventing unwanted values from being stored.

Constructor method   A system-defined function that instantiates a class, typically of the same name as the class for which it creates objects. Oracle generates a default constructor for each class defined.

Contention   A situation in which several users are trying to update the same record(s) or several processes are trying to use the same resources.

Control file   A small binary external file that contains physical database structure information. It's needed to mount and open a database. It also contains all options for a SQL*Loader run. A backup of a database's control file should be made every time a structural change is made to the database because a control file keeps track of the associated database's physical file structure.

Cursor   A handle or name for a private SQL area, an area in memory in which a parsed statement and other information for processing the statement are kept.

D

Data Control Language (DCL)   A category of SQL commands that deal with controlling access to the data and the database.

Data Definition Language (DDL)   A category of SQL commands that can be used to define the data structures.

Data file   A physical computer file holding data segments that can belong to one or more tablespaces.

Data Manipulation Language (DML)   A category of SQL commands that can be used to manipulate the data. DML mainly involves the commands SELECTINSERT, UPDATE, and DELETE.

Data warehouse   A database used for storing historical data, used for data analysis.

Database writer process (DBWR)   An Oracle background process responsible for buffer cache management writing buffers to data files.

DCL   See *Data Control Language (DCL)*.

DDL   See *Data Definition Language (DDL)*.

Dedicated server process   Same as a *shadow process*, it has a one-to-one relation with the client process. In a dedicated server configuration, a server process handles requests for a single-user process. A multithreaded server configuration, on the other hand, allows many user processes to share a small number of server processes, minimizing the number of server processes and maximizing the utilization of available system resources.

Delimiter   A character that can be used to mark the beginning or end of a data field (column) in an ASCII text file. See also *Comma-delimited*.

Discard file   In SQL*Loader, an optional file containing records that were filtered out by a WHEN clause specified in the file.

Dispatcher   An optional background process, present only when a multithreaded server configuration is used. Each dispatcher process is responsible for routing requests from connected user processes to available shared server processes and returning the responses back to the appropriate user processes.

DML   See *Data Manipulation Language (DML)*.

Drop   A process in which an existing data object or structure is deleted.

Dump   A process in which data is copied to another media.

Dynamic performance view   A set of "virtual" tables that record current database activity.

E

Exception handler   A block of code, found in an exception block, that manages a SQL or PL/SQL error condition.

Exception propagation   The behavior of an exception in which it "bubbles up" through the call stack until it's handled by a suitable exception handler or returned to the calling program.

Explicit cursor   A cursor that's explicitly declared in the PL/SQL code block by using the DECLARE CURSOR command.

Export   An Oracle utility designed to copy the DDL of database entities and data to a file.

Extent   A data structure that stores database information as a contiguous set of database blocks.

External file   A file that's external to the Oracle Server (located outside the server on which Oracle is installed).

F

Filter   A SQL*Loader capability to put conditions on the input data so that only certain data is loaded.

Flow   See *Mode*.

Free list   A linked list of blocks in a table, cluster, or index that is examined when space is required for new or relocated data.

Function   A named block of PL/SQL that returns a value when executed. Also, a particular kind of subroutine.

G

GRANT   A SQL command to give users privileges.

Grantee   A user who receives privileges.

Grantor   A user who grants privileges to access certain database objects.

H

Hash cluster   A cluster in which rows with the same hash key values are stored together.

Hot backup   See *Online backup*.

I

Identifier   The general name for programmatic objects (things that get operated on): variables, constants, cursors, and so on.

Implicit cursor   A SQL statement that's embedded inline in PL/SQL code.

Import   An Oracle utility designed to create database entities and insert data into tables. The Import utility reads files created by the Export utility. The imported data could be originally in Oracle format or non-Oracle format. The Export utility puts the data in Oracle format.

Index   A pointer or handle that provides fast access to table data, just like the index in a book.

Instance   A collection of background processes and the memory acquired for the System Global Area (SGA) to which they are attached.

Instantiate   The process of allocating memory for an instance of an object class.

Integrity constraint   A business rule on one or more columns that defines the valid values to be placed in those columns.

Iteration scheme   In a FOR...LOOP iterative statement, everything between the keywords FOR and LOOP (the loop control variable and the range condition).

L

Large object binary (LOB)   A special data type used to store binary data such as images, sound, and video.

Least recently used   See *LRU*.

Literal   Any hard-coded string enclosed in single quotation marks, a fixed decimal number, or the special values TRUE, FALSE, and NULL.

Location transparency   The process of setting up the Oracle distributed servers so that the client doesn't know the name or location of the server that is servicing its request.

Log file   A file that contains detailed information on the SQL*Loader run, including any parsed errors in the control file.

Loop control variable   A variable used to control or count the iterations of a loop, especially a FOR loop.

LRU   An algorithm by which the DBWR process writes the least recently used (LRU) buffers to disk. This buffer management scheme allows DBWR to improve the performance by finding free buffers while keeping recently used buffers resident in memory.

M

Memory structures   Memory units allocated for Oracle processes. These units are composed of Software Code Areas, the System Global Area (SGA), Program Global Areas (PGA), and Sort Areas.

Mode   Indicates how a subprogram parameter can be used—as read-only input (IN), write-only output (OUT), or both (IN OUT). Also known as *flow*.

Mount   A process in which the control file for the database is read and validated, and during which the data files and control file indicated by the control file are validated. However, the database isn't available for general use.

Multithreaded server (MTS)   An alternative way of supporting a large number of user processes by means of few server processes. There's a many-to-one relation between user processes and server processes.

Multiversioning   The enforcement of statement- and transaction-level read consistency by providing each statement or transaction with its "own" version of the data as of a specific point in time (the start of statement or transaction execution).

N

Named notation   The form of specifying subprogram parameters where the parameter name is given, followed by the association operator (=>), followed by the value. Parameters can thus be supplied in any order or skipped altogether.

NOAUDIT   Stops SQL statements from being audited as a result of the AUDIT command.

Node   (1) In a tree-structured table, one row. (2) The location on a network where a computer is attached.

Nonsystem process   A type of nonrequired background process that performs a specific service.

O

Object   An entity in the database, such as a table or a view.

Online backup   A process in which the database is open and handling database transactions while the external files are backed up.

Offline backup   A process in which the database is closed while the external files are backed up.

P

Package   A container for a collection of related subprograms and data.

Package body   The part of a package in which globally accessible cursors and subprograms are implemented. The body can also contain private cursors, variables, user-defined data types, and subprograms, available only to other items in the package body.

Package header   The part of a package where globally accessible cursors, variables, user-defined datatypes, and subprograms are declared. Also called a *package specification*.

Parameter   A value, a column name, or an expression—usually following a function or module name—that specifies additional functions or controls that should be observed by the function or module.

Parameter file   File that contains information used by the database during startup.

Parameter list   The list of variables, their modes, and data types that make up the interface between a subprogram and a calling context.

Parfile   The file used by Export and Import to contain keywords for a run.

PCTFREE   A portion of the data block that's not filled by rows as they are inserted into a table, but is reserved for later updates made to the rows in that block.

PCTUSED   The percentage of space in a data block, which Oracle attempts to fill before it allocates another block.

Persistence   The capability of variables to retain their existence and values for the duration of the session or connection. Such variables are declared within a package header or body, but outside any subprogram.

PGA   See *Process Global Area (PGA)*.

PL/SQL   Acronym for Procedural Language/Structured Query Language, the built-in programming language supported by Oracle Server.

PMON   A background process (Process MONitor) used for recovery when a process accessing a database fails.

Positional notation   The form of specifying subprogram parameters where it is sufficient to list every parameter in the exact order in which they appear. The position of each parameter is thus relative to the other parameters.

Pragma   A compiler directive that tells the compiler how to handle language-specific conditions and similar information. This information is applied at compile time, not runtime.

Privilege   A permission granted to an Oracle user to execute some action, such as inserting data into a table.

Procedure   A named block that performs a unit of work; a particular kind of subroutine.

Process Global Area (PGA)   Memory that's physically private to a process; it's not shared with other processes. Unlike SGA, it can grow at runtime. See also *System Global Area (SGA)*.

Profile   A named set of computer resource limitations.

Purity   A relative indication to the compiler that a packaged function has no side-effects.

Q

Quota   The amount of space allocated to a user in a tablespace.

R

RAID   A disk system that provides various options for striping, mirroring, and managing error-correcting codes (often called parity checks) for balanced disk access and fault tolerance. RAID is an acronym for a redundant array of independent (or inexpensive) disks.

Re-entrant   Executable code that can be shared in memory among users.

Record type   A user-defined composite data type, composed of one or more members.

Recursion   When a function calls itself until a final value is reached. Recursion provides an elegant solution for many iterative problems.

Redo log file   A file that records all transactions made in a database.

Referential integrity   A condition that guarantees that values in one column (of the child table) also exist in another column (of the parent table).

Replication   The process by which copies of data are consistently maintained in the different databases of a distributed system.

REVOKE   A SQL command that removes a privilege from a user.

Role   A named group of security privileges for a given security domain.

Rollback   Provides read consistency of data and the capability to undo some database activities.

Rollback segment   A data structure that stores undo information. It is used for transaction management.

Rowid   A value that points to the specific physical location of a row in a table by identifying its file number, block number, and relative row number in the block. For tables in tablespaces with more than 1,200 files, the file number is a relative number, and the rowid also includes an object ID number. ROWID is a pseudocolumn that can be referenced in SQL statements. Rowids are also stored in b*tree indexes.

S

Scalar   A variable or expression having exactly a single value of an atomic data type, such as VARCHAR2, DATE, NUMBER, BOOLEAN, and so on.

Schema A collection of objects associated with a particular user. In Oracle, the schema name always matches its username, so the two terms—schema and user—can generally be interchanged without confusion.

SCN See *System change number (SCN)*.

Scope The visibility of program objects (variables, cursors, block names) within blocks.

Security domain settings All security attributes of a user.

Segment A set of extents for a database object. A segment can store a table's data, an index, rollback information, or temporary sort information.

Server The node in a client/server environment that serves requests submitted to it by nodes that represent clients.

Server process An Oracle process that acts on behalf of the user process and executes all the necessary Oracle Server code to satisfy the user request.

Shadow process See *Dedicated server process*.

SMON The System MONitor process, in which one of the Oracle7 background processes is used to perform recovery and clean up unused temporary segments.

Snapshot A means of creating a local copy of remote data. You can use a snapshot to replicate all or part of a single table, or to replicate the result of a query against multiple tables.

SQL Acronym for *Structured Query Language*, a declarative language developed for expressing requests for data from a relational database.

Startup The process of starting an instance, with the intent of mounting and opening a database to make a database system available for use.

Stored subprogram A named PL/SQL block (a subprogram) whose executable code is stored in the database. This kind of program is precompiled and, when called, executes much more quickly than nonstored subprograms, which need to be compiled every time they are run.

System change number (SCN) A unit of time used and maintained by the database kernel to order the events occurring in the system.

System Global Area (SGA) Contains memory structures called the shared pool, database buffer cache, and redo log buffer.

System process A type of background process that is required for the proper functioning of the Oracle instance.

System resource A resource provided by the system, such as physical memory and hard disk space. System resources are controlled by profiles.

Subprogram A program unit callable by name. Also known as a *subroutine*.

Subtype A data type derived from a parent type, having the same internal representation as the parent type, but typically having some additional constraint—for example, INTEGER is a subtype of NUMBER.

T

Table A segment that contains user data organized in columns (fields) and rows (records).

Tablespace A logical database structure that holds related data.

Top-down design   The practice of defining procedural actions first at a general, high level, and then recursively refining the actions by creating more detailed routines at lower and lower levels until the actions are fully specified.

Transaction   A set of one or more commands issued against the database between bracketing commit or rollback commands. Consequently, all or none of the database changes made by a single transaction will become permanent.

U

UGA   Acronym for User Global Area.

User   A name used to access the database.

Overview of the Certification Process

You must pass rigorous certification exams to become an Oracle Certified Professional. These certification exams provide a valid and reliable measure of your technical proficiency and expertise. The computer-based exams have been developed in consultation with computer industry professionals who have on-the-job experience with Oracle products in the workplace. These exams are conducted by an independent organization—Sylvan Prometric—at more than 1,200 Authorized Prometric Testing Centers around the world.

Now Oracle offers one type of certification, based on Oracle 7.3 database administration: Oracle Certified Professional Database Administration Track (OCP). OCPs are qualified to provide installation, configuration, tuning, and backup/recovery for Oracle 7.3 databases. At the time of this writing, a test track for Oracle8 certification wasn't planned until in October 1998. After you earn your Oracle7.3 certification, you will be eligible to take the Oracle8: New Features for Administrators exam as early as August.

HOW TO BECOME AN ORACLE CERTIFIED PROFESSIONAL (OCP)

Becoming an OCP requires you to pass four separate exams:

- Test I: Introduction to Oracle SQL and Pl/SQL
- Test II: Oracle7 Database Administration
- Test III: Oracle7 Backup and Recovery Workshop
- Test IV: Oracle7 Performance Tuning Workshop

> **NOTE** **Need Info?** Need up-to-date information about Oracle's certification? Visit the Oracle Training and Certification Web site at http://www.education.oracle.com/certification. You also can call the following sources:
>
> - Oracle Certified Professional Program: 1-650-506-7000
> - Sylvan Prometric Testing Centers: 1-800-891-EXAM

Study Tips

Self-study involves any method that you use to learn a given topic. The most popular method is third-party books, such as the one you hold in your hand. Before you begin to study for a certification exam, you should know exactly what Oracle expects you to learn.

Pay close attention to the objectives posted for the exam. The entire set of objectives is listed in this book's introduction. The relevant subset of objectives also appears at the beginning of each chapter. Also, at the beginning of the book there's a handy tear-out card with an objective matrix that lists all the objectives and their page references in the book.

Another thing to think about is that humans vary in their learning styles. Some people are visual learners, others are textual, and still others learn best from aural sources. However, some basic principles of learning apply to everyone. For example, students who take notes at lectures have better recall on exam day—even if they did not study the notes later. Because they *encoded* the information as well as *decoded* it, they processed it in a deeper, more active fashion than those who simply listened to the lecture.

Hence, you should use the study techniques that you know work for you, but also take advantage of more general principles of learning. For example, if you are a visual learner, pay special attention to the figures provided in this book. Also, create your own visual cues by doing things such as diagramming processes and relationships.

A general principle of learning has to do with studying the organization of information separately from its details. Cognitive learning research has demonstrated that if you focus on learning just the organization of the information, followed by focusing on just learning the specific details, you will retain the information better than if you attempt to take in all the information at once. Use your study materials to prepare a detailed outline of the material on the exam. Study it first by learning the organization of the material, and then go back and focus on memorizing and understanding the details. Trying to do both at once only leads to the two types of information interfering with your overall learning.

Finally, follow common-sense practices in your studying as well:

◆ Study in bright light to reduce fatigue and depression.

◆ Establish a regular study schedule and stick to it as closely as possible.

◆ Turn off all forms of distraction, including radios and televisions, or try studying in a quiet room.

◆ Always study in the same place so your materials are always readily at hand.

◆ Take short breaks (approximately 15 minutes) every two to three hours. Studies have proven that your brain assimilates information better when you take these rest periods.

PRETESTING YOURSELF

Before taking the actual exam, you should test yourself many times in various ways. There are review questions at the end of each chapter. On the accompanying CD-ROM is an electronic test engine that emulates the actual Oracle exam and enables you to test your knowledge of the subject areas. Use this practice text repeatedly until you consistently score in the 90 percent range (or better).

This means, of course, that you can't start studying five days before the exam begins. You will need to give yourself plenty of time to read, practice, and allow for testing yourself several times.

We believe the New Riders' Top Score electronic testing engine is the best test preparation tool on the market. Top Score is described in detail in Appendix E, "All About Top Score."

HINTS AND TIPS FOR DOING YOUR BEST ON THE TESTS

When you take the actual exam, be prepared. Arrive early and be ready to show two forms of identification. Expect wordy questions. Although you have 90 minutes to take the exam, there are 60–70 questions that you must answer. This gives you just over one minute to answer each question. This may sound like ample, but remember that many of the questions can involve lengthy word problems, exhibits that must be referred to, and even, more recently, simulations. Your exam time can be consumed very quickly.

Things to Watch For

When you take the exam, *read very carefully!* Make sure that you understand just what the question requires, and notice the number of correct choices you need to make. Remember that some questions require that you select a single correct answer; other questions have more than one correct answer. Radio buttons next to the answer choices indicate that the answers are mutually exclusive—there is only one correct answer. On the other hand, check boxes indicate that there is more than one correct answer.

Again, read the questions fully. With lengthy questions, the last sentence often dramatically changes the scenario. When you're taking the exam, you are given pencils and two sheets of paper. If you are uncertain of what the question requires, map out the scenario on the paper until you have it clear in your mind. You must turn in the scrap paper at the end of the exam.

Choosing the Right Answer

Adopt a strategy for evaluating possible answers. Eliminate impossible or implausible answers, and then carefully evaluate those that remain. Be careful—some answers are true statements on their own, but might not be correct in the context of the question. The answers must match or relate to the question before they can serve as correct choices.

Marking Answers for Return

You can answer questions on the computer-based exam and refer back to them later. If you encounter a wordy question that will take a long time to read and decipher, mark it and return to it when you have completed the rest of the exam. This will prevent you from wasting time on it and running out of time—there are only 90 minutes allotted for the exam, and it ends whether or not you're finished.

Changing Answers

The rule of thumb here is: *Don't change your answers!* If you read the question carefully and completely and felt like you knew the right answer, you probably did. Don't second-guess yourself! As you check your answers, if one clearly stands out as incorrect, of course, you should change it. But if you are at all unsure, go with your first impression.

Good luck!

What's on the CD-ROM

This appendix offers a brief rundown of what you'll find on the CD-ROM that comes with this book. For a more detailed description of the newly developed Top Score test engine, exclusive to Macmillan Computer Publishing, see Appendix E, "All About Top Score."

TOP SCORE

Top Score is a test engine developed exclusively for Macmillan Computer Publishing. It is the best test engine available because it closely emulates the format of the standard Microsoft exams. In addition to providing a means of evaluating your knowledge of the exam material, Top Score features several innovations that help you to improve your mastery of the subject matter. For example, the practice tests allow you to check your score by exam area or category, which helps you determine which topics you need to study further. Other modes allow you to obtain immediate feedback on your response to a question, explanation of the correct answer, and even hyperlinks to the chapter in an electronic version of the book where the topic of the question is covered. Again, for a complete description of the benefits of Top Score, see Appendix E.

Before you attempt to run the Top Score software, make sure that autorun is enabled. If you prefer not to use autorun, you can run the application from the CD by double-clicking the START.EXE file from within Explorer.

EXCLUSIVE ELECTRONIC VERSION OF TEXT

As alluded to previously, the CD-ROM also contains the electronic version of this book in Portable Document Format (PDF). In addition to the links to the book that are built into the Top Score engine, you can use that version of the book to help you search for terms you need to study or other book elements. The electronic version comes complete with all figures as they appear in the book.

COPYRIGHT INFORMATION AND DISCLAIMER

Macmillan Computer Publishing's Top Score test engine: Copyright 1998 New Riders Publishing. All rights reserved. Made in U.S.A.

All About Top Score

The Top Score software included on the CD-ROM accompanying this book enables you to test your Oracle knowledge in a manner similar to that employed by the actual Oracle exam. Three applications are included:

◆ Practice exams provide you with simulated multiple-choice tests.

◆ Study cards provide the same sorts of questions (but let you control the number and types of questions) and provide immediate feedback. With this format, you can learn from your testing and control the topics on which you want to be tested.

◆ Flash cards provide this same sort of feedback and allow the same sort of control, but require short answers or essay answers to questions. You aren't prompted with multiple-choice selections or cued as to the number of correct answers to provide.

Although it is possible to maximize the Top Score applications, the default is to run them in smaller mode so that you can refer to your desktop while answering questions. Top Score uses a unique randomization process to ensure that each time you run the programs, you are presented with a different sequence of questions—thus enhancing your learning and preventing you from merely memorizing the expected answers without reading the question each and every time.

SCORING

The Top Score Practice Exam Score Report uses actual numbers from the Oracle Certified Professionals (OCP) exam. For that exam, the number of questions is 60–70, and the time limit is 90 minutes.

Index

A

B

I

J-K

L

P

Package header for the table DEPT listing, 170
packages, 167-181
  body, 171-176
  calling from SQL, 177-178
  database objects, 445
  headers, 168-171
  stored objects, getting information, 178-181
paradigms, 155
PARALLEL MAX_SERVERS parameter, 402
Parallel Query processing, 397, 399-400, 402
Parallel Server option, 402-406
PARALLEL_DEFAULT_MAX_SCANS parameter, 401
PARALLEL_DEFAULT_SCANSIZE parameter, 401
parameters, 147-149
  default values, 149
  named notation, 150-151
  positional notation, 149
password file, databases, 340
passwords
  DBAs, authentication, 205-207
  ORAPWD utility, 205-207
persistence, packages, 167
physical offline backup, database backup, 348
physical online backup, database backup, 349-350
pinging, 404
PL/SQL, 78
  blocks, 81-82
  collections, 92-99
  comments, 102-103
  conditional statements, 118-122
  cursor FOR loop, 127-128
  data type support, 90-92
  data types, conversion, 104-106

  exceptions
    blocks, 82
    defining, 111-112
    handlers, 82-84, 107-113
    naming, 112-113
    propagation, 107-108
  executable statements, 103-106
  explicit cursors, 115-117
  FOR loops, 123-126
  identifiers, 86-87, 89-90, 92-103
  implicit cursors, 113-115
  infinite loops, avoiding, 108, 129
  iteration schemes, 123
  iterative statements, 123-129, 131
  literal strings, 87-89
  loop control variables, 127
  nested logic, 121
  NULL values, 120-121
  output, getting, 131-134
  pragmas, 113
  records, 99-101
  reserved words, 78-81
  scope, 84, 86
  scoping rules, 81
  sequential logic, 121-122
  short-circuit evaluation, 119
  SQL, 113-117
  SQLCODE, capturing, 109
  subprogram, 103
  suitable, 107
  tables, 92
    dense, 96
    sparse, 96
  top-design syntax, 81-86
  unconditional loops, 128-129
  unconditional statements, 122-123
  variables
    assignment, 104
    based, 101-102